Generative AI and Multifactor Productivity in Business

Festus Fatai Adedoyin
Bournemouth University, UK

Bryan Christiansen
Southern New Hampshire University, USA

A volume in the Advances in Logistics, Operations, and Management Science (ALOMS) Book Series

IGI Global
PUBLISHER of TIMELY KNOWLEDGE

Published in the United States of America by
IGI Global
Business Science Reference (an imprint of IGI Global)
701 E. Chocolate Avenue
Hershey PA, USA 17033
Tel: 717-533-8845
Fax: 717-533-8661
E-mail: cust@igi-global.com
Web site: http://www.igi-global.com

Library of Congress Cataloging-in-Publication Data

Names: Adedoyin, Festus Fatai, 1989- editor. | Christiansen, Bryan, 1960- editor.
Title: GenerativeAI and multifactor productivity in business / edited by Festus Adedoyin, Bryan Christiansen.
Description: Hershey, PA : Business Science Reference, [2024] | Includes bibliographical references and index. | Summary: "This book aims to examine scholarly and practitioner-based contributions which push the boundaries of GenerativeAI in Business research. This includes applications of more powerful generative AI tools, language models and innovative technologies specific to businesses across sectors, scales, and regions"-- Provided by publisher.
Identifiers: LCCN 2024002062 (print) | LCCN 2024002063 (ebook) | ISBN 9798369311981 (hardcover) | ISBN 9798369311998 (ebook)
Subjects: LCSH: Business--Research. | Artificial intelligence. | Industrial productivity. | Information technology.
Classification: LCC HD30.4 .O64 2024 (print) | LCC HD30.4 (ebook) | DDC 658.500285/63--dc23/eng/20240309
LC record available at https://lccn.loc.gov/2024002062
LC ebook record available at https://lccn.loc.gov/2024002063

This book is published in the IGI Global book series Advances in Logistics, Operations, and Management Science (ALOMS) (ISSN: 2327-350X; eISSN: 2327-3518)

British Cataloguing in Publication Data
A Cataloguing in Publication record for this book is available from the British Library.

For electronic access to this publication, please contact: eresources@igi-global.com.

Advances in Logistics, Operations, and Management Science (ALOMS) Book Series

ISSN:2327-350X
EISSN:2327-3518

Editor-in-Chief: John Wang, Montclair State University, USA

MISSION

Operations research and management science continue to influence business processes, administration, and management information systems, particularly in covering the application methods for decision-making processes. New case studies and applications on management science, operations management, social sciences, and other behavioral sciences have been incorporated into business and organizations real-world objectives.

The **Advances in Logistics, Operations, and Management Science** (ALOMS) Book Series provides a collection of reference publications on the current trends, applications, theories, and practices in the management science field. Providing relevant and current research, this series and its individual publications would be useful for academics, researchers, scholars, and practitioners interested in improving decision making models and business functions.

COVERAGE

- Organizational Behavior
- Risk Management
- Political Science
- Marketing engineering
- Finance
- Networks
- Production Management
- Operations Management
- Computing and information technologies
- Information Management

IGI Global is currently accepting manuscripts for publication within this series. To submit a proposal for a volume in this series, please contact our Acquisition Editors at Acquisitions@igi-global.com or visit: http://www.igi-global.com/publish/.

The Advances in Logistics, Operations, and Management Science (ALOMS) Book Series (ISSN 2327-350X) is published by IGI Global, 701 E. Chocolate Avenue, Hershey, PA 17033-1240, USA, www.igi-global.com. This series is composed of titles available for purchase individually; each title is edited to be contextually exclusive from any other title within the series. For pricing and ordering information please visit http://www.igi-global.com/book-series/advances-logistics-operations-management-science/37170. Postmaster: Send all address changes to above address.

Titles in this Series

For a list of additional titles in this series, please visit:
http://www.igi-global.com/book-series/advances-logistics-operations-management-science/37170

State-of-the-Art Digital Twin Applications for Shipping Sector Decarbonization
Bill Karakostas (Inlecom, Belgium) and Takis Katsoulakos (Inlecom, Belgium)
Business Science Reference • © 2024 • 319pp • H/C (ISBN: 9781668498484) • US $165.00

Strategic Management and Policy in the Global Aviation Industry
Salim Kurnaz (Istanbul Aydın University, Turkey) Antonio Rodrigues (Instituto Superior de Gestão, Portugal) and Anıl Padhra (West London University, UK)
Business Science Reference • © 2024 • 325pp • H/C (ISBN: 9798369309087) • US $275.00

Strategic Innovations for Dynamic Supply Chains
Filiz Mızrak (Beykoz Univeristy, Turkey)
Business Science Reference • © 2024 • 342pp • H/C (ISBN: 9798369335758) • US $325.00

Convergence of Industry 4.0 and Supply Chain Sustainability
Muhammad Rahies Khan (Bahria University, Karachi, Pakistan) Naveed R. Khan (UCSI University, Malaysia) and Noor Zaman Jhanjhi (Taylor's University, Malaysia)
Business Science Reference • © 2024 • 491pp • H/C (ISBN: 9798369313633) • US $275.00

Drivers of SME Growth and Sustainability in Emerging Markets
Sumesh Dadwal (Northumbrian University, UK) Pawan Kumar (Lovely Professional University, India) Rajesh Verma (Lovely Professional University, India) and Gursimranjit Singh (Dr. B.R. Ambedkar National Institute of Technology, Jalandhar, India)
Business Science Reference • © 2024 • 308pp • H/C (ISBN: 9798369301111) • US $250.00

Navigating the Coaching and Leadership Landscape Strategies and Insights for Success
Andrew J. Wefald (Staley School of Leadership, Kansas State University, USA)
Business Science Reference • © 2024 • 306pp • H/C (ISBN: 9798369352427) • US $295.00

For an entire list of titles in this series, please visit:
http://www.igi-global.com/book-series/advances-logistics-operations-management-science/37170

IGI Global
PUBLISHER of TIMELY KNOWLEDGE

701 East Chocolate Avenue, Hershey, PA 17033, USA
Tel: 717-533-8845 x100 • Fax: 717-533-8661
E-Mail: cust@igi-global.com • www.igi-global.com

Christiansen Dedication

For Tanya, Stas, and Nicole

For Damilola and Morianugba

Table of Contents

Detailed Table of Contents

Transformative breakthroughs appear every few decades, revolutionizing the globe and vastly enhancing our quality of life. With the introduction of ChatGPT, another paradigm-shifting event has now occurred. This Study examine the importance of GPT-3 in the context of business. In essence, GPT-3 has the potential to transform a variety of business processes by streamlining workflows, enhancing client relationships, and spurring creative breakthroughs. This transformative tool can substantially advance businesses by amplifying effectiveness, refining customer engagements, fostering innovation, and simplifying an array of operations. This research will explore the capacity to influence diverse sectors, notably the financial market. Moreover, GPT-3 holds the potential to profoundly shape the functions of financial brokers, augmenting their efficiency, customer service, and decision-making protocols. Ultimately, we will examine how GPT-3 can elevate effectiveness, customer engagement, decision-making, and creative advancement

Transformers algorithms and deep learning architectures are increasingly spreading in different applications in several industries. One of the most well-known transformers widely used is ChatGPT. Transformers are designed to assist in problem solving by transforming sequence of inputs to a sequence of outputs. In this paper, transformer models will be studied for the purpose of integrating them to Business Intelligence (BI) architecture in Higher Education (HE) context. The purpose of integrating transformers is to minimise human interaction with data handling to benefit from time reduction and increase the quality of data. Quality Assurance (QA) in HE encompasses data gathering from several sources which requires data preparation to capture compliance with QA standards and measuring learning outcomes. This paper proposes an architecture for BI dashboards in HE with an integration with transformers models.

This chapter explores how OpenAI's technologies boost multifactor productivity (MFP) in Chinese firms. MFP measures output efficiency against inputs like capital and labour. The chapter examines China's fast tech adoption and evolving industry. It highlights how integrating OpenAI's algorithms and machine learning improves Chinese companies' operational efficiency, decision-making, and innovation. Case

Preface

In the ever-evolving landscape of business, where efficiency and growth are paramount, the integration of Artificial Intelligence (AI) stands as a transformative force with unparalleled potential. As Editors, it is our privilege to introduce this comprehensive volume dedicated to exploring the intersection of Multifactor Productivity (MFP) with several types and examples of Generative AI tools increasingly been used in businesses.

In today's dynamic environment, understanding and harnessing the power of AI-driven automation and innovation are imperative for organizations striving to thrive amidst economic challenges. This book delves deep into the realm of Generative AI usage and implications, shedding light on its role in reshaping organizational operations, accelerating innovation, and unlocking new avenues of growth.

The chapters assembled here present a diverse array of scholarly and practitioner-based contributions, each pushing the boundaries of types of Generative AI used in business research. From the applications of powerful generative AI tools to innovative technologies tailored to businesses of varying scales and sectors, this book offers insights into how Multifactor Productivity can be enhanced through technological advancements.

While the potential benefits of integrating Generative AI into business processes are vast, this volume does not shy away from addressing the challenges that come with it. From ethical considerations to the practical implications for labor markets and industry transformation, the chapters within provide a holistic view of the multifaceted relationship between examples of Generative AI, technological advancements, and MFP.

We extend our gratitude to the contributors who have shared their expertise and insights, enriching this compilation with valuable perspectives from academia, industry, and policy realms. Whether you are a business leader, academic researcher, policymaker, or industry practitioner, we believe that the contents of this book will offer valuable insights into the transformative power of Generative AI in driving multifactor productivity.

As Editors, it is our hope that this volume serves as a catalyst for further exploration and discussion, inspiring readers to navigate the complexities of AI integration with a nuanced understanding of its implications for productivity, innovation, and economic growth.

Chapter 1: Critical Analysis of Emerging and Disruptive Digital Technologies in an Era of Artificial Intelligence (IA)

Authors: José Vargas-Hernandez, Selene Castañeda-Burciaga, Omar Guirette-Barbosa, Omar Vargas-Gonzàlez

In this chapter, Vargas-Hernandez et al. conduct a critical analysis of the emergent and disruptive digital technologies within the era of artificial intelligence (IA). The authors delve into the opportunities and challenges posed by these technologies, highlighting their impacts on individuals, organizations, institutions, and society at large. Drawing from recent scientific literature, the chapter employs a method of critical analysis to examine issues such as bias, surveillance, and hacking. Ultimately, the authors advocate for a digital conversation and leadership regarding acceptable ethical behaviors, emphasizing the role of human guidance in navigating the ongoing digital transformation.

Chapter 2: AI-Powered Dialogue System for Business Exploring GPT3's Impact

Authors: Amir Dar, Akshat Jain, Mehak Malhotra, Mohammad Khan, Manzoor Khanday

Dar et al. explore the transformative potential of GPT-3 in business contexts. The chapter discusses how GPT-3 can streamline workflows, enhance client relationships, and foster creative breakthroughs across various sectors. Through empirical analysis and theoretical insights, the authors examine GPT-3's capacity to influence diverse sectors, including the financial market. Furthermore, they explore how GPT-3 can augment efficiency, customer service, and decision-making protocols within financial brokerage functions. Ultimately, the chapter aims to shed light on GPT-3's potential to elevate effectiveness, customer engagement, decision-making, and creative advancement in business operations.

Chapter 3: Integrating Artificial Intelligence Transformers with Business Intelligence Systems for Monitoring Learning Outcomes in Higher Education Institutions

Authors: Ali Sorour, Anthony Atkins

Sorour and Atkins propose an architecture for integrating transformer models into Business Intelligence (BI) systems within higher education contexts. The chapter discusses the potential benefits of integrating transformers to minimize human interaction with data handling and enhance data quality. Through empirical analysis, the authors highlight the importance of such integration for optimizing data processing and improving learning outcome monitoring in higher education institutions.

Chapter 4: Leveraging OpenAI for Enhanced Multifactor Productivity in Chinese Businesses

Author: Mohamad Zreik

Zreik explores how OpenAI's technologies enhance multifactor productivity (MFP) in Chinese firms. The chapter examines China's rapid tech adoption and evolving industry landscape, emphasizing the role of OpenAI's algorithms and machine learning in improving operational efficiency, decision-making, and innovation. Through case studies and analyses, the author demonstrates OpenAI's contributions to optimizing resources, enhancing output, and driving economic growth in key Chinese industries. Additionally, the chapter discusses AI-driven productivity's broader impact on China's GDP, global competitiveness, and transition to a knowledge-based economy, providing insights into future challenges and opportunities.

Chapter 5: Safeguarding Business in the Age of AI for Organizational Resilience and Risk Management

Authors: Dr. Pushan Dutta, Sulagna Das, Devraj Ganguly

Dutta et al. outline risk management frameworks to address cybersecurity risks associated with the proliferation of AI across sectors. The chapter emphasizes the need for updated cyber strategies centered on ethical governance to harness AI safely despite escalating threats. Through analysis of prominent threats and technical safeguards, the authors provide recommendations for managing cybersecurity risks and ensuring organizational resilience in the age of AI.

Chapter 6: A Policy Simulation Experiment on Innovations and Open AI-Driven Labour Force-Growth Nexus: OpenAI Capabilities through Patent and IT Exports

Authors: Festus Adedoyin, Victor Ogunbiyi, Aliu Adebiyi, Emmanuel Oluokun

Adedoyin et al. investigate the impact of AI-driven labor on economic growth, particularly in Switzerland. Through dynamic ARDL simulation and empirical analysis, the chapter explores the relationship between labor and growth, highlighting the potential benefits and challenges of OpenAI implementation. The authors advocate for a strategic approach to harnessing AI's potential benefits while addressing its challenges and emphasize the importance of investing in human capital for long-term economic growth.

Chapter 7: Enhancing Emotionally Intelligent Responses in AIML Systems through Idiom-Emoticon Integration and Analysis

Authors: Jonathan Bishop, Wahid Hassan, Robert Bilsland, Elias Alexander

Bishop et al. enhance AIML systems' understanding of English idioms and their emotional contexts. By integrating a database of idioms with emoticons, the authors aim to enable AI to interpret idioms beyond their literal meanings and respond appropriately to emotional undertones. Through methodology description and empirical analysis, the authors refine AIML systems' emotional intelligence, enhancing user interaction and response quality.

Chapter 8: The Impact of Open-AI and MFP on the Labour Market Dynamics of Trinidad and Tobago

Author: Roshnie Doon

Doon examines the integration of OpenAI technologies and Multifactor Productivity (MFP) in the labor dynamics of Trinidad and Tobago. Through secondary research, the chapter explores the impact of AI tools on labor dynamics, production processes, and the future of work in domestic industries. The author discusses the connection between AI tools, MFP, and labor dynamics, providing insights into the potential benefits and challenges of OpenAI adoption in the region.

Chapter 9: Crafting the Future: OpenAI's Strategies and Sustainable Innovation

Authors: Premavathi T., Ayush Shekhar, Aayush Raj, Shreya Agrawal, Damodharan Palaniappan

T. et al. examine OpenAI's strategies and their implications for sustainable innovation. The chapter highlights OpenAI's commitment to safety, transparency, and social benefit, emphasizing collaborative frameworks and community involvement in democratizing AI deployment. Through theoretical insights and practical examples, the authors explore the ethical implications and transformative potential of OpenAI's initiatives, informing readers about OpenAI's impact on global AI laws and standards.

In conclusion, this edited reference book serves as a testament to the transformative potential of Artificial Intelligence (AI) and its intersection with Multifactor Productivity (MFP) in contemporary business landscapes. Through the collective efforts of the contributors, this volume has provided a comprehensive exploration of the myriad ways in which AI technologies, particularly those developed by OpenAI, are reshaping organizational operations, driving innovation, and catalyzing growth across diverse sectors and industries.

As Editors, we have been privileged to witness the depth and breadth of scholarly and practitioner-based insights presented in this compilation. From critical analyses of emerging digital technologies to empirical investigations into AI-driven labor force dynamics, each chapter offers unique perspectives and actionable insights that contribute to our understanding of the complex interplay between AI and productivity.

Moreover, this volume does not shy away from addressing the ethical, societal, and economic implications of AI integration, underscoring the importance of responsible AI deployment and proactive measures to mitigate potential risks and challenges. By fostering dialogue and debate on these crucial issues, this book endeavors to empower readers with the knowledge and tools needed to navigate the evolving landscape of AI-driven business transformation with prudence and foresight.

We extend our heartfelt appreciation to all the contributors who have generously shared their expertise and perspectives, enriching this compilation with invaluable insights and analysis. Whether you are a business leader, academic researcher, policymaker, or industry practitioner, we trust that the contents of this book will inspire further exploration and discourse on the transformative power of AI in driving organizational resilience, innovation, and sustainable growth.

As Editors, we remain hopeful that this volume will serve as a catalyst for continued research, collaboration, and innovation in the field of AI and productivity, ultimately contributing to the advancement of knowledge and the betterment of society as a whole.

Editors:

Festus Adedoyin
Bournemouth University, United Kingdom

Bryan Christiansen
Southern New Hampshire University, United States

Chapter 1
Critical Analysis of Emerging and Disruptive Digital Technologies in an Era of Artificial Intelligence (AI)

José G. Vargas-Hernandez
Tecnológico Nacional de México, Mexico & Budapest Centre for Long-Term Sustainability, Hungary

Selene Castañeda-Burciaga
https://orcid.org/0000-0002-2436-308X
Universidad Politécnica de Zacatecas, Mexico

Omar A. Guirette-Barbosa
https://orcid.org/0000-0003-1336-9475
Universidad Politécnica de Zacatecas, Mexico

Omar C. Vargas-Gonzàlez
https://orcid.org/0000-0002-6089-956X
Tecnològico Nacional de Mèxico, Ciudad Guzmàn, Mexico

ABSTRACT

This study aims to analyze the emergent and disruptive digital technologies in an era of artificial intelligence (IA). It departs from the assumption that the emerging technologies create both opportunities and challenges with an impact on individuals, organizations, institutions, and society at large in terms of bias, surveillance, hacking, etc. The method employed is the critical analysis based on the recent developments reported in scientific literature. It is concluded that control over the ethical disruption of digital technologies and more specifically artificial strategy must require a digital conversation and leadership about acceptable ethical behaviors, under the assumption that digital transformation cannot be interrupted and must be guided by humans in in following years of the near future.

DOI: 10.4018/979-8-3693-1198-1.ch001

INTRODUCTION

I can do Everything for you!

Human development in recent decades has been accompanied by emergent and rapid disruptive technological changes leading to a growing proliferation of digitized devices and services. Emergent and disruptive digital technologies have become intrinsic to our current way for life and will be part of our future lifestyle, from mundane routines and activities to improvement of productive, contributing to manage the requirements of an economic growth in a more competitive and dynamic environment, and evaluating the balance of power for a more collective security.

Artificial intelligence (AI) has a significant impact on individuals, organizations, and societies by offering systematic capabilities of learning and reasoning based on inputs and the differences with the expected outputs, predicting and adapting to changes in the socio-ecosystems from its received external environment stimulus. Artificial intelligence is a digital transformation lead using emerging technologies that have broken into all areas and sectors worldwide leading to get benefits in terms of agility, efficiency, transparency, and social welfare, so it can be affirmed that the emerging and disruptive digital technologies play a preponderant role in our environment and can do everything for us!

Smart life on Everything.

Artificial intelligence (AI), internet of things (IoT), blockchain and Chat GPT, among others, are emergent and disruptive digital technologies that aid human beings and societies in quick and efficient way to increase economic productivity, support the social wellbeing by providing a more educated, productive and healthier lifestyle of individuals, anticipate and prevent responses to crisis and disasters, absorbing shocks, etc. (Sharifi, Khavarian-Garmsir, & Kummitha, 2021). An increased level of research in chatbots designed to respond to queries of the user by mapping the best possible response in real time feedback, are based on adopted language models and deep learning to address natural language processes (NLP) (Lokman & Ameedeen, 2018; Kushwaha & Kar, 2021).

TRANSFORMATIVE EFFECTS OF IOT, BLOCKCHAIN, ARTIFICIAL INTELLIGENCE AND CHAT GPT ON CLOUD COMPUTING: EVOLUTION, VISION, TRENDS, AND OPEN CHALLENGES

The pace of change is likely to accelerate because of the "frontier technologies" that are redefining our world, taking advantage of digitization and connectivity, include artificial intelligence (AI), big data, blockchain, the Internet of Things (IoT), 3D printing, robotics, drones, biotechnology, and nanotechnology. Emerging and disruptive technologies evolution has become the buzzword of the current economic and productivity growth, geopolitical landscape, and security architecture, to build resilience leading to conclude that there is a strong link between them. The design of future digital technologies is bound to change the technological socio-ecosystem and the society at large.

Organizations and states remain the major actors in technological innovation designing and implementing policies, strategies, tactics, and instruments, although the leading technological edge is currently and will be lead in the future by private firms, university research centers and academia while extending the possibility to involve the whole of society approach in operations.

The emerging technologies create both opportunities and challenges with an impact on individuals, organizations, institutions, and society at large in terms of bias, surveillance, hacking, etc. Digital technologies enhance economic, societal, and socio-ecological resilience in terms of health, education, connectivity, communication, etc.

Innovation and competition are the drivers of an emerging and disruptive digital technologies raising challenges and threats based on dynamic and organic processes that require creative destruction of established technologies and industries that takes considerable time in revealing its true features and ultimate effects (Schumpeter, 1949, 1994). Thus, the organic process of creative destruction applies to a new cycle of emerging and disrupting digital technologies that will win the competition leading to the entire transformation of the technological socio-ecosystem.

A positive impact of these technologies is the promotion of resilience with the identification of maintenance needs by inspecting critical infrastructure leading to respond to the emergencies with assistance of recovery efforts in crises and disasters, for example.

WHY IS THE DIGITAL ERA GOING WRONG? WHO CONTROLS THE FUTURE?

Any emergent technological outcome is a neutral tool before receiving connotations depending on how is being used. However, in this era of emerging and disruptive digital technologies we are witnessing heated debates on legal frameworks, standards, recommendations, methods, practices, problems, etc., marked by lack of agreement among the main actors due to divergent interests for control without a clear how to provide solutions.

Emerging, and disruptive digital technologies such as big data, biotechnologies, quantum, autonomous systems require separate international standardization principles of responsible use, which may require various regulatory levels in the space domains. However, the debate on whether ChatGPT's use must be restricted, legislated, and regulated is split. Technological innovation must be stalled by global standards to ensure performance and interoperability between the different emerging technological socio-ecosystems. In the elaboration of this standards must be driven by global governance mechanisms with the participation of other sectors such as private sector and academia.

Obviously, it is difficult to know how far human evil can go, incapacity and stupidity. Suffice it to remember that the largest sources of profit are related to death: war and drugs. Thus, the human being does not seem very trustworthy, as stated by Marín (2023).

Artificial Intelligence Focuses on Automation not on Creating Jobs and not on the Impact of Creating the Greatest Value.

The focus of emerging and disruptive digital technologies has been on automation and not in creating jobs must be amended. Artificial intelligence has been focused on automation and this focus should be changed to the net increase of jobs and job creation. The focus of long term artificial intelligence directions must have an impact on the greatest value of implementation by augmenting people in the jobs, enrichment of jobs and tasks, reimagine and redefine old tasks to create new job activities and transform culture to adapt artificial intelligence threats into new opportunities.

Warnings of job losses confuse artificial intelligence with automation overshadowing the augmentation benefit of a combination and complementation of human and artificial intelligence, where both combine and complement each other. Artificial intelligence has already a negative impact on the workplace by applying to highly repeatable routine tasks requiring copious quantities of data observations and decisions to be analyzed searching for patterns.

Applying artificial intelligence to less-routine with low repeatability and more varied tasks is yielding higher benefits in job creation and greater value. Using auto-generative artificial intelligence have different impacts depending on the industry sector such as to select data or curing diseases. The retailing industry sector is already expanding digital technology, artificial intelligence and human operation activities aimed to improve productivity the in-store check-out process while creating greater value. Applying artificial intelligence to nonroutine tasks tends to combine and complement humans and machines each other to perform more efficiently than either human experts or AI-driven devices and machines working alone.

Investments in artificial intelligence-enable technologies must evaluate the jobs lost, job creation and transformation of co-working collaboration and decision making processes between workers and digital technologies. Technological innovations are associated with a transition period of job loss followed by a recovery. Affected jobs by artificial intelligence varies according to the industry sector with manufacturing and services such as education and healthcare hit the hardest by eliminating middle- and low-level positions, but also creating more new positions of highly skilled, management, the entry-level and low-skilled variety.

Research suggests consumers still prefer the interaction with a knowledgeable human salesperson than using artificial intelligence in more specialized areas who make a significant impact on customer satisfaction. These efforts of applying artificial intelligence and robotics in retailing to replace human tasks prove not be successful to eliminate this job at all despite that operational activities are disrupted, reducing labor, making labor savings, and prompting to reinvest on training to enhance customer experience and satisfaction, creating higher value.

The impact of artificial intelligence and digital technologies in outsourcing are pressured to fundamental changes aimed to reinvent and invest on business models with the symbiosis of human activities instead of only automating practices to create new business opportunities. Improvement of nonroutine work by applying artificial intelligence and robotics must concentrate on leveraging knowledge of digital technologies about general purpose tools to be incorporated into work processes leading to develop a competitive relationship of intelligent employee-robot automation processes to identify and optimize labor-intensive and repetitive activities currently performed by humans.

This improvement resulting from expanding digital technologies, applying artificial intelligence and robotics combined and complemented with humans increment elevated levels of productivity, reducing labor costs and the most important, crate higher levels of value with the creation of new jobs. The entire decision process based on the interaction between human and machines driven by artificial intelligence and other digital technologies must be redesigned to have the advantage of combining and complementing strengths each other to increase agility and optimize the value creation.

Automation, robotics, artificial intelligence, and other digital technologies have a multiplier effect which requires to redefine and create more jobs to create higher value than displacing and killing them, to the extent that should augment the workforce, increasing the productivity and quality of their work, freeing up time to be employed on more strategic priorities. Artificial intelligence, robotics and other digital technologies improves the productivity of many jobs that already has become a positive motivator. Artificial intelligence, robotics, and automation in manufacturing as in any other sectors rather than removing humans from task processes, contribute to augment customer experiences of workers leading to improve productivity by reducing costs, reducing frictions in value chains, optimizing supply chains, and creating higher value opportunities.

ChatGPT Could Make These Jobs Obsolete: 'The Wolf is at the Door.'

The subtitle of this section is taken from Mitchell (2023) on a recent article of analysis, which I borrowed because it is very illustrative of the situation. Concerned with the emergence of a disruptive tool ChatGPT capabilities, surprising intelligent chat bot upended from and based on artificial intelligence, which since its release on the 30th of November 2022, proving to be a tool with capabilities to perform complex tasks and simplify them (Sagarikabiswas, 2023). Higher education, finance and banking, hospitality and tourism, and information technology industries are sectors in which artificial intelligence and its most recent tool ChatGPT are enhancing business management and marketing activities, among others (Yogesh, et al., 2023).

A competing battle is taking place between artificial intelligence chatbots already released such as ChatGPT, BARD powered by Google, Microsoft-powered Bing, ChatSonic and Ernie powered by China's Baidu App, which are leading to employees and workers to dreadful feelings of losing or getting replaced on their jobs.

OpenAI-powered ChatGPT and released GPT-4 fueling fear among the informational technology due to the replacement of programmers and other informational technology professionals by current ongoing massive layoffs (Sagarikabiswas, 2023). OpenAI's ChatGPT extends the capabilities through the integration of natural language models and deep learning based on a Generative Pre-training Transformer (GPT) architecture (Radford et al., 2018) of neural networks aimed to predict the sequence of words in human interactions through generative and discriminative algorithms (Vaswani et al., 2017) used to generate responses to queries that resembles a human expert.

The ChatGPT system is designed on a huge data set and continually improves itself using a simple text prompt to generate the ability to work through any problem and answer to any question with certain varying accuracy depending on its task Experts and analysts are warning that the improvement of these and other capabilities of the ChatGPT tool could spell doom for numerous job fields in industry.

According to the analysis of (Sagarikabiswas, 2023) by April of 2023, 503 technological companies worldwide have laid off 1,39,165 employees in 2023, in part due to the release of the artificial intelligence chatbot. However, other analysts such as Goldman Sachs, are more pessimistic concluding that at least three hundred million jobs are getting obsolete and replaced. Technology engineering and software design has undergone massive staff layoffs at the Silicon Valley (figure 1). Large firms like Microsoft have announced a large investment in the revolutionary technology of artificial intelligence replacing a substantial portion of its global well-paid white-collar workforce while leaving many employees and industries currently vulnerable, from the financial, health care and publishing sectors. Microsoft has already laid off thousands of workers (Mitchell, 2023).

Large firms, such as Microsoft left out of work ten thousand employees while at the same time investing on partnership with OpenAI to accelerate artificial intelligence breakthroughs in abroad set of products aimed to drive growth (Potter, 2023). Other technological firms going through the layoff of white collar employees to achieve cost-cutting measures, includes Amazon, Facebook, Apple, and Meta (Figure 1).

Figure 1. The Job Losses Across the Silicon Valley

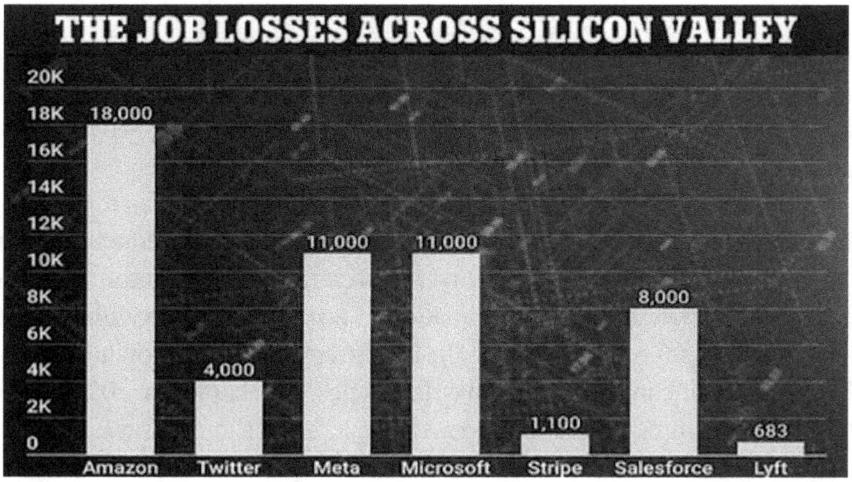

Technology analysts and experts are warning that the artificial intelligence tool ChatGPT are making white collar jobs obsolete and putting millions of people out of work (Potter, 2023). Humans must learn how to harness ChatGPT as a mind-blowing tool of the artificial intelligence technology which is rocking practices on the academia and social media, and leading to the risk that jobs in certain sectors can be supplemented and even replaced such as high education, financial services, journalism, software design engineering and graphics, etc., just to mention some of the affected sectors.

However, the efficient performance of ChatGPT in finding answers to complex questions and solutions to difficult problems in many working tasks and diverse roles of professional fields, there are some tasks and jobs requiring human interaction and empathy, critical thinking, and creativity that artificial intelligence cannot replace. Artificial intelligence cannot replace humans before it has consciousness, autonomy, the ability to act with intent, creativity.

There are some job roles that artificial intelligence is not able to replace in the current and future scenarios. Some of these jobs analyzed by Sagarikabiswas (2023) are programming, hardware technology, network engineering, cyber security analysis, risk analysis, project management and information technology training, among others.

Using ChatGPT is transforming the nature of work, in terms of knowledge, capabilities, competencies and roles of employees. Due to the disruptions already created ChatGPT as it stands today has been already banned or blocked the access in some schools concerned over cheating actions.

Consequences of Automation for Jobs, Wages, and Inequality.

Automation reduces human intervention in job performance by creating machines capable of replacing human attributes in the execution of more complex and repetitive operations with more certainty and security to work more efficiently by reproducing human tasks and leading to fully substitute workers in some cases.

Regarding research on the effects of automation, many studies forecast that in the following next years there will be a huge job destruction, reduction of wages and thus an increasing level of inequality. (See figures 2 and 3). Automation is often associated with job destruction. Automation of tasks will change with advances in artificial intelligence (Acemoglu, Hazell, & Restrepo (2022). Following automation is a decline in routine jobs (Acemoglu & Restrepo 2020; Humlum, 2020). Research on automation documents that is easier to implement it in routine tasks (Levy & Murnane, 2003) (Figure 2 and 3).

Figure 2. Existing Jobs at Potential Risk of Automation

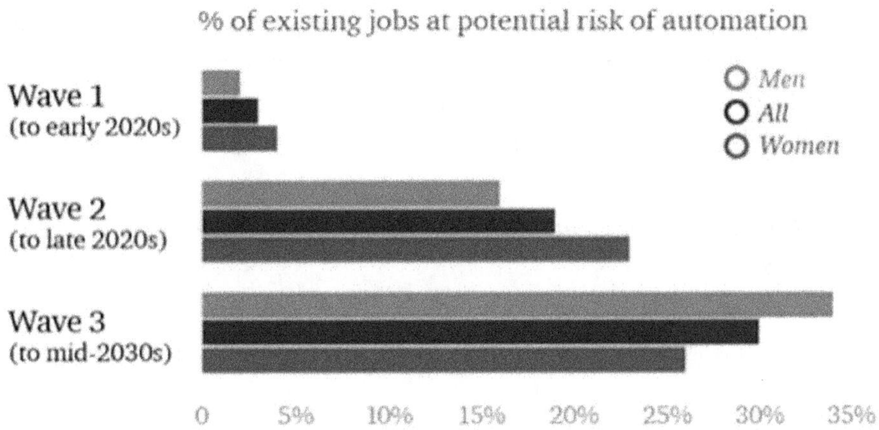

Figure 3. Existing Jobs at Potential Risk of Automation

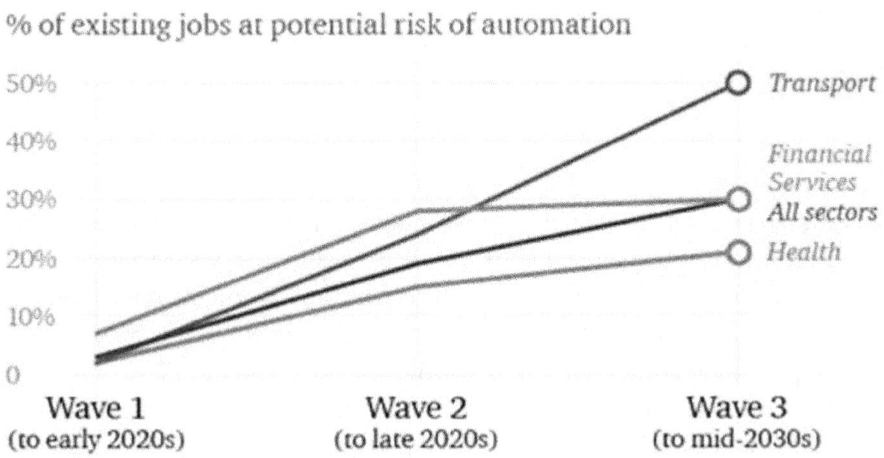

Digital automation technologies tend to expand the tasks performed by the efficient capital, while displacing jobs of certain worker groups for which they have comparative advantage or by reducing the relative, and real, wages of workers specialized in routine tasks in manufacturing industries undergoing digital automation, such as the blue-collar jobs and clerical workers. In contrast, workers with post-graduate studies not displaced from their jobs have wage gains. Wage inequality is rising sharply among the worker groups specialized in routine tasks in routine tasks of industries in economies experiencing rapid automation over the last decades (Acemoglu & Restrepo, 2022) (Figure 4).

Figure 4. Cumulative per Cent Change in Real Annual Wages, by Wage Group in United States

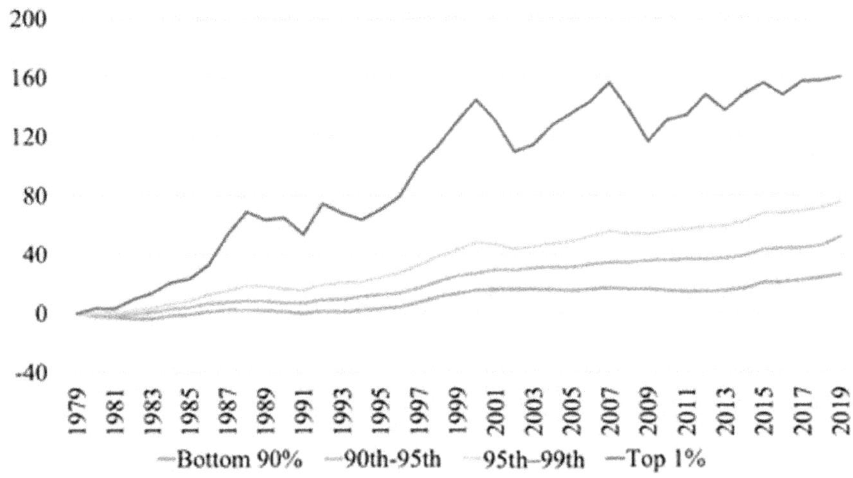

Wage inequality is the result of task displacement, rather than productivity growth and overall capital intensity. According to Acemoglu & Restrepo (2022) task displacement of workers driven by automation from employment opportunities has a defined role in the surge of wage inequality over the last decades. A model designed and developed by Brito & Curl, (2020) with data from 1984 to 2016 demonstrates that the most important consequence of automation is to lower the share of workers in real wages of medium-skilled and low-skilled jobs in domestic production which has steadily declined. Task allocation to diverse types of capital, labor and automation technologies expands tasks performance of capital at the expense of workers. Tax displacement leads to increase in wage inequality.

Generative AI can Reverse Long Term Trends on Inequality, Worker Power and Productivity Growth?

Artificial intelligence may reverse the trends of slowing global productivity, increasing the gap of inequality, and diminishing the worker power, undermining advancement of living standards. The living standards of people determines the wealth of nations which can be raised by lifting productivity, as the amount of output produced per worker.

Productivity is barely growing and will continue for some years due to economic and geopolitical uncertainty and the rising capital costs leading to holdback increases in economic growth and wages while widening the gap of inequality. Workplace shifts due to pandemic and investments into generative artificial intelligence eventually will produce compelling results unleashing an era of productivity growth despite that will take more than a decade to reap the benefits. There is an optimism on the use of digital technologies for the creation and development of new business models and workers switching tasks and jobs to yield better results in increasing productivity, augmenting wages, and reducing the inequality wage gap.

The implementation of the diverse tools of artificial intelligence in the productivity revolution will take a long-term period to pay off (Strauss, June 4, 2023)

Artificial intelligence tools like ChatGPT are easy to adopt ensuring integration with other everyday use apps, which can amplify inequality of resource access leading to asymmetric use and marginalizing groups that will not have represented data (Chen and Wellman, 2004; Weissglass, 2022).

Gopinath (Jun 5, 2023) from the International Monetary Fund foresees a boost of economic growth and benefits workers raising productivity by automating cognitive tasks and giving rise to new higher-productivity tasks to perform with machines taking care of routine and repetitive tasks. Humans could spend more time on being creative innovators and analytical people. Artificial Intelligence can spread the knowledge of experienced and productive workers. (Figure 5)

Figure 5. The Trend of Productivity Growth has been Lower Since Fiscal Crisis

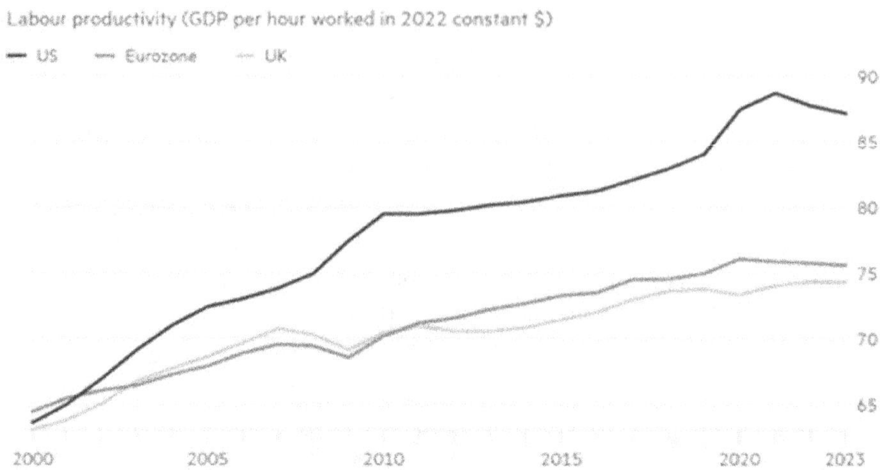

The potential of generative artificial intelligence as more tools are developed, brings about sweeping changes to the global economy, driving about 7%, or almost $7 trillion increase in global GDP lifting productivity growth by about 1.5 percentage points over a 10-year period. Generative AI tools could enhance productivity at office, sales, design building, manufacturing parts, improving healthcare in patient diagnosis, cyber fraud detection, etc. benefiting the global economy (Figure 6).

Figure 6. AI´s Impact on Labor Productivity Depends on its Capability and Adoption Timeline

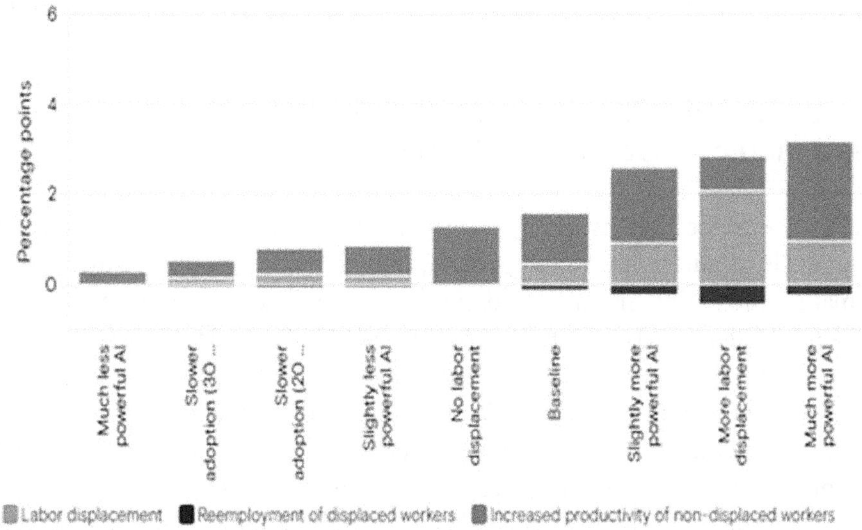

Effect of AI adoption on annual labor productivity growth, 10-year adoption period

Surveillance Intensifies.

A negative impact of the emerging technologies may be the empowerment of malicious actions and the erosion of individual privacy.

ACTIONS TO REDIRECT TECHNOLOGICAL INNOVATION AND CHANGE.

Change the Narrative.

At international level, the discussion on the standardization in the present of future digital technologies exists between communities considering that the measures must be evolutive and most of the times the narratives collide leaving space to black swan scenarios and uncertainties lurking back.

Some of the issues that should be considered in changing the narratives are the optimism instead of realism on strategies for technological supremacy among nations, governance, regulations, and standards, competing and cooperation values, congruent coordination of planning, patterns of interactions between governments, technological firms, start-ups, academic and scientific researchers, global market demand, inadequate protocols, revenues, etc., to address operational needs, solve challenges, create benefits for the actors involved and significant impact for the society at large.

Focus on Machine Learning and Intelligence Instead than on Machine Usefulness!

Artificial intelligence systems are characterized as machine-based systems with certain varying levels of autonomy which give support to humans in their objectives and tasks, making predictions, recommendations, decisions, etc., using data analytics also referred as big data based on a massive amount of alternative data sources. Artificial intelligence and machine learning in several industries build applications to take advantage of connections between artificial intelligence and machine learning, helping the companies to transform their processes and products. Machine learning models are techniques of artificial intelligence increasingly deployed in the use experience in big data automatically to learn and improve predictability in performance without being programmed by humans (OECD, 2021). Artificial intelligence and machine learning today are being used in a wide range of applications.

Artificial intelligence and machine learning are used to optimize inventories of retailers, in health organizations in image processing for improved cancer detection; in banking and finance are used for detecting fraud, predicting risk, and proactive financial advice; in sales and marketing for sales forecasting, campaign optimization, sentiment analysis, etc.; in cyber security protect organizations and their clients by detecting anomalies; in customer services, the use of chatbots and cognitive search to gauge customer intent, virtual assistance and answer questions; in transportation improve the efficiency of routs, predictive analysis, traffic forecasting, etc.; in manufacturing, artificial intelligence are used for predictive maintenance and efficiency of operations, etc.

Behind the scenes, the engine of machine learning attempts to reinforce known patterns in the member's behavior and adjusting accordingly when the member change patterns (Burns, 2023). The "Chat Generative Pre-Trained Transformer" (ChatGPT) is a tool of artificial intelligence, with usefulness as machine to overcome resistance to change resulting from the implementation process of digital innovations. As with most tools of artificial intelligence, ChatGPT sometimes works great and simply fine becoming an especially useful learning machine to provide support to human tasks.

An artificial intelligence chatbot performs some cognitive functions, like analysis and interpretation, better than human brains, with more efficiency, effectiveness, and quality, discerning some patterns that elude the human mind to become more useful in contributions to knowledge. Is in this sense, that from a more cheerful outlook, it is required to move from machine learning to machine usefulness.

Enhance Human Capabilities.

The relationship between humans and the artificial intelligence ecosystem is one of enhancement of human capabilities and not replacement. Artificial intelligence can be leveraged to enhance cognitive functions and human behavior in the analysis, interpretation, and decision-making. However, the digital traces of artificial intelligence require a knowing subject to interpret, analyze, and validate the outcomes.

Humans are uniquely adapted to constantly create becoming good at it, but when it comes to analyzing, interpreting, and understanding data, the larger the data set becomes, the worse humans perform (Williams, 2023). Humans visualizing data miss the smaller trends that have been averaged out besides that are innately biased through past experiences and preexisting assumptions such as spotting correlations to assume causations. While artificial intelligence takes care of the details data analysis and interpretation, humans can concentrate on creating what he-she does best, making best decisions and empowering to implement them, driving behavior change, improving the abilities to inspire, create habits and true accountability. It is difficult to hold accountability in artificial intelligence systems for any errors and problems with generated content because they lack awareness and consciousness as humans have.

Humans have a limited ability to scale only focusing on one item at a time while in comparison, artificial intelligence does not have limitations regarding scalability processing thousands of tasks in a fraction of a second. Thus, humans can have on artificial intelligence scalability as a trait.

Create Countervailing Powers.

The future of edge digital technologies from artificial intelligence to quantum information science have not clear definition which complicates the standardization and regulation because the global competition of major players to gain the largest global market share (Neaher, *et al.* 2021).

The new standards and regulations for the emerging and disruptive digital technologies must rise from a creative destruction of outdated advances leading to an overall scientific revolution to fully occur to instate no longer emergent the emerging technologies. This argument is supported by Kuhn (1962: 11) who stated that men whose research is based on shared paradigms are committed to the same rules and standards for scientific practice. That commitment and the apparent consensus it creates are prerequisites for normal science.

A new model of cooperation in partnerships between governments and firms sharing both risks and responsibilities, will enable to deliver more value in the digital technologies field by creating more benefits for the involved partners by ensuring proper alignment of interest involving the society at large. Private public partnership cooperation becomes the new structure and a tool for creating economic growth, social development, and socio-ecological resilience, while providing opportunities to balance the advantages for all the involved actors and the society at large.

Convergence of stakeholders in emerging and disruptive digital technology brings new conceptualizations and types of instrumentation of end products and services that will enable major changes in productivity and lifestyles for the wellbeing of the whole society.

ALIGNMENT ETHICS.

It is difficult to imagine how far the evil and stupidity of the human being can go. The rise of ChatGPT and their effects on individuals and society is an opportunity to discuss ethical issues when using these and other similar tools. In the field of artificial intelligence (AI) alignment ethics aims to steer artificial intelligence systems towards ethical principles based on humans' intended goals and preferences. An artificial intelligence system is considered ethically aligned if it advances the intended objectives of human development. Preceded debates are conducted with moral and ethical considerations on specific technologies, as for example, the Ethics of Artificial Intelligence Recommendation of UNESCO.

Artificial intelligence is a digital technology different from all previous technologies including neural networks, dep learning through algorithms and automatic learning, which have presented new and different risks and ethical concerns (Blackman, 2020) considering that humans have control over the machines, turning on and turning off. Humans need to make decisions on what is an acceptable behavior in the use of digital technologies and more precisely on the tools of artificial intelligence, to design, enact and enforce policies.

Avoiding biases on Data and Models of AI.

Artificial intelligence is already here to stay forever and from ethical alignment to be used responsible which requires the commitment to act and behave ethically at every turn. The increasing use of artificial intelligence is risen significant ethical alignment concerns sparking debates regarding issues from human data privacy to the use of algorithms in chat bots and chatGPT that not only perpetuates but tend to emphasize religious, ethnic, racial, gender and other bias. The ethics of responsible artificial intelligence has an orientation from utilitarianism to justify some threats posed by tools such as the ChatGPT, and similar chat bots that include black- box algorithms to validate copyright, infringement discrimination and biases, vulgarity, plagiarism, fake media, fabricated unauthentic textual content, etc., among others.

These ethical issues are being already reported by academics, organizations, and institutions worried with these developments and some measures are being proposed to deal with them. Among other measures to put into place and enforce to mitigate the negative effects, are the claims of disclosing data collected and transparency of what is done with that data, to establish committees dedicated to overseeing the use of artificial intelligence, to identify intelligent agents and chatbots as non-human entities, etc. (Carufel, Dec. 18, 2019).

Ways to Conduct Additional Training.

Academic, institutional, and organizational leaders are worried and concerned about the effect of artificial intelligence replacing the workforce and the ways to conduct additional training to employees that are rightly worried about being displaced from their jobs. Organizations adopting artificial intelligence must understand, analyze, manage, assess, and mitigate risks, monitor, and evaluate ethical reviews and bias screening considering the evolution of algorithms in nature which require training on the heterogeneous algorithm models that possess high velocity and variability. The diverse ways to conduct additional training is an issue that raises ethical concerns.

Permission to use Millions of Words and Material on Artificial Intelligence Training.

Reputation and legal risks of artificial intelligence using copyrighted or offensive content, loss of privacy, spreading false information, fraudulent transactions, lack of transparence, misuse, bias, etc. Regarding the integrity issues, to identify the actual scriptwriter by comparing the text created by ChatGPT is still elusive now. There many legal concerns and issues around copyright and ownership of content generated by artificial intelligence.

Laws and regulations are concerned with these ethical issues dealing with the content created by learning machines which create legal disputes over the ownership of rights to use and profit from the generated content. However, generative artificial intelligence content poses an elevated risk for intellectual property rights and copyright protection, which has serious implications for research to avoid potential infringement caused by the use. OpenAI has already declared that it does not take any responsibility for any infringement that may occur.

Long term Implications of Artificial Intelligence are not clear.

Artificial intelligence risk management frameworks must consolidate in the long-term the ethical theory to integrate socially responsible judgments leading to ensure reasoned, purposeful, cautious, and ethical leverage alignment to generative artificial intelligence models. Identification of artificial intelligence and management risks lead to design and implement ethical models to be used long-term to determine a path (Ashok et al., 2022). Utilitarism is an ethical approach used to decision making based on the positive and negative impact of actions that does best good and least harm to individuals, organizations, environment (B¨ohm et al., 2022).

Control over the ethical disruption of digital technologies and more specifically artificial strategy must require a digital conversation and leadership about acceptable ethical behaviors, under the assumption that digital transformation cannot be interrupted and must be guided by humans in in following years of the near future.

CONCLUSIONS

Machine learning in artificial intelligence tools, such as the chat GPT can offer prompt responses with an unforeseen combination of innovative and valuable texts produced from digital traces, with the likelihood of an exceptionally low selection subject to quality of data sources and training. These traces require a knowing subject to interpret, analyze, and validate the outcomes. As a stochastic and algorithm parrot, most of the tools of artificial intelligence are unconscious and not be able to produce self-knowledge, which by themselves do not constitute meaningful, valid, and legitimated scientific knowledge.

The development of ethical codes, law, and regulations for the governance of generative artificial intelligence systems is required aimed to minimize ethical concerns such as discrimination, false data and information, plagiarism, copyright infringement, etc. Further, questions regarding the copyright ownership, intellectual property rights, regulations for acceptable use norms, etc., are issues that must be raised, discussed, analyzed, and addressed.

Research and practice must be extended to explore innovative approaches for using artificial intelligence tools and other digital disruptive and breakthrough technologies for finding solution to all ills leading to potential enhancement of human development, creating social and environmental benefits, increasing productivity. These opportunities to conduct future research calls for more transdisciplinary approaches with implications in educational programs that must be challenged using an ethical perspective of digital technologies and artificial intelligence tools aimed to benefit humanity.

REFERENCES

Acemoglu, D., Hazell, J., & Restrepo, P. (2022). Artificial Intelligence and Jobs: Evidence from Online Vacancies. *Journal of Labor Economics, 40*(S1), S293–S340. doi:10.1086/718327

Acemoglu, D., Lelarge, C., & Restrepo, P. (2020). Competing With Robots: Firm-Level Evidence from France. *AEA Papers and Proceedings. American Economic Association, 110*, 383–388. doi:10.1257/pandp.20201003

Acemoglu, D., & Restrepo, P. (2022). Tasks, automation, and the rise in U.S. wage inequality. *Econometrica, 90*(5), 1973–2016. doi:10.3982/ECTA19815

Ashok, M., Madan, R., Joha, A., & Sivarajah, U. (2022). Ethical framework for Artificial Intelligence and Digital technologies. *International Journal of Information Management, 62*, 102433. doi:10.1016/j.ijinfomgt.2021.102433

B'ohm, S., Carrington, M., Cornelius, N., de Bruin, B., Greenwood, M., Hassan, L., & Shaw, D. (2022). Ethics at the centre of global and local challenges: Thoughts on the future of business ethics. *Journal of Business Ethics*, 180(3), 835–861.

Blackman, R. (2020, October 15). *A Practical Guide to Building Ethical AI.* Retrieved from https://hbr.org/2020/10/a-practical-guide-to-building-ethical-ai.

Brito, D., & Curl, R. F. (2020). *Automation Does Not Kill Jobs. It Increases Inequality*. Baker Institute Report no. 11.06.20. Rice University's Baker Institute for Public Policy, Houston, Texas.

Burns, E. (2023). Machine Learning. *TechTarget network.* https://www.techtarget.com/searchenterpriseai/definition/machine-learning-ML

Carufel, R. (Dec. 18, 2019). Companies embrace AI, but execs cite challenges on alignment, ethics. Agility, PR Solutions. Retrieved from: https://www.agilitypr.com/pr-news/public-relations/companies-embrace-ai-but-execs-

Chen, W., & Wellman, B. (2004). The global digital divide–within and between countries. *ITandSociety, 1*(7), 39–45.

Gopinath, G. (Jun 5, 2023). *The Power and Perils of the "Artificial Hand": Considering AI Through the Ideas of Adam Smith Speech to commemorate 300th anniversary of Adam Smith's birth University of Glasgow.* International Monetary Fund. Retrieved from https://www.imf.org/en/News/Articles/2023/06/05/sp060523-fdmd-ai-adamsmith?cid=em-COM-123-46688

Humlum, A. (2020). *Robot Adoption and Labor Market Dynamics*, Working paper, University of Chicago.

Kuhn, T. (1962). *The structure of scientific revolutions*. University of Chicago Press.

Kushwaha, A. K., & Kar, A. K. (2021). *MarkBot–A Language Model-Driven Chatbot for Interactive Marketing in Post-Modern World*. Retrieved January 31, 2023, from Information Systems Frontiers. . doi:10.1007/s10796-021-10184-y

Levy, D. H. F., & Murnane, R. J. (2003). The Skill Content of Recent Technological Change: An Empirical Exploration. *The Quarterly Journal of Economics, 118*(4), 1279–1333. https://www.jstor.org/stable/25053940. doi:10.1162/003355303322552801

Lokman, A. S., & Ameedeen, M. A. (2018). *Modern chatbot systems: A technical review. Proceedings of the Future Technologies Conference* (pp. 1012–1023). Cham: Springer, (November).10.1007/978-3-030-02683-7_75

Marín, F. M. (2023). *De las humanidades digitales a la Inteligencia Artificial General*. University of Texas at San Antonio.

Mishel, L., & Bivens, J. (2021). The Productivity-Median Compensation Gap in the United States: The Contribution of Increased Wage Inequality and the Role of Policy Choices. *International Productivity Monitor*, (41), 61+. https://link.gale.com/apps/doc/A689169156/AONE?u=anon~10ba8f08&sid=googleScholar&xid=5119dfa8

Mitchell, A. (January 25, 2023). ChatGPT could make these jobs obsolete: 'The wolf is at the door.' *New York Post*. Retrieved from https://nypost.com/2023/01/25/chat-gpt-could-make-these-jobs-obsolete/

Neaher, G., Bray, D., Mueller-Kaler, J. & Schatz, B. (2021). *Standardizing the future: How can the United States navigate the geopolitics of international technology standards?* Atlantic Council Report.

OECD. (2021). *Artificial Intelligence, Machine Learning and Big Data in Finance: Opportunities, Challenges, and Implications for Policy Makers,* https://www.oecd.org/finance/artificial-intelligence-machine-learning-big-data-in-finance.htm

Potter, W. (27 January 2023) 'This is not crying wolf... the wolf is at the door': Fears AI could make white collar jobs obsolete as Microsoft pumps multibillion-dollar investment into ChatGPT after laying off 10,000 workers. *Dailymail.com*. retrieved from https://www.dailymail.co.uk/news/article-11683901/ChatGPT-make-white-collar-jobs-obsolete-Microsoft-pumps-billions-AI.html

Radford, A., Narasimhan, K., Salimans, T. and Sutskever, I. (2018) *Improving Language Understanding with Unsupervised Learning*. Technical Report, OpenAI.

Sacks, G. (05 April 2023). Generative AI could raise global GDP by 7% Artificial Intelligence Retrieved from https://www.goldmansachs.com/intelligence/pages/generative-ai-could-raise-global-gdp-by-7-percent.html

Sagarikabiswas (02 Apr 2023). ChatGPT: 7 IT Jobs That AI Can't Replace. Retrieved from https://www.geeksforgeeks.org/chatgpt-7-it-jobs-that-ai-cant-replace/

Schumpeter, J. (1949). *The Theory of Economic Development, An Inquiry into Profits, Capital, Credit, Interest and the Business Cycle*. Harvard University Press.

Schumpeter, J. (1994). *Capitalism, Socialism and democracy*. Routledge.

Sharifi, A., Khavarian-Garmsir, A. R., & Kummitha, R. K. R. (2021). Contributions of smart city solutions and technologies to resilience against the COVID-19 pandemic: A literature review. *Sustainability (Basel)*, *13*(14), 1–28. doi:10.3390/su13148018

Strauss, D. (June 4, 2023). Generative AI's 'productivity revolution' will take time to pay off. Financial Times. Retrieved from https://www.ft.com/content/21384711-3506-4901-830c-7ecc3ae6b32a

Vaswani, A., Shazeer, N., Parmar, N., Uszkoreit, J., Jones, L., Gomez, A. N., & Polosukhin, I. (2017). *Attention is all you need. Advances in neural information processing systems,* 30. 31st Conference on Neural Information Processing Systems. CA, USA: Long Beach, (Available at) https://proceedings.neurips.cc/paper/2017/file/ 3f5ee243547dee91fbd053c1c4a845aa-Paper.pdf.

Weissglass, D. E. (2022). Contextual bias, the democratization of healthcare, and medical artificial intelligence in low- and middle-income countries. *Bioethics*, *36*(2), 201–209. doi:10.1111/bioe.12927 PMID:34460977

Williams, J. (2023). How AI Will Enhance Human Capabilities. *Forbes*. Retrieved from https://www.forbes.com/sites/forbescommunicationscouncil/2018/03/19/how-ai-will-enhance-human-capabilities/?sh=1d37cd1e366f

Yogesh, K., & ... . (2023). "So, what if ChatGPT wrote it?" Multidisciplinary perspectives on opportunities, challenges, and implications of generative conversational AI for research, practice, and policy. *International Journal of Information Management*, *71*, 102642. https://www.sciencedirect.com/science/article/pii/S0268401223000233. doi:10.1016/j.ijinfomgt.2023.102642

Chapter 2
AI-Powered Dialogue System for Business Exploring GPT3's Impact

Amir Ahmad Dar
https://orcid.org/0000-0002-0379-2272
Lovely Professional University, India

Akshat Jain
Lovely Professional University, India

Mehak Malhotra
Lovely Professional University, India

Mohammad Shahfaraz Khan
University of Technology and Applied Sciences, Oman

Manzoor Ahmad Khanday
https://orcid.org/0000-0002-0053-098X
Lovely Professional University, India

ABSTRACT

Transformative breakthroughs appear every few decades, revolutionizing the globe and vastly enhancing our quality of life. With the introduction of ChatGPT, another paradigm-shifting event has now occurred. This Study examine the importance of GPT-3 in the context of business. In essence, GPT-3 has the potential to transform a variety of business processes by streamlining workflows, enhancing client relationships, and spurring creative breakthroughs. This transformative tool can substantially advance businesses by amplifying effectiveness, refining customer engagements, fostering innovation, and simplifying an array of operations. This research will explore the capacity to influence diverse sectors, notably the financial market. Moreover, GPT-3 holds the potential to profoundly shape the functions of financial brokers, augmenting their efficiency, customer service, and decision-making protocols. Ultimately, we will examine how GPT-3 can elevate effectiveness, customer engagement, decision-making, and creative advancement

DOI: 10.4018/979-8-3693-1198-1.ch002

1. INTRODUCTION

ChatGPT was developed by the AI research organization OpenAI (a San Francisco-based research lab and company). It is a product of OpenAI which is a natural language processing (NLP) model that amalgamates GPT-2, a language model rooted in transformers, with supervised and reinforcement learning techniques for fine-tuning. This approach is a facet of transfer learning and was applied to the extensive collection of large language patterns known as GPT-3, also developed by OpenAI. This model's sophisticated NLP capabilities encompass a diverse spectrum of potential applications, which can support efficiency, interactions with customers, decision-making processes, and innovative pursuits (Kumar and Sharma, 2023; George and George, 2023).

GPT-3, "Generative Pre-trained Transformer 3," is a state-of-the-art artificial intelligence model for language processing. This version marks the third instalment in the GPT series and signifies a notable stride forward in comprehending and generating natural language. It is constructed upon the foundational framework of a deep learning architecture known as a transformer. Transformers are purpose-built for processing sequential data, encompassing sentences and paragraphs, and are particularly adept at tasks entailing contextual understanding and extensive linkages. The primary breakthrough of GPT-3 resides in its extensive scale and capabilities, establishing it as one of the most sizable language models to date.

GPT-3 boasts an immense scale, characterized by its incorporation of a staggering 175 billion parameters. These parameters represent the adaptable weights utilised by the model to formulate predictions grounded in input data. The substantial quantity of parameters equips GPT-3 with the ability to grasp and produce intricate language structures. Much like its forerunners, GPT-3 undergoes pre-training by exposure to an extensive corpus of text data. This process enables the model to internalize language patterns and contextual intricacies (George and George, 2023).

The model doesn't possess precise information about its training data, but it learns to create logical and contextually fitting text. Following initial training, the model can be specialized for tasks using more specific data. GPT-3 can handle tasks with only a few examples given as prompts. It can draw broad conclusions from just a handful of instances, even for tasks it wasn't specifically taught. This capability has enabled its use in various applications such as language translation, answering questions, generating code, etc.

GPT-3 can produce text resembling human language when given prompts. It can extend text, respond to queries, craft poetry, and generate code segments. The model can grasp and retain context across lengthy text segments, resulting in more consistent and contextually appropriate replies. Despite its substantial advancements in language handling, GPT-3 is not exempt from constraints (Kumar and Sharma, 2023; George & George, 2023).

The model's output may occasionally sound reasonable but contain inaccuracies or lack coherence. Furthermore, it can unintentionally magnify biases embedded in the training data. GPT-3's proficiencies have resulted in its application across diverse domains, encompassing content generation, chatbots for customer support, translation services, code writing, virtual aides, and beyond (Kumar and Sharma, 2023; George and George, 2023).

Enterprises can leverage chatbots like ChatGPT to automate routine operations or enhance intricate interactions, like designing email sales campaigns, debugging code, or elevating customer support. Gartner, a research firm, forecasts that the AI software market will approach approximately $134.8 billion by 2025. Furthermore, the market expansion rate is projected to surge from 14.4% in 2021 to 31.1% in 2025, surpassing the general growth rate of the software market (Weblink).

A significant portion of the market will comprise chatbot technology, leveraging artificial intelligence (AI) and natural language processing to provide answers to user inquiries. These responses closely resemble human language and are presented in prose format. Advanced versions of these programs enable interactions involving subsequent questions and replies, and they can be customized to suit particular business needs. A key distinction between ChatGPT and GPT-3, as summarized by a senior solutions architect at TripStax, lies in their scale and capabilities (Weblink).

This research focuses on the utilization of ChatGPT within the business context. It will also examine into the impact of GPT-3 on the financial market. The field of artificial intelligence (AI) has undergone substantial progress in recent times, resulting in the emergence of various applications and novel technologies. Furthermore, the study will explore the contribution of GPT in the realm of business, highlighting its potential to assist brokers in generating precise and contextually relevant answers.

1.1 Objectives of the Study

ChatGPT is a natural language processing (NLP) model that operates on an open-source framework, originating from the efforts of OpenAI. The document titled "ChatGPT: Generative Pre-training for Conversational Response Generation" offers a thorough exploration of the creation and applications of this inventive technological advancement (George & George, 2023). The objectives are: a) Investigate the impact of GPT-3 on financial markets and its potential to assist brokers in making informed decisions. b) Assess how GPT-3 can improve efficiency, decision-making processes, and innovation in various business contexts. Also, c) the aim is to understand the role and impact of GPT-3 on various aspects of business operations.

2. METHODOLOGY

This literature review adopts a systematic approach to investigate the utilization of ChatGPT and the impact of GPT-3 on the financial market within the context of business. The review focuses on analyzing scholarly articles, research papers, and reports that discuss the applications of ChatGPT and GPT-3 in business operations and their influence on the financial market. Key concepts include the functionality of ChatGPT, the sophistication of GPT-3, business applications, and financial market implications. Selected literature must provide insights into ChatGPT, GPT-3, their applications in business, and their effects on the financial market. Only articles published in English and accessible through academic databases will be included. Overall, this methodology ensures a systematic and comprehensive analysis of the literature related to ChatGPT, GPT-3, and their implications for business and the financial market.

3. GPT-3 AND FINANCIAL MARKET

The author provides some insights into how GPT-3 might have affected the financial market (Williams, 2023; Riserbato, 2022).

Investment Research: GPT-3 can help by quickly combining data from several sources to create investment research summaries and reports. This capability could enable investors and analysts to maintain current awareness of pertinent news and trends as they unfold (Dai et al., 2023).

Sentiment Analysis: Sentiment analysis could leverage GPT-3 to interpret and comprehend market sentiment using extensive textual data accessible on the internet. Through the examination of news articles, posts on social media platforms, and financial documents, GPT-3 could assess market sentiment, potentially leading to predictions about market trends (Leippold, 2023).

Automated Trading Algorithms: Automated trading algorithms empowered by GPT-3's natural language processing abilities have the potential to create advanced trading strategies. These strategies would involve real-time analysis of news articles, financial statements, and social media sentiments to enhance decision-making in trading. Yet, the success of these algorithms hinges on the precision of the foundational language models and the quality of the data they are trained on (Haluza, & Jungwirth, 2023).

Customer Support and Financial Advisory: GPT-3 could enhance customer support and financial advisory services for financial institutions. By employing GPT-3-driven chatbots, these institutions could swiftly address customer inquiries, offer fundamental financial guidance, and aid in managing accounts more effectively (Kumar et al., 2023).

Regulatory Compliance: GPT-3 could expedite the process of summarizing regulatory modifications and their implications, aiding financial organizations in promptly comprehending a diverse range of regulations. This capability could empower companies to effectively adjust to evolving compliance prerequisites.

Risk Assessment: GPT-3 holds the potential to enhance the complexity of risk assessment models by analyzing intricate financial documents and pinpointing potential risks that might not be readily apparent.

Market News Summaries: GPT-3 has the potential to automate the task of condensing financial news articles, press releases, and earnings reports. This would be beneficial for traders and investors who need to stay abreast of a continuous flow of information, as it would help them save time and effort.

4. GPT-3 AND BUSINESS

GPT-3 possesses the capability to profoundly influence diverse aspects of businesses across various industries. It is sophisticated natural language processing abilities open doors to a broad spectrum of applications that can optimise effectiveness, customer engagement, decision-making processes, and innovative endeavours ((George et al., 2022a; George et al., 2022b). Here are several avenues through which GPT-3 can be utilised within a business context:

1. **Enhanced Customer Support and Chatbots:** Leveraging GPT-3, chatbots can deliver effective and individualized customer support by comprehending and addressing customer questions in a manner akin to human interaction. These automated chatbots can manage diverse inquiries, offer guidance in resolving issues, and even contribute to suggesting product choices (Kumar et al., 2023).
2. **Utilization in Virtual Assistants:** GPT-3 can be incorporated into virtual assistants designed to assist with tasks such as arranging appointments, overseeing assignments, issuing prompts, and even composing emails for users (Okerlund et al., 2022).
3. **Automated Content Creation:** GPT-3 can streamline content generation by producing blog entries, articles, promotional content, and social media posts. This ability can aid businesses in upholding a vibrant online identity and crafting captivating content (Kumar and Sharma, 2023).

4. **Automated Language Translations:** The language translation proficiency of GPT-3 can empower businesses to enhance communication with global clients and customers by furnishing instantaneous translations (Katar et al., 2022).
5. **Utilization in Market Analysis and Insights:** Enterprises can harness GPT-3 to scrutinize and condense market research documents, industry patterns, and customer input. It can aid in extracting valuable understandings from substantial quantities of text-based information (Haluza, & Jungwirth, 2023).
6. **Creativity and Design:** GPT-3 can contribute to devising inventive concepts for design undertakings, collaborative idea sessions, and the creation of products. It can aid in conceiving taglines, product labels, and even design blueprints (Kumar and Sharma, 2023).
7. **Code Creation Support:** In the technology industry, GPT-3 can provide aid in producing code fragments, supplying programming guidance, and even contributing to tasks related to software development (Khan and Uddin, 2022).
8. **Automated Data Handling:** GPT-3 has the potential to automate data entry responsibilities by extracting pertinent details from documents and forms, mitigating the need for manual labour and the risk of mistakes (Jaimovitch-López et al., 2023).
9. **Analysis of Market Sentiments:** GPT-3 can evaluate social media updates, news pieces, and digital conversations to offer an understanding of market sentiment, thereby assisting businesses in making well-informed choices (Leippold, 2023).
10. **Evaluating Risks and Ensuring Adherence to Regulations:** Particularly in the financial and legal domains, GPT-3 can provide support in scrutinizing intricate documents, contracts, and updates in regulations. This aids in the assessment of potential risks and the guarantee of regulatory compliance (Leippold, 2023).
11. **Cultivating Innovation and Conceptualization:** GPT-3 can play a role in stimulating idea-generation sessions by formulating novel concepts, notions, and attributes for products. This contributes to nurturing an atmosphere of innovation within businesses (Dai et al., 2023).

Overall, the integration of GPT-3 into financial markets can enhance efficiency, decision-making processes, and risk management practices, ultimately leading to improved performance and better outcomes for market participants.

Investors often rely on sentiment analysis to gauge market sentiment and make informed trading decisions. Traditionally, sentiment analysis involves manually analyzing news articles, social media posts, and other sources of information to assess whether the overall sentiment is positive, negative, or neutral.

However, this process can be time-consuming and prone to biases. By integrating GPT-3 into sentiment analysis tools, financial institutions can automate and enhance this process.

Let's say a hedge fund wants to gauge market sentiment regarding a specific stock, such as Tesla (TSLA). They can utilize GPT-3 to analyze a large volume of news articles, social media posts, and analyst reports related to Tesla in real time.

GPT-3 can accurately identify and categorize the sentiment expressed in each piece of content, taking into account the context, tone, and language used. For example

a) Positive sentiment: "Tesla's latest earnings report exceeded analysts' expectations, driving the stock price higher." b) Negative sentiment: "Concerns about Tesla's production delays and quality control issues have led to a sell-off in the stock." c) Neutral sentiment: "Tesla announced plans to expand its production facilities, which could potentially boost future revenue."

By aggregating and analyzing this sentiment data, the hedge fund can gain valuable insights into market sentiment towards Tesla. They can use this information to adjust their trading strategies, such as buying or selling Tesla stock based on whether the sentiment is bullish or bearish.

5. ROLE OF GPT3 IN THE DEVELOPMENT OF THE BUSINESS

GPT-3 can have a substantial impact on business growth through its ability to boost effectiveness, enhance customer engagements, foster innovation, and optimize diverse operations, as depicted in Figure 1. The following are particular avenues where GPT-3's contributions to business development are evident:

Figure 1. Role of GPT3

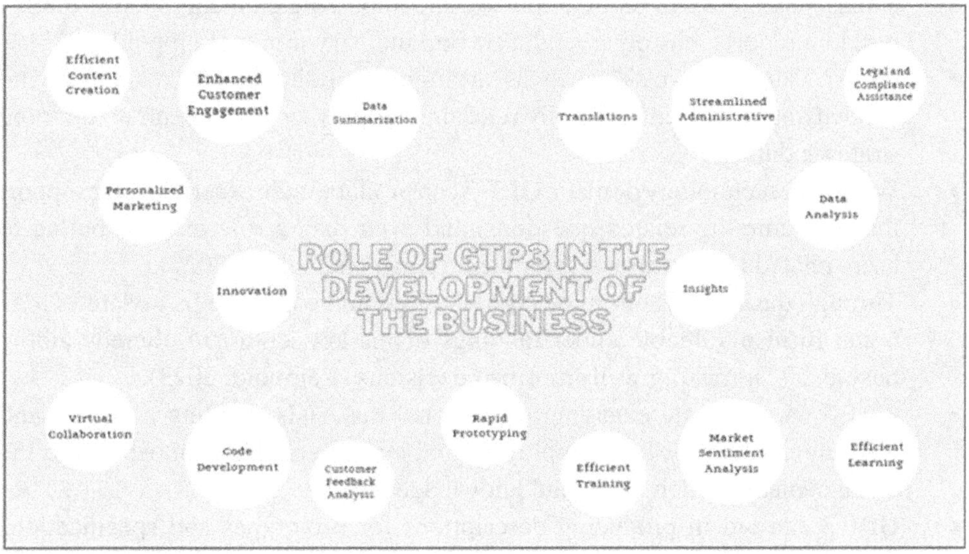

- Through the utilization of chatbots and virtual assistants driven by GPT-3, businesses can offer immediate responses to customer queries, resulting in enhanced levels of customer interaction and contentment. This approach allows enterprises to provide continuous support without the need to expand their human customer service workforce (Bansal 2024).
- GPT-3 can assist in tailoring marketing efforts for specific customers through the study of client data and preferences, resulting in promotions that are more potent and accurately targeted (Haluza, & Jungwirth, 2023).
- By generating premium articles, blog posts, updates for social media sites, and promotional content, GPT-3 can automate content generation. Businesses may be able to save time and resources as a result of this efficiency, allowing them to continue producing fresh and interesting content (Kumar and Sharma, 2023).
- GPT-3 can contribute to brainstorming sessions and innovation endeavours by offering novel suggestions for ideas, product attributes, and imaginative concepts. This can foster a culture of creative thinking within teams.
- For enterprises engaged in global markets, GPT-3 can offer immediate translations, streamlining communication with clients and customers from around the world (Katar et al., 2022).

- GPT-3 can assist businesses in extracting valuable understandings from extensive amounts of text-based data, encompassing elements such as market research reports, customer feedback, and industry trends (Leippold, 2023).
- GPT-3 can aid in tasks such as arranging appointments, data input, and condensing documents, thereby releasing employees to concentrate on more strategic duties.
- Within the technology domain, GPT-3 can produce code excerpts, offer support for programming-related questions, and even play a role in contributing to tasks related to software development (Khan and Uddin, 2022).
- Through the analysis of online conversations and social media updates, GPT-3 can furnish valuable understandings of market sentiment, thereby aiding businesses in making well-informed decisions (Leippold, 2023).
- GPT-3 can generate engaging educational materials, training modules, and learning content for both employees and customers. This contributes to the enhancement of their skills and knowledge levels.
- GPT-3 can aid in producing descriptions for prototypes and specifications of products, thereby accelerating the initial phase of product development where prototypes are created.
- GPT-3 can analyze customer feedback collected from diverse channels and offer practical insights that can be used to enhance products, services, and overall customer experiences.
- In industries with complex legal requirements, GPT-3 can contribute by examining contracts, legal papers, and updates to regulations. This assistance aids in ensuring compliance and diminishing potential risks.
- GPT-3 can provide concise summaries of extensive reports, articles, and research outcomes, expediting the process for business professionals to swiftly understand essential information.
- Virtual assistants powered by GPT-3 can streamline communication and teamwork by coordinating meetings, disseminating updates, and overseeing task management among teams.

It's essential to acknowledge that although GPT-3 presents numerous benefits, it isn't flawless. There might be instances where its responses are incorrect or contextually unsuitable, and it could perpetuate biases inherent in the training data. Businesses need to meticulously weigh these aspects when incorporating GPT-3 into their processes, guaranteeing the presence of human supervision and mechanisms for maintaining quality control. When applied thoughtfully, GPT-3 can indeed play a role in fostering business expansion, operational efficiency, and inventive advancements.

6. GPT3 AND ITS ROLE ON FINANCIAL BROKERS

GPT-3 holds considerable potential in revolutionizing the functions of financial brokers, thereby augmenting their operational efficiency, customer service, and decision-making procedures. Below are the ways GPT-3 can be harnessed within the realm of financial brokerage:

1. **Customer Support and Communication:** By utilizing chatbots and virtual assistants driven by GPT-3, financial brokers can offer immediate responses to client queries concerning matters such as account balances, transaction records, and investment opportunities. This advancement enhances customer service by delivering rapid and precise information, extending assistance even beyond standard business hours (Boman, 2023).
2. **Portfolio Management Suggestions:** Utilizing GPT-3, brokers can assess a client's risk tolerance, investment objectives, and financial status. They can then create tailored portfolio suggestions encompassing diverse asset categories and considering prevailing market conditions (Zhang et al., 2020).
3. **Investment Research and Analysis:** GPT-3 can aid brokers in conducting thorough investment research by condensing market-related news, financial documents, and analyst advice. This capability streamlines the process, saving time and enabling brokers to remain well-informed about prevailing market trends (Leippold, 2023).
4. **Trading Strategy Generation:** GPT-3 can support brokers in crafting trading strategies by evaluating historical data, current market conditions, and client preferences. It can introduce fresh viewpoints and insights to aid in making informed trading choices conditions (Zhang et al., 2020).
5. **Automated Report Generation:** GPT-3 can be used by brokers to automate the creation of investment reports, performance summaries, and client communication materials. This ensures that clients get timely and accurate updates on the condition of their investments.
6. **Risk Assessment and Compliance:** GPT-3 can aid in examining regulatory documents, compliance directives, and potential risks linked to investment selections, thereby supporting brokers in arriving at better-informed decisions.
7. **Market Sentiment Analysis:** GPT-3 may examine market sentiment from news stories, social media posts, and financial reports, providing insightful information about how the market is responding to recent events and emerging trends (Leippold, 2023).
8. **Real-time Market Updates:** GPT-3 can provide brokers with immediate updates on stock prices, market indexes, and financial news, allowing them to stay informed and react quickly to market changes.

9. **Client Education:** Brokers can use GPT-3 to create instructional tools and resources geared at assisting clients in understanding financial concepts, investment strategies, and market dynamics.
10. **Data Analysis and Insights:** To help brokers identify patterns, correlations, and prospective market opportunities from large datasets, GPT-3 was developed (Leippold, 2023).
11. **Customized Investment Recommendations:** Brokers can use GPT-3 to make tailored investment recommendations that take into account a client's financial goals, level of risk tolerance, and the current state of the market.
12. **Algorithmic Trading Strategies:** By carefully examining historical data and market trends, GPT-3 can contribute to the creation of algorithmic trading methods, helping brokers create more effective trading algorithms (Leippold, 2023).
13. **Client Engagement and Relationship Building:** GPT-3 can assist brokers in delivering clients personalized messages, updates, and financial advice to foster stronger client connections.

Although GPT-3 presents various benefits, it's crucial to recognize its constraints. It may not consistently generate accurate or contextually fitting answers, and its suggestions must be cross-checked by financial professionals. Furthermore, utmost care should be taken to ensure the utmost security and confidentiality when dealing with sensitive financial data.

7. DISCUSSION

GPT-3, as a cutting-edge language model, has significantly impacted the development of businesses, particularly within the financial brokerage sector. Its advanced natural language processing capabilities enable financial brokers to streamline various aspects of their operations. One primary area where GPT-3 contributes is in data analysis. Financial markets generate vast amounts of data from various sources such as news articles, earnings reports, social media, and market trends. GPT-3 can sift through this data quickly, extracting valuable insights and patterns that aid brokers in making informed decisions. By analyzing historical data alongside current market conditions, GPT-3 can help brokers identify potential opportunities and mitigate risks more effectively.

Moreover, GPT-3 plays a crucial role in risk assessment. Processing complex financial data and market indicators can assist brokers in evaluating the potential risks associated with different investment strategies or portfolio allocations. This helps brokers make more informed decisions aligned with their clients' risk profiles and investment objectives. Additionally, GPT-3 contributes to customer service automation for financial brokers. Through the development of AI-powered chatbots, brokers can offer round-the-clock support to clients, addressing inquiries, providing account information, and even offering basic financial advice. This not only enhances customer satisfaction but also reduces operational costs for brokerage firms.

Furthermore, GPT-3 aids in compliance and regulatory adherence. Financial markets are subject to stringent regulations, and compliance is paramount for brokerage firms. GPT-3 can assist in analyzing legal documents, identifying compliance issues, and ensuring adherence to relevant regulations, thereby minimizing the risk of penalties and reputational damage. In summary, GPT-3's role in the financial brokerage sector is multifaceted. From data analysis and risk assessment to customer service automation and regulatory compliance, its advanced capabilities empower brokers to operate more efficiently, make better-informed decisions, and ultimately provide superior services to their clients in the ever-evolving landscape of the financial market.

CONCLUSION

The release of GPT-3 has spurred interest in and debates about artificial intelligence, natural language processing, and the moral issues related to AI-generated content. This represents a significant development in the progress of AI models that can interpret and produce writing that is similar to human language, blurring the line between content created by humans and that created by machines.

Nevertheless, it's crucial to emphasize that despite GPT-3's valuable functionalities, its application should be undertaken thoughtfully, taking into account its inherent constraints. The model's output may not consistently yield accurate or contextually suitable responses, and the biases ingrained in the training data can impact its outcomes.

It's crucial to remember that GPT-3 has some limitations as well as its capabilities. The predictions made by the model could be affected by biases contained in the training data, and it's possible that it doesn't always understand context completely. Additionally, a variety of factors, such as world events, economic statistics, and geopolitical developments, affect and complicate financial markets. While GPT-3 might provide insightful information, it might not be able to accurately forecast market moves.

Integrating GPT-3 into financial brokerage activities can elevate the level of service extended to clients, refine decision-making procedures, and in the end, play a role in advancing well-informed and prosperous investment strategies.

A FUTURE VISION

By 2050, conversational GPT technology is poised to become an essential communication component. It will emerge as the primary tool for businesses, institutions, and individuals alike, facilitating rapid interactions with computers and yielding meaningful, top-notch outcomes. Conversational GPT will empower users to engage in natural conversations through both text and voice modes with AI-driven bots that comprehend their inputs. This innovation will enable seamless, real-time discussions spanning a myriad of subjects—ranging from mundane tasks like ordering food or reserving tickets to complex discussions about topics like quantum mechanics. Notably, conversational GPT will substantially curtail customer service expenses by automating numerous tasks that currently demand manual intervention. Furthermore, its adaptability will render it highly flexible, capable of adapting to diverse contexts and delivering tailored interactions with users. The potential implications are limitless—conversational GPT could potentially transform our future interactions with computers (George, A. S., & George, A. H. (2023).

REFERENCES

Bansal, R. (2024). Unveiling the Potential of ChatGPT for Enhancing Customer Engagement. In *Leveraging ChatGPT and Artificial Intelligence for Effective Customer Engagement* (pp. 111–128). IGI Global. doi:10.4018/979-8-3693-0815-8

Boman, S. (2023). Improving customer support efficiency through decision support powered by machine learning.

Dai, Y., Liu, A., & Lim, C. P. (2023). Reconceptualizing ChatGPT and generative AI as a student-driven innovation in higher education.

George, A. H., Hameed, A. S., George, A. S., & Baskar, T. (2022). Study on Quantitative Understanding and Knowledge of Farmers in Trichy District. *Partners Universal International Research Journal, 1*(2), 5–8.

George, A. S., & George, A. H. (2023). A review of ChatGPT AI's impact on several business sectors. *Partners Universal International Innovation Journal, 1*(1), 9–23.

George, A. S., George, A. H., Baskar, T., & Pandey, D. (2022). The Transformation of the workspace using Multigigabit Ethernet. *Partners Universal International Research Journal, 1*(3), 34–43.

Haluza, D., & Jungwirth, D. (2023). Artificial Intelligence and Ten Societal Megatrends: An Exploratory Study Using GPT-3. *Systems, 11*(3), 120. doi:10.3390/systems11030120

Jaimovitch-López, G., Ferri, C., Hernández-Orallo, J., Martínez-Plumed, F., & Ramírez-Quintana, M. J. (2023). Can language models automate data wrangling? *Machine Learning, 112*(6), 2053–2082. doi:10.1007/s10994-022-06259-9

Katar, O., ÖZKAN, D., YILDIRIM, Ö., & Acharya, U. R. (2023). Evaluation of GPT-3 AI language model in research paper writing. *Turkish Journal of Science and Technology, 18*(2), 311–318.

Khan, J. Y., & Uddin, G. (2022, October). Automatic code documentation generation using gpt-3. In *Proceedings of the 37th IEEE/ACM International Conference on Automated Software Engineering* (pp. 1-6).

Kumar, A., Gupta, N., & Bapat, G. (2023). Who is making the decisions? How retail managers can use the power of ChatGPT. *The Journal of Business Strategy.*

Kumar Sharma, A., & Sharma, R. (2023). The role of generative pre-trained transformers (GPTs) in revolutionising digital marketing: A conceptual model. *Journal of Cultural Marketing Strategy, 8*(1), 80–92.

Leippold, M. (2023). Sentiment spin: Attacking financial sentiment with GPT-3. *Finance Research Letters, 55*, 103957. doi:10.1016/j.frl.2023.103957

Majumder, E. (2022). ChatGPT-what is it and how does it work exactly?. *Geek Culture, 18.*

Okerlund, J., Klasky, E., Middha, A., Kim, S., Rosenfeld, H., Kleinman, M., & Parthasarathy, S. (2022). What's in the chatterbox? Large language models, why they matter, and what we should do about them.

Weblink: https://www.computerworld.com/article/3687614/how-enterprises-can-use-chatgpt-and-gpt-3.html

Williams, J. (2023). ChatGPT and Its Use in the Finance and Banking Industry [2023]. Its ChatGPT, 3.

Zhang, Z., Zohren, S., & Roberts, S. (2020). Deep learning for portfolio optimization. *The Journal of Financial Data Science.*

Chapter 3
Integrating Artificial Intelligence Transformers With Business Intelligence Systems for Monitoring Learning Outcomes in Higher Education Institutions

Ali Sorour
Staffordshire University, UK

Anthony S. Atkins
https://orcid.org/0000-0002-8447-4822
Staffordshire University, UK

ABSTRACT

Transformers algorithms and deep learning architectures are increasingly spreading in different applications in several industries. One of the most well-known transformers widely used is ChatGPT. Transformers are designed to assist in problem solving by transforming sequence of inputs to a sequence of outputs. In this paper, transformer models will be studied for the purpose of integrating them to Business Intelligence (BI) architecture in Higher Education (HE) context. The purpose of integrating transformers is to minimise human interaction with data handling to benefit from time reduction and increase the quality of data. Quality Assurance (QA) in HE encompasses data gathering from several sources which requires data preparation to capture compliance with QA standards and measuring learning outcomes. This paper proposes an architecture for BI dashboards in HE with an integration with transformers models.

DOI: 10.4018/979-8-3693-1198-1.ch003

1. INTRODUCTION

Quality Assurance (QA) in Higher Education Institutions (HEIs) is a complex procedure which covers several tasks. It encompasses tasks such as strategic planning, monitoring institutional financial performance, and teaching and learning quality processes. One of the most important tasks related to the QA process in HEIs revolves around the assessment of teaching and learning processes. Throughout the assessment of teaching and learning processes, HEIs develop their educational Learning Outcomes (LOs). These LOs are developed under the umbrella of the institutional strategic direction toward the achievement of educational mission. However, HEIs find several challenges related to the assessment of LOs. This chapter discusses these challenges and outlines how AI transformers can be utilised for this purpose. A conceptual framework for LO assessment in HEIs is presented in this chapter. Additionally, Business Intelligence (BI) architecture and monitoring LOs is proposed. This chapter will also explore how the integration of AI in HEIs can contribute to enhanced business productivity outcomes, highlighting the strategic importance of AI-driven educational tools.

2. UNDERSTANDING LEARNING OUTCOMES MEASURING IN QUALITY ASSURANCE IN HIGHER EDUCATION

Quality Assurance (QA) in Higher Education Institutions (HEIs) encompasses different activities related to the assessment of the level of quality of the services provided by the HEI. QA standards typically include several administrative and academic measures which are intended to assess overall quality of HEIs. HEIs in several countries such as United Kingdom, United States, The Kingdom of Saudi Arabia, and Australia are required to comply with QA standards in order to achieve academic accreditation. LOs plays an important role in the accreditation process as it assists in measuring the educational effectiveness of programmes. For example, in the United Kingdom, The Quality Assurance Agency for Higher Education (QAA) developed The Frameworks for Higher Education Qualifications of UK Degree-Awarding Bodies, which is known as The Frameworks (QAA, 2019). These frameworks include qualification descriptors, which identifies the minimum expectations for institutions awarding bachelor's degrees with honours. HEIs develop and approve their intended LO statements which are drawn from the qualification descriptors (QAA, 2019). The QAA standards in the UK, Learning and Teaching activities were outlined for HEIs to understand how they can link LOs to the institutional learning objectives (QAA, 2018b, 2018a). Individual HEIs will develop their own LOs for course (module) level, department level, and the institutional level. The process of LOs development is discussed in Section 2.3 in this chapter. In the Kingdom of Saudi Arabia (KSA), the National Centre for Academic Accreditation and Evaluation (NCAAA) has developed QA standards which all HEIs in KSA are required to comply with. There are 8 QA standards in the NCAAA 2022 version (NCAAA, 2022). The Teaching and Learning process has been assigned standard 3 from the NCAAA 2022 standards. The assessment of LOs in HEIs is an essential part of the Learning and Teaching activities which all HEIs are required to comply with for accreditation purposes.

Among QA activities, institutions usually measure the achievement of learning outcomes (LOs) as a part of their QA systems. HEIs compare their student performance against standards in order to ensure that qualifications are awarded in relation to the specified LOs of the course (Quality Assurance Agency, 2014). Therefore, HEIs develop teaching and learning KPIs which include several measurements for monitoring the achievement of LOs in the institution (Alzubaidi, 2017; Ayadat, Ahmed, Chowdhury, & Asiz, 2020). LOs are documented in the programme specifications as a part of QA to be submitted for accreditation. They assist in in reporting the level of achievement of students' performance of the programme studied. In this section, a definition of LOs in HEIs will be addressed. Additionally, a discussion of the techniques that are being used by HEIs in measuring LOs will be outlined. At the end of this section, the challenges in monitoring LOs will be discussed.

2.1 Definition of Learning Outcomes in HEIs

Learning Outcomes (LOs) are defined as '*statements of what a learner knows, understands, and is able to do after completion of learning*' (Cedefop, 2009). This definition shows that the main component of the LOs is the measurement of the knowledge obtained by the learner. As HEIs are measuring LOs as a part of their QA requirements, LOs can be defined as: '*statements describe the required knowledge that the learner must obtain for the purpose of achieving learning objectives defined by the higher education institution*'. This definition stresses that the LOs are not only statements that identifies what a learner should know or understand, but it also emphasizes the relationship between these LOs, and the learning objectives identified by the HEI. As a part of strategic management in HEIs, they develop educational objectives, which are usually determined after an environmental analysis. Environmental analysis might include several research activities that are aimed to determine the requirements in labour market and sustainability needs in the nation. After determining these requirements, HEIs develop their LOs and research objectives to direct their resources toward the achievement of these objectives. HEIs develop their curriculums and programmes for the purpose of assuring that their LOs will be reflected in the provided courses. Therefore, HEIs are concerned with the assessment of these LOs to be able to determine the level of achievement for their educational mission.

2.2 How Learning Outcomes are Measured in HEIs

There are several methods that HEIs are using for the purpose of measuring LOs. These methods are classified as direct and indirect methods of measurements (Breslow, 2014; Keshavarz, 2011; Ramadhan & Suhendra, 2021). In the direct measurement tools, HEIs tie each LO to a certain type of measurement such as examination and/or assignment questions. The grades obtained by students related to these questions are directly measuring the LO. However, the indirect methods encompass measuring achievement of LOs by using measurements such as programme completion rate. Programme completion rate indicates the percentage of students who successfully completed the programme completion requirements to students who initially admitted the programme. This percentage may give an indication of the achievement of the LOs of the programme indirectly as it is not tied to a specific LO.

The nature of LOs as direct and indirect measurements leads to a challenge related to measure and reporting on these LOs. In a certain course, several direct methods of assessment might be related to the LOs, which can be aggregated to determine the achievement of LOs at the course level. However, the measurement of LOs at the institutional level by aggregating all courses LOs and programmes LOs as well as the indirect measurements is a complex process. HEIs may find it challenging to report this information for decision makers to be able to take corrective actions if required. Therefore, several HEIs tend to use technological solutions for the purpose of automating the assessment process and to ease the reporting to decision makers.

2.3 Use of Technology in Measuring LOs

Currently, most HEIs have developed spreadsheets for the purpose of measuring LOs (Sheehan & Tessmer, 1997; Sonntag, 2008; Sulindawati, 2021; Wong, 2013). Some Learning Management Systems (LMS) are capable to automatically calculate LOs. However, these LMSs cannot be relied upon to solely as the educational process might include assessment methods outside the LMS such as administering face-to-face/oral examinations. The use of spreadsheets assists in matching the measurement tool to each specific LO. In the Kingdom of Saudi Arabia (KSA), for example, all HEIs are required to measure LOs for each academic programme provided by the institution. This process follows a bottom-up approach to measure learning outcomes as outlines in Figure 1.

Figure 1. Learning Outcomes Measurement in HEIs in KSA

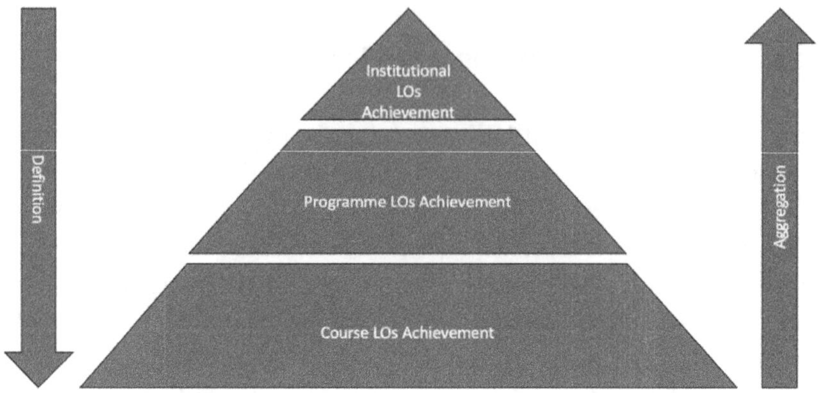

Figure 1 shows the process of measurement of LOs in HEIs in the KSA. This process is used in HEI that adopts the Total Quality Management (TQM) philosophy (Almurshidee, 2017; Santarisi & Tarazi, 2008). The definition of the institutional LOs is a strategic function that is defined by HEI top management. Each faculty develops its own LOs for each programme provided based on the requirements of institutional LOs. For each programme provided, LOs are defined for each course provided in the programme curriculum. Therefore, the definition of the LOs follows a top-down approach. However, the measurement of the LOs of the institution starts at the course level. Each course LOs are measured and aggregated to measure the achievement of LOs of the programme. All LOs related to the programmes provided by the HEI are then measured and aggregated to determine the achievement level of the LOs for the whole institution. Thus, the measurement process follows a bottom-up approach (Cedefop, 2009).

As discussed in Section 2.2, LOs can be assessed using direct methods and indirect methods. The use of direct methods encompasses measurements such as examinations, quizzes, and assignments. These methods may use objective measurement, such as Multiple-Choice Questions (MCQs) or True and False statements. Also, subjective measurements such as written essays may be used. Typically, a combination of both subjective and objective measurements may be found to be used in a single course. Objective measurements can be easily mapped to a specific LO. For example, a tutor may decide to assess specific LO through developing an MCQ question that is directly related to the knowledge and theories related to the LO. The percentage of correct answers of students will indicate the degree of achievement of this LO. However, the use of subjective measurement such as written essay might be challenging. Two tutors may grade the same student answer in different way as it is dependent upon their own judgment. Therefore, Assessment Rubrics are being used for the purpose of assessing subjective measurements which is explained in Section 2.4.

2.4 Challenges in Monitoring Learning Outcomes

Through the measurement of LOs, tutors evaluate subjective measurements using Assessment Rubrics (Breslow, 2014). Assessment Rubrics define set of criteria by which the tutor can objectively evaluate students submissions by giving the student a grade on their submission based on pre-defined criteria (Breslow, 2014; Keshavarz, 2011). The use of rubrics assisted in the measurement of LOs and to transfer subjective judgment (qualitative) into objective measurement (quantitative). An example of a rubric is shown in Figure 2. However, each tutor may have their own judgment which might differ than another evaluator. Therefore, the process of designing fair rubrics is considered to be complicated.

Figure 2. Assessment Rubric Example

Assessment Criteria	Exceeds Expectations	Meets Expectations	Some Expectations	Unsatisfactory
Quantity 500 Words	**5.0 Points** Submission length was (±5%)	**4.0 Points** Submission length was (±6~10%)	**3.0 Points** Submission length was (±11~20%)	**1.0 Point** Submission length was (±21%+)
Content	**5.0 Points** The student demonstrated excellent knowledge of theories and concepts related to the topic	**4.0 Points** The student demonstrated knowledge of theories and concepts	**2.0 Points** The student demonstrated satisfactory knowledge of theories and concepts	**0 Point** The student shown misunderstanding of the theories and concepts
Language	**5.0 Points** The writing was well organized, clear, with no errors	**4.0 Points** Some errors was found but wasn't significant	**2.0 Points** Major errors found in the submission which affects the clarity	**0 Point** The submission is not readable

In this chapter, a discussion of the use of AI transformers in terms of evaluating submissions related to the measurement of LOs are outlined. The aim of using AI transformers is to offer fair judgment on evaluating students' submissions that are not following objective assessment methods.

3. AI TRANSFORMERS

This section discusses AI transformers' definition and examples. Additionally, it explores the uses of transformers in Higher Education context. It also discusses the role of AI in HEIs and provides examples of using AI in Higher Education.

3.1 What are AI Transformers?

Artificial Intelligence (AI) transformers were introduced in 2017 by Vaswansi et.al. (2017) to change the way machines understand and generate human-like text. AI transformers are considered to be part of Natural Language Processing (NLP) field. Vaswani et.al. (2017) defined transformers as '*a model architecture eschewing recurrence and instead relying entirely on an attention mechanism to draw global dependencies between input and output*'.

AI transformers allow the system to make predictions by focusing on different parts of the input sequence of statements, this is known as the attention mechanism. Compared with earlier architectures such as Recurrent Neural Network (RNN) and Long Short-Term Memory Networks (LSTMs), the transformers can be able to handle long-range dependencies in sequential data. The transformer consists of an encoder-decoder structure and self-attention layers. Additionally, transformers addressed the challenge of sequential data processing, which enables the transformer to understand the order of the words in the input data (Vaswani et al., 2017).

The attention mechanism is the backbone of the transformer's architecture. It allows making predictions based on focusing on different parts of the input sequence. This advancement allows understanding the context of the statements provided, especially if it is used in machine translations. As discussed by Vaswani et.al. (2017), the transformer model comprises an encoder-decoder structure and self-attention layer. Encoder-decoder structure is responsible for processing the input sequence and representing the information in a way that the model can be able to understand (encode). It also generates the output sequence based on the information represented by the encoder (decode). Alternatively, self-attention mechanism allows assigning different weights to the input sequence. This procedure allows the system to give more attention to certain words and consider dependencies between all pairs of words in the input sequence.

3.2 Examples of Using Transformers

There are several well-known examples of using transformers. Bidirectional Encoder Representations from Transformers (BERT), which was introduced by Google researchers in 2018 is a pre-trained transformer which provides unique understanding of the tasks in Natural Processing Language. It was based on neural network architecture introduced by Vaswani et.al. (2017). BERT is different from previous language models in terms of processing of the text. Unlike previous models which process text in a unidirectional manner, BERT capture bidirectional context. BERT can be found in several applications in sentiment analysis, automated Questions and Answers (Q&As), and text classification (Devlin, Chang, Lee, & Toutanova, 2018).

Another well-known example of transformers is Generative Pre-trained Transformer (GPT) which was developed by OpenAI in 2018. GPT is a type of Large Language Model (LLM) which aims to replicate human language processing abilities. It is widely used in natural language generation tasks (Rasul et al., 2023). Additionally, it enables content creators to be able to generate human like texts and is widely used in chatbots for generating responses to users automatically. This can also be used for writing programming codes.

3.3 The Role of AI in HE

Artificial Intelligence (AI) is reshaping various sectors, and its impact on Higher Education sector is found in several applications. AI technologies, including advanced models like transformers, have been essential in changing the way HEIs operate, from providing personalised learning experiences to achieve administrative efficiency. In this chapter, examples of AI in HE will be explored, including the use of transformers, and the implications for the future of learning will be discussed.

3.3.1 AI Transformers in Higher Education

AI technologies can enhance the process of learning and teaching in HEIs. In the NLP context, AI transformers are used in HEIs as they are capable in capturing language patterns, which can be employed in several educational tasks, including plagiarism checkers (Rasul et al., 2023).

Transformers such as BERT can be used for the purpose of designing automated grading systems. These transformers are capable to understand and evaluate written contents submitted by students in HEIs (Devlin et al., 2018). Therefore, it can achieve faster and more accurate grading of the assignments.

Furthermore, transformers are used in HEIs for the purpose of developing intelligent tutoring systems. These systems provide guidance for students through their studying journey by tailoring programmes based on their special needs. Additionally, they provide real-time feedback on performance with personalised content recommendations (Li, 2023). HEIs may also use GPT for operating chatbots to respond to students' concerns during their study.

3.3.2 Implications for the Future

The integration of AI transformers in HEIs provides significant opportunities which can shape the future of educational processes. However, the use of AI technologies also raises concerns related to the ethical use of these technologies (Rasul et al., 2023). There is a dispute regarding the ethicality of using AI transformers in HEIs. While there are some HEIs that are considering the use of AI transformers as an academic misconduct, it can be found that several HEIs are teaching their students' how to use ChatGPT properly to assist them in finding sources and planning for structuring the written essays (Rasul et al., 2023).

In the context of utilising OpenAI and Multifactor productivity in business, the utilisation of AI in HEIs can be directly related to the improved productivity in various business domains (Dwivedi & Joshi, 2019; Smolansky et al., 2023). Improving the quality and efficiency of LOs allows AI applications such as transformers to support the development of faculty members to be better trained and more capable. Therefore, multifactor productivity will be given increased attention in the business sector as a result.

The future of using transformers in HEIs is expected to be the dominating issue through the upcoming years. HEIs could tend to review their policies and curriculum under the light of new innovations in this field. These enhancements in their policies should incorporate proper and improper use of transformers. Additionally, there will be a need to study the costs related to the adaptation of transformers in the context of HEIs. A Cost-Benefit Analysis (CBA) models may be used for this purpose in order to identify the relative advantage and the costs related to these innovations.

The integration of AI transformers in HEIs not only shapes the future of educational processes but also has significant implications for business productivity. By improving the quality and efficiency of LOs, AI applications such as transformers support the development of more skilled and capable graduates, therefore, it should enhance multifactor productivity in the business sector.

3.4 Ethical and Privacy Considerations

The integration of AI technologies in the context of HE must be taken with consideration for ethical standards and privacy regulations. The use of these technologies might address data governance issues such as using information without obtaining the required informed consent for data usage. Also, the AI technologies might access information without giving proper credit to the actual bearer of copyrights.

Further developments and applications of AI in the context of HEIs must consider ethical and privacy issues while adopting these technologies. It is essential for gaining trust and facilitate the wider adoption of AI technologies.

4. GPT AND AI DRIVEN ASSESSMENT METHODS OF LEARNING OUTCOMES

This section outlines how AI-driven methodologies can be utilised for the purpose of assessment of LOs in HEIs. Additionally, AI-Enhanced learning analytics are discussed. A conceptual framework of Business Intelligence in Higher Education is presented in this section.

4.1 Assessment of Learning Outcomes Using GPT

The most well-known application of Generative Pre-Trained Transformers (GPT) is ChatGPT. There are several versions of ChatGPT, and the latest version currently is ChatGPT V4. There is lack of studies that discussed the use of ChatGPT in the learning process in Higher Education. However, most HEIs in the world consider the use of ChatGPT by students to assist them in the preparation of written assignments as a plagiarism. There is a doubt about the current plagiarism checkers' ability to detect human-like phrases generated by ChatGPT.

In the context of Higher Education, ChatGPT can assist in the process of assessment of LOs. For example, Tsai et.al. (2021) suggested that ChatGPT may be used in the generation of questions and predicting the achievement of learning outcomes.

4.2 AI-Enhanced Learning Analytics

The use of BI dashboards in providing advanced analytics using trained transformers lacks scientific background. However, there are many applications of BI dashboards in HEIs including visualising sustainability, performance management, monitoring compliance with QA requirements, and providing visual representations of sentiment analysis from social media content. In this chapter, BI architecture in HE will be discussed to explore how it can be used for the purpose of integrating transformers to provide advanced analytics. These BI dashboards should also be able to present the achievement of the LOs in HEIs from the requirements of the mandatory QA KPIs in the country where the HEI operates. BI architecture in HE consist of three main layers; data source layer, data movement, storage, and processing layer, and data visualisation and reporting layer (Sorour, Atkins, Stanier, & Alharbi, 2019). The use of transformers can assist in the automation of the Extract, Transform, Load (ETL) process of BI systems. Using transformers might be integrated with the BI architecture to assist in processing LO analytics to monitor the achievement of the LOs at the institutional level. The drill-down capabilities of BI dashboard would allow drill-down of the learning analytics to monitor programme LOs and each specific course LOs. Figure 3 shows the conceptual framework of BI dashboard for the purpose of visualising LOs.

Figure 3. Conceptual Framework of Business Intelligence in Higher Education for Monitoring Learning Outcomes

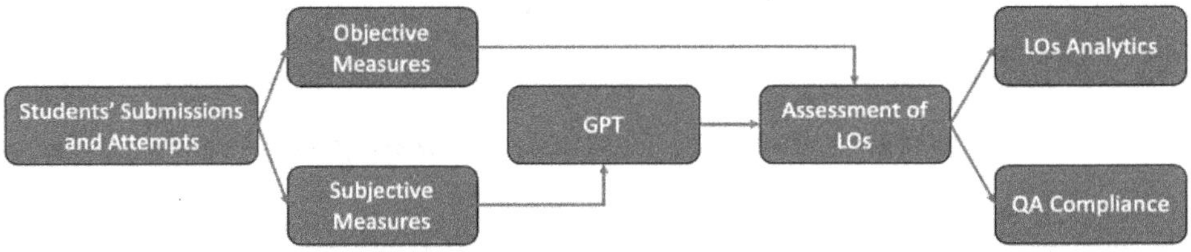

As discussed in Section 2.2, LOs can be measured using objective measures such as the Multiple-Choice Questions (MCQs) which can be correlated directly to a specific LO. Also, LOs might be measured through subjective measurements, which require using rubrics to assist in determining fair evaluation of the student submission to determine achievement of LO. The conceptual framework shown in Figure 3 suggests that student submission can be analysed with the use of GPT transformers to provide fast, accurate, and fair evaluation of the submissions made by students. The transformer ability to analyse inputs will guarantee that each input will be treated in the same manner and compared with the pre-defined criteria (rubrics). The quantitative outputs provided by the system will feed the BI system to visualise the LO analytics. The visualisation of LO analytics should assist decision makers in HEIs in determining the level of achievement at institutional, programme, and course levels.

4.3 Practical Applications of AI in Business

AI applications in business context are diverse and impactful. AI is found in our daily life in several applications that we might not realise. For example, several websites use AI chatbots to respond to our inquiries and provide tailored feedback based on our specific concerns. Also, in manufacturing, AI monitors information from machines and devices to predict when and where maintenance could be needed (Wan, 2023). In the HEI sector, AI-driven analytics for monitoring learning outcomes can inform curriculum development, ensuring that the skills taught align with current and future business needs.

A practical example of using AI in HEIs is the AI chatbots (Hakiki et al., 2023; Rasul et al., 2023). Academic advisership in HEIs require significant time and resources that can be replaced by utilising AI technologies such as AI chatbots. HEIs might use AI chatbots to assist students in advising in their curriculum. Also, chatbots such as ChatGPT can improve LOs of students by providing interactive and personalised learning experience in technology learning (Hakiki et al., 2023).

5. IMPLEMENTING AI FOR MONITORING LEARNING OUTCOMES

In this section, the use of AI for monitoring Quality Assurance in HEIs is discussed. A proposed BI architecture for monitoring LOs in HEIs is presented in relation to the conceptual framework discussed in Section 4.2. The presented architecture considers the integration of AI transformers for the purpose of presenting LO analytics.

5.1 Integrating AI in HE QA Monitoring

The assessment of LOs in HEIs is considered a crucial part of Quality Assurance (QA) process. Most international QA standards including these for example the USA, KSA, UK, and New Zealand include the assessment of teaching and learning, which is known as assessment of LOs (Sorour, Atkins, Stanier, Alharbi, & Campion, 2022). However, QA monitoring is not limited to monitoring LOs. There are several issues that HEIs monitor while determining compliance with QA standards such as administrative services quality, facilities quality, and public opinions expressed in social media (Cao & Li, 2014; Qiu, Ravi, & Qiu, 2015). In several international QA standards, Teaching and Learning KPIs are an essential part in the QA process in HEIs (Sorour et al., 2022). The measurement of LOs' KPIs assist decision makers in HEIs top management in determining the achievement level of educational objectives of the HEI.

Currently, HEIs are giving increased attention to public opinions expressed on social media platforms (Qiu, Ha, Ravi, Qiu, & Badr, 2016; Qiu et al., 2015). Monitoring public opinions expressed in social media channels allows HEIs to determining the level of satisfaction of dissatisfaction of the quality of services provided by the HEI. For example, there are hundreds of thousands of tweets which are published on X platform daily where HEIs may be mentioned. The monitoring process, which includes analysis of text sentiments, is challenging for HEIs as some of the comments may be critical and affect the reputation of the HEIs. The HEIs need to monitor these published comments on social media to enable them to take corrective actions. As data obtained from social media contains human generated text, AI-driven sentiment analysis is used to analyse text published on social media. This process assist in identifying patterns in the text in order to aggregate opinions related to satisfaction and dissatisfaction of the services provided by the HEI (Qiu et al., 2016, 2015; Sorour, Atkins, Alharbi, Stanier, & Campion, 2020).

5.2 Proposed Architecture for AI-Driven Monitoring of Learning Outcomes in HE

In this chapter, an architecture is proposed to show how AI transformers can assist in the process of assessment of LOs in HEIs. The proposed architecture suggests that LOs can be measured from the mandatory KPIs relating to the Teaching and Learning standard. The NCAAA 2022 standards has 6 mandatory KPIs relating to Teaching and Learning process. The proposed architecture allows HEIs to monitor the LOs through the use of developed assessment methods for the courses and programmes for individual HEIs. The proposed architecture integrates the use of AI and BI dashboards for the purpose of providing advanced analytics related to the measurement of compliance with QA requirements in HEIs. As discussed in Section 4.2, there are three main layers in BI systems. The integration of transformers appears in the automation of the processes undertaken in the data movement, storage, and processing layer. As BI systems in HE handle data from different sources including social media, external sources, and cloud services (Sorour et al., 2019), handling LO data should follow a mechanism that guarantees proper quantification of human-generated text to assist in visualise LOs in the BI dashboard. Therefore, a proposed BI architecture is shown in Figure 4.

Figure 4. Business Intelligence Architecture in Higher Education for Monitoring Learning Outcomes

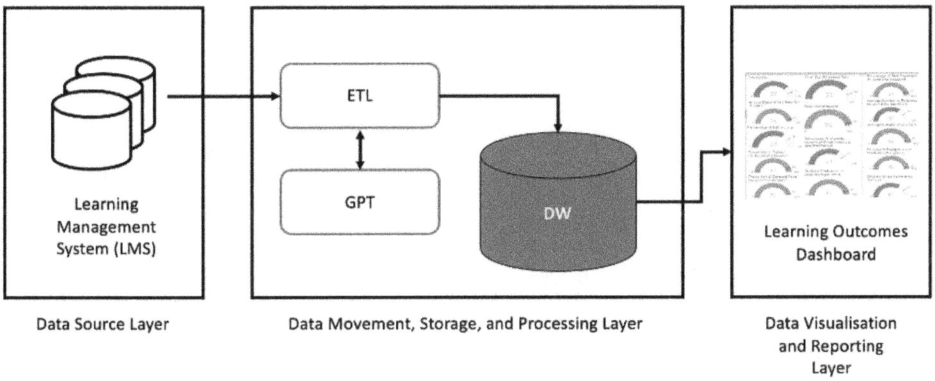

The proposed architecture in Figure 5 shows the use of GPT transformer in understanding human-generated text and compare it with the pre-defined criteria, which will be the assessment rubric in this case. The ETL will be responsible for extracting data from the Learning Management System (LMS), which is the typical platform for students' submission of their written essays. The ETL layer should load all objective assessments of LOs directly to the Data Warehouse (DW) for further processing. Subjective assessments will be transferred to the GPT transformer. The GPT transformer will assist in assessing inputs based on assessment criteria and transform the assessment from subjective manner into numerical representations. The ETL layer should transform the numerical data into the DW. The DW conducts Online Analytical Processing (OLAP) for the numerical data representing assessment of LOs. The dashboard presented in the data visualisation and reporting layer will provide aggregated analytics of LOs at institutional, programme, and course level. The user of BI dashboard can drill-down each level to monitor LO achievement (Sorour & Atkins, 2024).

The use of this BI architecture is designed to achieve several benefits as follows:

1. To improve the QA process related to assessment of LOs, which is part of teaching and learning process. The improvement of this process encompasses providing real-time reporting through the BI dashboards for decision makers in HEIs. These dashboards will be able to assess the LOs continuously.
2. To provide more sophisticated reports related to LOs. The BI dashboards should provide assessment of LOs and be able to show more intuitive reports compared with the traditional reporting methods such as the use of spreadsheets.

3. Assessment of students' submissions through the GPT should provide unbiased assessment of LOs for each specific course. Although, HEIs use rubrics for the purpose of quantifying written essays by giving it numerical representation for each of the grading criteria, and the use of GPT should provide bias-free analysis of submissions. Therefore, numerical assessment of written submissions will be assigned in a similar manner for each student. Additionally, this feature might be integrated with Optical Character Recognition (OCR). The use of OCR allows the system to be able to read handwritten essays. This should lead to increased use of digital technologies in HEIs which automates the QA processes.

CONCLUSION

This chapter outlined the use of Learning Outcomes in Higher Education Institutions for the purpose of determining the achievement of learning objectives at institutional/ programme/ course level. The chapter shows how the LOs are developed in HEIs and the different methods of assessment of LOs which include the use of spreadsheets in determining the level of achievement of the desired LOs. The challenges associated with the current methods for assessment was outlined in the chapter. The use of AI in Higher Education was discussed with examples of application in Higher Education. Also, this chapter outlined examples of using AI chatbots in the context of HE. This chapter also discussed the integration of AI transformers in BI applications in HE. The increasing importance of social media in HE was discussed in terms of the challenges for top management in monitoring public opinions and carrying out agile remedial strategies to protect the reputation of the institutions. Learning Outcomes assessment in Higher Education conceptual framework was outlined to show how to integrate AI transformers in the process of assessment. The chapter proposes a BI architecture for monitoring LOs in HEIs with the use of transformers technologies. The use of transformers in the assessment process in HEIs should provide improved reporting related to the level of achievement. There are several benefits of using transformers in the assessment of LOs in HEIs such as providing bias-free assessment of students' submissions and achieve real-time monitoring of Teaching and Learning processes through the use of BI dashboards. This chapter has demonstrated the critical role of AI transformers in enhancing the assessment of LOs in HEIs, their application in educational settings, and their implications for business productivity. The proposed BI architecture for monitoring LOs represents a significant step forward in leveraging AI technologies for Quality Assurance in Higher Education, showing the benefits for both educational and business outcomes.

REFERENCES

Almurshidee, K. A. (2017). The Implementation of TQM in Higher Education Institutionsin Saudi Arabia: Marketing Prospective, *17*(1), 0–8.

Alzubaidi, L. (2017). Program outcomes assessment using key performance indicators. *Proceedings of 62nd ISERD International Conference*, (January 2017), 20–24.

Ayadat, T., Ahmed, D., Chowdhury, S., & Asiz, A. (2020). Measurable performance indicators of student learning outcomes: A case study. *Global Journal of Engineering Education*, *22*(1), 40–50.

Breslow, L. (2014). Methods of Measuring Learning Outcomes and Value Added, *44*(3), 72. Retrieved from www.et-foundation.co.uk%5Cn10.1080/02615470020028364%5Cnhttp://ludwig.lub.lu.se/login?url=http://search.ebscohost.com/login.aspx?direct=true&AuthType=ip,uid&db=a9h&AN=4139623&site=ehost-live%5Cnhttp://dx.doi.org/10.1016/j.tate.2014.08.004%5Cnhttp://dx.doi

Cao, Y., & Li, X. (2014). Quality and quality assurance in Chinese private higher education. *Quality Assurance in Education*, *22*(1), 65–87. doi:10.1108/QAE-09-2011-0061

Cedefop. (2009). *The shift to learning outcomes: Policies and practices in Europe. European Centre for the Development of Vocational Training*. doi:10.1108/et.2009.00451cab.002

Devlin, J., Chang, M. W., Lee, K., & Toutanova, K. (2018). BERT: Pre-training of deep bidirectional transformers for language understanding.

Dwivedi, V. J., & Joshi, Y. C. (2019). Productivity in 21st Century Indian Higher Education Institutions. *International Journal of Human Resource Management and Research*, *9*(4), 61–80. doi:10.24247/ijhrmraug20197

Hakiki, M., Fadli, R., Samala, A. D., Fricticarani, A., Dayurni, P., Rahmadani, K., & Astiti, A. D. (2023). Exploring the impact of using Chat-GPT on student learning outcomes in technology learning: The comprehensive experiment. *Advances in Mobile Learning Educational Research*, *3*(2), 859–872. doi:10.25082/AMLER.2023.02.013

Keshavarz, M. (2011). Measuring course learning outcomes. *Journal of Learning Design*, *4*(4), 1–9. doi:10.5204/jld.v4i4.84

LiJ. (2023). Advancing Personalized Learning with Multi-modal Embedding Open Learner Model and GPT Prompt. doi:10.36227/techrxiv.24087288.v1

NCAAA. (2022). Key Performance Indicators for Higher Education Institutions. https://www.etec.gov.sa/ar/service/Institutional accreditation/servicedocuments

QAA. (2018a). UK Quality Code for Higher Education: Advice and Guidance -. *Learning and Teaching*, (November), 1–11. https://www.qaa.ac.uk/en/Publications/Documents/quality-code-brief-guide.pdf

QAA. (2018b). UK Quality Code for Higher Education: Advise and Guidance - Assessment, (November), 1–14. Retrieved from https://www.qaa.ac.uk/en/Publications/Documents/quality-code-brief-guide.pdf

QAA. (2019). Annex D: Outcome classification descriptions for FHEQ Level 6 and FQHEIS Level 10 degrees, 1–9. Retrieved from https://www.qaa.ac.uk/docs/qaa/quality-code/annex-d-outcome-classification-descriptions-for-fheq-level-6-and-fqheis-level-10-degrees.pdf?sfvrsn=824c981_10

Qiu, R. G., Ha, H., Ravi, R., Qiu, L., & Badr, Y. (2016). A Big Data based Smart Evaluation System using Public Opinion Aggregation. *Proceedings of the 18th International Conference on Enterprise Information Systems, 1*(Iceis), 520–527. 10.5220/0005867805200527

Qiu, R. G., Ravi, R. R., & Qiu, L. L. (2015). Aggregating and visualizing public opinions and sentiment trends on the US higher education. *Proceedings of the 17th International Conference on Information Integration and Web-Based Applications &Services - IiWAS '15*, 1–5. 10.1145/2837185.2837261

Quality Assurance Agency. (2014). The Frameworks for Higher Education Qualifications of UK Degree-Awarding Bodies. *The Frameworks for Higher Education Qualifications of UK Degree-Awarding Bodies*, (October). Retrieved from https://www.qaa.ac.uk/docs/qaa/quality-code/qualifications-frameworks.pdf

Ramadhan, R., & Suhendra. (2021). The effect of distance learning during Covid-19 pandemics on the mathematical learning results. *Journal of Physics: Conference Series, 1806*(1), 012096. Advance online publication. doi:10.1088/1742-6596/1806/1/012096

Rasul, T., Nair, S., Kalendrs, D., Robin, M., Santini, F. de O., Ladeira, W. J., ... Heathcote, L. (2023). The role of ChatGPT in higher education: Benefits, Challenges, and future research directions. *Journal of Applied Learning & Teaching, 6*(1), 41–56. https://doi.org/https://doi.org/10.37074/jalt.2023.6.1.29

Santarisi, N. S., & Tarazi, A. H. (2008). The Effect of TQM Practices on Higher Education Performance : The Faculty of Engineering and Technology at the University of Jordan as a Case Study. *Dirasat. Engineering and Science, 35*(2), 84–96.

Sheehan, J., & Tessmer, M. (1997). A Construct Validation of the Mental Models Learning Outcome Using Explaratory Factor Analysis. *Eric*, 363–381.

Smolansky, A., Cram, A., Raduescu, C., Zeivots, S., Huber, E., & Kizilcec, R. F. (2023). Educator and Student Perspectives on the Impact of Generative AI on Assessments in Higher Education. *L@S 2023 - Proceedings of the 10th ACM Conference on Learning @ Scale*, 378–382. 10.1145/3573051.3596191

Sonntag, G. (2008). We Have Evidence, They Are Learning: Using Multiple Assessments to Measure Student Information Literacy Learning Outcomes. *World Library and Information Congress: 74th IFLA General Conference and Council*, 14.

Sorour, A., & Atkins, A. (2024). Big data challenge for monitoring quality in higher education institutions using business intelligence dashboards. *Journal of Electronic Science and Technology*, *22*(1).

Sorour, A., Atkins, A. S., Stanier, C., & Alharbi, F. (2019). The Role of Business Intelligence and Analytics in Higher Education Quality: A Proposed Architecture. *International Conference on Advances in the Emerging Computing Technologies, Islamic Un*(February 10-12).

Sorour, A., Atkins, A. S., Stanier, C., Alharbi, F., & Campion, R. (2022). The Development of Business Intelligence Dashboard for Monitoring Quality in Higher Education Institutions in Saudi Arabia Including Sentiment Analysis From Social Media. *INTED2022 Proceedings, 1*(March), 1391–1399. 10.21125/inted.2022.0413

Sorour, A., Atkins, A., Alharbi, F., Stanier, C., & Campion, R. (2020). Integrated Dashboards With Social Media Analysis Capabilities For Monitoring Quality in Higher Education Institutions. *12th International Conference on Education and New Learning Technologies, 6-7 July*, 2862–2870. 10.21125/edulearn.2020.0861

Sulindawati, N. L. G. E. (2021). Improving Learning Outcomes through Learning Media in Making Financial Reports at the Hospitality Board. *Journal of Education Research and Evaluation*, *5*(4), 580–586. doi:10.23887/jere.v5i4.34888

Tsai, D. C. L., Huang, A. Y. Q., Lu, O. H. T., & Yang, S. J. H. (2021). Automatic question generation for repeated testing to improve student learning outcome. *Proceedings - IEEE 21st International Conference on Advanced Learning Technologies, ICALT 2021*, (1), 339–341. 10.1109/ICALT52272.2021.00108

Vaswani, A., Shazeer, N., Parmar, N., Uszkoreit, J., Jones, L., Gomez, A. N., ... Polosukhin, I. (2017). Attention is all you need. *31st Conference on Neural Information Processing Systems (NIPS 2017).*

Wan, C. (2023). How Predictive Maintenance Is Transforming Manufacturing. Retrieved January 31, 2024, from https://www.thefastmode.com/expert-opinion/32863-how-predictive-maintenance-is-transforming-manufacturing

Wong, L. (2013). Student Engagement with Online Resources and Its Impact on Learning Outcomes. *Journal of Information Technology Education: Innovations in Practice*, *12*, 129–146. doi:10.28945/1829

Chapter 4
Leveraging OpenAI for Enhanced Multifactor Productivity in Chinese Businesses

Mohamad Zreik
https://orcid.org/0000-0002-6812-6529
Sun Yat-sen University, China

ABSTRACT

This chapter explores how OpenAI's technologies boost multifactor productivity (MFP) in Chinese firms. MFP measures output efficiency against inputs like capital and labour. The chapter examines China's fast tech adoption and evolving industry. It highlights how integrating OpenAI's algorithms and machine learning improves Chinese companies' operational efficiency, decision-making, and innovation. Case studies show OpenAI's role in optimizing resources, enhancing output, and economic growth in key Chinese industries. The chapter also discusses AI-driven productivity's impact on China's GDP, global competitiveness, and its shift to a knowledge-based economy. It ends with a future outlook on challenges and opportunities in this area.

1. INTRODUCTION

The efficiency and effectiveness with which a mixture of inputs, including as money, labour, equipment, and technology, are transformed into outputs can be assessed using Multifactor Productivity (MFP), a comprehensive statistic. MFP provides a more complete picture of productivity than metrics that isolate individual

DOI: 10.4018/979-8-3693-1198-1.ch004

components, like labour productivity, by taking into consideration the interaction and cumulative impact of several resources. Because of this, it is a more complex and reliable indicator of economic health and company success as a whole.

The MFP is an important metric for measuring the efficiency of a company. It sheds light on the efficiency with which a business or economy generates goods and services by analysing its resource utilisation. A higher MFP indicates that a company is more efficient and effective since it can produce more with the same amount of inputs (Sahay, 2005). Having a firm grasp on how to make the most of available resources is crucial in the modern corporate world, where every second counts.

When it comes to finding ways to improve a company, MFP is also an important tool. Companies may find out which inputs are making the largest impact on output and where they can make improvements by looking at MFP. For example, if the MFP is low, it could mean that there is room for improvement in integrating technology or making better use of capital and labour (Pan & Koehler, 2007).

Furthermore, MFP is relevant in the context of economic growth and development. A shift towards greater value-added industries may be signalled by gains in MFP for economies, especially those making the shift from a manufacturing-based to a knowledge-and technology-driven economy, such as China. In order to achieve sustainable growth over the long run, it is essential for an economy to be able to innovate and become more efficient.

Using the ever-changing landscape of Chinese companies as an example, this chapter delves further into how OpenAI technologies are transforming MFP. The sophisticated algorithms and machine learning skills offered by OpenAI are playing a crucial role in the dynamic Chinese corporate environment, which is characterised by the country's quick adoption of new technologies and innovative manufacturing processes. For instance, JD.com, a leading Chinese e-commerce company, has significantly enhanced its MFP by integrating AI into its logistics and delivery systems. The company's use of drone delivery and automated warehouses has reduced labour costs and increased efficiency.

In this chapter, the focus will primarily be on examining how Chinese enterprises have incorporated OpenAI's innovative technology into their main operating plans. Production efficiency, decision-making, and innovation-driving are just a few areas that have benefited greatly from this integration, which represents the digital transformation in China's corporate sector. This chapter will demonstrate how top Chinese companies are using OpenAI to improve economic development, optimise resource allocation, and boost production quality through a series of in-depth case studies.

Furthermore, this chapter seeks to shed light on the wider consequences of AI-driven productivity gains for China's GDP, its position in the global competitive landscape, and its shift towards an economy that is more knowledge-and technology-based. This chapter aims to give a thorough knowledge of how OpenAI is changing the Chinese business scene by exploring these elements. Taking a look ahead, the chapter will discuss possible obstacles and new prospects in this field. To pave the way for future conversations and studies in this dynamic area, the goal is to offer a nuanced perspective on how OpenAI can influence China's future business efficiency and economic growth. This chapter not only explores the current impact of AI and ML in Chinese businesses but also projects future trends and the potential transformative effects of these technologies in the coming years.

2. UNDERSTANDING MULTIFACTOR PRODUCTIVITY

A more nuanced approach to calculating productivity than only looking at labour or capital alone is multifactor productivity, sometimes known as total factor productivity. It is a measure of how well a set of inputs is utilised to create a set of outputs in a manufacturing process. To know not only the output but also the efficiency of the production process, MFP is essential. Capital, labour, equipment, and technology are the mainstays of MFP, and they all have important and unique roles to play in manufacturing:

Capital is the term used to describe the assets and financial resources that are put into manufacturing. It encompasses investments in structures, gear, instruments, and ancillary apparatus (Creamer, Dobrovolsky, & Borenstein, 2015). Capital plays a pivotal role in MFP since it dictates the scope and capacity of production capacities.

Human beings engaged in physical work as part of a production process are known as labour. Employee knowledge, experience, and hard work are all a part of it (Townley, 2019). When discussing MFP, the emphasis is on how productive and efficient the labour is rather than simply the quantity of hours worked.

The tangible implements, such as tools and machinery, that are a part of any manufacturing process are referred to as equipment. Equipment efficiency, modernism, and appropriateness greatly affect MFP because these factors have direct effects on production speed, quality, and volume (Beaudreau, 2020).

In MFP, "technology" is incorporating scientific understanding into the manufacturing process. All the necessary software, hardware, procedures, and approaches are part of it (Mehrabi, Ulsoy, & Koren, 2000). By streamlining operations, increasing accuracy, and easing the way for new ideas, cutting-edge tech has the potential to revolutionise MFP.

All of these parts work together in intricate ways; they are not independent. One way in which technology is improving capital utilisation is by making labour and equipment more effective. Because MFP is based on the harmony and balance of several factors, it is a more comprehensive metric than ones that just look at the inputs.

For companies to reach their full potential in terms of efficiency and production, it is crucial to comprehend and enhance these elements.

In order to have a more complete and accurate view of how efficient and productive an organisation is, MFP is essential when evaluating overall performance. Instead of concentrating on labour or capital productivity as isolated metrics, MFP takes a holistic view that takes into account a variety of inputs. Because it can capture the efficiency of all inputs utilised in production, MFP is crucial for measuring company success. Using inputs like capital, labour, equipment, and technology and how efficiently they are used to generate outputs, MFP provides a picture of how well a business is doing in terms of its operational strategies. Success in today's complicated corporate contexts is determined by the interplay of many resources, therefore this is particularly crucial.

In addition, MFP is useful for pinpointing the sources of revenue development for a business. It helps companies figure out what's driving their production the most and where they might make changes for the better. In order to make smart choices about investments, resource distribution, and long-term planning, this knowledge is essential. For instance, rather than hiring more people, a company may discover that investing in technology boosts productivity more than hiring more workers (Drucker, 2018). Furthermore, MFP plays a crucial role when comparing and benchmarking. Companies can utilise MFP to evaluate how they are doing in comparison to other companies or industry norms. Through this comparison, a company may find out where it stands in contrast to its competitors and where it could use some development.

Increases in MFP, in the grand scheme of things, can indicate that a business is getting serious about innovation, competitiveness, and value-added operations. Metrics like MFP are crucial for economies like China's that are moving towards information and technology-driven models, as they show the progress towards more efficient and advanced manufacturing.

3. THE CHINESE BUSINESS LANDSCAPE

China has one of the world's most dynamic and rapidly changing economic landscapes right now, thanks to its business climate that is defined by swift innovation and transition (Zreik, 2023a). Various important variables, such as changes in government regulations, technology developments, and global economic trends, are driving this transformation and shaping China's distinctive business ecosystem.

The central role of the Chinese government in directing economic growth stands out among China's business climate features. Various policies have been put in place by the Chinese government to encourage innovation, boost important industries, and bring in international investment. Particularly in industries powered by technology, these regulations have contributed to a more favourable climate for company expansion (Fu, Woo, & Hou, 2016). Tech giants like Tencent and Alibaba are leading in AI adoption. Tencent's AI Lab focuses on four key areas: machine learning, computer vision, speech recognition, and natural language processing, impacting everything from gaming to content creation. Alibaba, with its AI-powered 'City Brain' project, is optimizing urban traffic flow in Hangzhou, demonstrating real-world utility of AI in urban management.

Another pillar of China's economic environment is technological innovation. Thanks to heavy spending on R&D and an emphasis on innovation, the country has risen to the position of technological leader on a global scale. Innovations in renewable energy, artificial intelligence, and telecommunications are spearheaded by Chinese enterprises (Johannessen, 2021). Chinese companies are positioned as major participants on the global arena thanks to their technological prowess, which also defines the domestic market. Additionally, a consumer-driven economy is becoming more prominent in China's corporate climate. The choices and behaviours of consumers are becoming increasingly influential in driving market dynamics, thanks to an expanding middle class and higher purchasing power (Cavusgil et al., 2018). A thriving online retail industry has emerged as a result of this change, and services and consumer goods have taken front stage.

The business climate in China is also affected by global economic developments. Chinese companies are strengthening their presence around the world as a result of the growing interconnection of economies. The Belt and Road Initiative is a prime example of China's increasing clout in international trade and finance; it seeks to improve connectivity and cooperation in certain regions (Zreik, 2023b). But there are also obstacles in China's economic climate, such as a lack of clarity in regulations, intense competition, and the need for ongoing innovation to meet consumers' ever-shifting wants. The business climate is also susceptible to outside influences, such as trade disputes and variations in the world economy (Shenkar, Luo, & Chi, 2021). There has been a remarkable period of technical adoption and industrial growth in China's corporate landscape, with new technologies being integrated across different sectors at a quick pace. As a result of this shift, the country's economy is changing, and it is becoming known as a centre of technical innovation.

The extensive use of machine learning and artificial intelligence (AI) across several sectors in China is one of the most remarkable developments in the country's technology adoption. Operations are being optimised, consumer experiences are being enhanced, and innovation is being driven by the utilisation of AI across several industries, including manufacturing, healthcare, finance, and retail (Oosthuizen et al., 2021). A growing number of Chinese entrepreneurs and tech behemoths are driving innovation in AI applications and shaping industry trends worldwide.

As the internet economy grows, it will play an increasingly important role in China's adoption of new technologies. Digital technology's meteoric rise has disrupted long-established markets and given rise to innovative new forms of company organisation. For example, thanks to sophisticated online payment methods, extensive transportation networks, and an increasingly tech-savvy customer base, online shopping has experienced phenomenal growth (Kuah & Wang, 2017). Similarly, digital lending, internet banking, and mobile payments are all part of fintech's revolution in the financial services sector.

One area where China is making great strides is in sophisticated manufacturing technology, which is commonly referred to as Industry 4.0 or the Fourth Industrial Revolution. This encompasses the incorporation of robotics, automation, 3D printing, and the IoT into production procedures (Martinelli, Mina, & Moggi, 2021). With the use of these technologies, Chinese firms are able to compete on a worldwide scale by increasing the efficiency, quality, and adaptability of their manufacturing processes. Another area where China is making great advances is in renewable energy and green technologies. The country is making significant investments in renewable energy sources such as solar and wind power in order to lessen its impact on the environment and take the lead in the worldwide movement towards sustainable energy (Zreik, 2023c).

The emphasis on infrastructure development, especially in the telecommunications sector, is another feature of China's technological landscape. An excellent illustration of this is the deployment of 5G networks, which will facilitate a plethora of new apps and services while radically altering the nature of communication. Problems arise, nevertheless, as a result of these fast developments. These include dealing with data security and privacy issues, finding one's way through regulatory landscapes, and the demand for competent human resources. The need to adjust to new regulatory landscapes and market dynamics is becoming more apparent to Chinese enterprises as they seek to expand internationally.

4. INTEGRATION OF OPENAI IN CHINESE BUSINESSES

The impact and significance of OpenAI technologies, which are renowned for their innovative AI developments, are growing in the context of business applications. From improving decision-making and process optimisation to engaging customers and fostering creativity, these technologies aim to improve many parts of corporate operations.

Natural language processing (NLP) algorithms and deep learning frameworks are sophisticated machine learning models that are at the core of OpenAI's solutions (Lauriola, Lavelli, & Aiolli, 2022). Insights that were previously unavailable to firms are now within reach, thanks to these tools' capacity to analyse and understand massive amounts of data. Automating customer care with chatbots, analysing market trends from social media chats, and even generating informative reports from raw data are all made possible by OpenAI's natural language processing and understanding capabilities.

Automation and process optimisation are two more important areas where OpenAI technologies are being used. By analysing company processes for patterns and inefficiencies, AI systems can propose changes or automate mundane jobs (Jarrahi, 2018). In the long run, this improves productivity and creativity because it boosts efficiency and frees up human resources to work on more complicated and creative activities. The predictive analytics industry is also seeing a shift thanks to OpenAI's machine learning algorithms. These models are able to accurately predict market trends, customer behaviour, and possible business dangers by utilising massive volumes of data. Businesses can use this predictive power to their advantage by staying ahead of the curve, making proactive decisions, and keeping their competitive edge. In addition, OpenAI technologies are vital for tailoring experiences to each individual consumer. Businesses may better cater to their customers' unique needs by using AI-driven tools to study their preferences and behaviours. Enhancing client pleasure, driving sales, and fostering brand loyalty are all outcomes of this personalised strategy.

When it comes to R&D, OpenAI has you covered with tools that let you test and prototype new ideas quickly. Its sophisticated algorithms can model different situations and forecast their results, assisting companies in the cost-effective and risk-reducing development of new goods and strategies. Concerns about data security and privacy, as well as ethical considerations, must be carefully considered when businesses use OpenAI technologies. Businesses must employ AI ethically and in accordance with regulatory norms as the technology becomes more integrated into their operations.

China has taken a giant leap forward in its technological and economic development with the incorporation of OpenAI technology into its corporate operations. Chinese businesses in many kinds of industries are embracing OpenAI's AI and machine learning features to boost productivity, innovate, and transform their operations (Lauterbach, 2019). The automation of corporate operations is one of the most important areas seeing the influence of OpenAI technology. In order to save time and effort and cut down on manual labour, Chinese businesses are implementing AI algorithms. In manufacturing, Haier, a global home appliances manufacturer, integrated AI in its production lines. This integration has led to predictive maintenance, reducing machine downtime by 20% and improving overall production efficiency (Davenport, 2018). The use of automation and robotics powered by artificial intelligence is revolutionising production lines in the manufacturing industry, leading to better quality control, lower operational costs, and higher throughput.

Data analytics and decision-making are two other areas where OpenAI has found substantial use in Chinese companies. Businesses are making better strategic decisions with the help of AI by processing and analysing massive amounts of data. Foreseeing market trends, comprehending consumer demands, and making well-informed decisions quickly and efficiently are all made possible through this, which includes consumer behaviour insights, predictive modelling, and market analysis.

Another area where OpenAI technologies are being used is in customer service and engagement. In order to boost customer happiness, personalise communication, and offer 24/7 customer assistance, Chinese enterprises are incorporating AI-powered chatbots and virtual assistants (Lee, Pan, & Hsieh, 2022). These AI solutions can improve the customer service experience by handling various interactions with customers, such as answering questions and making product recommendations.

Targeted marketing campaigns and sales optimisation are two areas where the sophisticated algorithms developed by OpenAI are finding usage in the marketing and sales industries. AI solutions sift through mountains of consumer data in search of trends and preferences, letting businesses zero in on certain demographics and create ads and products that speak directly to them. Furthermore, OpenAI technologies are making a mark on China's innovation scene. Machine learning models are being used by businesses to speed up the development of new products, optimise design processes, and test new concepts as part of their AI research and development efforts (Verganti, Vendraminelli, & Iansiti, 2020). The innovation cycle is shortened and the risks and expenses of developing new products are decreased as a result of this (Åström, Reim, & Parida, 2022).

Concerns about data privacy, handling AI's ethical implications, and filling the AI and ML talent gap are some of the obstacles that arise from integrating these technologies. Businesses in China who are interested in using OpenAI should prioritise creating strong policies that address issues like data security, responsible AI usage, and employee skill development. Looking ahead, developments in quantum computing and AI are poised to offer unprecedented computational power, opening new frontiers for complex problem-solving in business environments.

5. IMPACT ON PRODUCTION EFFICIENCY AND DECISION-MAKING

With its cutting-edge AI technologies providing game-changing answers to both old and new manufacturing problems, OpenAI is playing an ever-more-important role in improving production processes. Organisations can attain enormous gains in effectiveness, reliability, and extensibility by incorporating OpenAI's algorithms and machine learning models into their production systems. For instance, predictive maintenance powered by AI can anticipate machine failures in advance, reducing unscheduled downtime and increasing equipment lifespan (Converso et al., 2023). Artificial intelligence algorithms enhance operations in assembly lines, leading to more efficient use of resources and less waste. Another essential part of production, quality control, is also being transformed by AI. It can detect faults more consistently and precisely than human inspectors, which means that product quality is going to be much improved (Javaid et al., 2022). In addition, AI can analyse data in real-time, which allows industrial processes to react to changing market needs or operational situations swiftly (Bécue, Praça, & Gama, 2021). Not only does this flexibility boost manufacturing efficiency, but it also allows for product customisation, meeting the increasingly individual expectations of consumers. To put it simply, OpenAI's technologies are revolutionising production by giving companies unprecedented levels of accuracy, efficiency, and adaptability; as a result, they are raising the bar for manufacturing excellence.

Businesses are moving towards data-driven, intelligent strategies, thanks to OpenAI's impact on decision-making. With OpenAI's state-of-the-art AI and ML capabilities, companies can analyse massive amounts of data, discover profound insights, and make better strategic decisions. Improved data analytics is one of the main ways OpenAI influences decision-making. Insights and patterns in market trends, customer behaviour, and internal performance measures can be found with the use of OpenAI's robust algorithms. With this kind of analysis, businesses may see into the future and anticipate changes in the market and consumer wants and needs, rather than relying solely on past performance. Baidu, with its Apollo self-driving platform, uses AI for predictive vehicle maintenance, which has increased its operational efficiency and reduced the decision-making time in logistics management.

Furthermore, the decision-making processes are made more precise and efficient by OpenAI's technology. Businesses can benefit from the timely insights provided by AI models since they can process and assess possibilities significantly faster than traditional techniques. The capacity to make quick, effective decisions is a huge competitive advantage in today's fast-paced corporate climate, thus this speed is vital. In addition, OpenAI allows for decision-making that is more tailored to the individual and focused on their needs (Jungwirth & Haluza, 2023). Increased customer satisfaction and loyalty can be achieved when organisations gain granular insights into consumer preferences and behaviours. This allows them to better cater their products, services, and marketing activities to fit the unique demands of each customer.

Strategic planning and decisions made with the long term in mind are also affected by OpenAI. To better prepare for the future, organisations can use OpenAI's tools to simulate numerous scenarios and forecast results. This allows them to examine the possible impact of different tactics. It is important to carefully balance human judgement with AI insights when using OpenAI for decision-making. Business executives must always factor in context, experience, and ethical concerns when making decisions, even while AI offers useful data-driven insights. In the future, AI-driven decision-making tools are expected to become more autonomous, capable of making complex decisions with minimal human intervention, thus further streamlining business operations.

6. CASE STUDIES: OPENAI IN CHINESE INDUSTRIES

The successful application of OpenAI technology across different industries with real-world examples from China can be observed:

The use of AI by Foxconn, a leading electronics manufacturer and supplier to well-known multinational companies, stands out in the manufacturing sector (Crawford, 2021). For predictive maintenance and quality control, Foxconn has integrated AI-driven technologies into its production lines. By detecting any equipment faults early on and ensuring high product quality standards, these technologies greatly improve operating efficiency.

Alibaba, a prominent Chinese e-commerce platform, has made heavy use of AI to tailor the purchasing experience for its millions of customers. Customised product suggestions, improved search results, and simplified inventory and logistics management are all outcomes of data analysis performed by Alibaba's AI algorithms (Feldman et al., 2022). Both the company's operational efficiency and customer happiness have been enhanced by this.

Among China's "big four" banks, China Construction Bank has used AI to do risk assessments and detect fraud. The use of artificial intelligence algorithms allows the bank to better monitor client transactions for signs of suspicious or fraudulent behaviour (Li et al., 2021).

Also benefiting greatly from AI's incorporation is China's healthcare system. To aid in the analysis of medical photographs, for instance, Ping An Good Doctor—a prominent healthcare and technology company—uses diagnostic tools powered by artificial intelligence (Chang, 2020). These resources have helped countless people get the high-quality medical treatment they need by increasing the reliability of diagnosis.

Various Chinese industries have benefited from OpenAI technology, as shown by these real-world examples from Foxconn, Alibaba, China Construction Bank, and Ping An Good Doctor, which have improved operational efficiencies, customer experiences, and overall performance. In the finance sector, China Merchants Bank has implemented AI for personalized customer service and fraud detection. The bank's AI system analyzes customer transactions in real-time, reducing fraudulent activities by 60% and enhancing customer engagement. There have been huge gains from implementing OpenAI technology across a range of Chinese sectors, which have improved overall performance and revolutionised operational operations.

Utilisation of OpenAI technology in predictive maintenance and quality control has greatly enhanced manufacturing industry efficiency, as demonstrated by companies such as Foxconn. To cut down on maintenance expenses and downtime, predictive maintenance uses artificial intelligence to detect and fix possible equipment problems before they happen. Better product quality and happier customers are the outcomes of AI-enhanced quality control, which has led to more precise defect detection.

Alibaba and other retail and e-commerce behemoths have reaped enormous gains from incorporating AI into their operations. Sales and consumer engagement have skyrocketed thanks to AI-powered personalisation of the shopping experience. The shopping experience becomes more natural and enjoyable for customers as they obtain personalised product recommendations. Delivery services have also become more efficient and less expensive as a consequence of AI-driven logistics optimisation, which has simplified supply chain management.

Banks like China Construction Bank have used AI to better control risks and increase security in the financial sector. To safeguard the bank and its clients from possible financial risks, AI algorithms allow for more efficient and precise detection of fraudulent transactions. In addition, AI has made it easier to create customised financial products, which better match services to each customer's unique requirements and preferences and ultimately boost trust and loyalty.

Artificial intelligence has led to remarkable developments in the healthcare industry, as seen in examples such as Ping An Good Doctor. With the help of AI-powered diagnostic technologies, doctors are now able to detect illnesses earlier and with better accuracy. The time and resources needed for proper diagnosis are reduced, which improves patient outcomes and contributes to more effective healthcare service delivery.

There has been a general upward trend in efficiency, service or product quality, customer experience, and risk management across all of these sectors since they began utilising OpenAI technology. As a result of these advantages, these sectors are more innovative and competitive, putting them in the front of the global digital economy.

7. ECONOMIC GROWTH AND GDP IMPACT

A revolutionary change in China's economic landscape is illustrated by the quantifiable and considerable impact of AI-driven productivity on the country's GDP. The widespread use of AI has significantly increased productivity and efficiency, which has had a direct impact on China's economic growth. One industry that stands to gain the most from AI implementations is manufacturing, where estimates indicate a 20% boost in production efficiency. According to a report by McKinsey, AI has the potential to add 0.8 to 1.4 trillion dollars to the Chinese economy by 2030, representing a significant portion of China's GDP growth (Liang, Yang, & Ding, 2022). The sector's contribution to the GDP is greatly boosted by this upgrade, which not only decreases operational costs but also enhances output. An increase in productivity of just a few percentage points can have a profound impact on a sector that is vital to China's economy, leading to a boost in GDP worth billions of dollars.

AI-driven personalisation and supply chain optimisations have increased sales by an estimated 10-15% in China's retail and e-commerce sector, a major contributor to the country's GDP (Akhtar et al., 2022). Sales have increased, which is a sign of both more consumer spending and more efficient market operations, two factors that contribute significantly to GDP development.

Artificial intelligence's role in detecting fraud and managing risks in the financial sector has been significant. Artificial intelligence is indirectly helping the economy by decreasing fraud losses, which can reach billions of yuan yearly (Hilal, Gadsden, & Yawney, 2022). In addition, the financial services industry is so large and important that the efficiency benefits from AI are predicted to boost sector productivity by about 15% (Chang, Taghizadeh-Hesary, & Mohsin, 2023). This would be a significant contribution to GDP. There has been a 20-30% increase in service efficiency in the healthcare industry's use of AI for patient care and diagnostics (Yang et al., 2022). In addition to adding to GDP directly, this boost helps the economy expand in the long run by encouraging a healthy workforce, which is key to sustaining and enhancing productivity across all industries.

Artificial intelligence has a substantial overall effect on China's GDP. Research indicates that artificial intelligence has the potential to boost China's economy by 1.0-1.5 trillion yuan each year, which would constitute a significant portion of the country's GDP growth (Griffiths et al., 2022). This impact extends beyond immediate monetary gain to encompass indirect advantages such as increased productivity, novel ideas, and the birth of whole new markets and employment possibilities.

The impact of OpenAI technologies on China's ability to compete globally is far-reaching and strong, elevating the country's standing in the global economy. Businesses and industries in China are improving internal efficiencies and raising product and service quality to reach or surpass global standards by utilising AI. In the field of innovation, OpenAI makes a significant contribution to China's global competitiveness. Chinese businesses that use AI to create innovative products and solutions can frequently beat their international rivals to market (Wang et al., 2022). This is especially true in areas such as renewable energy, technology, and telecommunications, where Chinese enterprises have recently established themselves as market leaders. By maintaining its status as a world leader in technology and innovation, China is able to entice investment and collaboration from around the world (Al Shaher, Yanzhe, & Zreik, 2023).

The use of OpenAI technology has completely altered manufacturing processes, allowing Chinese firms to create better things at cheaper prices. The increased competitiveness of Chinese products on the global market is a direct result of this efficiency, which has helped the country capture a larger portion of many different industries. AI in manufacturing improves accuracy and quality, which helps establish and sustain a stellar reputation in international trade. Also, Chinese banks are killing it in the global financial market because to AI-powered personalised loans and better risk management (Hentzen et al., 2022). As a result of the safety and efficiency offered by these AI-powered services, China's reputation in the global financial services industry is rising.

Chinese businesses are pioneering innovative approaches to customer care and engagement in the digital services and e-commerce space by leveraging artificial intelligence to provide customers with one-of-a-kind, tailored online shopping experiences. This has made them not just unstoppable in their home market, but also a serious threat on a worldwide scale. Additionally, it is impossible to ignore AI's contribution to cultivating a competent labour force. Creating a more tech-savvy and inventive workforce, Chinese corporations are investing in upskilling their staff as they adopt more AI technologies. To stay ahead in today's knowledge-driven global economy, this innovation is essential. AI is projected to play a crucial role in driving sustainable economic growth in China, with potential impacts on GDP growth rates and the overall economic landscape.

8. TRANSITION TO A KNOWLEDGE AND TECHNOLOGY-BASED ECONOMY

There has been a dramatic change in the global economic landscape, with nations like China leading the way towards an information and technology-driven economic model. These changes are changing the basis of economic growth and competitiveness through a greater focus on innovation, technological improvement, and the creation of a skilled workforce.

Knowledge and technology play a pivotal role in the generation of value in this new economic model. New sectors are emerging and old ones are changing as a result of technology breakthroughs, which are reshaping traditional industries. In the manufacturing sector, for example, "smart factories" have emerged as a result of the integration of AI, the Internet of Things (IoT), and automation, which significantly increases output per worker (Ashima et al., 2021). This development highlights the shift from labour-intensive to knowledge-intensive procedures. R&D plays a crucial role in this economic paradigm. Companies and nations that pour resources into research and development are more likely to be at the forefront of innovation, creating ground-breaking goods and services that compete on a global scale. The tech industry is a prime example of this, as staying ahead of the competition requires constant innovation.

The rising importance of the digital economy is another indicator of this change. The proliferation of e-commerce, digital platforms, and online services is indicative of a more systemic shift in the way companies function and communicate with their clientele. it becomes an invaluable asset in this setting, and the capacity to analyse and utilise it efficiently gives one a distinct edge over the competition. Human resources are highly valued in the knowledge and technology-driven approach. There is a growing need for competent individuals who can design, oversee, and make use of increasingly complex technological systems. As a result, there is now a stronger push for STEM (science, technology, engineering, and mathematics) education and training, along with initiatives to encourage students to keep studying throughout their lives and improve their existing set of skills (Morrison, Roth McDuffie, & French, 2015).

On the other hand, there are issues that come with this transformation. One of them is the possibility that jobs could be lost to automation. Another is the widening gap between people who have access to technology and those who don't. To make sure that everyone can reap the benefits of the economy powered by information and technology, it is essential to tackle these difficulties. An information and technology-driven economic paradigm is now under development, and AI plays a complex and revolutionary role in this shift. This change is accelerated by AI, which allows economies and enterprises to achieve new heights of efficiency, creativity, and competitiveness.

One important aspect of this shift is the ability of AI to handle and analyse massive volumes of data. Artificial intelligence's capacity to derive meaningful conclusions from intricate datasets is priceless in this age of data being a vital asset. From healthcare to banking, this skill improves decision-making and spurs innovation by revealing previously unseen trends and opportunities. When it comes to production and manufacturing, AI is a game-changer for better, more efficient procedures. Automation driven by AI not only reduces waste but also maximises efficiency, which in turn reduces costs and has a positive impact on the environment (Javaid et al., 2022). More evidence of AI's ability to build production and distribution networks that are responsive, efficient, and integrated can be seen in its application to supply chain management. The emergence of AI-driven fintech startups in China, such as Ant Financial, is reshaping the financial services sector. These companies are leveraging AI to offer personalized financial products, contributing to the growth of a technology-driven financial ecosystem.

When it comes to encouraging creativity, AI is also crucial. AI shortens the time and money needed to bring novel medicines to market by speeding up the processes of medication discovery and development in sectors like pharmaceuticals (Mak & Pichika, 2019). AI drives innovation in the tech industry, which in turn creates new goods and services that expand the limits of what technology can do. The demands for and supply of workers are also changing as a result of AI. A transition to higher-level, more creative, and technically-oriented occupations will be required as AI automates formerly manual processes. To ensure that the workforce can adapt and operate alongside more advanced AI systems, this transition highlights the necessity of STEM education, lifelong learning, and skill development.

One cannot ignore the impact of AI on increasing global competitiveness. The world's leading economies and businesses are those that masterfully use AI. Their ability to think outside the box, keep operations running smoothly, and adapt quickly to changes in the market gives them an edge in global competition. Ethical questions, privacy worries, and the possibility of more inequality are some of the problems that can arise from integrating AI. In order to guarantee that AI is utilised responsibly and that its advantages are shared fairly, it is essential to tackle these difficulties. As China transitions towards a knowledge and technology-based economy, the integration of AI in various sectors is expected to accelerate, leading to the emergence of new industries and job roles centred around AI and technology.

9. CHALLENGES AND OPPORTUNITIES

Leveraging OpenAI in Chinese businesses, while offering numerous benefits, also presents several challenges that need careful consideration and strategic management. Integrating AI solutions with pre-existing company infrastructure is a major obstacle. Legacy system and workflow integration with AI can be a resource-intensive and complicated process. In order to avoid interruptions to their current operations, businesses should check that the AI solutions they are considering are compatible with their existing infrastructures.

Another major issue with AI is the security and privacy of user data. The security of this data and the preservation of user privacy become of utmost importance as AI systems rely on massive amounts of data to operate efficiently (Braun et al., 2018). To avoid data breaches, Chinese companies must adhere to strict data protection legislation and put strong cybersecurity safeguards in place. Concerns about AI's moral application are another obstacle. Problems like algorithmic bias, lack of transparency, and responsibility are rising to the forefront as AI grows in popularity (Felzmann et al., 2020). To avoid prejudice in AI decisions and keep public faith, Chinese companies must set explicit ethical standards for AI usage. DJI, a world leader in commercial drone manufacturing, faced and overcame significant data security challenges by implementing end-to-end encryption across its data transmission systems, ensuring user privacy and security.

Another significant obstacle is the lack of trained AI professionals. A workforce with specialised skills is needed to design, administer, and understand AI systems due to the rapid growth of AI. But companies may struggle to effectively deploy and oversee AI technology due to a lack of such trained personnel. Furthermore, unsafe reduction in human oversight, especially in crucial decision-making circumstances, can result from reliance on AI. Finding the right mix of AI-driven automation and human judgement and involvement is critical for companies. Additionally, AI implementation and maintenance costs can be prohibitive for many businesses, particularly SMEs. Data management, system upgrades, and employee training are all part of the continuing expenses associated with AI, which extend beyond the original setup (Daugherty & Wilson, 2018). Businesses need to stay up with the latest advances in AI if they want to be competitive. AI is constantly changing, so they need to adapt. This necessitates ongoing expenditure on R&D, which can be difficult for companies, particularly those with low resources, to accomplish.

A combination of hope and strategic foresight characterises the debate of potential future prospects and growth areas as they pertain to businesses' use of OpenAI technologies. Businesses have the opportunity to reach new heights of efficiency, creativity, and market leadership as AI continues to grow, opening up a spectrum of possibilities. Expanding the use of AI in the customer service process is a promising new direction. Businesses may improve their customer connections by learning more about AI and using that knowledge to make interactions more personalised, engaging, and frictionless. In addition to making customers happier, this also creates new opportunities to make money and build brand loyalty.

The development of AI also bodes well for the improvement of operational efficiency. Automation of supply chain management and human resources are only two of the many business operations that can benefit from further advancements in artificial intelligence. More automation means more time for people to focus on strategic and creative work, which in turn means more growth for the company. Data analysis and AI-powered decision-making is another promising field. Businesses will be able to make better decisions with the help of increasingly sophisticated AI systems that offer insights that are more accurate, timely, and actionable. When it comes to data-driven decision-making, this capability can be game-changing in sectors like transportation, healthcare, and finance.

AI also opens up a world of possibilities for new product and service development. Using AI's speed and accuracy in analysing consumer tastes and market trends, companies may create products and services that cater to customers' ever-changing demands. Industries such as consumer goods, technology, and medicines may feel the effects of this the most. There is also a lot of room for development in AI's function as a tool for sustainability and environmental protection. To achieve both economic growth and environmental responsibility, businesses can employ AI to optimise resource consumption, decrease waste, and develop sustainable practices. Nevertheless, to harness these possibilities, the problems surrounding AI must be addressed. These problems include managing ethical concerns, closing the skills gap, and protecting personal data. In addition to addressing these issues, companies should prioritise creating an environment that encourages creativity and lifelong learning so that they can stay up with the rapid development of AI. Future advancements in AI will bring both challenges, such as the need for advanced cybersecurity measures, and opportunities, such as the creation of new markets and AI-based services.

10. CONCLUSION

This chapter has examined the revolution brought about by OpenAI technologies in China's corporate landscape. Industries ranging from manufacturing to retail, banking to healthcare have been explored to understand how these advanced AI tools and algorithms are reshaping them, fostering innovation and efficiency. The incorporation of OpenAI has led to enhancements in manufacturing processes, decision-making, customer communication, and operational optimization. The transformation seen in companies like JD.com, Haier, and China Merchants Bank exemplifies the profound impact of AI in enhancing multifactor productivity, optimizing operations, and driving economic growth in China.

The real-world advantages of OpenAI in enhancing output quality, optimizing resource allocation, and contributing to economic growth have been observed through comprehensive case studies from prominent Chinese enterprises. A knowledge and technology-based economy has emerged in China, and AI-driven productivity has had a significant influence on GDP, global competitiveness, and this transition. However, there are a number of obstacles that come with this shift, including concerns about data security, the ethical application of AI, and the necessity of ongoing skill training.

Looking ahead, numerous opportunities for further integration and creativity with OpenAI in Chinese businesses emerge. The Chinese business landscape will change over time as companies deal with AI's problems and prospects. This will have an impact on economic trends and practices around the world. AI and ML will not only continue to transform existing industries but also pave the way for new forms of business innovation, economic models, and global market dynamics. The significance of adopting AI technologies for future economic and business success is ultimately highlighted in this chapter. There will be constant learning and adjusting along the road to incorporating OpenAI into Chinese companies. This trip will show how AI will play a significant part in the future of business and economic growth, and it will also define how businesses operate in China in the future.

REFERENCES

Akhtar, W. H., Watanabe, C., Tou, Y., & Neittaanmäki, P. (2022). A New Perspective on the Textile and Apparel Industry in the Digital Transformation Era. *Textiles*, *2*(4), 633–656. doi:10.3390/textiles2040037

Al Shaher, S., Yanzhe, M., & Zreik, M. (2023). Navigating the Digital Frontier: Responsible Innovation in China's Digital Silk Road. *Migration Letters : An International Journal of Migration Studies*, *20*(S9), 1297–1315.

Ashima, R., Haleem, A., Bahl, S., Javaid, M., Mahla, S. K., & Singh, S. (2021). Automation and manufacturing of smart materials in Additive Manufacturing technologies using Internet of Things towards the adoption of Industry 4.0. *Materials Today: Proceedings*, *45*, 5081–5088. doi:10.1016/j.matpr.2021.01.583

Åström, J., Reim, W., & Parida, V. (2022). Value creation and value capture for AI business model innovation: A three-phase process framework. *Review of Managerial Science*, *16*(7), 2111–2133. doi:10.1007/s11846-022-00521-z

Beaudreau, B. C. (2020). *The Economics of Speed: Machine Speed as the Key Factor in Productivity*. Springer. doi:10.1007/978-3-030-26713-1

Bécue, A., Praça, I., & Gama, J. (2021). Artificial intelligence, cyber-threats and Industry 4.0: Challenges and opportunities. *Artificial Intelligence Review*, *54*(5), 3849–3886. doi:10.1007/s10462-020-09942-2

Braun, T., Fung, B. C., Iqbal, F., & Shah, B. (2018). Security and privacy challenges in smart cities. *Sustainable Cities and Society*, *39*, 499–507. doi:10.1016/j.scs.2018.02.039

Cavusgil, S. T., Deligonul, S., Kardes, I., & Cavusgil, E. (2018). Middle-class consumers in emerging markets: Conceptualization, propositions, and implications for international marketers. *Journal of International Marketing*, *26*(3), 94–108. doi:10.1509/jim.16.0021

Chang, A. C. (2020). *Intelligence-based medicine: artificial intelligence and human cognition in clinical medicine and healthcare*. Academic Press.

Chang, L., Taghizadeh-Hesary, F., & Mohsin, M. (2023). Role of artificial intelligence on green economic development: Joint determinates of natural resources and green total factor productivity. *Resources Policy*, *82*, 103508. doi:10.1016/j.resourpol.2023.103508

Converso, G., Gallo, M., Murino, T., & Vespoli, S. (2023). Predicting Failure Probability in Industry 4.0 Production Systems: A Workload-Based Prognostic Model for Maintenance Planning. *Applied Sciences (Basel, Switzerland)*, *13*(3), 1938. doi:10.3390/app13031938

Crawford, K. (2021). *The atlas of AI: Power, politics, and the planetary costs of artificial intelligence*. Yale University Press.

Creamer, D. B., Dobrovolsky, S. B., & Borenstein, I. (2015). *Capital in manufacturing and mining: Its formation and financing*. Princeton University Press.

Daugherty, P. R., & Wilson, H. J. (2018). *Human+ machine: Reimagining work in the age of AI*. Harvard Business Press.

Davenport, T. H. (2018). *The AI advantage: How to put the artificial intelligence revolution to work*. MIT Press. doi:10.7551/mitpress/11781.001.0001

Drucker, P. F. (2018). The new productivity challenge. In *Quality in Higher Education* (pp. 37–46). Routledge. doi:10.4324/9781351293563-2

Feldman, J., Zhang, D. J., Liu, X., & Zhang, N. (2022). Customer choice models vs. machine learning: Finding optimal product displays on Alibaba. *Operations Research*, *70*(1), 309–328. doi:10.1287/opre.2021.2158

Felzmann, H., Fosch-Villaronga, E., Lutz, C., & Tamò-Larrieux, A. (2020). Towards transparency by design for artificial intelligence. *Science and Engineering Ethics*, *26*(6), 3333–3361. doi:10.1007/s11948-020-00276-4 PMID:33196975

Fu, X., Woo, W. T., & Hou, J. (2016). Technological innovation policy in China: The lessons, and the necessary changes ahead. *Economic Change and Restructuring*, *49*(2-3), 139–157. doi:10.1007/s10644-016-9186-x

Griffiths, S., Sovacool, B. K., Kim, J., Bazilian, M., & Uratani, J. M. (2022). Decarbonizing the oil refining industry: A systematic review of sociotechnical systems, technological innovations, and policy options. *Energy Research & Social Science*, *89*, 102542. doi:10.1016/j.erss.2022.102542

Hentzen, J. K., Hoffmann, A., Dolan, R., & Pala, E. (2022). Artificial intelligence in customer-facing financial services: A systematic literature review and agenda for future research. *International Journal of Bank Marketing*, *40*(6), 1299–1336. doi:10.1108/IJBM-09-2021-0417

Hilal, W., Gadsden, S. A., & Yawney, J. (2022). Financial fraud: A review of anomaly detection techniques and recent advances. *Expert Systems with Applications*, *193*, 116429. doi:10.1016/j.eswa.2021.116429

Jarrahi, M. H. (2018). Artificial intelligence and the future of work: Human-AI symbiosis in organizational decision making. *Business Horizons*, *61*(4), 577–586. doi:10.1016/j.bushor.2018.03.007

Javaid, M., Haleem, A., Singh, R. P., Suman, R., & Gonzalez, E. S. (2022). Understanding the adoption of Industry 4.0 technologies in improving environmental sustainability. *Sustainable Operations and Computers*, *3*, 203–217. doi:10.1016/j.susoc.2022.01.008

Johannessen, J. A. (2021). *China's innovation economy: artificial intelligence and the new silk road*. Routledge. doi:10.4324/9781003211907

Jungwirth, D., & Haluza, D. (2023). Artificial intelligence and public health: An exploratory study. *International Journal of Environmental Research and Public Health*, *20*(5), 4541. doi:10.3390/ijerph20054541 PMID:36901550

Kuah, A. T., & Wang, P. (2017). Fast-Expanding "Online" Markets in South Korea and China: Are They Worth Pursuing? *Thunderbird International Business Review*, *59*(1), 63–77. doi:10.1002/tie.21779

Lauriola, I., Lavelli, A., & Aiolli, F. (2022). An introduction to deep learning in natural language processing: Models, techniques, and tools. *Neurocomputing*, *470*, 443–456. doi:10.1016/j.neucom.2021.05.103

Lauterbach, A. (2019). Artificial intelligence and policy: Quo vadis? *Digital Policy. Regulation & Governance*, *21*(3), 238–263. doi:10.1108/DPRG-09-2018-0054

Lee, C. T., Pan, L. Y., & Hsieh, S. H. (2022). Artificial intelligent chatbots as brand promoters: A two-stage structural equation modeling-artificial neural network approach. *Internet Research*, *32*(4), 1329–1356. doi:10.1108/INTR-01-2021-0030

Li, Y., Yi, J., Chen, H., & Peng, D. (2021). Theory and application of artificial intelligence in financial industry. *Data Science in Finance and Economics*, *1*(2), 96–116. doi:10.3934/DSFE.2021006

Liang, S., Yang, J., & Ding, T. (2022). Performance evaluation of AI driven low carbon manufacturing industry in China: An interactive network DEA approach. *Computers & Industrial Engineering*, *170*, 108248. doi:10.1016/j.cie.2022.108248

Mak, K. K., & Pichika, M. R. (2019). Artificial intelligence in drug development: Present status and future prospects. *Drug Discovery Today*, *24*(3), 773–780. doi:10.1016/j.drudis.2018.11.014 PMID:30472429

Martinelli, A., Mina, A., & Moggi, M. (2021). The enabling technologies of industry 4.0: Examining the seeds of the fourth industrial revolution. *Industrial and Corporate Change*, *30*(1), 161–188. doi:10.1093/icc/dtaa060

Mehrabi, M. G., Ulsoy, A. G., & Koren, Y. (2000). Reconfigurable manufacturing systems: Key to future manufacturing. *Journal of Intelligent Manufacturing*, *11*(4), 403–419. doi:10.1023/A:1008930403506

Morrison, J., Roth McDuffie, A., & French, B. (2015). Identifying key components of teaching and learning in a STEM school. *School Science and Mathematics*, *115*(5), 244–255. doi:10.1111/ssm.12126

Oosthuizen, K., Botha, E., Robertson, J., & Montecchi, M. (2021). Artificial intelligence in retail: The AI-enabled value chain. *Australasian Marketing Journal*, *29*(3), 264–273. doi:10.1016/j.ausmj.2020.07.007

Pan, H., & Koehler, J. (2007). Technological change in energy systems: Learning curves, logistic curves and input–output coefficients. *Ecological Economics*, *63*(4), 749–758. doi:10.1016/j.ecolecon.2007.01.013

Sahay, B. S. (2005). Multi-factor productivity measurement model for service organisation. *International Journal of Productivity and Performance Management*, *54*(1), 7–22. doi:10.1108/17410400510571419

Shenkar, O., Luo, Y., & Chi, T. (2021). *International business*. Routledge. doi:10.4324/9781003034315

Townley, B. (2019). Foucault, power/knowledge, and its relevance for human resource management. In *Postmodern management theory* (pp. 215–242). Routledge. doi:10.4324/9780429431678-11

Verganti, R., Vendraminelli, L., & Iansiti, M. (2020). Innovation and design in the age of artificial intelligence. *Journal of Product Innovation Management*, *37*(3), 212–227. doi:10.1111/jpim.12523

Wang, J., Lu, Y., Fan, S., Hu, P., & Wang, B. (2022). How to survive in the age of artificial intelligence? Exploring the intelligent transformations of SMEs in central China. *International Journal of Emerging Markets*, *17*(4), 1143–1162. doi:10.1108/IJOEM-06-2021-0985

Yang, J., Luo, B., Zhao, C., & Zhang, H. (2022). Artificial intelligence healthcare service resources adoption by medical institutions based on TOE framework. *Digital Health*, *8*, 20552076221126034. doi:10.1177/20552076221126034 PMID:36211801

Zreik, M. (2023a). Navigating HRM Challenges in Post-Pandemic China: Multigenerational Workforce, Skill Gaps, and Emerging Strategies. In A. Even & B. Christiansen (Eds.), *Enhancing Employee Engagement and Productivity in the Post-Pandemic Multigenerational Workforce* (pp. 171–188). IGI Global., doi:10.4018/978-1-6684-9172-0.ch008

Zreik, M. (2023b). Sustainable and Smart Supply Chains in China: A Multidimensional Approach. In B. Bentalha, A. Hmioui, & L. Alla (Eds.), *Integrating Intelligence and Sustainability in Supply Chains* (pp. 179–197). IGI Global., doi:10.4018/979-8-3693-0225-5.ch010

Zreik, M. (2023c). Harnessing the Power of Blockchain Technology in Modern China: A Comprehensive Exploration. In L. Ferreira, M. Cruz, E. Cruz, H. Quintela, & M. Cunha (Eds.), *Supporting Technologies and the Impact of Blockchain on Organizations and Society* (pp. 94–112). IGI Global., doi:10.4018/978-1-6684-5747-4.ch007

KEY TERMS AND DEFINITIONS

OpenAI:: A research institute focused on developing and promoting friendly AI in a way that benefits humanity as a whole. OpenAI creates and advances digital intelligence technologies, particularly artificial intelligence.

Multifactor Productivity (MFP):: A measure of economic performance that compares the amount of goods and services produced (output) to the amount of combined inputs used to produce these goods and services. MFP considers multiple factors like labour, capital, and technology.

Artificial Intelligence (AI):: The simulation of human intelligence processes by machines, especially computer systems. These processes include learning, reasoning, self-correction, and problem-solving.

Machine Learning:: A subset of AI that involves the development of algorithms that allow computers to learn and make predictions or decisions based on data.

Predictive Analytics:: The use of data, statistical algorithms, and machine learning techniques to identify the likelihood of future outcomes based on historical data.

Automation:: The technology by which a process or procedure is performed with minimal human assistance, often through the use of AI and robotics.

Data Analytics:: The process of examining data sets to draw conclusions about the information they contain, often with the aid of specialized systems and software.

E-Commerce:: The buying and selling of goods or services using the internet, and the transfer of money and data to execute these transactions.

Supply Chain Management:: The management of the flow of goods and services, involving the movement and storage of raw materials, of work-in-process inventory, and of finished goods from point of origin to point of consumption.

Cybersecurity:: The practice of protecting systems, networks, and programs from digital attacks aimed at accessing, changing, or destroying sensitive information.

Algorithmic Bias:: Systematic and repeatable errors in a computer system that create unfair outcomes, such as privileging one arbitrary group of users over others.

Digital Transformation:: The integration of digital technology into all areas of a business, fundamentally changing how businesses operate and deliver value to customers.

Internet of Things (IoT):: The interconnection via the internet of computing devices embedded in everyday objects, enabling them to send and receive data.

Fintech:: A combination of "financial technology," it refers to new tech that seeks to improve and automate the delivery and use of financial services.

Sustainability:: Meeting our own needs without compromising the ability of future generations to meet their own needs, especially pertaining to environmental conservation and resource management.

Chapter 5
Safeguarding Business in the Age of AI for Organizational Resilience and Risk Management

Pushan Kumar Dutta
https://orcid.org/0000-0002-4765-3864
School of Engineering and Technology, Amity University, Kolkata, India

Sulagna Das
JIS University, India

Devraj Ganguly
JIS University, India

ABSTRACT

As AI proliferates across sectors, it creates new cybersecurity risks from growing attack surfaces, data flows, and system complexity. This chapter outlines risk management frameworks to harness AI safely despite escalating threats. It establishes why traditional controls now fall short, necessitating updated cyber strategies centered on ethical "Secure AI by Design" governance. First, prominent threats like malware and denial-of-service attacks are analyzed. Technical safeguards such as authentication, encryption, and blockchain applications are suggested alongside auditing, transparency, and proactive risk monitoring to manage threats. Real-world critical infrastructure attack cases reveal current susceptibilities. esilience demands optimization coupled with defense-in-depth approaches across people, processes and system that gives advisory on adapting cybersecurity and a guide to securing AI innovation potential, aligning with the book's focus on OpenAI outlines steps around pipelines, red teams, and internal/external trust via auditing and transparency for cyber risk management

DOI: 10.4018/979-8-3693-1198-1.ch005

1.INTRODUCTION

The advent of artificial intelligence (AI) and machine learning introduces vast opportunities for business innovation and productivity gains. However, these technologies also usher in new cyber risks that demand a thoughtful risk management approach. Corporate strategy must evolve to address heightened threats to confidentiality, integrity, and availability of data and systems. Proactive investment in cybersecurity and resilience is crucial even during early adoption of AI/ML. Techniques like secure system design, robust access controls, data encryption, and ongoing vulnerability testing must become ingrained in tech development and deployment lifecycles. Fostering a "security first" culture top to bottom is key. Further, the complexity of AI demands more holistic safeguards beyond just technical controls. Careful governance through impact assessments, ethics boards, and internal/external audits can uncover risks like unfair bias. It also supports transparency and accountability with stakeholders. Overall, integrated cyber risk management enables companies to harness AI's potential while building trust and mitigating harm. The strategies firms put in place today to protect people and data will largely determine whether AI remains an open, productive frontier or a source of instability and insecurity. By self-regulating early, businesses can lead the way toward ethical and responsible AI while securing lasting competitive advantage. The privacy and security of sensitive information may be threatened, as well as financial and reputational harm. The motto of cybersecurity is to maintain

- **Confidentiality:** Ensuring that only certified people or systems have access to sensitive information. To avoid unapproved disclosure, this calls for precautions like encryption, access restrictions, and secure communication protocols.
- **Integrity:** Upholding the reliability, correctness, and consistency of data and systems. To guard against unauthorized alteration or tampering, integrity measures include data validation, checksums, digital signatures, and secure coding techniques.
- **Availability:** Ensuring that data and systems are available to authorized users at all times. Measures including redundant systems, backup and recovery procedures, and defenses against denial-of-service (DoS) assaults are used to protect availability.

To achieve all these cybersecurity employs a range of practices, technologies, and methodologies, including:

- **Network Security:** The use of firewalls, intrusion detection systems (IDS), and virtual private networks (VPNs) to safeguard computer networks, limit access, and monitor network traffic is known as network security.
- **Endpoint Protection:** Using firewalls, intrusion prevention systems (IPS), and antivirus software to guard against malware infections and unauthorized access on specific devices including laptops, smartphones, and tablets.
- **Secure Coding and Application Security:** To find and fix vulnerabilities in software and applications, adhere to secure coding standards, carry out regular security audits, and do penetration tests and vulnerability assessments.
- **Control of Threats:** Cybersecurity groups should cooperate and share threat intelligence to stay up-to-date on new threats and respond to them. This will help identify, control, and recover from security issues.
- **Risk Assessment:** Risk assessment and management entail identifying possible threats and vulnerabilities through risk assessments, and successfully prioritizing and reducing risks through the use of risk management procedures (What is Cybersecurity, n.d.).

Frames the cyberattacks in context of undermining organizational productivity gains and resilience by highlighting emerging exposure areas that AI systems create. As the book explores, while OpenAI promises enhanced efficiency and decision-making, cases demonstrate AI also expands attack surfaces if not managed securely. The field of cybersecurity is dynamic and constantly developing to address threats from new technologies like AI. It necessitates a proactive, multi-layered strategy spanning people, processes and solutions. By putting strong practices in place, organizations can lessen cyber risk exposures and protect digital assets that drive performance. However, AI-powered systems also introduce new attack vectors that legacy controls fall short on. Vast data flows, interconnectivity and machine learning model vulnerabilities increase threats to critical functions like:

- **Data Protection**: Safeguarding sensitive information from compromise that damages consumer trust and business continuity.
- **Fraud Prevention**: Blocking unauthorized transactions or data manipulation, which incur financial and reputational losses.
- **Availability/Continuity**: Withstanding disruptions from malware, denial-of-service attacks or related threats that undermine productivity. The cases profiled spotlight exactly such susceptibilities that counter the performance gains promised by AI adoption. They underscore why securing OpenAI systems against escalating cyber risks is integral to actualizing multifactor productivity improvements.

We create a Pseudo-Algorithm: Integrating AI with Cybersecurity for Organizational Resilience

Step 1: Introduction

- Define the dual nature of AI and machine learning as both enablers of innovation and sources of new cyber risks.
- Emphasize the need for a "security first" culture and integrated risk management strategies.
- Highlight the importance of confidentiality, integrity, and availability in cybersecurity.

Step 2: Understanding Cyber Threats

- Enumerate common cyber threats: malware, phishing, man-in-the-middle attacks, DDoS, DNS attacks, and SQL injection.
- Discuss the prevalence of cybercrime globally and its impact on various countries, with a focus on India.
- Present statistics on cybersecurity concerns and breaches among small and medium-sized businesses.

Step 3: Identifying Sources of Cyber Threats

- List sources of cyber threats: nation-states, criminal groups, hackers, terrorist groups, hacktivists, malicious insiders, and corporate detectives.
- Explore scams operated by scammers for financial gain.

Step 4: Examining Vulnerabilities and High-Profile Cases

- Detail specific cases of cybersecurity breaches within India, highlighting the vulnerabilities exploited.
- Discuss the implementation of cybersecurity technologies in banking to protect against fraud and ensure system reliability.

Step 5: Facing Organizational Challenges

- Address challenges businesses face in securing their operations, including employee errors, malware, and the high cost of security measures.
- Discuss the significance of staying updated with security practices and compliance with data regulations.

Step 6: Implementing Best Practices for Protection

- Suggest best practices for cybersecurity, including the development of insider threat programs, employee training, maintaining compliance, and building a cyber incident response plan.
- Emphasize the importance of regular updates, data backups, phishing simulations, and securing sites with HTTPS.

Step 7: Applying Cybersecurity Across Fields

- Describe the application of cybersecurity in cloud security, virtualization security, machine learning technologies, data-centric security, and network security.
- Highlight key strategies such as encryption, monitoring, compliance, and the use of firewalls and VPNs.

Step 8: Looking Towards the Future

- Discuss the future of cybersecurity in India, focusing on digital transformation, skill development, emerging technologies, data protection regulations, collaboration, and cybersecurity in critical sectors.
- Highlight the need for public awareness and cyber hygiene.

Step 9: Conclusion

- Reiterate the importance of integrating cybersecurity into the organizational strategy for AI and machine learning adoption.
- Summarize the need for a proactive approach to cybersecurity to harness the benefits of AI while ensuring data protection and system integrity.

II. CYBER THREATS IN ORGANIZATIONS

A cybersecurity threat is an individual or organization's attempt to obtain unauthorized access to a network to hurt, disrupt, or steal sensitive data. The top cyber security threats are the most widespread, and must be considered by modern businesses:

Figure 1. Cyber Threats
Source: Author

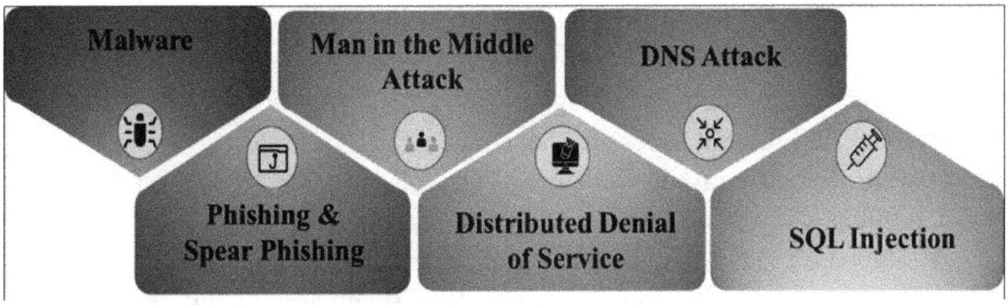

- **Malware:** Malicious software is the most common form of cyberattack, including spyware, ransomware, and viruses. ***Spyware*** is a type of computer program that enables hackers to track computer activities by sending data from a hard drive. Malicious malware known as ransomware encrypts files and requests a fee to unlock them. ***Backdoors*** are a term used to describe attackers who can access a system without using authentication processes, giving them the ability to remotely update malware. ***Trojans*** are harmful programs that impersonate trustworthy programs or files to deceive users into installing and running them. A ***Computer Virus*** is a harmful program that spreads from one device to another. ***Worms*** are a type of virus that transfers itself from computer to computer when a user clicks on a phishing link or email. It can refuse access to network components, damage the computer, and export sensitive data to unexpected places.
- **Phishing and Spear Phishing:** Phishing occurs when someone is duped into disclosing personal information such as usernames and passwords, bank account data, social security numbers, and credit card numbers. Hackers send phishing emails that appear to be from trusted sources in an attempt to fool customers into clicking on links to bogus websites that request personal information or download malware. Hackers could be able to install malware or remotely manage equipment if fraudulent email attachments are opened. A more sophisticated type of phishing called ***Spear Phishing*** targets privileged people like system administrators and C-suite executives. Phishing techniques include Smishing which is the practice of phishers utilizing SMS, whereas Vishing is a social engineering assault in which the attacker calls the target and impersonates a financial institution representative to acquire information. To get access to the victim's device, the attacker frequently asks the victim to install screen-sharing applications. The other techniques are

domain spoofing, URL phishing, watering hole phishing, clone phishing, and evil twin phishing.

- **Man in the Middle Attack:** MITM attacks are eavesdropping attacks where hostile actors infiltrate a two-way communication and intercept incoming data. They may construct bogus Wi-Fi networks or implant malware on victims' PCs to gain access to their data.
- **Distributed Denial of Service:** A DDoS attack attempts to take down a company's website by flooding its servers with requests from hacked IP addresses. This assault can slow down or even take down the servers, preventing customers from accessing the website and placing purchases.
- **DNS Attack:** A DNS attack is a type of cyberattack that exploits DNS weaknesses. Attackers take advantage of DNS flaws to redirect visitors to malicious websites (DNS Hijacking) and steal information from vulnerable systems (DNS Tunneling).
- **SQL Injection:** SQL injection attacks allow fraudsters to gain access to a database by uploading malicious SQL scripts, allowing them to access, edit, or remove data (What are Cybersecurity Threats?, 2022). According to a report published by Digital Ocean, (An MNC specializing in technology and provider of cloud service to small and medium-scale businesses, startups, and developers. It has fifteen data centers worldwide and is headquartered in New York, USA) on Small Business and Cybersecurity (Small businesses and cybersecurity, 2023), survey done on 550 Small scale and medium-scale business owners and employees, it has been observed that 54% of the sample stated increasing concern about cybersecurity in comparison to the previous years. The biggest security concern was the lack of time to manage security (25%), followed by data loss or data theft (23%), ransomware attacks (12%), and DDoS attacks (10%).

Figure 2. Biggest Security Concern
Source: Digital Ocean

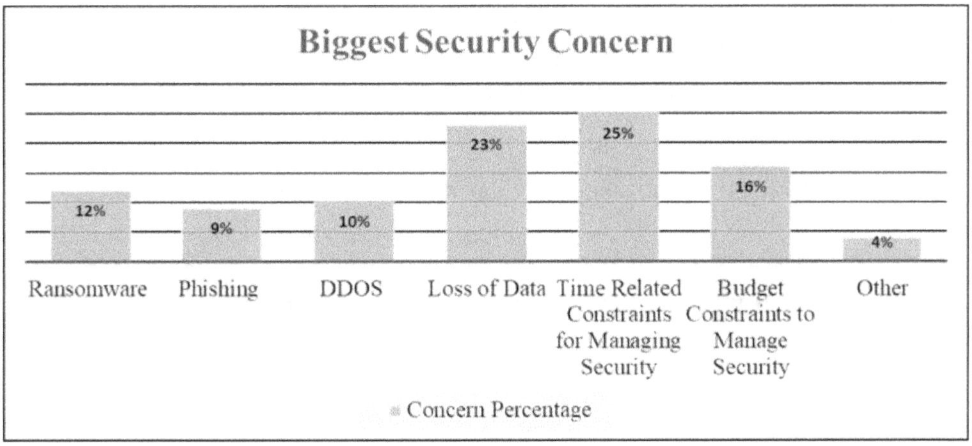

The most prevalent type of security breach in the previous year was phishing attacks (44%), followed by DDoS attacks (30%) and ransomware attacks (10%). 8% had suffered a security breach, 87% had not suffered, and 4% were unsure. The most common type of breach was phishing or corporate email compromise attacks (44%).

Figure 3. Security Breach Experience
Source: Digital Ocean

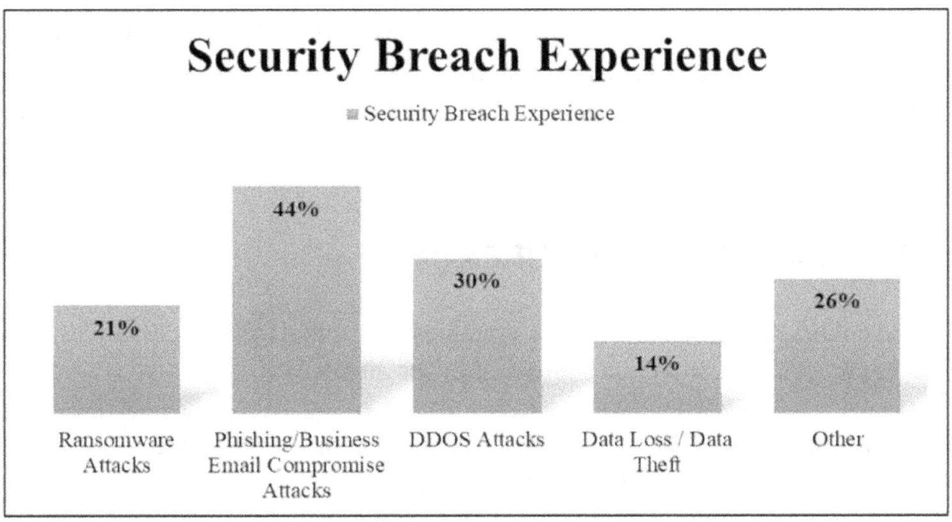

Worldwide around four out of ten internet users have experienced cybercrime in the year 2022, and India was the most likely country to experience cybercrime, with nearly 70% of internet users reporting having experienced it. The United States came in second, with 49% reporting having been victims. Australia is third with 40%, followed by New Zealand with 38%, the United Kingdom and

Figure 4. Cybercrime Experienced by Internet Users' Country Wise
Source: Statista

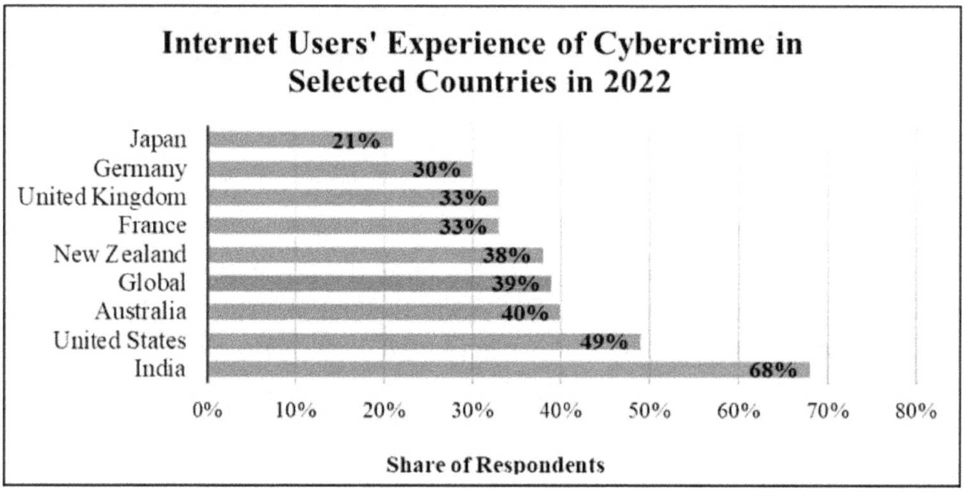

France with 33%, Germany with 30%, and Japan with only 21%. Cybercrime has become a major threat to the banking industry, as the technology and expertise used by hackers are becoming increasingly advanced, making it impossible to prevent attacks consistently.

III. SOURCES OF CYBER THREATS

Understanding threat actors and their strategies is essential for a successful response to cyberattacks. Below are the sources of cyber threats:

- **Nation States:** Cyberattacks can disrupt communications, military activities, and day to day life of the common people.
- **Criminal Group:** Criminal groups utilize phishing, spam, spyware, and malware to steal identities, commit online fraud, and extort money from computer systems.

Figure 5. Sources of Cyberthreats
Sources: Author

- **Hackers:** Hackers use cyber methods to circumvent security measures and exploit vulnerabilities in a computer system or network for personal benefit, vengeance, stalking, financial gain, or political action. Furthermore, they create unique ways of attack to compete or gain prestige in the hacking community.
- **Terrorist Groups:** Terrorists employ cyberattacks to harm, infiltrate, or exploit critical infrastructure, putting national security and the economy at risk and causing mass casualties.
- **Hacktivists:** Cyberattacks are used by hacktivists to target industries, organizations, and individuals that do not support their political beliefs, opinion, and purposes.
- **Malicious Insider:** The majority of IT executives are concerned about the fact that employees, outside suppliers, contractors, and other business partners have legal access to corporate assets and data yet misuse it by stealing or destroying information for monetary or personal benefit.
- **Corporate Detectives:** Industrial or corporate espionage is used by corporate spies to get access to a competitor's infrastructure, gather trade secrets, and gain access.

III a) Scams Operated by Scammers to Earn Money from Victims (Individual / Organization):

- **Scams Involving Lotteries and Sweepstakes:** Scammers tell their victims they have won a lottery or sweepstakes when they never even entered. Before the alleged wins can be claimed, the con artists demand upfront payment of fees or taxes, but there is no genuine award.
- **Romance Scams:** To lure victims into love relationships, con artists build false accounts on dating websites or social media platforms. Once they have gained the victim's trust, they exploit their emotions and demand money for a variety of things, including crises, trips, or investments. After getting the money, the con artists vanish.
- **Investments and Ponzi Schemes:** Scammers get victims to invest their money in dishonest schemes by promising great returns on investments. They can design complex investment possibilities or Ponzi schemes that employ money from new participants to pay returns to previous investors. The con eventually fails, and the money is taken by the con artist.
- **Scams Involving Charities:** During times of emergencies or natural disasters, con artists create fictitious charities or impersonate real ones to take advantage of people's goodwill. Donations are requested, but the fraudsters keep the money because it never gets to the designated beneficiaries.
- **Identity Theft:** Scammers steal people's identities by obtaining personal information such as social security numbers, license information, or bank account numbers. They could use the victim's name to create false credit accounts, seek loans, or carry out unauthorized activities.

b) Vulnerabilities

- **Jawaharlal Nehru Port Container Terminal (JNPCT) Case (Attack on February 2022):** Jawaharlal Nehru Port Container Terminal (JNPCT), the sole state-owned and controlled container terminal in India, reportedly started turning away ships as a result of a ransomware assault. One of five container terminals, JNPCT is the biggest container port in India. Half of all containers in India were handled by the Jawaharlal Nehru Port Trust. The attack was detected by local sources on February 21 and ships were immediately diverted to other terminals in a complex close to Mumbai.
- **SpiceJet Airline Case (Attack on May 2022):** Ransomware assaults were launched against SpiceJet, an Indian airline, on May 24 or Tuesday night, delaying the departure of aircraft the next morning. It frustrates hundreds of travelers who are trapped at the airport and in other parts of the nation. The airline acknowledged that ransomware assaults had been made against its system in a tweet (Mishra, 2022).

- **Water Resources Department in Goa (Attack on July 2022):** On June 21, a ransomware assault was launched on Goa, India's Water Resources Department, the most accountable institution. This organization is in charge of setting up flood monitoring systems throughout Goa. The data must be delivered in exchange for bitcoin, according to these ransomware perpetrators.
- **Tata Power Case (Attack on October 2022):** On October 14th, ransomware assaults hit Tata Power, the largest integrated power business in India. Their IT system and infrastructure were affected by these attacks. They moved right away to recover or restore the systems. (Top 5 Ransomware Attacks in India to Watch Out for in 2023, 2023)
- **All India Institute of Medical Service or AIIMS Case (Attack on November 2022)**: The All India Institute of Medical Service, often known as AIIMS, is the top public medical institution in India. On November 23, it was the target of a cyberattack. Numerous patients and clinicians who use basic healthcare services, such as the discharge, billing, and patient admission systems, are impacted by this attack.
- **• Air India Data Breach Case (Attack on May 2021):** A cyberattack on the systems of airline data service provider SITA resulted in the disclosure of customer personal information. Passengers weren't made aware of the data collection until March, even though it took place between August 2011 and February 2021. The incident also had an impact on Cathay Pacific, Malaysia Airlines, Singapore Airlines, and Lufthansa.
- **Trading platform Upstox Case (Attack on April 2021):** Upstox, an Indian trading website, has acknowledged a KYC data breach. Financial services organizations gather KYC data to verify clients' identities and prevent fraud or money laundering. Upstox notified clients that their passwords would be changed and extra precautions would be implemented. (Ghosh, 2021)

To safeguard confidential financial information, avoid fraud, and guarantee the reliability of banking systems, technology in cybersecurity must be implemented. The following are some essential technologies that are frequently used in the banking industry's cybersecurity environment.

- Firewalls are used to create a barrier between internal and external networks by regulating incoming and outgoing network traffic. They are also used in conjunction with intrusion detection systems (IDS) and intrusion prevention systems (IPS). IDS/IPS technologies can be used to stop or prevent possible attacks by scanning network traffic for suspicious activity.
- Secure communication channels over the internet are provided by the Transport Layer Security (TLS) and Secure Socket Layer (SSL) protocols,

respectively. They protect the security and integrity of sensitive data, including login passwords and financial transactions, as it is sent between servers and clients.

- MFA (multi-factor authentication) and two-factor authentication (2FA) Beyond the usual username and password combinations, some authentication techniques are used. By requesting additional authentication elements from users, such as biometrics (fingerprint, facial recognition), hardware tokens, SMS codes, or mobile apps, they increase security by lowering the possibility of unauthorized access.
- Blockchain technology offers a distributed, unchangeable ledger for securely documenting financial transactions. It can improve banking operations' security and transparency, especially in areas like identity verification, international payments, and smart contracts.

According to a study by Digital Ocean, 37% of company executives have established password or access controls, 41% have deployed firewalls or other security measures, and 59% have used two-factor authentication. Only 6% of companies have increased their security spending or staffing, indicating that many small- and medium-sized companies lack the means to prioritize security.

Figure 6. Measures to Increase Security
Source: Digital Ocean

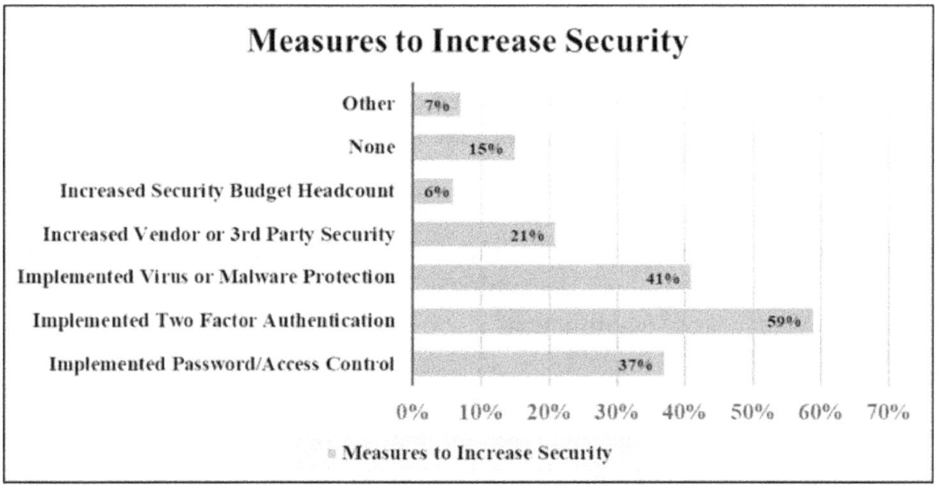

The below graph is a study by Statista, where has been observed that the rate of growth of different cyber security products market in between the year 2019 to 2022.

Figure 7. The Growth of Cyber Security Products in India
Source: Statista

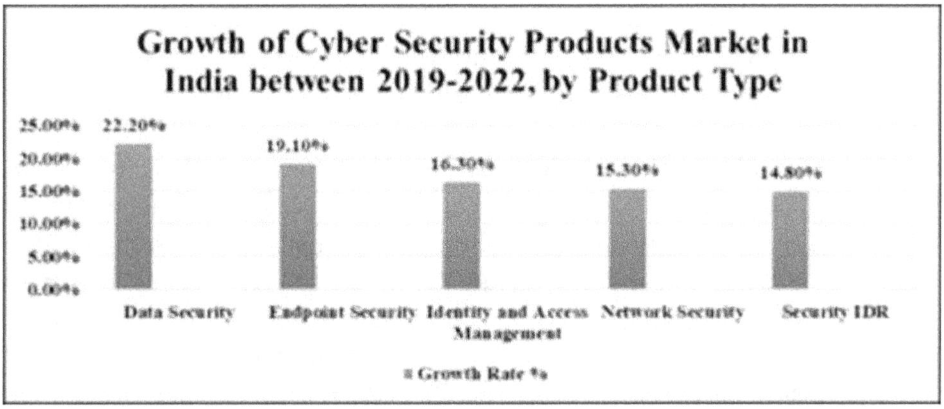

The growth rate for data security products is the maximum (22.20%), in comparison to endpoint security (19.10%), Identity and Access Management (16.30%), Network Security (15.30%), and security IDR (14.80%).

IV. CHALLENGES FACED BY AN ORGANIZATION TO SECURE THEIR BUSINESS:

Businesses invest in data security to protect critical company data, but there are several hurdles in maintaining its security on any form of infrastructure. A data breach can be devastating, so businesses invest in data security. The most important idea is to protect corporate data, from three challenges:

- **Employees:** The first and foremost reason for data breach is the mishandling of data, by the Employees with genuine system access credentials. There is a growing need for qualified cybersecurity experts. As human error continues to be a major cybersecurity risk. To inform staff about new dangers, phishing tricks, and security best practices, organizations will need to invest in thorough cybersecurity training programs. Campaigns to raise awareness of cybersecurity will be necessary to develop a security-conscious organizational culture. Artificial intelligence and automation will also play a part in enhancing cybersecurity capabilities, streamlining procedures, and addressing the skills problem.
- **Malware:** Malware is a type of harmful software that infiltrates a system once a user clicks on a malicious link or email. It can block access to essential

network components, harm the system, and acquire private information. It is the most common cyber security danger. Malware-based cyberattacks can be prevented by protecting users with antivirus, endpoint security, anti-malware, and email spam filters ensuring all updates and patches are up-to-date, updating workers with regular cybersecurity awareness training, and restricting user access and application rights.

- **Cost of Implementing and Maintaining High-Security Measures:** Strong, multi-layered security can be expensive to implement internally owing to license fees, hardware costs, and human requirements (Bhattacharya et al., 2023). Businesses use secure cloud service providers to provide enterprise-grade protection for a fraction of the cost. The cloud provider frequently controls cloud infrastructure and security improvements, minimizing labor and freeing up time for the internal IT staff. Businesses must work with a secure cloud service provider to acquire enterprise-grade cloud security, which should offer exceptional security and support for sensitive data.(The 3 Biggest Challenges to Securing Company Data, n.d.)

Regarding the report of Digital Ocean, Organizations face a variety of challenges when it comes to securing their operations, such as a lack of time to focus on security, the cost of security solutions, a lack of security experience, and vendor security. The most significant challenges that organizations face in securing their operations observed that a lack of time to focus on security was the most frequently cited challenge (53 percent), followed by coping with changing threats (48 percent), the value of security solutions and scarce security expertise (40 percent) and (19 percent) said determining vendor security was difficult. (Small businesses and cybersecurity How startups and SMBs are viewing security threats in 2023, 2023)

Figure 8. Challenges in Securing Business
Source: Digital Ocean

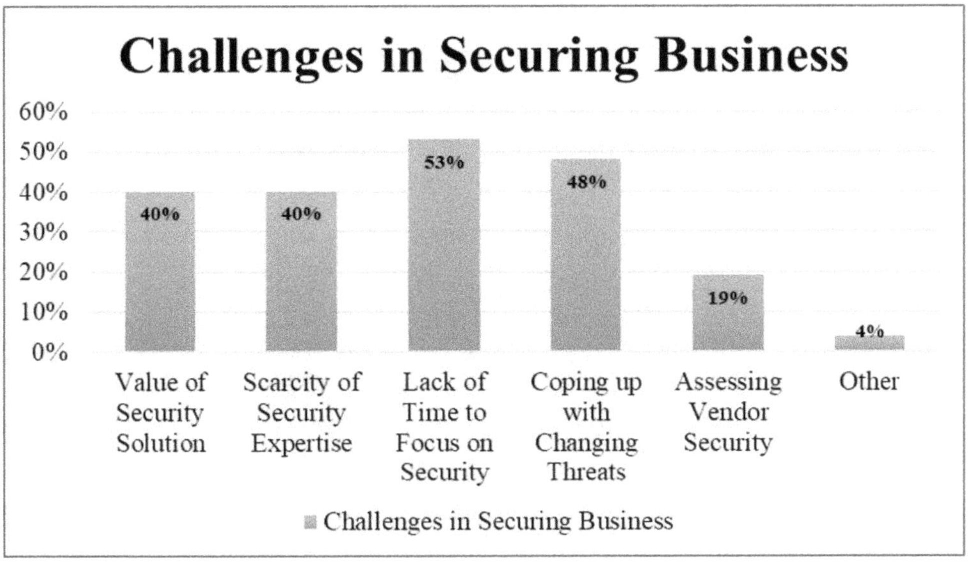

IV b. Protection from Cyber Threats by Use of Cybersecurity Best Practices

Organizations must modify their cybersecurity strategy to stay up-to-date with new technology and attack techniques, and these best practices can help prepare for cyber-attacks and ensure business continuity.

- **Development of an insider threat Program:** To prevent workers from utilizing access credentials to steal or destroy business data, organizations must implement an insider threat program, and IT security staff should not wait for clearance from senior management.
- **Training of Employees:** Employees are the first line of defense against cyber-attacks, therefore companies must develop cybersecurity awareness programs to teach them how to detect and respond to them. This will improve their cybersecurity and resilience.
- **Maintain Compliance:** Firms must maintain compliance with data rules applicable to their industry and geographical region, and remain educated about changing compliance rules to reap the benefits.

Figure 9. Protection from Cyber Threats
Source: Author

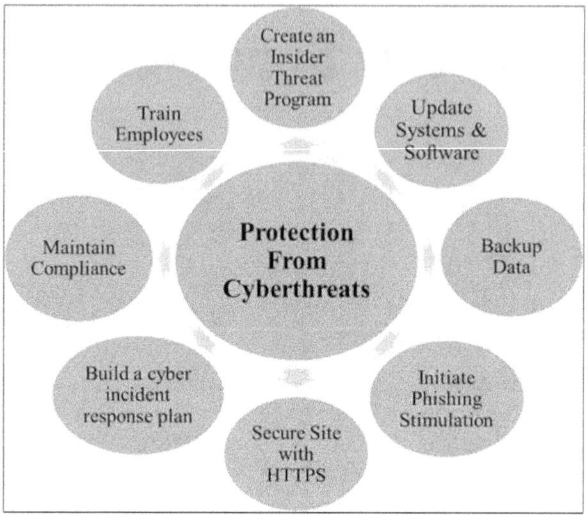

- **Building of Cyber Incident Response Plan:** Businesses must build an effective Cyber Security Incident Response Plan (CSIRP) to anticipate, respond to, and recover from cyberattacks.
- **Regular Updating of System and Software:** To defend a business from cyberattacks, the security network, systems, and software should be kept up to date, as cyber threats grow fast.
- **Data Backup:** Regular backups of data including, backups of websites, applications, databases, emails, attachments, files, calendars, and other data can help reduce the risk of data breaches.
- **Start a Phishing Simulation:** Businesses must run phishing simulations to inform staff members about the dangers of downloading files and clicking on dubious links, as well as to help them understand the repercussions of a phishing attempt.
- **Securing Sites with HTTP:** Organizations must use SSL (secure sockets layer) certificates to protect their website, while HTTPS ensures the integrity and confidentiality of data exchanged between a user and a website.

IV c) Implementation of Cybersecurity in Different Fields:

Figure 10. Cyber Security in Different Fields
Source: Author

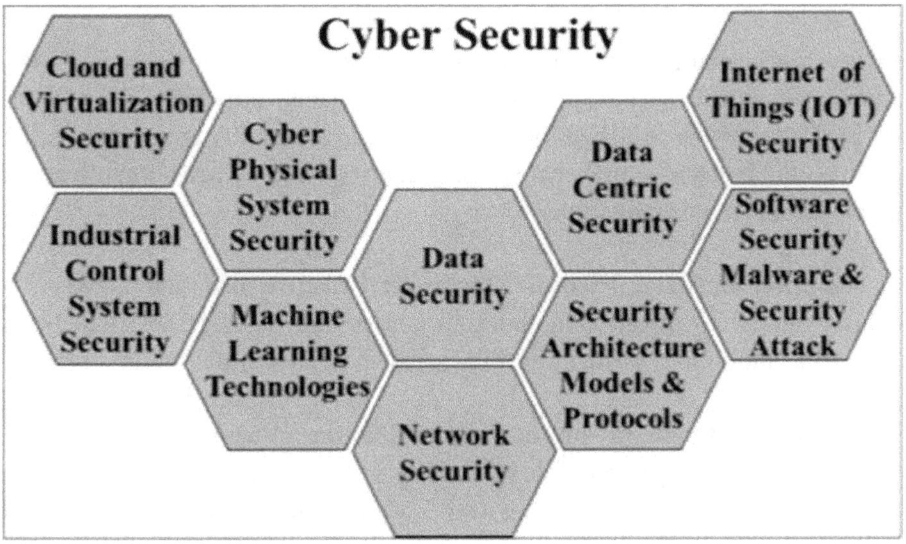

a) Cloud Security:

The term "cloud security" refers to a collection of procedures, tools, and regulations created to guard cloud computing environments and the information stored there from a variety of dangers and weaknesses. The main goals of cloud security are to protect the privacy, availability, and integrity of data and resources in cloud-based systems. Following are some crucial elements of cloud security:

1. **Data security:** To safeguard data while it is in transit and at rest, cloud service providers use a variety of encryption techniques. Sensitive information is protected using robust encryption techniques like the AES (Advanced Encryption Standard).
2. **Compliance and Auditing:** To ensure compliance, cloud service providers comply with industry-specific compliance laws (such as GDPR, and HIPAA). Within the cloud environment, customers may also keep an eye on and check the state of their compliance.
3. **Monitoring and Reaction to Events:** To quickly identify and address security issues, procedures for continuous monitoring, log management, and real-time

threat detection are put into place. Systems for managing security information and events (SIEM) are frequently used to collect and examine security event data.

b) Virtualization Security:

Security for virtualized systems, where numerous virtual machines (VMs) or containers operate on a single physical server, is the main emphasis of virtualization security. Better resource utilization, flexibility, and scalability are made possible by virtualization, but it also presents special security issues. The following are some crucial factors for virtualization security:

1. **Isolation Between Virtual Machines:** Effective isolation between VMs is essential to thwart unauthorized access and possible assaults. Network segmentation and virtual firewalls are security tools that assist enforce VM isolation.
2. **Monitoring the Behaviour of Virtual Machines** (VMs) can assist identify any suspicious activity or possible security concerns. Malware, unauthorized access attempts, and resource abuse within VMs may all be found using monitoring tools.
3. **Security of Virtual Networks:** It's crucial to protect the virtual networks that VMs utilize. The communication paths between VMs and external networks are secured via network segmentation, access restrictions, and virtual firewalls.

c) Machine Learning Technologies

A combination of methods and algorithms known as "machine learning technologies" enables computers to learn from data and make predictions without having to be programmed. Due to their capacity to analyze vast volumes of data and derive insightful information, these technologies have significantly increased in popularity across a variety of industries.

Data security is the protection of data from unauthorized access, use, disclosure, disturbance, alteration, or destruction. It involves putting in place safeguards and best practices to guarantee the availability, confidentiality, and integrity of data. An overview of data security is provided below:

1. **Encryption Data:** It is encrypted using cryptographic methods into an incomprehensible format. It ensures that even if data is accessed by unauthorized parties, they will be unable to use or understand it without the encryption keys.

Data that is stored, sent through networks, and used are all encrypted forms of data at rest and in use, respectively.

2. **Data Loss Prevention** (DLP) systems work to stop sensitive data from being unintentionally or intentionally transmitted outside of the company. To spot and stop any data breaches, these systems keep an eye on data that is being used, in motion, and at rest. When policies are violated, DLP systems can issue warnings and enforce policies, such as restricting or encrypting specific types of data.
3. **Compliance and Regulatory Measures:** Organisations must abide by pertinent data protection laws as well as compliance standards that are particular to their business. Implementing certain security controls, performing audits, and ensuring proper data handling practices are all examples of compliance measures.

The practices and policies used to safeguard computer networks and their infrastructure from unauthorized access, abuse, interruption, and assaults are referred to as network security. Security technologies, policies, and procedures must be implemented to protect network resources. An overview of network security is provided below:

1. **Firewalls:** Firewalls are essential for implementing network security regulations, keeping track of and regulating both incoming and outgoing network traffic. Firewalls can be hardware or software programs and are essential for protecting private networks from public networks. They are essential for implementing network security regulations.
2. **Virtual Private Networks (VPNs):** VPNs provide secure access to private networks over public networks. They safeguard and protect communications by encrypting network traffic between branch offices or distant users and the corporate network.
3. **Wi-Fi Protected Access:** Security issues with wireless networks are particularly difficult to solve. To safeguard wireless networks, it's crucial to use Wi-Fi Protected Access (WPA/WPA2) or the more secure WPA3 encryption protocols, use strong passwords, disable pointless functionality, and do routine wireless network security audits.

d) Data-Centric Security:

Data-centric security, often referred to as data-centric protection, is a security strategy that places more of an emphasis on safeguarding the data itself than just on perimeter-based security measures. It emphasizes protecting data at every stage of its lifespan, including production, storage, transport, and destruction. Data-centric security aims to protect data's confidentiality, integrity, and availability across all systems and networks, regardless of where it is located. Key components of data-centric security include:

1. **Data-Centric Security:** The crucial element of data-centric security is encryption. Cryptographic techniques are used to convert data into an unreadable format. With encryption, you can make sure that even if someone gets access to your data without your permission, they won't be able to read it or use it. Data at rest, in transit, and use are all securely stored, transmitted, and processed.
2. **Anonymization and Data Masking:** Anonymization involves modifying or replacing sensitive data with fictitious or altered data while maintaining its format and structure. Anonymization techniques make it difficult to connect datasets to specific people by removing or obscuring personally identifying information (PII). These methods aid in safeguarding data whether it is shared with third parties or used for testing or development.
3. **Data Retention and Destruction:** Adequate rules for data retention and destruction guarantee that data is safely preserved for as long as necessary and disposed of when it is no longer needed. To prevent unauthorized access to data during disposal, safe data destruction techniques including shredding physical media or securely deleting digital storage devices are used.

Future of Cybersecurity in India:

India's cybersecurity industry has both possibilities and problems in the future. The following significant factors are anticipated to have an impact on India's cybersecurity in the future:

- **Digital Transformation and Cybersecurity**: As more industries in India, including banking, healthcare, and e-commerce, rapidly digitize, the attack surface for cyber threats is growing. To safeguard sensitive data and crucial infrastructure throughout this digital revolution, the future will need strong cybersecurity measures.
- **Development of Cybersecurity Skills**: India is funding programs to advance cybersecurity skill development. A greater need is being seen for qualified cybersecurity experts who can counter advanced online threats. To close the cybersecurity skills gap, there will be a greater emphasis in the future on training initiatives, certifications, and partnerships between academics and businesses.(Filipkowski, 2023)

- **Emerging Technologies**: India is facing new cybersecurity challenges due to the adoption of AI, IoT, and 5G technologies. Proactive steps including applying security-by-design principles, performing frequent risk assessments, and providing privacy protection will be needed to secure these systems.
- **Data Protection and Privacy Regulations**: To provide a thorough data protection framework, India has established the Personal Data Protection Bill. In the future, there will be a greater focus placed on data privacy laws, including the adoption of strict data protection policies, user consent processes, and enforcement tools to secure personal data.
- **Information Sharing and Collaboration**: Because cybersecurity threats are global in scope, cooperation between public and private sector organizations and foreign partners is essential. India's partnership efforts to exchange threat intelligence, and best practices, and take part in global cybersecurity projects are anticipated to get stronger.
- **Cybersecurity in Critical Sectors**: Preventing cyber-attacks in industries as vital as energy, transportation, and healthcare will be a top concern. In the future, there will be more money invested in safeguarding vital infrastructure, putting in place sophisticated threat detection systems, and creating sector-specific cybersecurity standards. (Banafa, 2023)
- **Public Knowledge and Cyber Hygiene**: It will be crucial to increase public knowledge of cybersecurity dangers and to encourage appropriate cyber hygiene practices. In-depth cybersecurity awareness campaigns will be used in the future to inform people, companies, and organizations about the best ways to stay secure online.

To combat increasing cyber threats and create a safe digital environment, India's future in cybersecurity would necessitate a proactive and all-encompassing approach that combines technology, experts, strict rules, and cooperative efforts.

While artificial intelligence promises enhanced efficiency and decision-making, real-world cases demonstrate AI also expands attack surfaces. As the chapters explores, implementing OpenAI requires carefully weighing new productivity gains against emerging risk exposures across interconnected systems (Tyagi et al., 2023). Recent attacks on Indian organizations showcase susceptibilities arising from AI adoption that underscore why cybersecurity must be an integral part of any AI strategy. Though technologies like advanced machine learning analytics help secure networks, the same promise greater access and disruption potential for malicious actors if governance and safeguards falter.

This section profiles seminal cases where vulnerabilities introduced by AI systems, data flows or autonomous controls were potentially exploited amidst the digital transformation journey. The lessons gleaned serves as a harbinger for organizations on the imperatives of defense in-depth measures tailored for an increasingly automated business landscape supported by OpenAI.

REFERENCES:

Banafa, A. The Future of Cybersecurity: Predictions and Trends. BBVA Openmind. 2023. Available from: https://www.bbvaopenmind.com/en/technology/digital-world/future-of-cybersecurity-predictions-trends. Accessed 19 Jun 2023.

Bhattacharya, P., Chatterjee, S., Datt, R., Verma, A., & Dutta, P. K. (2023). A Permissioned Blockchain Approach for Real-Time Embedded Control Systems. In S. Kadry & R. Prasath (Eds.), Lecture Notes in Computer Science: Vol. 13924. *Mining Intelligence and Knowledge Exploration. MIKE 2023*. Springer., doi:10.1007/978-3-031-44084-7_32

CrowdStrike. Small Business Cyberattack Analysis: The Most Targeted SMB Sectors. CrowdStrike Blog. Available from: https://www.crowdstrike.com/blog/small-business-cyberattack-analysis-most-targeted-smb-sectors/. Accessed 17 Aug 2023.

Filipkowski, B. What is the future of cybersecurity? Fieldeffect. 2023. Available from: https://fieldeffect.com/blog/what-is-the-future-of-cyber-security. Accessed 19 Jun 2023.

Ghosh, S. The biggest data breaches in India, CSO Online tracks recent major data breaches in India. CSO Online. 2021. Available from: https://www.csoonline.com/article/3541148/the-biggest-data-breaches-in-india.html

Mishra, A. Cyber-attacks that shook Indian firms in 2022: Critical infra, healthcare most targeted. ET Insights. 2022. Available from: https://etinsights.et-edge.com/cyber-attacks-that-shook-indian-firms-in-2022-critical-infra-healthcare-most-targeted/

The 3 Biggest Challenges to Securing Company Data. WHOA.com. Available from: https://whoa.com/the-3-biggest-challenges-to-securing-company-data. Accessed 15 Jun 2023.

Top 5 Ransomware Attacks in India to Watch Out for in 2023. LinkedIn. 2023. Available from: https://www.linkedin.com/pulse/top-5-ransomware-attacks-india-watch-out-2023

Tyagi, S., Tyagi, D. R. K., Dutta, D. P. K., & Dubey, D. P. Next Generation Phishing Detection and Prevention System using Machine Learning. *1st International Conference on Advanced Innovations in Smart Cities (ICAISC)*, Jeddah, Saudi Arabia; 2023. p. 1-6. 10.1109/ICAISC56366.2023.10085529

What are Cybersecurity Threats? RiskOptics (reciprocity.com). 2022. Available from: https://www.reciprocity.com/what-are-cybersecurity-threats. Accessed 15 Jun 2023.

What is Cybersecurity? Cisco. Available from: https://www.cisco.com/c/en_in/products/security/what-is-cybersecurity.html

What is cybersecurity? IBM. Available from: https://www.ibm.com/topics/cybersecurity

Chapter 6
A Policy Simulation Experiment on Innovations and OpenAI-Driven Labour Force-Growth Nexus:
OpenAI Capabilities Through Patent and IT Exports

Festus Fatai Adedoyin
https://orcid.org/0000-0002-3586-2570
Bournemouth University, UK

Victor oyewumi Ogunbiyi
https://orcid.org/0009-0007-2966-0941
De Montfort University, UK

Aliu Adebiyi
https://orcid.org/0000-0002-6340-098X
University of Ibadan, Nigeria

Emmanuel Oluokun
Bournemouth University, UK

ABSTRACT

The hypothesis that advancement in Artificial intelligence can enhance the quality of labour and consequently its contribution to multifactor productivity and economic growth has continued to attract attention in recent times. However, not much empirical evidence is available in the literature to support this hypothesis considering

DOI: 10.4018/979-8-3693-1198-1.ch006

current economic realities. This study investigates the impact of AI-driven labor on economic growth in Switzerland. Data from 1960-2022 is used to analyze the relationship between labor and growth. Dynamic ARDL simulation is employed for policy simulation and prediction. The findings suggest that the short-term implementation of OpenAI may cause economic shocks, but a strategic approach can lead to long-term benefits. The study emphasizes the importance of investing in human capital through education and training programs. It also recommends a proactive and balanced approach to harness the potential benefits of AI while addressing its challenges.

1. INTRODUCTION

The advent of technology has spurred a paradigm shift in how things are done globally. It has affected every facet of human life. A major aspect of technology that has made much impact is Artificial Intelligence (AI). The AI system has been defined by the OECD (2019) as

"...a machine-based system that is capable of influencing the environment by producing an output (predictions, recommendations, or decisions) for a given set of objectives. It uses machine and/or human-based data and inputs to (i) perceive real and/or virtual environments; (ii) abstract these perceptions into models through analysis in an automated manner (e.g., with machine learning), or manually; and (iii) use model inference to formulate options for outcomes. AI systems are designed to operate with varying levels of autonomy".

Essentially, AI is structured to perform tasks which only humans could perform such as problem solving and reasoning. AI has been found to have the potential to assist humans, both in completing their cognitive tasks as well as automating tasks which have been identified as difficult to do for humans.

The introduction of Artificial Intelligence has been greeted with much enthusiasm on the possible positive and negative effects that the introduction holds for the future of work and how this will affect growth in the overall analysis. It is trite to say that it is agreed that the advancements in AI have proven to be superior to human cognitive capacities (Somer, 2018). They have proven to excel in the performance of tasks at the human level in areas including, but not limited to, speech recognition, visual image recognition, fault detection in humans and even automobiles, translation, product packaging, driving, and bodyguarding. For example, Somer (2018) referred to a situation in 2016 when a Google program defeated the world's best Go master and another in 2017 when AlphaZero, an AI-powered program, defeated the world's best chess engine. Also, the Google fleet of self-driving cars, the Waymo One, is said to have collectively logged over 3 million autonomous miles on the road. These examples point to the change that AI portends for labour productivity as well as the economy.

It is however unclear what the role of AI will be in the labour-growth nexus. The arguments have varied in this regard. Brynjolfsson et al. (2019) noted that AI will play a positive role in the labour-growth nexus by enhancing productivity and inadvertently leading to economic growth. AI, the authors opine, will achieve this through the removal of the bottlenecks that come with human handling of tasks. Becker (2015) and Bloom *et al.* (2019) reviewed the role AI can play in the enhancement of productivity and the promotion of economic growth from the viewpoint of intellectual property rights, pointing out that investments in AI can be deployed in the building of intangible capital asset that is an ingredient for growth. The two studies proved that these returns from the intellectual property rights on AI have the potential to significantly contribute to intangible capital accumulation and put the economy on the pathway to boom. A report by Goldman Sachs noted that AI "*could drive a 7% (or almost $7 trillion) increase in global GDP and lift productivity growth by 1.5 percentage points over 10 years*" (Goldman Sachs, 2023). Gries and Naudié, (2018) and Gordon (2018) do not however share in this optimism that AI will enhance productivity and engender significant growth. Where there is skills obsolescence of labour, technological progress, or AI, will only have a negative impact on economic growth (de Grip and van Loo 2002). On their own, Brynjolfsson and Petropoulos (2022) that using the quantum to which economic growth is engendered as a framework to measure the contribution of AI to productivity is not suitable enough, particularly when all that is considered are goods and services offered at positive prices. Mert (2015) holds a middle ground in this argument. The study argued that technological advancement generally has the potential to positively and negatively affect labour productivity, and inadvertently economic growth.

Whichever side one is tempted to hold in the AI labour productivity-growth nexus, it is incontrovertible that heavy leaps have been made in AI in the last decade. In the last decade, countries like South Korea, China, the United States, and Japan have been at the forefront of breaking new ground in AI globally. Interestingly, Switzerland which is one of the developers of AI has not been at the forefront of countries breaking new frontiers in AI (Rauflaub, 2023). This is despite that the country ranks third in AI professional density by country (Stiftung, 2021) and the third position in countries with top AI patents per million population (OECD, 2021). The Swiss Government is not oblivious to this and has started making concerted efforts towards promoting AI as well as resolving all ethical issues that may arise from the use of same. One effort that points towards the attainment of this goal is the creation of the "Swiss Digital Trust Label" which is saddled with the responsibility of restoring and boosting user confidence in the use of AI through the provision of adequate information on AI and creating an atmosphere of transparency within the confines of accepted ethical practices. Niniane Paeffgen, Director of Swiss Digital Initiative, the organisation behind the "Swiss Digital Trust Label, stated that "*We want to help guarantee that ethical and responsible behaviour also becomes a competitive advantage for businesses,*"(Rauflaub, 2023). This position was corroborated in the recommendation of a working committee to the Federal Council where it was stated that "*It is important that Switzerland utilises the opportunities of AI to the full,... We have to establish the best possible framework conditions that allow Switzerland to play a leading role in the research, development and application of AI. At the same time, the risks have to be addressed and effective measures introduced.*" This shows the level of commitment put into the advancement of AI by the Swiss Government.

2. LITERATURE REVIEW

2.1 Labour and Economic Growth Theory

This study deploys the labour and economic theory. This theory is premised on the nexus that exists between labour and economic growth. The theory runs on the assumption that there is a connection between labour and economic growth. The further assumption is that a decrease in labour productivity will result in a reduction in the contribution to GDP while an increase in labour productivity will increase how much it affects economic growth. There have been several studies to justify this assumption about the impact of labour productivity on economic growth.

Several studies have argued that there is a positive causal relationship between labour and economic growth. Korkmaz and Korkmaz (2017) and Jorgenson (2009) both argued that the relationship between the two is a positive one where labour influences economic growth positively. Korkmaz and Korkmaz (2017) review the impact of labour productivity on economic growth. The study investigated the contributions of labour productivity to economic growth in seven OECD countries between the period of 2008 and 2014, using the panel data analysis method. The result of the study establishes a unidirectional causal relationship between the two. OECD (2021) examined the level to which labour productivity affects economic growth. The study finds out that the contributions of labour to GDP were lower between the 2007 and 2009 financial crisis and that the recoveries observed in the post-financial crisis were sustained increases in employment. In other words, a drop in labour productivity affects GDP growth rates. Christensen, Cummings, and Jorgenson (1980) reviewed international comparisons of sources of economic growth among industrialized countries and concluded that labour productivity was key in the growth.

There have been some area-specific studies, considering how labour productivity affects economic countries in specific countries or groups of countries. Jorgenson (1991) interrogated how labour productivity affected economic growth between 1947 and 1985 in the United States and observed that the increase in labour productivity was the second major factor that affected economic growth. Similarly, Alani (2012) in his study of economic growth in Uganda between 1972 and 2008 observed that the increase in labour played a pivotal role in ensuring this. Su and Heshmati (2011) also interrogated the impact of labour productivity on economic growth in China between 2000 and 2009, using the Least Square Dummies Variables (LSDV) method. The study observed, based on the result from the analysis, that economic growth was significantly impacted by labour productivity.

The results from the study by Auzina-Emsina (2014) toed a different line of thought. The study interrogated the impact of labour productivity on the economic growth of European Union countries during the pre-financial crisis and the post-financial crisis periods. Their finding revealed during the pre-financial crisis period, a weak relationship was observed between labour and economic growth while no relationship was observed between the two during the early stages of the post-financial crisis period. Ayila, Ngutsav, and Ijirshar (2018) interrogated the impact of labour productivity on economic growth in Nigeria between 1980, using the Autoregressive Distributed Lag (ARDL) model. Their study did a sectoral analysis of the impact of labour productivity on four different sectors – agriculture, oil and gas, service, and manufacturing - and their findings revealed that labour productivity had a significant impact on growth in the agricultural sector and the service sector while labour productivity did not have any significant impact on growth in the oil and gas sector as well as the manufacturing sector.

This theory therefore foregrounds this study on the premise that labour can have a significant or less significant positive or negative relationship on economic growth. The quantum to which AI can cause a paradigm shift in labour productivity and the future of work will go a long way in determining how this can birth economic growth in a country.

Technological Advancement and Labour Productivity

The question of how the advancement in technology has impacted labour productivity has garnered much scholarly attention. Scholars have tried to x-ray the dimension of the impact that the advancement in technology will have or have had on labour productivity. The positions of scholars in this regard can be seen in two perspectives. Some opine that technological advancements have a negative effect on labour productivity. There are also those whose research concluded that although technological advancement has (had) a negative influence on labour productivity, it should not be discarded because the gains outweigh the cost.

Needless to say the concern over the negative impact of technological advancement on labour productivity borders largely on job losses. Mart (1995) pointed out that people, since the beginning of the Industrial Revolution, have predicted that the introduction of machines to work would lead to job loss. They maintained that the investment in machines, though would aid increased productivity, would only lead to the creation of an army of unemployed people. Chabra (2000) noted that the advancement in technology has brought about organizational complexities and a complication of work mode. To this end, new skills are often required to fit in into the new order and those who do not are eased out into the labour market. Mert (2017) re-echoes this when they emphasized that the negative effect of technological advancement is that it leads to the obsolescence of labour. Philiph (2010) also concluded that machines only eradicate the need for human effort and so cannot be said to create jobs but rather do away with them.

Different studies have been conducted in different countries to justify this. Kitur and Rotich (2014) interrogated the impact of technological advancement on human productivity in Kenya. It looked at how the introduction of tea harvesters has affected labour productivity in the tea harvesting firm. The findings of the study revealed that the introduction of tea harvesters has had both positive and negative impacts on labour productivity in the country. Hence, the introduction of the machines brought about an increase in production in the tea estates, a reduction in the cost of labour, and an improvement in the wages of workers. Equally, the introduction of the machine has affected productivity as it resulted in job loss for workers. Two studies have looked at the possible job loss effect of technological advancement. Using different methodologies for their research, Frey and Osborne (2017) and Arntz, Gregory, and Zierahn (2016) concluded that the developments in AI pose a risk at 47% and 9% of US employment respectively. The findings from Pajarinen, Rouvinen, and Ekeland (2015) concluded technological advancement will affect 35% of employment in Finland. Brzeski and Burk (2015) maintained that recent advancements in AI will cost 59% of jobs in Germany. Bowles (2014) proposed that automation will possibly affect between 45% to 60% of employment across the whole of Europe.

Naone (2009), Frase (2016), and Farrell (2013) agreed that automation will lead to job loss no doubt but a cost-benefit analysis will reveal that the benefits outweigh the cost that automation comes with. David and Dom (2013) contend that technology has the potential to increase employment opportunities for those whose job description is not in competition with automation. Bartelsman, Haltiwanger, and Scarpetta (2004) also concluded that while it is incontrovertible that advancement in technology will lead to job loss, it will create new opportunities that portend more benefits. It is to this end that Kulundu (2006) it will be disastrous to human jobs if we decide to go on full automation or mechanization. Thus, he advocates a partial implementation of the deployment of technology to the workspace.

Different methodologies have been deployed by authors in assessing the impact of technological advancement on labour productivity. Jiang et al. (2021) use SBM-GML to measure GTFP and decompose it into green technology progress index (GTP) and green technology efficiency index (GTE). Camiña et al. (2020) investigate overall long-term productivity augmenting and the existence of overall labour-reducing and human capital-labour-augmenting effects. Li et al. (2022) deploy an empirical model to quantitatively investigate the impact of ICT on total factor productivity (TFP).

2.2 OpenAI and Multifactor Productivity

There have been several experiments that have been conducted to test the impact of AI on productivity. These experiments have often looked at specific areas in the application of Artificial Intelligence. For example, Maggie Fu et al. (2021) discovered that the adoption of industrial robots records significant benefits for productivity and employment in developed economies while it records insignificant effects in developing economies. Their findings revealed that the adoption of industrial robots led to an increase in the contribution of labour to the GDP of developed countries while the reverse is the case in developing countries. They further discovered that the adoption of industrial robots led to higher income inequalities in both developing and developed economies. Johnson et al. (2022), in their study, discovered that automation of agricultural processes helps in the development and improvement of the quality of lives of farmers as well as create employment opportunities to match up the new process. Li et al. (2022), using data from Chinese-based A-share-listed manufacturing companies, argued that there is a positive correlation between ICT and TFP. Phiph (2010) revealed from its findings that the deployment of advanced technology like AI has proven to be of immense help for people who have found themselves in life-risking professions like space exploration and mining. The use of AI, he opines, has helped in reducing the risk level associated with the jobs.

It is in a similar vein that Korinek (2023) concluded that economists now stand a chance to be between 10% and 20% more productive in their jobs by using language models. It is also observed that writing tasks can now be completed faster and with more clarity of ideas using ChatGT (Noy and Zhang, 2023). So, writing can be done with only little effort from the writer who is just expected to give an overview of what s/he wants while ChatGT works on that to come up with a befitting write-up based on the user's specification. A study also revealed that software engineers now have the potential to code twice as fast as they used to before using Codex (a coding tool) (Kalliamvakou, 2022). This means that coding becomes easier and faster than what was obtainable before.

A recent study by Brynjolfsson, Li, and Raymond (2023) observed that call centre agents record more productivity when they use technology. Thus, a well-experienced call centre operator becomes at least 14% more productive while using technology while a less experienced operator may record up to 30% more productivity when technology is deployed. Also, when an operator uses generative AI as an aid when attending to a customer, the findings of the study were that customer satisfaction is easily achieved because the system tends to provide the operator with all that is needed to help meet the customer's needs. This is a departure from when an operator has to rely on learning on the job and is susceptible to many errors.

A Goldman Sachs study (2023) reveals that employee productivity will be improved by 66% by the adoption and deployment of AI. The study undertook three different studies namely: customer service agents resolving customer inquiries in an enterprise software company; experienced business professionals (e.g., marketers, HR professionals) writing routine business documents (such as press releases) that take about half an hour to write; and programmers coding a small software project that took about three hours to complete without AI assistance. The productivity results of the three studies show that support agents who used AI could handle 13.8% more customer inquiries per hour; business professionals who used AI could write 59% more business documents per hour; and programmers who used AI could code 126% more projects per week.

These examples, it must be noted, are pointers to the gains inherent in the deployment of technology, nay AI.

2.3 Research Gap

Based on what we have shown so far in this study, much literature suffices with evidence on how technological adoption has affected productivity across both developed and developing countries as well as the gender adoption across those countries and influence on educational exposure in technology adoption. More importantly, there has been a gamut of literature in this area for the frontline states in the development of AI like the United States, Japan, and China, among others. However, there has been less literature on this concerning Switzerland, one of the developers of AI.

Also, while there has been sizeable evidence on the effect of technological adoption on productivity and the long-term and short-term effects, there has been less than a border on the deployment and state of AI in Switzerland. There has also been less literature that shows how the deployment of technology can be a mediating factor in the labour productivity-economic growth nexus. Much of the literature has kept us making assumptions on the level to which the deployment of AI affects labour productivity and what the effect of such impact will be on economic growth.

This study therefore adds to the body of literature that shows how AI affects productivity. While there is evidence on the relationship between AI and productivity, there is a need for more evidence of; the effect of technological adoption on productivity across sectors, and the short-term/long-term effect of open AI on productivity, provides evidence for technological unemployment. It also opens up a study in this regard in Switzerland.

3. DATA, MODELS AND METHODS

3.1 Data and Variables

As it relates to this study, Table 1 presents the variables employed for a period of 43 years. These are GDP per capita, which is measured in constant 2010 dollars, capital investment which is billions in USD, percentage of labour force participation rate, trade balance and government spending in billions of USD, information technology export, which is the per cent of total good exports, and also the number of residents that are given patent application. Also, the descriptive statistics are next to the column of the variable descriptions in Table 1. This shows that the mean of GDP per capita is \$73905.96 with a standard deviation of 9005.18 which ranges from \$59259.16 to \$88464.03. Capital investment has a mean of \$113.26 billion with a standard deviation of \$57.41 billion, a minimum of \$31.83 and a maximum of \$220.49. The mean of labour force participation rates is given as 67.76%, the standard deviation is 0.43%, the minimum is 66.97%, and the maximum is 68.56%. Regarding trade balance and government spending, they have their respective mean to be \$29.41 billion and \$47.28 billion and their respective standard deviation to be \$31.00 billion and \$27.44 billion. Also, the average of information technology exports is 5.45%, the standard deviation is 4.74%, the minimum is 0.95%, and the maximum is 15.23%. Lastly, a patent application by a resident has a mean number of 2285 and a standard deviation of 858 which ranges from 1283 minimum value to 4049 maximum value.

Presenting the descriptive statistics of the variable is not only for reporting sake but also to assess the characteristics of the variables that would be deployed in the model, as regards this, it could be observed that only the labour force has a lower standard deviation among the variables. This means that there is too wide dispersion in the variables, hence necessitating the need to transform them to natural logarithms to reduce the heterogeneity effect among the observations. The correlation matrix of the transformed variables is presented in the lower pane of Table 1. According to this, economic growth is positively correlated with capital investment, labour force, trade balance, and government expenditure. On the other hand, information technology exports and patent applications have a negative correlation with economic growth.

Finally, Figure 1 exposes the trend behaviour of the variables. It shows the upward movement of GDP per capita, capital investment, government spending, and trade balance. Also, while information technology exports and patent applications continue to decline, there is a seasonal pattern detected in the labour force. In general, the trend line indicates the value information about the nature of variables for further scrutiny before being deployed into the model which is discussed in the next section.

Table 1. Description of Variables

Variable	Unit of measurement	Obs.	Mean	Std. Dev.	Min	Max
GDP per capita	constant 2010 dollars	43	73905.96	9005.176	59259.16	88464.03
Capital investment	billion USD	43	113.264	57.40867	31.83	220.49
Labor force participation rate	percentage	43	67.76628	0.43151	66.97	68.56
Trade balance	billion USD	43	29.40512	31.00705	-3.25	137.44
Government spending	billion USD	43	47.27628	27.44019	10.71	104.46
Information technology exports	per cent of total goods exports	43	5.446976	4.738265	0.95	15.23
Patent applications by residents	Number of residents	43	2285.814	858.6255	1283	4049
	Correlation matrix					
	LGDP	LCAP	LLAB	LTRA	LGOV	LIFT
LGDP	1					
LCAP	0.9558*	1				
LLAB	0.1702	0.1702	1			
LTRA	0.8756*	0.8410*	-0.1834	1		
LGOV	0.9546*	0.9887*	0.1355	0.9048*	1	
LIFT	-0.9719*	-0.9228*	-0.0743	-0.9199*	-0.9363*	1
LPAT	-0.9657*	-0.8992*	-0.0941	-0.8978*	-0.9178*	0.9800*

Figure 1. Trend of Variables

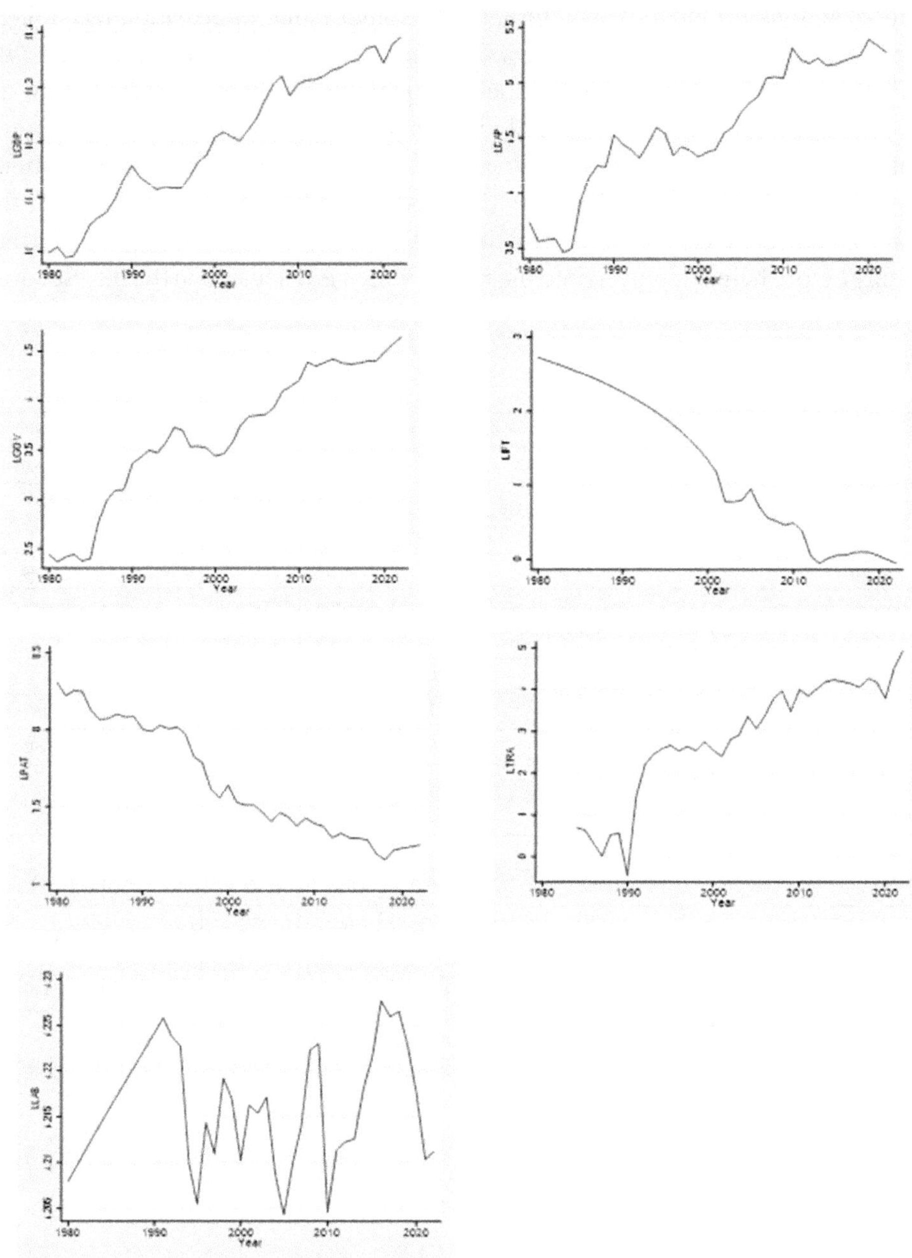

3.2 Model and Methods

In estimating the economic growth function, different models, considering the nature of time series data used in this study, are adopted. These are the usual ARDL model, the dynamic ARDL model for policy simulation, and in addition, Kernel-based regularized least squares (KRLS) which is a machine learning model. The analysis passes through several steps which are depicted in the empirical scheme shown in Figure 2. The steps will be explained, but then the economic growth function employed in this study is expressed as follows:

GDP= f (CAP, LAB, TRA, GOV, IFT)

GDP= f (CAP, LAB, TRA, GOV, PAT)

GDP= f (CAP, LAB, TRA, GOV, IFT, PAT)

From the above, GDP denotes economic growth, CAP denotes capital investment or gross fixed capital formation, TRA denotes trade balance, GOV denotes government spending, IFT denotes information technology export and PAT denotes patent application by residents.

Figure 2. Empirical Scheme

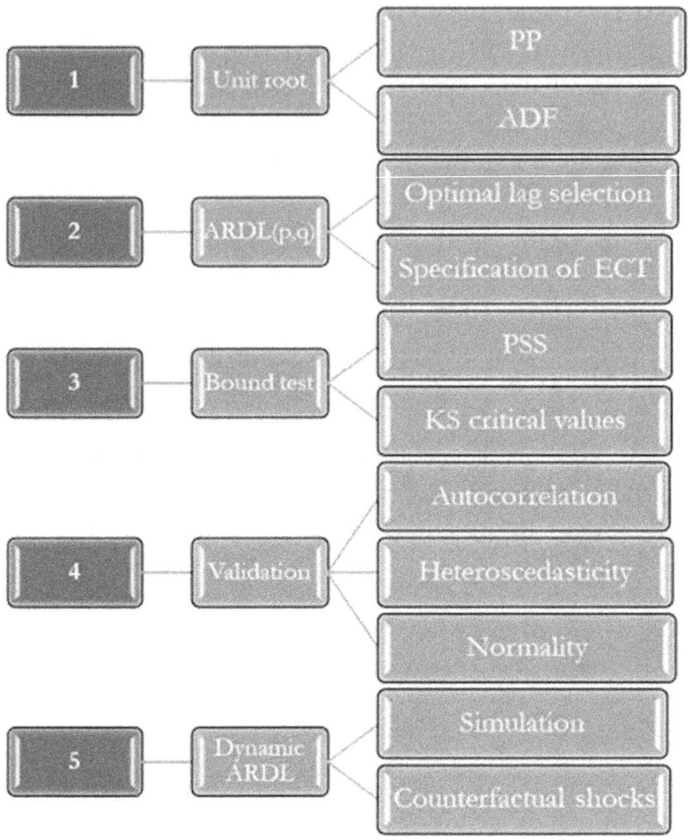

As indicated in the empirical scheme, the first step toward the dynamic ARDL model is testing for the stationary of the time series variables using the Augmented Dickey-Fuller (ADF) test and Phillips-Perron test. The general expression of a unit root test is given as:

$$y_t = D_t + z_t + \varepsilon t \quad (1)$$

Where y_t is the series (LGDP, LCAP, LLAB, LTRA, LGOV, LIFT, and LPAT) to be tested for some time t. D_t is the presence of deterministic component (trend movement, seasonal variation) in the model, z_t is the random or stochastic component, and εt is the stationarity error process. The problem to is examine whether the zt has unit root (non-stationary) in the series (*K*očenda and Alexandr, 2014). If true, the null hypothesis of the unit root will be upheld, and the test will be performed again on the first difference of the series. In ARDL, model, the dependent variable must be integrated of order I(1) while the predictors may either be I(0) or I(1).

Proceeding to step two, the optimal lag of the stationarity variables is performed and the parameters of ARDL regression are estimated. Using the optimal lag, the bound test (step three) which is the presence of cointegration in the ARDL regression is performed following the recommendation of Philips (2018) on the application of the Pesaran et al. (2001) ARDL bound test. To achieve this, Pesaran, Shin, and Smith (PSS) bound test with novel Kripfganz & Schneider (KS) critical values and approximate p – p-values are used while formulating the null hypothesis of no level cointegration between lag of dependent and independent variables. The goal is to either reject or uphold the null hypothesis-based critical value at 10%, 5%, and 1% levels of significance.

Thereafter, the validity of the ARDL model is evaluated to confirm the degree of parameter estimation. These validity tests get rid of problems that could affect the output of results in dynamic ARDL simulations. These are serial correlation or autocorrelation by Breusch- Godfrey LM test; a heteroscedastic error by Cameron & Trivedi's decomposition of IM-test; a test of normality by skewness or kurtosis test as well as the quantile of residual plots.

After confirming that the model is devoid of any errors, the novel dynamic ARDL simulation is then run based on 20% shocks in information technology export and patent application by residents. Following Sarkodie et al. (2019), the given expression for the dynamic ARDL model is:

Using the natural log-transformed of the variables,

$$\begin{aligned} LGDP_t = {} & \beta_0 (LGDP)_{t-1} + \beta_1 (LCAP)_t + \beta_2 (LCAP)_{t-1} + \beta_3 (LLAB)_t \\ & + \beta_4 (LLAB)_{t-1} + \beta_5 (LTRA)_t + \beta_6 (LTRA)_{t-1} + \beta_7 (LGOV)_t \\ & + \beta_8 (LGOV)_{t-1} + \beta_9 (LIFT)_t + \beta_{10} (LIFT)_{t-1} + \beta_{10} (LPAT)_t + \beta_{10} (LPAT)_{t-1} + \mu_t \end{aligned} \tag{2}$$

Where all variables have their usual meaning, βT is the vector of estimated parameters, and μt $_i$s the residual in the model. Also, the simulation experiments provide a counterfactual interface that could result in GDP per capita based on 20% shocks in LIFT and LPAT.

4. RESULTS AND DISCUSSION

The unit root test, as presented in Table 2, was conducted on the logged values of the target variables. At the levels, according to the Phillips Perron (PP) tests, all variables except LLAB exhibit non-stationarity. Similarly, at the levels, the results of the Augmented Dickey-Fuller (ADF) tests indicate that only LLAB is stationary. The presence of a unit root at the levels arose from accepting the null hypothesis and provided sufficient justification for further differencing of the variables. Following the first difference, it was confirmed that all the variables are stationary, thus indicating integration of I(1). Consequently, the ARDL model is deemed suitable for estimation. Moreover, the optimal lag for the ARDL (1,0,0,1,0) regression, as shown in Table 2, is estimated. The estimation comprises three models, namely the model with technological export (column 2), the model with patent application by residents (column 3), and the model with all variables included (Column 3). A detailed interpretation of the results will be presented in the subsequent section.

Table 2. Stationary Test

Variable	Level. PP	Δ. PP	Level.ADF	Δ. ADF
LGDP	-0.717	-5.329***	-0.720	-5.396***
LCAP	-0.984	-6.037***	-0.978	-6.036***
LLAB	-3.233**	-6.530***	-3.149**	-6.495***
LTRA	-1.721	-7.019***	-1.721	-6.824***
LGOV	-1.040	-4.829***	-1.048	-4.904***
LIFT	-0.699	-4.874***	-0.701	-4.989***
LPAT	-1.490	-6.838***	-1.433	-6.826***

Level.PP is the level of the PP unit root, Δ. PP is the first-difference value; Level.ADF level of ADF, Δ.ADF is the first difference; ***, **, * significance at 10%, 5%, and 1% respectively

4.1 ARDL Model Estimation

Table 3 shows the different variants of the model to have a more robust study. The more encompassing model is the full model with all the variables present. The result indicated that, for a model with information technology export (IFT), while LLAB is a positive and significant predictor of GDP in both the short run and the long run, LTRA, LGOV, and LIFT are only significant in the short run while no evidence of significant influence is recorded for LCAP in the short run and the long run. By indication, economic growth is positively influenced by the labour force, trade balance and information technology export while it is negatively influenced by government spending.

Under the model with a patent application by residents (PAT), LLAB, LCAP, and LPAT are significant predictors of GDP in both the short run and the long run. In particular, an increase in gross fixed capital formation leads to an increase in economic growth in the short run and long run. On the other hand, an increase in the percentage of patent applications by residents decreases economic growth in the short run and the long run, and while the labour force significantly reduces economic growth in the short run, its influence, in the long run, is positive. Still on the model with PAT, trade balance and government spending are reported to be positively and negatively significant predictors of economic growth, respectively in the short run only.

Regarding the full model, while only LTRA and LGOV have positive and negative influences on economic growth in the short run, LLAB has a positive influence on economic growth in the long run only. The rest of the predictors are not significant in both long run and short run.

Throughout the three models, the negative and significant coefficient of the error correction term (ECT) serves as an indication of a long-term dynamic in the short-term estimation of the ARDL model. This finding is supported by the outcomes presented in Table 4, which represent the model diagnostics of the cointegration relationship. The employed Shin, Pesaran, and Smith (PSS) bound tests, in conjunction with the Kripfganz and Schneider (KS) critical value, demonstrate the existence of long-term cointegration. The combined F-statistic (4.485) of the short-term parameters exceeds the I(1) critical values at the 10% and 5% levels of significance, further confirming the presence of long-term cointegration. Additionally, various tests were conducted to evaluate the internal validity of the ARDL (1,0,0,1,0) regression model. These tests include the Breusch-Godfrey LM serial correlation test (Table 5), which indicates the absence of serial correlation between the variables and their lags at the 5% level of significance ($p > .05$). The decomposition of the IM-test by Cameron and Trivedi (Table 6) reveals that the residuals of the model are homoscedastic at the 5% level of significance. Furthermore, the skewness and kurtosis tests (Table 7) demonstrate that the residuals satisfy the normality assumptions at the 5% level of significance ($p > .05$).

Table 3. ARDL Regression

Variables	The model with Information technology exports	Model with Patent Application by residents	The model with All Variables
Error Correction Term	-0.838**	-0.370***	0.579***
	(0.261)	(0.284)	(0.732)
Short Run			
D.LCAP	0.0533	0.131**	0.0960
	(0.0615)	(0.0419)	(0.113)
D.LLAB	0.564*	-0.888**	0.609
	(0.238)	(0.338)	(0.661)
D.LTRA	0.0613***	0.0855***	0.0695**
	(0.0109)	(0.00723)	(0.0173)
D.LGOV	-0.383***	-0.383***	-0.413*
	(0.0677)	(0.0617)	(0.133)
D.LIFT	0.0700**		0.0413
	(0.0268)		(0.0554)
D.LPAT		-0.0647*	-0.0319
		(0.0324)	(0.0563)
Long Run			
L.LCAP	-0.0793	0.325**	-0.0237
	(0.221)	(0.132)	(0.493)
L.LLAB	2.485***	3.126***	2.377**
	(0.0740)	(0.193)	(0.482)
L.LTRA	-0.0679	0.185	-0.0877
	(0.0446)	(0.128)	(0.136)
L.LGOV	0.344	-0.571	0.294
	(0.359)	(0.336)	(0.837)
L.LIFT	-0.0449		-0.0802
	(0.0372)		(0.0631)
L.LPAT		-0.242***	0.0652
		(0.0601)	(0.203)
Observations	32	32	32
R-squared	0.988	0.986	0.990

Standard errors are in parentheses. *** p<0.01, ** p<0.05, * p<0.1 represents statistical significance at 1%, 5% and 10% respectively.

Table 4. Model Diagnostics Tests **a. Pesaran, Shin, and Smith bounds testing.**

		10%		5%		1%		*p-value*	
	K	**I (0)**	**I (1)**	**I (0)**	**I (1)**	**I (0)**	**I (1)**	**I (0)**	**I (1)**
F	4.485	2.036	3.33	2.492	3.972	3.619	5.544	0.003	0.029
t	-3.939	-1.613	-3.669	-1.984	-4.119	-2.735	-5.045	0.001	0.067

I (0) is the lower bound critical value; I (1) is the upper bound critical value; ** indicates the significance of KS critical values at the 0.01 significance level.

Table 5. Model Diagnostic Tests **b. Breusch-Godfrey LM test for autocorrelation**

lags(p)	**F**		**df.**	**Prob > F**
1	0.003		(1, 29)	0.9599
2	0.606		(2, 28)	0.5525
3	0.408		(3, 27)	0.7484
4	0.351		(4, 26)	0.8412

H0: no serial correlation

Table 6. Model Diagnostics Tests c. **Cameron & Trivedi's decomposition of IM-test.**

Source	**chi2**	**df.**	*p-value*
Heteroskedasticity	26.02	20	0.1651
Skewness	8.02	5	0.1549
Kurtosis	0.31	1	0.5806
Total	34.35	26	0.1264

Table 7. Model Diagnostics Tests **d. Skewness/Kurtosis tests for normality**

Variable	**Obs.**	**Pr. (skewness)**	**Pr. (kurtosis)**	**Joint adj. chi^2(2)**	**Prob>chi2**
Residuals	38	0.3178	0.9569	1.05	0.5907

4.2 ARDL Regression: Post-estimation diagnostics

The examination of skewness and kurtosis in the residuals confirms their adherence to a normal distribution. This is further supported by the standardized normal probability plot (Figure 3) and the comparison of the residuals' quantiles with those of the normal distribution (Figure 4) in the ARDL(1,0,0,1,0) model. Both graphs reveal the presence of evenly distributed residuals, as evidenced by the well-fitted observations around the regression line.

Figure 3. Standardized Normal Probability Plot

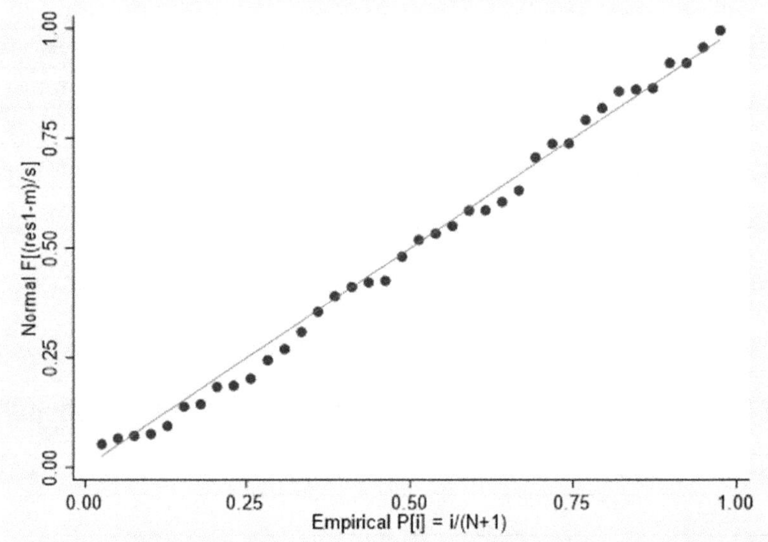

Figure 4. Quantiles of Residuals Against Quantiles of Normal Distribution

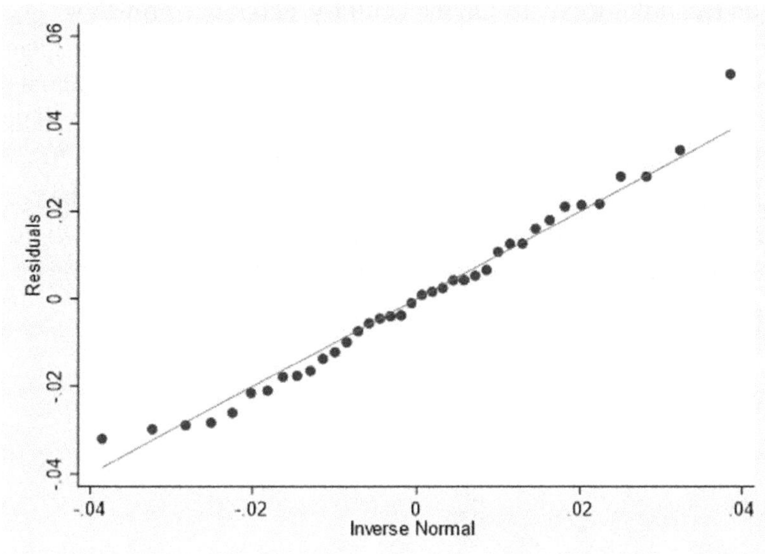

5. OPENAI CAPABILITIES (MEASURED THROUGH PATENT AND IT EXPORTS) POLICY SIMULATIONS[1]

Simulation is conducted on IFT and PAT to test the changes in the predicted growth of Switzerland's economy for a 20% shock over the next 10 years (2023-2033).

5.1 Dynamic ARDL Simulations

The dynamic ARDL simulation as it pertains to this study is conducted on IFT and PAT to test the changes in the predicted growth of Switzerland's economy for a 20% shock over the next 10 years (2023-2033). The long run and the short run of the estimated parameters are presented in Figure 4. It shows that information technology export is positive in the short run and long run and while the labour force has a negative effect in the long run, its effect in the short run is negative. For government expenditure, its effect on economic growth in the long run and short run is negative. Gross fixed capital formation, has negative and positive effects on economic growth in the long run and short run, respectively. Also, while economic growth is positively influenced by trade balance in both the short run and long run, the effect of patent application in the same period is negative. Both ARDL and dynamic ARDL simulation almost give identical results, but dynamic ARDL indicates that policies that encourage openAI in Switzerland will increase economic growth due to an increase in gross fixed capital formulation, trade balance, and information technology export. On the contrary, economic growth will be reduced by the increase in the percentage of patent applications, government spending, and labour force in the short run. Furthermore, using the 20% counterfactual shocks in IFT and PAT for the window period of 2023 – 2033, the dynamic ARDL produce a simulation plot in Figure 5 and Figure 6. Both plots depicted that 20% of shocks in the estimated IFT and PAT on economic growth decreases over the period from 2023 to 2033 which means that adopting this policy of IFT and PAT in the long run would decrease the economic growth in Switzerland. This goes by the negative effect of open AI replacing the working force in the future.

Figure 5. Dynamic ARDL Parameter Estimates

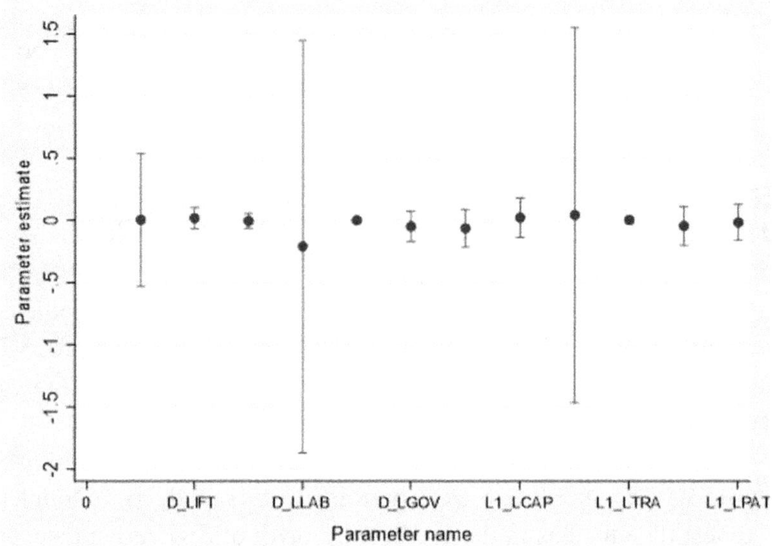

Figure 6. Counterfactual Shock in Predicted Growth and Information Technology and AI Policy Shocks using Dynamic ARDL Simulations

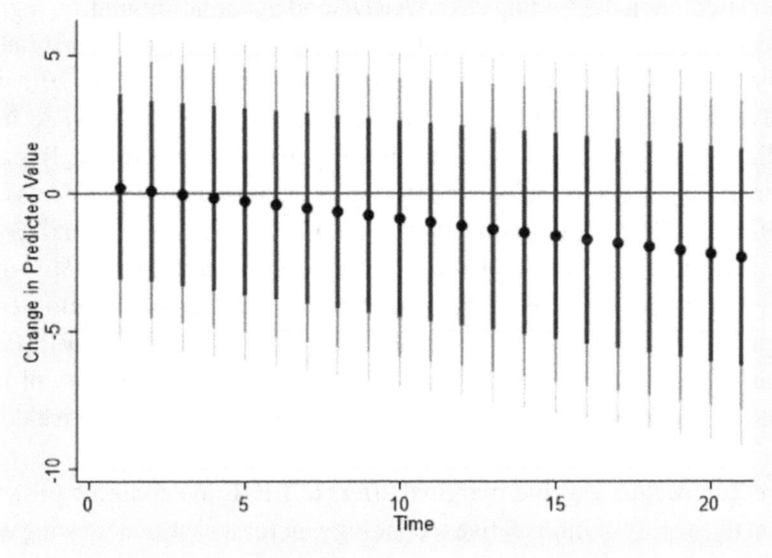

Figure 7. Counterfactual Shock in Predicted Growth and Number of Patent Applications by Residents and AI Policy Shocks using Dynamic ARDL Simulations

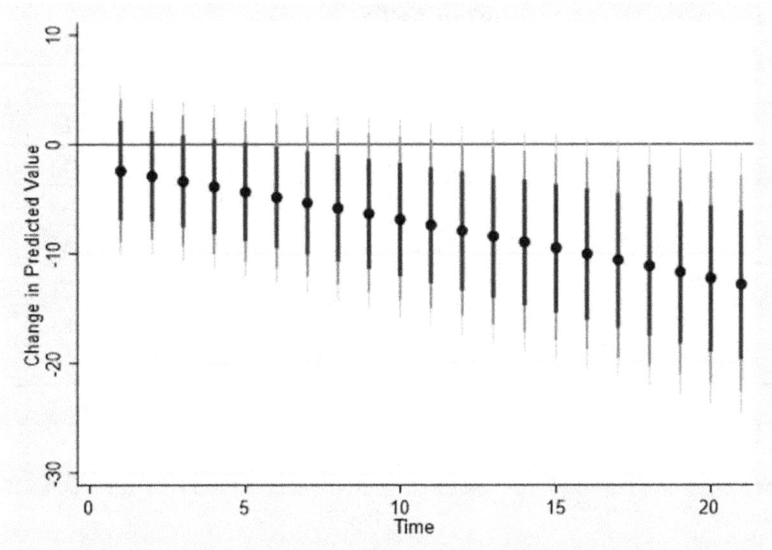

5.2 Kernel-based regularized least squares (KRLS)

To further strengthen the findings from ARDL and dynamic simulation regression, a machine learning methodology is adopted to assess and establish causal relationships among the target variables. In this regard, pointwise derivatives were estimated using KRLS. The overall predicting power of the model (Table 6) is 0.9888 indicating that predictors explained 98.88% of the disparity in economic growth. Reporting the average marginal effect, it is observed the mean pairwise marginal effects of LCAP, LLAB, LTRA, LGOV, LIFT, and LPAT are 0.04%, 0.95%, 0.02%, -0.02%, -0.01%, and -0.11% respectively. The probability value of each variable at a 1% significance level means that all variables, except government spending and information technology export, are not significant, hence evidence of a causal-effect relationship is spotted in two variables. Furthermore, the long-term effects of the variability of LIFT and LPAT on economic growth are examined using the plots of pointwise derivatives in Figure 9 and Figure 10.

Figure 7 shows the varying marginal effect of LIFT on economic growth, and it shows that the export of informative technology increases with increasing economic growth. Figure 8 shows the varying marginal effect of LPAT on economic growth. It showed that, at first, a higher percentage of patent applications is associated with low economic output until it reaches a certain point where a lower percentage of patent applications gives rise to higher economic output. Both figures confirmed the counterfactual shocks of dynamic simulation presented in Figure 5 and Figure 6.

Table 8. Pointwise Derivatives using KRLS

LGDP	Avg.	SE	t	P>t	P-25	P-50	P-75
LCAP	0.042983	0.009456	4.546	0.000	0.027571	0.044765	0.059833
LLAB	0.945392	0.333662	2.833	0.008	-1.35852	0.307355	1.45193
LTRA	0.020032	0.004024	4.978	0.000	0.008245	0.021044	0.035672
LGOV	-0.01621	0.007977	-2.032	0.051	-0.0362	-0.00765	0.005235
LIFT	-0.00981	0.005538	-1.772	0.086	-0.02617	-0.01159	0.010756
LPAT	-0.10555	0.014457	-7.301	0.000	-0.14975	-0.11883	-0.0634
Diagnostics							
Lambda	0.06357	Sigma	6	R^2	0.9888	Obs.	38
Tolerance	0.038	Eff. Df	17.46	Looloss	0.155		

Avg. is the average marginal effect; SE is the standard error; P-25, P-50, and P-75 represent the 25th, 50th, and 75th percentile.

Figure 8. Lowess Smoother

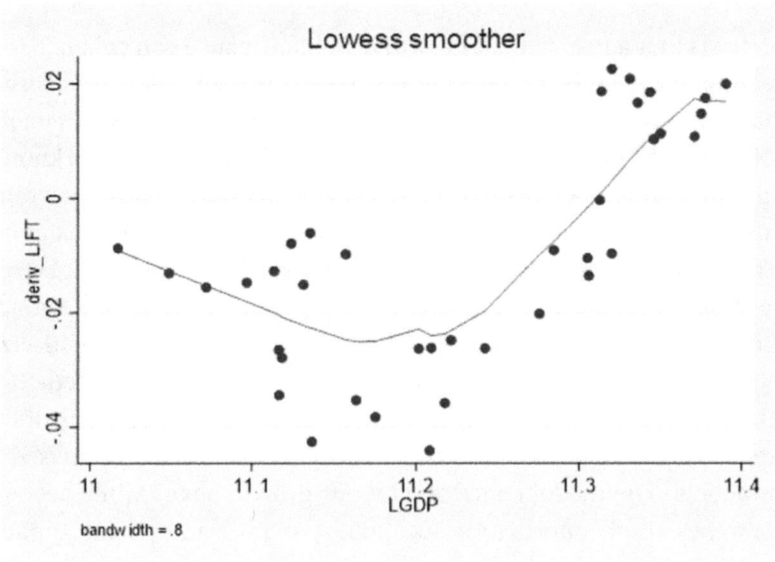

Figure 9. Lowess Smoother

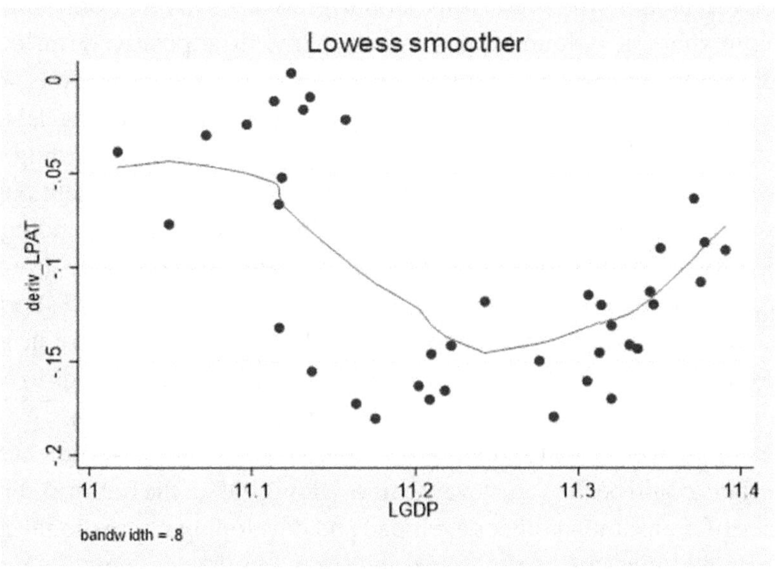

6. CONCLUSION AND POLICY DIRECTIONS

The hypothesis that advancement in Artificial intelligence can enhance the quality of labour and consequently its contribution to multifactor productivity and economic growth has continued to attract attention in recent times. It is however unclear what the role of AI will be in the labour-growth nexus. This study advances knowledge by exploring how an intelligent labour force influenced by Generative and other forms of AI can contribute significantly and accelerate measurable indexes of economic growth. Yearly data from 1960 – 2022 collected from the World Bank Development Indicators database are used on a Labour-Growth Model. The Dynamic Autoregressive Distributed Lag Model and the Machine Learning Kernel-Based Regularized Least Squares techniques are used for the policy simulation and policy predictions.

The findings from the ARDL model, after affirming the stationary of the series, the existence of cointegration, and the validity of the model, are based on three different models. The model contains a labour-growth nexus while accounting for OpenAI proxies (both information technology export and patent application by residents. With this, the findings revealed no evidence of the significant effect of OpenAI on boosting economic growth and while government spending is reported to reduce the economic growth of Switzerland in the short run, the trade balance is reported to increase the economic growth in the short run, and labour force is found to boost the growth in the long run.

As for the model which contains labour-growth nexus and only information technology export, it is found that economic growth is positively influenced by labour force, trade balance and information technology export while it is negatively influenced by government spending. Interestingly, the effect of the labour force on economic growth is both the short run and the long run. Regarding the third model, which contains the labour force-growth nexus and only patent application by residents as OpenAI, the findings revealed that government spending reduces economic growth in the short run, trade balance increases economic growth in the short run, and capital investment boosts the economic growth in both short run and long run. Also, while patent applications by residents hampered economic growth in both the run and long run, this makes the labour force disadvantageous to economic growth in the short run, but later has positive effects in the long run.

Interestingly from these findings, it is common that higher government spending in Switzerland could be the surest way to have a low GDP in the future except if there are balance of trade among other developed and developing international countries, and huge capital investment is pumped into growing the economy. Regarding the labour-growth nexus in the face of OpenAI, the negative influence of the labour force on economic growth in the short run is in line with some previous studies, such as Auzina-Emsina (2014) who reported a weak relationship between labour productivity and economic growth in EU economies. Also, this could be explained by the threat of OpenAI to employees' productivity wherein there is a risk of job loss and laziness of employees which could ultimately lead to dampened revenues generated from the government and AI-based industry (Osborne, 2017; Arntz et al., 2016; Bartelsman et al., 2004). Hence, partial implementation of the OpenAI technology could be introduced into the workplace.

On the contrary, the strong influence of labour-growth nexus in the long run is commensurate with several studies, such as Jorgenson (1980) using industrialized companies, Korkmaz and Korkmaz (2017) using OECD economies, Alani (2012) in Uganda, Su and Heshmati (2011) in China, and Ayila et al. (2018) in Nigeria. Also, this could be explained from the view of technological advancement and labour productivity as posed by Chabra (2000). While it seems there to be a conflicting result about the labour-growth nexus in Switzerland, dynamic ARDL simulations give credence to the argument as it revealed the 20% shocks in OpenAI (information technology export and patent application by residents) concurrently bring down the economy growth due to their effect on replacing labour market. Surprisingly, the same findings are reported from the negative marginal means effect of OpenAI variables using the KRLS machine learning model. This further confirmed that OpenAI in labour productivity in Switzerland could reduce the country's economic growth, hence supporting the view of Mert (2017) and Philiph (2010). The following policy direction is highlighted.

Policy direction

The findings of the study underscore the importance of implementing OpenAI technologies in the labour force in a measured and balanced manner. Although there may be short-term disruptions, the long-term advantages are significant. As a result, policymakers should carefully strategize the integration of AI to alleviate initial shocks. It is crucial to invest in human capital to equip the workforce with the necessary skills for the digital economy. Encouraging innovation and providing support for research and development activities can stimulate economic expansion. Incentives should be offered for patent applications and technological advancements to drive innovation. Adapting the labour market to the challenges posed by AI is essential. Policies should facilitate the transition for displaced workers, promote flexible work arrangements, and ensure that AI complements human labour. Adaptive policies should be responsive to changing circumstances to maximize the benefits of AI. International collaboration on AI-related policies can establish common standards and best practices, mitigating any negative spillover effects and enhancing global cooperation for sustainable economic growth. In conclusion, policymakers should adopt a proactive and balanced approach to harness the potential benefits of AI while addressing its challenges, ensuring that AI technologies contribute positively to long-term economic growth and societal well-being.

REFERENCES

Aghion, P., & Howitt, P. (1990). A Model of Growth through Creative Destruction. NBER Working Paper 3223 (National Bureau of Economic Research, Cambridge, MA).

Aghion, P., & Howitt, P. (1994). Growth and Unemployment. *The Review of Economic Studies*, *61*(3), 477–494. doi:10.2307/2297900

Alani, J. (2012). Effects of Productivity Growth on Employment Generation, Capital Accumulation and Economic Growth in Uganda. International Journal of Trade. *Economics and Finance*, *3*(3), 170–175. doi:10.7763/IJTEF.2012.V3.194

Arntz, M., Gregory, T., & Zierahn, U. (2016). The Risk of Automation for Jobs. In *OECD Countries: A Comparative Analysis. OECD Social, Employment and Migration Working Paper, 189*. OECD Publishing., Available at www.ifuturo.org/sites/default/files/docs/automation.pdf

Auzina-Emsina, A. (2014). Labour Productivity, Economic Growth and Global Competitiveness in Post-crisis Period. *Procedia: Social and Behavioral Sciences*, *156*, 317–321. doi:10.1016/j.sbspro.2014.11.195

Avent, R. (September 19, 2016). A world without work is coming – It could be utopia or it could be hell. The Guardian. Available at https://www.theguardian.com/commentisfree/2016/sep/19/world-without-work-utopia-hell-human-labour-obsolete

Bartelsman, E., Haltiwanger, J., & Scarpetta, S. (2004). *Microeconomic Evidence of Creative Destruction in Industrial and Developing Countries*. World Bank.

Becker, B. (2015). Public R&D Policies and Private R&D Investment: A Survey of the Empirical Evidence. *Journal of Economic Surveys*, *29*(5), 917–942. doi:10.1111/joes.12074

Bessen, J. (2018). AI and Jobs: The role of demand. NBER Working Paper No. 24235. Available at https://www.nber.org/papers/w24235. Accessed September 07, 2023.

Bloom, N., Van Reenen, J., & Williams, H. (2019). A toolkit of policies to promote innovation. *The Journal of Economic Perspectives*, *33*(3), 163–184. doi:10.1257/jep.33.3.163

Bowles, J. (July 24, 2014). The computerisation of European Jobs. Bruegel blog. Available at bruegel.org/2014/07/the-computerisation-of-european-jobs/.

Brynjolfsson, E., Li, D., & Raymond, L. R. (2023) Generative AI at Work. National Bureau of Economic Research working paper 31161. https://www.nber.org/papers/w31161

Brynjolfsson, E., Mitchell, T., & Rock, D. (2018). What can machines learn and what does it mean for occupations and the economy. *The American Economic Review*, *108*, 43–47.

Brynjolfsson, E. and G. Petropoulos (2021) 'The coming productivity boom', MIT Technology Review, 10 June

Brynjolfsson, E., & Petropoulos, G. (2021). *The coming productivity boom*. MIT Technology Review.

Brynjolfsson, E., & Petropoulos, G. (2022). Advancing a More Productive Tech Economy. A White Paper for the Stanford Institute for Human – Centered Artificial Intelligence and the Stanford Digital Economy Lab.

Brynjolfsson, E., Rock, D., & Syverson, C. (2021). The Productivity J-Curve: How Intangibles Complement General Purpose Technologies. *American Economic Journal. Macroeconomics*, *13*(1), 333–372. doi:10.1257/mac.20180386

Brynjolfsson, E., Rock, D., & Syverson, C. (2021). The Productivity J-Curve: How Intangibles Complement General Purpose Technologies. *American Economic Journal. Macroeconomics*, *13*(1), 333–372. doi:10.1257/mac.20180386

Brzeski, C., & Burk, C. (2015). Die Roboter kommen: Folgen der Automatisierung für den deutschen Arbeitsmarkt (The Robots are coming: Consequences of Automation for the German Labor Market) [German.]. *INGDiBa Econ Res*, *30*, 1–7.

Christensen, L. R., Cummings, D., & Jorgenson, D. W. (1980). Economic Growth, 1947-1973: An International Comparison. In J. W. Kendrick & B. Vaccara (Eds.), *New Developments in Productivity Measurement* (pp. 17–131). University of Chicago Press.

Dauth, W., Findeisen, S., Südekum, J., & Woessner, N. (2017). German robots – The impact of industrial robots on workers. IAB Discussion Paper 30/2017 (Institute for Employment Research, Nuremberg, Germany).

Dauth, W., Findeisen, S., & Suedekum, J. (2017). Trade and Manufacturing Jobs in Germany. *The American Economic Review*, *107*(5), 337–342. doi:10.1257/aer.p20171025

David, H., & Dorn, D. (2013). The Growth of Low-Skill Service Jobs and the Polarization of the US Labor Market. *The American Economic Review*, *103*(5), 1553–1597. doi:10.1257/aer.103.5.1553

De Grip, A., & Van Loo, J. (2002), "The economics of skills obsolescence: A review", de Grip, A., van Loo, J. and Mayhew, K. (Ed.) The Economics of Skills Obsolescence (Research in Labor Economics, Vol. 21), Emerald Group Publishing Limited, Bingley, pp. 1-26. doi:10.1016/S0147-9121(02)21003-1

Farrell, C. (February 11, 2013). Will Robots Create Economic Utopia? Bloomberg. Available at https://www.bloomberg.com/news/articles/2013-02-11/will-robotscreate-economic-utopia

Frase, P. (2016). *Four Futures: Life after Capitalism*. Verso Books.

Frey, C.B. and Osborne, M.A. (2017). "The future of employment: How susceptible are jobs to computerisation?" Technol Forecast Soc Change, 114, Pp, 254–280.

Gordon, R. J. (2016). *The rise and fall of American growth: The US standard of living since the Civil War*. Princeton University Press. doi:10.1515/9781400873302

Gordon, R. J. (2018). Why Has Economic Growth Slowed When Innovation Appears to be Accelerating? NBER Working Paper 24554. National Bureau for Economic Research.

Graetz, G., & Michaels, G. (2018). Robots at work. *The Review of Economics and Statistics*, *100*(5), 753–768. doi:10.1162/rest_a_00754

Gries, T., & Naudié, W. (2018). Artificial intelligence, jobs, inequality and productivity: Does aggregate demand matter? IZA DP No. 12005, Bonn.

Griliches, Z. (1990). Patent statistics as economic indicators: A survey. *Journal of Economic Literature*, *18*, 1661–1707.

Ip, G. (August 2, 2017). We survived spreadsheets, and we'll survive AI. Wall Street Journal. Available at https://www.wsj.com/articles/wesurvived-spreadsheetsand-well-survive-ai-1501688765

Jackson, K. (April 25, 1993). The World's First Motel Rests Upon Its Memories. Seattle Times. Available at www.community.seattletimes.nwsource.com/archive/?date=19930425&slug=1697701

Jorgenson, D. W. (2009). *Productivity and Economic Growth*. doi:10.4337/9781784712891

Kočenda, E., & Alexandr, Č. (2014). *Elements of Time Series Econometrics: An Applied Approach*. Karolinum Press.

Korkmaz, S., & Korkmaz, O. (2017). The Relationship between Labor Productivity and Economic Growth in OECD Countries. *International Journal of Economics and Finance*, *9*(5), 71–76. doi:10.5539/ijef.v9n5p71

Makridakis, S. (2017). The forthcoming artificial intelligence (AI) revolution: Its impact on society and firms. *Futures*, *90*, 46–60. doi:10.1016/j.futures.2017.03.006

Mert, M. (2017). "Technological Progress, Labour Productivity And Economic Growth: Disentangling The Negative And Positive Effects" *28th International Academic Conference*, Tel Aviv. 10.20472/IAC.2017.028.012

Naone, E. (November 11, 2009). "The Dark Side of The Technology Utopia". MIT Technology Review. Available at https://www.technologyreview.com/s/416244/the-dark-side-of-the-technology-utopia/

Ngutsav, S. A. (2018, June). And Ijirshar, V.U. "Labour Productivity and Economic Growth in Nigeria: A Disaggregated Sector Analysis". *Lafia Journal of Economics and Management Sciences*, *3*(1), 256–276.

NoyS.ZhangW. (2023). Experimental Evidence on the Productivity Effects of Generative Artificial Intelligence. Available at SSRN: https://ssrn.com/abstract=4375283 or doi:10.2139/ssrn.4375283

OECD. (2019). AI Policy Observatory. Available at https://oecd.ai/en/ai-principles

OECD. (2021). Productivity and economic growth. In OECD Compendium of Productivity Indicators 2021. OECD Publishing., Retrieved September 09, 2023, from, doi:10.1787/f8c31e3c-

Pajarinen, M., Rouvinen, P., & Ekeland, A. (2015). "Computerization threatens one-third of Finnish and Norwegian employment". ETLA Brief 34. Available at https://www.etla.fi/wp-content/uploads/ETLA-Muistio-Brief-34.pdf

Peng, S., Kalliamvakou, E., Cihon, P., & Demirer, M. (2023). The Impact of AI on Developer Productivity: Evidence from GitHub Copilot. Available at Arxiv: https://arxiv.org/abs/2302.06590 or https://doi.org//arXiv.2302.06590 doi:10.48550

Pesaran, M. H., Shin, Y., & Smith, R. J. (2001). Bounds testing approaches to the analysis of level relationships. *Journal of Applied Econometrics*, *16*(3), 289–326. doi:10.1002/jae.616

Philips, A. Q. (2018). Have your cake and eat it too? Cointegration and dynamic inference from autoregressive distributed lag models. *American Journal of Political Science*, *62*(1), 230–244. doi:10.1111/ajps.12318

Rauflab, C. (2023). The Ethics of Artificial Intelligence. Available at https://www.swissinfo.ch/eng/45808880/45808880

Sachs, G. (2023). Generative AI could raise global GDP by 7%. Available at https://www.goldmansachs.com/intelligence/pages/generative-ai-could-raise-global-gdp-by-7-percent.html

Sarkodie, S. A., Strezov, V., Weldekidan, H., Asamoah, E. F., Owusu, P. A., & Doyi, I. N. Y. (2019). Environmental sustainability assessment using dynamic autoregressive-distributed lag simulations—Nexus between greenhouse gas emissions, biomass energy, food and economic growth. *The Science of the Total Environment*, *668*, 318–332. doi:10.1016/j.scitotenv.2019.02.432 PMID:30852209

Somers, J. (2018). "How the Artificial-Intelligence Program AlphaZero Mastered Its Games". The New Yorker. Available at: https://www.newyorker.com/science/elements/howthe-artificial-intelligence-program-alphazero-mastered-its-games

Su, B., & Heshmati, A. (2011). "Development and Sources of Labor Productivity in Chinese Provinces". IZA Discussion Paper, (No 6263), 1-30. Retrieved from http://ftp.iza.org/dp6263.pdf

ENDNOTE

1 The Working Group also recognises that AI will change the labour market in a different way from previous technological developments. In this sense, the skills and competencies of the workforce need to adapt quickly to the changing needs of the labour market. Existing measures are already in place to actively screen and monitor the skills demanded in the labour market. The State Secretariat for Economic Affairs (SECO) monitors the challenges and addresses emerging issues within the existing competencies in AI. Furthermore, in November 2017, the Federal Council decided to monitor the impact of digital transformation on the labour market. A report will publish the results of the monitoring by the end of 2022. Source: https://ai-watch.ec.europa.eu/countries/switzerland/switzerland-ai-strategy-report_en

Chapter 7
Enhancing Emotionally Intelligent Responses in AIML Systems Through Idiom-Emoticon Integration and Analysis

Jonathan Bishop
https://orcid.org/0000-0002-9919-7602
Crocels Community Media Group, UK

Wahid Hassan
https://orcid.org/0009-0001-8609-8322
Independent Researcher, UK

Robert Bilsland
Independent Researcher, UK

Elias Alexander
Clarisa Technologies, India

ABSTRACT

This research enhances Artificial Intelligence Markup Language (AIML) systems' understanding of English idioms and their emotional contexts. By integrating a database of 3,500 idioms with 16 emoticons representing different emotions, the study aims to enable AI to interpret idioms beyond their literal meanings and respond appropriately to their emotional undertones. The methodology includes collecting idioms from various online sources, using Python for extraction, and XML for data

DOI: 10.4018/979-8-3693-1198-1.ch007

structuring. The emoticons, sourced from the Crocels Troller-Sniper Emotion Index 16, are selected to encompass a wide range of emotions, and then encoded with idioms in the XML database for dynamic, context-sensitive AI responses. Using Python, idioms and emoticons are combined and processed through the OpenAI API. The responses are analysed for sentiment and emotional alignment using Python, Pandas, and NLP tools, refining the AIML system's emotional intelligence. Additionally, a Python Flask API Gateway is developed for AIML parser integration, enhancing user interaction by providing emoticon-aligned responses. This research demonstrates the effective use of AI models and programming tools in creating a nuanced, emotionally intelligent dataset of idioms, significantly advancing AI's linguistic capabilities and understanding.

INTRODUCTION

In the ever-evolving landscape of Artificial Intelligence, the quest for creating systems that closely mimic human understanding and expression remains a pinnacle of technological advancement (Kirchschläger, 2021). This project represents a significant stride in this direction. It focuses on imbuing AI with a nuanced grasp of English idioms, coupled with the ability to discern and express associated emotional undertones, a feat that bridges the gap between mechanical processing and human-like comprehension. Idioms, by their very nature, encapsulate cultural richness and linguistic complexity. They often defy literal interpretation, thereby posing a unique challenge in AI comprehension. Recognising this, the project sets out to compile an extensive and diverse collection of over 3,500 English idioms. The aim was to enable AIML to recognise these phrases and understand their contextual meanings and emotional connotations. This understanding is crucial in rendering AIML-based interactions more natural, empathetic, and effective. To achieve this, the authors embarked on a meticulous process of data collection, extraction, and compilation. The authors scoured a variety of reliable online sources to gather idioms, ensuring a broad representation of cultural and linguistic diversity. Each idiom was then carefully encoded into an XML-based AIML dataset. This dataset serves as the bedrock of the authors' project, providing a rich repository from which the AI can draw to enhance its linguistic processing capabilities. Further, the authors integrated a set of 16 emoticons, each representing a distinct emotional state, selected from the Crocels Troller-Sniper Emotion Index 16 (adapted from Bishop, 2019). With the help of these emoticons, the AIML parser can understand the idioms and respond in a way that is consistent with the intended emotional tone. This integration marks a pivotal enhancement in the parser's ability to engage in more human-like, emotionally resonant interactions. The system advances beyond earlier systems, which looked up idioms while a user was taking part in social situations (Bishop & Reddy, 2003; Bishop, 2015).

BACKGROUND

The background of the research lies in advancing the capabilities of the Artificial Intelligence Markup Language (AIML) by focusing on its ability to perceive and articulate emotional nuances. Distinct from prior versions of AIML, which lacked visual elements, this innovative approach incorporates emoticons and emojis to enhance emotional expression in user interactions. The authors have developed a comprehensive database featuring over 3,500 English idioms, each methodically paired with 16 carefully chosen emoticons. This unique pairing generates a dynamic matrix of emotional responses, leveraging the OpenAI API's GPT-3.5 Turbo model to produce 16 distinct responses for every idiom. The research underscores the importance of idioms, which play a crucial role in conveying culturally rich and nuanced meanings beyond their literal interpretations. By integrating these idiomatic expressions with a diverse range of emoticons, we aim to significantly enrich the AIML system's understanding of the subtleties of human language. The selection of 16 emoticons introduces a spectrum of emotional expressions for each idiom, aiding the AI in generating contextually relevant responses. The use of Python programming in this project allows for scalable and adaptable solutions in the ever-evolving domain of AI and communication.

Incorporating emoticons into the Artificial Intelligence Markup Language (AIML) is a major step forward in AI and natural language processing. This analysis explores the essential role of emoticons in AI communication. It examines how emoticons, by providing emotional context, can make AI interactions richer—a crucial aspect often missing in digital communication. The study also points out gaps in current research, particularly in the detailed understanding of emoticons within AIML. Highlighting the need for more research in this area, the analysis emphasizes how emoticons can significantly improve AI's emotional intelligence, making AI-human interactions in the digital world more engaging and meaningful.

Advanced Affective Computing in AI

Rosalind Picard's groundbreaking work in 2000 catalysed the field of affective computing, fundamentally shifting the landscape of AI research. Picard's insights underscored the importance of integrating emotional intelligence into AI systems, positing that the ability of machines to interpret and respond to human emotions would be a game-changer in technology-human interactions. Her work laid the essential groundwork for subsequent research, establishing affective computing as a feasible area of study and as a critical component in the evolution of AI.

Evolution in Emotion Recognition Techniques

The subsequent development in the field of emotion recognition within AI has been substantial, largely due to contributions from researchers like Cambria et al. (2014) and Calvo & D'Mello (2010). Cambria and colleagues introduced SenticNet, an innovative framework for sentiment analysis, which leveraged common-sense reasoning and contextual information. This approach marked a significant shift from traditional methods, offering a more nuanced and accurate interpretation of sentiments expressed in text. Calvo and D'Mello's contributions, on the other hand, focused on the interdisciplinary aspects of affect detection, merging insights from psychology, computer science, and linguistics. Their comprehensive review of models and methods in affect detection highlighted the multifaceted nature of this task, encompassing everything from facial expression analysis to textual sentiment analysis and physiological response detection.

Emoticons in AI and Communication

The study by Derks et al. (2008) marked a pivotal moment in understanding the role of emoticons in digital communication. Their research illuminated how these simple symbols could effectively articulate a wide range of human emotions, filling the void left by the absence of non-verbal cues in online text-based interactions. This study demonstrated that emoticons go beyond mere decorative characters; they play a crucial role in conveying tone, intent, and emotional nuances, which might otherwise be lost in digital communication. Emoticons, as explored in this study, emerged as a key tool in enhancing the emotional clarity of messages, reducing misunderstandings, and adding a layer of emotional depth to online conversations.

Kralj Novak et al. (2015) advanced the conversation by examining how AI systems interpret emoticons, linking them to specific emotional states. This research was instrumental in demonstrating how AI could be trained to recognize and understand the emotional content conveyed by emoticons. Their findings revealed the potential of emoticons to serve as reliable indicators of sentiment in text, offering valuable insights for sentiment analysis algorithms. However, the study also highlighted a significant gap in research, particularly the need for AI to comprehend the nuanced use of emoticons in idiomatic and culturally specific contexts. This gap points to the complexity of human communication and the challenges AI faces in interpreting the subtleties of language and emotion, especially when emoticons are used in conjunction with idiomatic expressions, sarcasm, or humour.

Examination of AIML's Progress

The introduction of AIML between 1995 and 2002 marked a significant milestone in the development of AI chatbots (Wallace, 2008). AIML, or Artificial Intelligence Markup Language, was designed as a specialised language for creating chatbot conversations, primarily focusing on pattern-matching techniques. This innovation provided a structured yet flexible way of scripting dialogues and responses, enabling developers to create more interactive and engaging chatbot experiences. Wallace's work laid the foundational architecture for AIML, emphasizing its ability to simulate human-like conversations. This approach revolutionized how chatbots were developed, moving away from rudimentary response systems to more sophisticated, conversational entities capable of engaging users in a more human-like manner.

Building on the initial framework of AIML, subsequent research, notably by Shawar and Atwell in 2007, sought to integrate more advanced Natural Language Processing (NLP) techniques into AIML. This integration aimed to enhance the chatbot's understanding of language nuances, context, and user intent. The incorporation of NLP methodologies enabled AIML-based chatbots to parse and interpret user inputs more effectively, allowing for more nuanced and contextually relevant responses. However, despite these advancements in NLP integration, a significant area that remained underexplored in AIML's evolution was the realm of emotional intelligence. While AIML had advanced in its linguistic capabilities, its ability to understand, interpret, and respond to emotional cues or affective states in user interactions was not deeply developed. This gap in emotional intelligence within AIML highlights an area ripe for exploration, where future enhancements could lead to more empathetic and emotionally aware AI conversational agents. Integrating affective computing aspects into AIML could dramatically improve the human-like quality of chatbot interactions, making them more responsive to the emotional and psychological needs of users.

Gaps in Existing Research

A critical observation in current AI research is the notable deficiency in the integration of affect awareness within AIML, particularly concerning the use of emoticons. While AIML has evolved significantly in terms of linguistic processing capabilities, its development in understanding and responding to emotional cues, a fundamental aspect of human communication, remains limited. This gap is especially evident when considering the use of emoticons, which are increasingly prevalent in digital communication. Emoticons, as non-verbal cues, offer a rich source of emotional context that, if effectively interpreted, could significantly enhance the interactive quality of AIML-based chatbots. Current AIML systems, however, lack the sophistication to decode the subtleties that emoticons convey, missing out on a crucial dimension of human-like interaction.

Another under-explored area in AI research is the nuanced use of emoticons in interpreting and responding to idiomatic expressions. Idioms, inherently laden with cultural and contextual meanings, pose a unique challenge in AI communication. The potential of emoticons to provide additional emotional context to these idiomatic expressions is immense yet barely tapped into. Current AI systems, including those based on AIML, often struggle to grasp the full meaning and tone conveyed through idioms, leading to responses that can be out of context or emotionally misaligned.

The research into how emoticon meanings and interpretations differ across various cultures is remarkably sparse, particularly in the context of AIML applications. Emoticons, while seemingly universal, can carry different connotations and emotional significance in different cultural settings. This lack of cultural sensitivity in AIML's emoticon interpretation can lead to misunderstandings or incorrect emotional readings in cross-cultural interactions. This gap in research highlights the need for a more global and culturally nuanced approach in developing AIML systems capable of understanding and adapting to diverse emotional expressions.

There is a significant void in understanding how emoticons and idioms interact within AI systems, particularly regarding how emoticons can help clarify the emotional context of idioms. This interaction is critical as idioms often carry implicit emotional tones that can be misinterpreted by AI systems. Emoticons could serve as crucial indicators, providing additional emotional cues that aid in deciphering the true sentiment behind idiomatic expressions. Exploring this dynamic is essential for developing more emotionally intelligent and contextually aware AIML systems that can engage in more natural and empathetic conversations.

Future Research Pathways

Future research should focus on developing methodologies for integrating emoticons into AIML to enhance affective awareness in AI systems. This integration would involve the technical embedding of emoticon recognition within the AIML framework and understanding the emotional weight emoticons carry in digital communication. Research could explore algorithmic approaches to interpret emoticons as emotional indicators, allowing chatbots to respond more empathetically. Such advancements would be pivotal in enabling chatbots to understand the nuanced emotional context of user interactions, making conversations more natural and relatable.

Another promising area of research is conducting cross-cultural studies to explore how emoticon meanings and interpretations vary globally. These studies could inform the development of AIML systems that are culturally sensitive and capable of adapting to diverse emotional expressions. Understanding these variations is crucial for creating AI systems that can effectively communicate across cultural boundaries, recognizing and responding appropriately to the expressive content conveyed through emoticons. This research could lead to more inclusive and universally applicable chatbot technologies.

Researching the role of emoticons in enhancing the comprehension of idiomatic expressions is a critical area for future exploration. Emoticons could provide additional clues to the emotional undertones of idioms, which are often culturally specific and laden with implied meanings. Investigating how AIML can leverage emoticons to understand and interpret idioms would significantly improve the conversational capabilities of AI systems. This research could involve linguistic analyses of idiomatic expressions in conjunction with emoticons, aiming to develop algorithms that can accurately discern the emotional subtexts of such phrases.

There is a growing need to advocate for the use of advanced NLP techniques in the integration of emoticons and idioms within AI systems. Future research should focus on developing sophisticated NLP methodologies that can process the complex interplay between idiomatic language and emoticons. This integration requires a deep understanding of language semantics, pragmatics, and emotional expressions. The goal would be to enhance AI's ability to parse idiomatic expressions enriched with emoticons, leading to more accurate and emotionally intelligent responses.

Emoticons, as a bridge for emotional expression in digital communication, offer a unique opportunity to enhance the emotional intelligence of AI systems. Specifically, their application in interpreting idiomatic expressions can lead to significant advancements in AI's ability to understand and interact with humans on a more empathetic level. The prospect of AI systems adept at decoding the emotional nuances of language and expressions promises to revolutionize AI-human interactions. By venturing into this uncharted territory, the future of AI could see a paradigm shift toward more intuitive, contextually aware, and emotionally responsive communication, transforming the landscape of digital interactions.

RESEARCH OBJECTIVE AND METHODOLOGY

The primary objective of this research is to enhance the capabilities of Artificial Intelligence Markup Language (AIML) systems in processing and understanding English idioms and their associated emotional contexts. This involves compiling a comprehensive list of 3,500 English idioms and integrating a set of 16 emoticons, each representing a distinct emotional state, into the AIML system. The goal is to enable the AI system to comprehend the literal meaning of idioms and to appropriately respond to them in a context-sensitive manner that aligns with the emotional undertones conveyed by the emoticons.

Research Methodology

Data Collection of English Idioms

1. Source Identification and Selection:
    a. Utilise a systematic approach to identify reliable and diverse online sources, including linguistic databases, online dictionaries, idiom-specific websites, and digital libraries.
    b. Apply criteria such as authenticity, comprehensiveness, and cultural diversity to evaluate and select sources.
2. Idiom Extraction and Compilation:
    a. Develop Python scripts to automate the extraction process from selected sources.
    b. Perform manual verification and cross-checking to ensure accuracy and relevance, including removing duplicates and validating meanings and usage contexts.
3. Data Structuring and Storage:
    a. Utilise XML format for structuring the idiomatic data, enabling seamless integration with AIML systems.
    b. Incorporate tags for categorising idioms based on emotional connotations and usage contexts.
4. Quality Assurance and Validation:
    a. Conduct multiple rounds of validation to ensure the XML database's consistency, accuracy, and completeness.
    b. Implement error-correction mechanisms to rectify any identified anomalies.

Creating the List of 16 Emoticons

1. Dataset Analysis:
    a. Analyse the Crocels Troller-Sniper Emotion Index 16 (adapted from Bishop, 2019) to identify a set of 16 emoticons representing various emotional states.
    b. Ensure the selected emoticons cover a wide range of emotions, from positive to negative and from mild to intense.
2. Emoticon Selection and Emotional Categorisation:
    a. Examine each emoticon's associated emotions and select those that best represent the desired emotional spectrum.

   b. Align each emoticon with specific emotions based on the Crocels TS-EI-16 classifications (adapted from Bishop, 2019).
3. Integration into AIML System:
   a. Encode each emoticon alongside idioms in the XML database, allowing for dynamic and context-sensitive AI responses.
   b. Focus on the AI system's ability to understand and express appropriate emotional responses in line with the emoticons.

Data Import and Mapping Using Python

1. Importing Idiom Data from XML:
   a. Use Python's `xml.etree.ElementTree` module to parse the XML file and extract idioms and associated information.
   b. Store extracted idioms in Python data structures for easy manipulation.
2. Importing Emoticons and Emotions:
   a. Import the emoticon-emotion data into Python, using the `pandas` library for efficient handling and structuring.
   b. Create a DataFrame linking each emoticon to its corresponding emotions.
3. Creating Emoticon-Emotion Maps:
   a. Develop Python dictionaries mapping each emoticon to its set of emotions, critical for later AI processing stages.

Generating Prompts and Utilising OpenAI API

1. Concatenating Emoticons with Idioms:
   a. Implement Python loops to concatenate each of the 3,500 idioms with the 16 emoticons, resulting in 56,000 unique combinations.
   b. Ensure each combination represents a distinct emotional context.
2. Utilising OpenAI API's Asynchronous Function:
   a. Use Python's `asyncio` library to send asynchronous requests to the OpenAI API for each idiom-emoticon combination.
   b. Focus on efficient processing of the large volume of prompts and timely retrieval of responses.
3. Retrieving and Saving Responses:
   a. Store each response in a text file named after the respective idiom, containing 16 responses for the 16 emoticons.
   b. Use Python's file-handling capabilities for organised and efficient data storage.

Development of Python Flask API for AIML Parser Integration

1. API Design and Development:
    a. Utilise Python Flask, a lightweight and adaptable web framework, to develop an Application Programming Interface (API) that interfaces with the AIML parser.
    b. Design the API to handle requests for idiomatic expressions and provide corresponding emoticon-emotion-aligned responses.
2. Setting Up the Flask Environment:
    a. Install Flask and set up a dedicated environment for the API development, ensuring isolation and consistency during the development process.
    b. Organise the application structure for efficient and maintainable code management, including routes, templates, and necessary static files.
3. Designing and Implementing API Endpoints:
    a. Define specific endpoints in the Flask application that cater to various functionalities of the AIML parser, such as fetching responses for given idioms.
    b. Associate each route with a Python function that manages HTTP requests, interacts with the AIML system, and processes the emoticon-emotion data.
4. Integrating AIML Parser with Flask:
    a. Embed Python scripts within the Flask application to communicate with the AIML parser, ensuring seamless interaction and data exchange.
    b. Utilise the structured idiom and emoticon-emotion data from the XML database and Python dictionaries for dynamic response generation.
5. API Functionality Testing and Validation:
    a. Implement rigorous testing protocols to validate the API's functionality, focusing on endpoint reliability, data handling accuracy, and response appropriateness.
    b. Conduct integration tests to ensure the API's compatibility and seamless operation with the AIML parser and the underlying data structures.
6. User Interface and Accessibility:
    a. Develop user-friendly interfaces that allow users to interact with the API effortlessly, enhancing the usability of the AIML system.
    b. Ensure the interfaces are intuitive, responsive, and cater to a diverse user base.
7. Deployment and Maintenance:
    a. Deploy the Flask API on a suitable server, configuring necessary settings and environment variables.

b. Establish maintenance procedures for regular updates, performance monitoring, and troubleshooting.

DATA COLLECTION: COMPILING A COMPREHENSIVE LIST OF 3,500 ENGLISH IDIOMS

The data collection phase of the research project involved an extensive and meticulous process of gathering a wide array of English idioms. This phase was pivotal in establishing a foundational database for enhancing the Artificial Intelligence Markup Language (AIML) system with a nuanced understanding of idiomatic expressions and their emotional connotations.

The authors' initial step was to identify reliable and diverse sources from the internet that provided a rich repository of English idioms. This included exploring linguistic databases, online dictionaries, idiom-specific websites, and digital libraries. The criteria for source selection were based on the authenticity, comprehensiveness, and cultural diversity of the idiomatic content. Each source was rigorously evaluated to ensure that it met the authors' stringent standards for accuracy and relevance.

Once the sources were finalised, the process of idiom extraction commenced. This task was performed with a combination of automated and manual methods. Custom scripts were written in Python to crawl through the identified websites and extract idioms. These scripts were designed to parse web pages, identify idiomatic expressions, and retrieve them along with their meanings and usage examples. Manual intervention was essential in this phase to ensure the quality of the data. This involved reviewing the extracted idioms for accuracy, removing duplicates, and cross-verifying the meanings and usage contexts. The manual process also helped in discerning culturally significant idioms that automated scripts might have overlooked.

The next crucial step was the structuring and storage of the collected idioms. To achieve this, we opted for an XML (Extensible Markup Language) format, which offers flexibility and ease of integration with AIML systems. Each idiom was carefully encoded into the XML file with its corresponding details, such as meaning, usage, and emotional undertone. The XML file was designed to be comprehensive yet intuitive, facilitating easy access and retrieval of idioms for the subsequent phases of the project. It included tags for categorising idioms based on their emotional connotations and usage contexts, which would later assist in pairing them with the appropriate emoticons.

To ensure the integrity and quality of the authors' idiom database, a thorough quality assurance process was implemented. This involved multiple rounds of validation where the XML file was checked for consistency, accuracy, and completeness. Any anomalies or errors detected during this stage were rectified, ensuring that the database was of the highest standard. The data collection phase was executed with a focus on precision, diversity, and comprehensiveness. The meticulous process of sourcing, extracting, structuring, and validating over 3,500 idioms laid the groundwork for enhancing the AIML system's capability to understand and express the emotional dimensions of language, marking a significant advancement in the field of AI and linguistic processing.

CREATING THE LIST OF 16 EMOTICONS: A DETAILED EXPLORATION

The development of the emoticon list for this project was a nuanced process, intricately tied to understanding the spectrum of human emotions. We derived a comprehensive list of 16 emoticons from the Crocels Troller-Sniper Emotion Index 16 (adapted from Bishop, 2019), each representing a distinct emotional state or response. The focus was to ensure that these emoticons encompassed a wide range of feelings, from positive to negative, and from mild to intense.

Dataset: Emoticons and Their Emotions

Below is a table representing the 'Emoticons' and their associated 'Emojis', as part of the Crocels Troller-Sniper Emotion Index 16 (adapted from Bishop, 2019).

Table 1. Emoticon/Emoji List

Emoticon	Emoji Representation	Emotions Associated
:-""'	Trident Emblem	Shame, Guilty, Obscene, Hurt, Scornful, Rejected, Resent
:@	Angry Face	Anger, Enraged, Hate, Outrage, Rage, Violent
^o)	Unamused Face	Disgusted, Displeased, Ridicule
8o)	Persevering Face	Disdainful, Hostile, Jealousy, Menace, Nasty, Obnoxious
:∞	Boy	Detached, Moral, Pride, Reserved, Snob
l-)	Smiling Face With Sunglasses	Rigid, rude, selfish, serious, sceptical, though.
;-)	Winking Face	Erotic, Merry, Romantic, Sexy
:-(	Disappointed Face	Depressed, Despairing, Distressed, Gloom, Helpless, Horror, Misery, Regretful, Sad, Stress, Suicide, Unhappy, Upset, Pity
:-0	Man	Devoted, Hopeful, Repentant, Wise
8-)	Mage	Elated, Excitement, Lively, Optimism, Triumphant
:-o	Astonished Face	Grateful, Kind, Reverent, Subdued, Thoughtful, Timid, Warmth
:-)	Smiling Face	Friendly, Impressed, Natural, Nice, Pleasure, Relaxed, Satisfied
:ℵ	Ghost	Embarrassment, Startled, Insecure
:-#	Fearful Face	Afraid, Discouraged, Fear, Loneliness, Nervous, Scared, Terrified
:-D	Face with Tears of Joy	Enjoyment, Happy, Joy, Joyful, Mischief, Silly, Tease, Wit
:-l	Tired Face	Fatigued, Rusty, Sleep

Source: Adapted from Bishop (2019).

Emoticon Selection and Emotional Categorisation

The selection of emoticons was a critical step in the methodology. We delved into the Crocels TS-EI-16 dataset (adapted from Bishop, 2019), which classifies emoticons based on various character types like 'Explorer', 'E-Venger', 'Iconoclast', and more. Each character type was associated with specific emotions, providing a rich framework for the selection process. For instance, the emoticon ':-""'' (Trident Emblem), associated with the character types 'Explorer' and 'Traveller', was chosen for its representation of emotions such as shame, guilt, and scorn. This emotion was is instrumental in depicting emotions related to personal interpretation and expression of complex situations. Another example is the emoticon ':@' (Angry Face), linked to the character type 'E-Venger', epitomising feelings of anger, outrage, and violence. This emoticon was vital for expressing responses driven by vengeance and the need to reveal truths. The emoticon '^o)' (Unamused Face), representing the 'Iconoclast' character, was selected for its association with disgust and displeasure, fitting for situations where the AI needs to express disagreement or debunk myths.

Emoticon-Emotion Alignment

Each emoticon was meticulously aligned with its respective emotions, as defined in the Crocels TS-EI-16 (Bishop, 2019). This alignment was not just about selecting an emoticon but understanding the depth and variety of emotions it could represent. For example, the emoticon '8o)' (Persevering Face), linked with the character type 'Snert', was chosen for its ability to convey emotions like hostility and jealousy, essential for responses that are meant to show disdain or disapproval. The emoticon ':∞' (Boy), associated with 'Trickster' and 'Pecker', was selected for its representation of pride and moral superiority, useful in situations where the AI needs to express self-assuredness or ethical stances. The range of emotions covered by these 16 emoticons included anger, shame, disgust, pride, despair, joy, embarrassment, fear, and more, ensuring that the authors' AI system could respond appropriately to a wide spectrum of human interactions.

Integration into the AIML System

The final step was the integration of these emoticons into the AIML system. Each emoticon is encoded alongside the idioms in the XML database, allowing for a dynamic and context-sensitive response mechanism. Creating the emoticon list was a detailed process that involved careful selection, emotional categorisation, and integration into the authors' AIML system. This process was instrumental in enhancing the AI's ability to communicate with a deeper understanding of human emotions, making it a significant step forward in the field of AI and emotional intelligence.

DATA IMPORT AND MAPPING USING PYTHON

Importing Idiom Data from XML

The initial step in the methodology involves the importation of idiom data from an XML file. This file, meticulously compiled during the data collection phase, contains over 3,500 English idioms. Python, renowned for its data processing capabilities, is the chosen programming language for this task. To import this data, Python's `xml.etree.ElementTree` module is used. This module is adept at parsing XML files, enabling the extraction of idioms and their associated information. The process commences with loading the XML file into Python, followed by iterating over each element – in this case, idioms. Each idiom is then extracted and stored in a Python data structure, such as a list or dictionary, for easy access and manipulation.

Importing Emoticons and Emotions

Following the idiom importation, the next step is to import the emoticons and their corresponding emotions. This data, derived from the Crocels TS-EI-16 dataset, is crucial for mapping each emoticon to its respective emotional spectrum. The emoticons and their linked emotions are imported into Python, possibly through a CSV file or directly from a database, depending on the storage format. Python's `pandas` library, known for its robust data manipulation capabilities, is employed to handle this dataset. The library allows for efficient data import and provides functionalities for creating a structured format, such as a DataFrame. This DataFrame serves as a map, linking each of the 16 emoticons to its array of corresponding emotions.

Creating Emoticon-Emotion Maps

The creation of emoticon-emotion maps is a critical part of this phase. Each emoticon is mapped to its respective set of emotions, forming a key-value pair in a Python dictionary. This mapping is vital for later stages where the AI system needs to understand the emotional context of each response.

GENERATING PROMPTS AND UTILISING OPENAI API

Concatenating Emoticons with Idioms

With the idioms and emoticon-emotion maps ready, Python's looping structures come into play. A loop iterates through the list of 3,500 idioms. For each idiom, another nested loop concatenates it with each of the 16 emoticons. This process results in 56,000 unique combinations – each a fusion of an idiom with an emoticon, representing a distinct emotional context.

Utilising OpenAI API's Asynchronous Function

The concatenated idiom-emoticon pairs are now used to prompt the OpenAI API. Given the large number of prompts (3,500 idioms x 16 emoticons), the API's asynchronous function is employed. This function allows multiple requests to be sent to the API simultaneously, significantly speeding up the process of obtaining responses. Python's `asyncio` library is used for this purpose. It enables the sending of asynchronous requests to the OpenAI API, ensuring that each idiom-emoticon pair is processed efficiently. This approach is essential to handle the sheer volume of prompts and to retrieve responses promptly.

Retrieving and Saving Responses

As responses are received from the OpenAI API, they are captured and stored. Each response, aligned with a specific idiom-emoticon pair, is saved in a text file. These text files are named after the respective idioms, ensuring easy identification and retrieval. Each text file contains 16 responses, corresponding to the 16 emoticons paired with that particular idiom. This organisation method allows for a structured and accessible way to store the vast amount of data generated by the API. The process of saving these responses involves Python's file-handling capabilities. A loop iterates through the received responses, writing each one into the corresponding text file. Python's efficient file handling ensures that this process is executed smoothly, maintaining the integrity and organisation of the data.

This mechanism leverages Python's powerful data processing and asynchronous capabilities to handle a large dataset of idioms and emoticons. By creating unique combinations of idioms and emoticons and utilising the OpenAI API to generate responses, we can collect a vast and diverse range of responses for this dataset.

ANALYSIS OF TEXT FILES USING PYTHON, PANDAS, AND NLP

Text File Processing and Data Cleaning

Once the text files containing the responses of idioms paired with emoticons are generated, the next crucial step is to analyse these files for data quality and relevance. Python, along with its libraries Pandas and Natural Language Processing (NLP) tools, plays a pivotal role in this phase. Initially, Python scripts are employed to load these text files. Given the extensive number of files (one for each idiom), automation is key. Python's file handling capabilities enable efficient loading of each text file into a Pandas DataFrame. This transformation is crucial for organising the data and facilitating its analysis. Once loaded into DataFrames, the data undergoes a cleaning process. This involves scanning for and removing any gibberish or out-of-place special characters. Gibberish responses, often manifested as random strings of characters or nonsensical word combinations, can skew the analysis and provide inaccurate insights. Similarly, special characters that do not contribute to the meaning or emotional tone of the response are also removed. This cleaning process ensures that the data is as accurate and relevant as possible for further analysis.

Sentiment Analysis and Emotional Alignment

The core of this phase involves sentiment analysis, a facet of NLP. Sentiment analysis tools are used to determine the emotional tone of each response – whether it is positive, negative, or neutral. This step is critical in understanding how well the response aligns with the intended emotion of the paired emoticon. Python's NLP libraries, such as NLTK or TextBlob, are adept at performing sentiment analysis. They can evaluate the text of the responses and assign a sentiment score to each. This scoring allows us to quantitatively assess the emotional tone of the responses.

FEEDBACK LOOP FOR RESPONSE OPTIMIZATION

Comparison with Emoticon Emotions

The sentiment analysis results are then compared with the intended emotions of the emoticons. This comparison is pivotal in determining the appropriateness of the responses. If the sentiment of a response aligns well with the emotion represented by the emoticon, the response is deemed suitable. However, if there is a mismatch – for instance, a positive response where a negative one was expected, or vice versa – the response is flagged as incorrect. It helps in maintaining the integrity and reliability of the AI system in terms of emotional intelligence.

Feedback Loop for Response Refinement

The flagged responses, identified as mismatches, feed into a feedback loop. This loop is an integral part of the response optimisation process. Using the previously established response pipeline, the AI is prompted to generate new responses for the idioms paired with the respective emoticons. The feedback loop operates iteratively. Each new set of responses generated is again subject to sentiment analysis and compared with the intended emoticon emotions. This iterative process continues until the responses align satisfactorily with the emoticon emotions, effectively weeding out inappropriate responses.

Continuous Improvement and System Evolution

The feedback loop is not just a mechanism for immediate correction; it also serves as a tool for continuous improvement of the AI system. By repeatedly refining the responses, the AI learns and adapts, becoming more adept at understanding and aligning with the nuanced emotional contexts of different idiomatic expressions.

The analysis of the text files using Python, Pandas, and NLP tools is a critical step in ensuring the quality and emotional accuracy of the AI responses. The sentiment analysis, combined with a rigorous feedback loop, forms a robust mechanism for refining the AI's responses.

ENHANCING AIML WITH EMOTION ATTRIBUTES AND COMPILING RESPONSES

Integrating Emotional Context in AIML

The advancement in Artificial Intelligence Markup Language (AIML) through the integration of an emotional context marks a significant enhancement in its existing format. The addition of a new attribute, 'emotion', to the AIML schema is a pivotal part of this enhancement. This attribute aligns with one of the emoticons associated with each idiom response, enabling AIML to support and recognize multiple emotionally contextualised responses for each idiom. This innovative step in the AIML format enriches AI interactions, making them more nuanced and akin to human-like communication. It allows the AIML system to respond not just based on the textual content of user queries but also to interpret and reflect the underlying emotional tone of the conversation.

Selection and Compilation of Responses

In the compilation process of responses for the 3,500 idioms, each paired with 16 emoticons, systematic formatting is key. For every idiom, one of the 16 responses is earmarked as the default response, based on its relevance and the predominant emotion it represents in typical dialogues. Each idiom and its corresponding responses are then formatted into the AIML structure, incorporating the newly added 'emotion' attribute within AIML tags. This structured approach ensures that the AIML system can effectively process and utilise these responses in interactions.

Implementing Additional AIML Tags

In addition to the 'emotion' attribute, other attributes like 'avatar' are also incorporated, further enhancing the richness of the responses. The 'avatar' attribute aligns an emoji or graphical representation with the emotional tone of the response, adding a visual dimension to the textual interaction.

Example of Enhanced AIML Structuring

For illustration, consider the idiom "He is the apple of my eye". Its AIML structure, accommodating multiple responses for various emotions, is as follows:

Figure 1. AIML Formatting

```
<!-- Category: He is the apple of my eye :-\" -->
<category>
    <pattern>He is the apple of my eye</pattern>
    <template>
        <random>
            <li emotion=':-\"' avatar="●" default="true">Oh no, what happened that makes you feel this way?</li>
            <li emotion=":@" avatar="●">Yikes, sounds like you are really furious at him! Take a deep breath.</li>
            <li emotion="^o)" avatar="●">Hmm, not sure what's the disgust for. Maybe you should talk to him?</li>
            <li emotion="8o)" avatar="●">Whoa, there seems to be some hostility there! Are you jealous of something?</li>
            <li emotion=":∞" avatar="●">Got it, you admire him from a distance. That's respectable.</li>
            <li emotion="|-)" avatar="●">Straight-faced, huh? Maybe you just need to loosen up a bit.</li>
            <li emotion=";-)" avatar="●">Oh, someone's got a little romance going on! That's sweet!</li>
            <li emotion=":-(" avatar="●">I'm really sorry to hear that you are sad about this.</li>
            <li emotion=":-0" avatar="●">You seem really devoted to him. That's great!</li>
            <li emotion="8-)" avatar="●">Wow, you sound super excited and happy about him! Enjoy the good times!</li>
            <li emotion=":-o" avatar="●">Oh, that's really kind! Sounds like you appreciate him a lot.</li>
            <li emotion=":-)" avatar="●">I'm glad to hear you're happy about him! That's awesome.</li>
            <li emotion=":-#" avatar="●">Seems like you're feeling scared or nervous about something.</li>
            <li emotion=":-D" avatar="●">You seem so joyful and happy about him! Cherish those moments.</li>
            <li emotion=":X" avatar="●">Are you feeling embarrassed or startled?</li>
            <li emotion=":-|" avatar="●">Feeling kind of meh about it, huh? Sometimes it's just one of those days.</li>
        </random>
    </template>
</category>
```

In this AIML example, each `<li>` tag within the `<random>` tag contains a unique response associated with a specific emotion and avatar, allowing the AI system to choose a response that matches the emotional context of the user's input. Legacy AIML parsers will pick any of the statements at random and the authors' proprietary system picks the one marked `default="true"` where no input emotion has been matched to an emoticon.

ENHANCING THE FLEXIBILITY AND RESPONSIVENESS OF AIML

Implementing Multi-Response Capability

The capability of AIML to accommodate multiple responses for a single idiom, enabled by the 'emotion' attribute, significantly enhances its flexibility and adaptiveness. This multi-response feature introduces a degree of dynamism previously unattainable, allowing the AI system to select from a variety of emotionally nuanced responses depending on the context of the conversation.

Addressing Technical Implementation Challenges

Implementing these enhancements necessitates modifications to the AIML parser to recognize and process the new attributes, such as 'emotion' and 'avatar'. This task requires a profound understanding of AIML's architecture and meticulous coding to ensure seamless integration with existing AIML standards and functionality. Ensuring that the emotional responses are contextually appropriate is a critical challenge in this implementation. The AI system is tasked with accurately interpreting the user's emotional state and selecting a response that aligns with that emotion, requiring sophisticated algorithms capable of discerning intricate language and emotional nuances. Moving forward, this approach to enhancing AIML paves the way for more advanced stages of development, focusing on refining the system's ability to navigate and respond to the complex emotional landscape of human interactions. This progression towards a more emotionally intelligent AI holds significant implications for the future of AI and human-computer interaction.

EXTENDING PYAIML FOR EMOTION AND AVATAR TAGS

Enhancing PyAIML for New Attributes

As the authors' project advances, they delve into enhancing the PyAIML parser, a Python adaptation of AIML, to support the novel 'emotion' and 'avatar' attributes integrated into the AIML structure. This enhancement is pivotal for processing these innovative tags within AIML files, marking a significant step in the evolution of AI communication. The 'emotion' attribute empowers the PyAIML parser to grasp and reflect the emotional tone of user interactions, while the 'avatar' tag introduces a visual element to the AI's responses. These enhancements bring a dynamic and more human-like quality to the interactions facilitated by the AI system.

Implementing Advanced Pattern Matching

A key aspect of enhancing PyAIML is the improvement of its pattern-matching capabilities through the integration of Regular Expressions (Regex). This enhancement enables the parser to adeptly handle and interpret complex and varied user inputs, accommodating natural language variations including colloquial expressions and unstructured phrases. Further, the enhancement for recognizing common words effectively is implemented, ensuring the AI system maintains coherent and contextually relevant dialogues across a wide range of conversational inputs.

Database Integration for Enhanced Functionality

The next enhancement phase involves adapting PyAIML to function seamlessly with relational databases, such as MySQL or Microsoft SQL Server. This integration significantly uplifts the AIML system's functionality and scalability, especially considering the voluminous data comprising numerous idioms and their corresponding responses.

COMPILING AND STORING AIML IN A RELATIONAL DATABASE FORMAT

Saving Compiled AIML to Database

The next critical step involves saving the compiled AIML files, now rich with 'emotion' and 'avatar' attributes, into a relational database. This process transforms the AIML data into a format congruent with relational database structures, optimising data management and retrieval capabilities. The database structure is tailored to align with the AIML file format, encompassing categories, patterns, templates, and the newly integrated attributes. This organisation ensures coherent and accessible data storage.

Enhancing Data Retrieval and Management

Storing AIML data in a relational database streamlines the retrieval and management of AI responses. The database facilitates swift access to specific idioms and their related responses, enhancing the AI's interaction efficiency. Robust data management tools provided by the database, including backup, recovery, and maintenance capabilities, ensure the long-term durability and integrity of the AIML data, a critical factor given the dynamic nature of AI interactions.

Synchronising PyAIML with Database

The final enhancement involves synchronising PyAIML with the relational database. This synchronisation guarantees that updates in the AIML files are accurately reflected in the database, achieved through database connectors and synchronisation scripts within PyAIML. Moving forward, these enhancements in PyAIML set the stage for subsequent phases of the project, aiming to refine and optimise the AI's interactive abilities and emotional intelligence.

DEVELOPING THE PYTHON FLASK API FOR AIML INTERACTION

Introduction to API Development with Python Flask

The next crucial step in the project involves creating an Application Programming Interface (API) using Python Flask. This API serves as a gateway for users to interact with the AIML mechanism developed with PyAIML and integrated with a MySQL database. Flask, a lightweight and powerful web framework for Python, is an ideal choice for this purpose due to its simplicity, flexibility, and ease of use.

Setting Up the Flask Environment

The first phase in developing the API involves setting up the Flask environment. This setup includes installing Flask using Python's package manager, pip, and creating a new Flask application instance. The structure of the Flask application is organised into various components, including routes, templates, and static files, facilitating a modular and maintainable codebase.

Designing API Endpoints

The core of the Flask application lies in designing API endpoints that users can access to interact with the AIML system. These endpoints are defined as routes in Flask, each corresponding to a specific functionality of the AIML mechanism. For instance, an endpoint might be created for submitting user queries to the AIML system and retrieving responses. Each route is associated with a Python function that handles the incoming HTTP requests, processes them using the PyAIML and MySQL setup, and returns the appropriate responses. Care is taken to ensure these functions are efficient and secure, providing a seamless and safe user experience.

Integrating PyAIML and MySQL with Flask

The integration of PyAIML and MySQL with the Flask application is a critical aspect of the API development. This integration allows the Flask application to interact with the AIML mechanism, processing user inputs and fetching responses from the MySQL database. To achieve this integration, Python scripts are written within the Flask application that connects to the MySQL database using appropriate connectors. These scripts utilise PyAIML functionalities to parse user inputs, match them with the AIML patterns stored in the database, and generate the relevant AI responses.

IMPLEMENTING THE API AND ENSURING ROBUST FUNCTIONALITY

A vital feature of the Flask-based Gateway API is processing user inputs. When a user submits a query through the API, the Flask application receives this input and passes it to the PyAIML engine. The engine, in turn, processes the input, matches it against the AIML patterns, and retrieves the corresponding response. Special attention is given to handling various types of user inputs, including those with different emotional contexts, as identified by the 'emotion' and 'avatar' tags in the AIML setup. The system is designed to understand and respond to these inputs accurately, reflecting the emotional intelligence of the AI.

Security is a paramount concern in API development. Measures are implemented to safeguard against common web vulnerabilities, such as SQL injection and cross-site scripting (XSS). Flask provides several built-in tools to help secure the application, which are utilised to their full potential. Scalability is another crucial factor considered in API development. The Flask application is designed to handle a significant number of concurrent user requests without compromising performance. This scalability is crucial for the widespread adoption and usability of the API.

While the backend functionality is critical, providing a user-friendly interface for interacting with the API is equally important. The Flask application includes templates that render user interfaces for inputting queries and displaying responses. These interfaces are designed to be intuitive and easy to use, catering to a wide range of users.

Before deployment, the Flask API undergoes thorough testing to ensure its functionality and robustness. This testing includes unit tests for individual components and integration tests for the entire application. Special attention is given to testing the API's interaction with the PyAIML engine and the MySQL database, ensuring that the entire system works seamlessly together. Once tested, the Flask API is deployed on a suitable web server. The deployment process involves configuring the server settings, setting up the necessary environment variables, and ensuring that the API is accessible to users. The creation of a Python Flask API for interacting with the AIML mechanism developed with PyAIML and MySQL represents a significant milestone in the project. The focus on user experience, security, scalability, and robust testing and deployment strategies ensures that the API is efficient, secure, and capable of handling diverse user interactions.

RESULTS AND ANALYSIS

The project's initial phase involved collecting 3,500 English idioms, presenting a significant opportunity to explore the processing of free-form text using Python and pandas. This process illustrated the efficiency of automation in data handling compared to manual methods. Through Python scripts, we could swiftly crawl, extract, and structure idiomatic data.

A pivotal aspect of the project was leveraging the OpenAI GPT-3.5-turbo API to generate responses for idioms paired with 16 predefined emoticons from the Crocels list (adapted from Bishop, 2019). This approach significantly accelerated the creation of the dataset. The API's capability to process and understand the nuanced meanings of idioms in conjunction with emotional contexts, as represented by emoticons, was instrumental in constructing a diverse and rich dataset. This advancement underscored the utility of advanced AI models in handling complex linguistic tasks.

The AI model provided multiple response options for each idiom-emoticon pair, from which we could select the most suitable ones. This multi-response feature of the AI model was crucial in ensuring that the chosen responses accurately reflected the intended emotional tone and context. It demonstrated the model's ability to offer varied and contextually relevant responses, enhancing the quality and reliability of the dataset.

Utilising Natural Language Processing (NLP) methodologies, we could efficiently validate the appropriateness of the responses generated by the AI model. This approach was significantly time-saving compared to manual review. NLP tools analyzed the sentiment and contextual relevance of the responses, ensuring their suitability. This automated validation process underscored the importance and effectiveness of NLP in streamlining linguistic data analysis.

The incorporation of a Gateway API and a relational database played a crucial role in system testing and access. This setup allowed for efficient testing of the AIML parser and the integration of the idioms and emoticons database. The database provided a structured platform for storing and retrieving the AI responses, while the Gateway API facilitated seamless interaction with the AIML parser. This architecture was key in evaluating the system's performance and ensuring its functionality.

Implications, Limitations and Future Research Directions

The project highlighted the ease and efficiency of processing extensive datasets of English idioms. Automation tools in Python proved to be effective in managing and structuring large volumes of text. The OpenAI GPT-3.5-turbo API demonstrated its value as a powerful platform for generating responses to a wide range of text prompts. Its scalability and ability to handle complex linguistic tasks were particularly noteworthy. While the AI model generally produced accurate responses, instances of inaccuracies and unclear responses were observed. The implementation of NLP libraries and Python for testing and validation was essential in identifying and correcting these errors. This process emphasized the need for robust testing mechanisms in AI systems to ensure the quality and reliability of outputs.

The current study, while successful in implementing an affect-aware API Gateway using PyAIML and Python Flask, reveals certain limitations that pave the way for future research directions. The primary constraints stem from the inherent limitations of the chosen technologies compared to more advanced cloud-based solutions like Microsoft Azure.

Firstly, scalability and performance emerge as critical areas. The Python Flask and PyAIML framework is constrained by the physical server resources, limiting its ability to dynamically adapt to increased loads or complex computational demands. This aspect highlights the need for future research into cloud-based solutions that offer better scalability and performance management.

Another significant limitation is the range of integrated services and features. Microsoft Azure, for example, provides a plethora of integrated AI and machine learning capabilities, along with extensive data analytics and security features. These integrated services could enhance an affect-aware API parser's functionality, particularly in areas like advanced natural language processing and sentiment analysis. Future research could explore integrating these advanced services to enhance the capabilities of the API Gateway. Reliability and uptime are also areas of concern. The study's setup might be more prone to downtime due to its reliance on a single server or limited infrastructure. This limitation underscores the importance of future research into distributed cloud infrastructure, like that offered by Azure, to ensure higher reliability and continuous service availability. The maintenance and support of the system present another challenge. Unlike Azure, which offers professional support and regular updates, maintaining a PyAIML and Flask-based system requires significant effort. Future research could focus on developing more automated maintenance processes or exploring cloud-based solutions that offer comprehensive support.

Security and compliance standards are paramount, especially when handling sensitive data. The current system, while secure, may not meet the same level of compliance as Azure's cloud infrastructure. Future research should investigate ways to enhance security protocols and compliance standards in Python Flask and PyAIML systems. Integration with other services and applications is somewhat limited in the current setup. Microsoft Azure allows for seamless integration with a wide range of services, enhancing the overall functionality of an API parser. Future studies could explore methods to facilitate better integration with other services and applications in PyAIML and Flask-based systems.

Lastly, the development and deployment processes in the current system are more manual and time-consuming compared to the streamlined tools provided by Azure. Future research directions could include the development of tools and processes that simplify and accelerate the development cycle, making it more comparable to cloud-based solutions.

DISCUSSION

As we culminate the project, it is pertinent to reflect on the strides made and the future implications of this endeavour. This project, ambitious in its scope and meticulous in its execution, has significantly advanced the capability of Artificial Intelligence in comprehending and employing idiomatic English. The completion of this venture marks a noteworthy milestone in the journey towards creating AI systems that can interact with a level of understanding and emotional intelligence akin to that of humans. The comprehensive collection and processing of over 3,500 English idioms, each paired with emotionally resonant emoticons, stand as a testament to the project's success. The use of Python for data handling, the application of the OpenAI GPT-3.5-turbo API for generating responses, and the integration of Natural Language Processing for response validation have collectively demonstrated the power of technology in enhancing AI's linguistic capabilities. The ability of the AI system to not just recognize idioms but also to understand their contextual and emotional nuances is an achievement that bridges a significant gap in AI-human interaction.

REFERENCES

Bishop, J. (2015). Supporting communication between people with social orientation impairments using affective computing technologies: Rethinking the autism spectrum. In *Assistive technologies for physical and cognitive disabilities* (pp. 42–55). IGI Global. doi:10.4018/978-1-4666-7373-1.ch003

Bishop, J. (2019). Assisting human interaction (United States Patent) [Review of Assisting human interaction]. https://patents.google.com/patent/US10467916B2

Bishop, J., & Reddy, M. (2003). The role of the Internet for educating individuals with social orientation impairments. *Journal of Computer Assisted Learning*, *19*(4), 546–556. doi:10.1046/j.0266-4909.2003.00057.x

Calvo, R. A., & D'Mello, S. (2010). Affect detection: An interdisciplinary review of models, methods, and their applications. *IEEE Transactions on Affective Computing*, *1*(1), 18–37. doi:10.1109/T-AFFC.2010.1

Cambria, E., Olsher, D., & Rajagopal, D. (2014). SenticNet 3: A common and common-sense knowledge base for cognition-driven sentiment analysis. *Proceedings of the AAAI Conference on Artificial Intelligence*, *28*(1). Advance online publication. doi:10.1609/aaai.v28i1.8928

Derks, D., Fischer, A. H., & Bos, A. E. R. (2008). The role of emotion in computer-mediated communication: A Review. *Computers in Human Behavior*, *24*(3), 766–785. doi:10.1016/j.chb.2007.04.004

Kirchschläger, P. G. (2021). *Digital transformation and ethics: ethical considerations on the robotization and automation of society and the economy and the use of artificial intelligence*. Nomos Verlag. doi:10.5771/9783845285504

Kralj Novak, P., Smailović, J., Sluban, B., & Mozetič, I. (2015). Sentiment of Emojis. *PLoS One*, *10*(12), e0144296. Advance online publication. doi:10.1371/journal.pone.0144296 PMID:26641093

Picard, R. W. (2000). *Affective computing*. MIT Press. doi:10.7551/mitpress/1140.001.0001

Wallace, R. S. (2008). The Anatomy of A.L.I.C.E. In Parsing the Turing test: Philosophical and methodological issues in the quest for the thinking computer (pp. 181–210). essay, Springer.

Chapter 8
The Impact of OpenAI and MFP on the Labour Market Dynamics of Trinidad and Tobago

Roshnie Anita Doon
https://orcid.org/0000-0002-3285-0355
Global Labor Organization, Germany

ABSTRACT

Open Artificial Intelligence (AI) is a research and operation company that seeks to ensure that persons around the world can reap the benefits of AI. Its focus is on developing a range of models that have the potential to revolutionize the labour market productivity of business enterprises across industries in Trinidad and Tobago. The use of AI-based tools can not only optimize every stage of the management and production process but from the perspective of Multi-Factor Productivity (MFP) can boost its efficiency. Even with such benefits, increased use of AI can displace workers, intensify educational and skills mismatch, and stimulate inequality between unskilled and highly skilled workers. This chapter examined the impact of Open AI and MFP on the Labor Dynamics of Trinidad and Tobago, using a secondary research methodology. This chapter delves into the connection between AI tools and MFP, its integration into the management and production process, and the impact that it has on the labour dynamics of domestic industries, and the future of work in Trinidad and Tobago.

DOI: 10.4018/979-8-3693-1198-1.ch008

INTRODUCTION

Artificial Intelligence (AI) has the potential to revolutionize the way businesses, industries and economies operate the world over. In the past decade, with the formation of Open AI, came the creation of a suite of AI-based programs such as ChatGPT, GPT-3, and DALL.E, whose APIs have formed the foundation of several AI applications in many different areas from automated story and resume generators to automated customer support systems, image generation and customization, as well as chatbots (George et al., 2023).

The diverse array of AI-based technologies implies that it has the potential to change the future of domestic industries in Trinidad and Tobago in a variety of ways, including the automation of tasks within the manufacturing and financial sector, the personalization of products and services, and optimizing the decision making and supply chain process (Fasso et al., 2021). These collective changes can have a notable impact on the productivity and efficiency of domestic businesses, as with the assistance of AI both employees and employers can realize their full potential, which can manifest itself as growth in Multi-Factor Productivity (MFP) as well as overall economic growth and stability in more technologically advanced countries like the United States (US) and China (Seaman's & Raj, 2018).

Within the literature, there is a dearth of knowledge on the impact that AI has on both the MFP and the labour market of Caribbean countries. To address this issue, the primary aim of this article will be to close this gap in the literature by discussing what impact Open AI has on the MFP and labour market of Trinidad and Tobago. To do this, this study uses a qualitative research methodology, to build a conceptual framework to gain a deeper understanding of such an impact. This study uses a host of existing scholarly literature to discuss and analyze the present information on AI in the context of countries like Trinidad and Tobago which may not have the financial and technical capacity to integrate AI into its industries to increase their MFP. In the context of this study, such a research methodology is appropriate because it generates new insights and provides a deeper understanding of the labour market situation that is likely to emerge from the integration of AI in domestic industries in Trinidad and Tobago while using fewer resources.

That being said, this chapter is structured as follows, first a review of the history and evolution of Open AI is provided, second the concept of MFP and its measurements are discussed, third the potential impact that AI is likely to have on MFP is explored, fourth the possible ways in which AI-based technologies can be integrated in Trinidad and Tobago's major revenue earners, i.e., the energy and manufacturing sector is examined, fifth the impact that such an integration may have on the domestic labour market, and the future of work in Trinidad and Tobago is considered, after which the study is concluded.

THE EVOLUTION OF OPEN AI

Open AI is an Artificial Intelligence (AI) research organization based in the United States (US) (OpenAI, 2023a). Established in 2015, the main goal of the organization is to create and provide Artificial General Intelligence (AGI) based solutions and systems, that are not only more intelligent and resourceful than human beings but can assist in the generation and implementation of solutions to the global problems of extreme poverty, climate change, deforestation, food security and hunger in the long run (OpenAI, 2023b; Gray, 2017). In the space of 8 years, Open AI has advanced the integration of AI-based tools and has become a driver of human inventiveness and resourcefulness, that allows everyone to tap into their unsung potential. In the long run, it is hoped that AI will be able to accelerate not only the growth and development of different fields of expertise such as science, medicine, finance, retail, manufacturing, education, and agriculture but also its progress (Altman, 2023).

The main driver of such growth lies in the approach that Open AI has taken to advance the field of AI, which is to share their patents and intellectual property, as well as open-sourcing their research in 2015, with researchers, scientific innovators, and institutions in the field of AI (OpenAI, 2023c). In doing so, Open AI has bolstered the rate at which AI technology systems have developed in real-time, which allows AI systems to evolve alongside the changes that occur in economies and societies around the world. This has led to the creation of several AI-based systems such as generative models, and language models during 2016-2022 (OpenAI, 2023c). For this chapter, emphasis will be placed on the main AI models developed by Open AI since its inception in 2015.

During the 2016-2017 timeframe, Open AI developed several systems, two of which include OpenAI Gym, and Generative models, while concentrating on the training of AI by learning from simulations, robotics, image-based robotics, competitive self-play and awareness, human preferences, and imitation (OpenAI, 2023d). The use of toolkits such as OpenAI Gym used robots and online games like Flappy Bird, and Pacman, to develop and reinforce learning algorithms that enable AI agents to achieve their goals in uncertain environments (Brockman et al., 2016). Since reinforcement occurs in a simulated environment, agents will not only be able to play in a multitude of different environments, and scenarios but also allow algorithms to be trained faster, which enhances the learning process (Chuchro & Gupta, 2017).

Generative models, in comparison to OpenAI Gym, concentrate on learning the underlying patterns found in data, to create related data points that can be found in the real world. Operated on neural networks, these types of models such as Generative Adversarial Networks (GANs), and Gaussian Mixture Model (GMM), produce new data by using a feedback loop that adjusts its data based on the dataset used. GANs in particular provided a means to detect deep representations without needing broad training data (Creswell et al., 2018). As a form of unsupervised learning, generative models automatically learn the features of the dataset and internalize the meaning of this information to produce an output that contains valuable information (Karpathy et al., 2016). These models have many real-world applications, such as in image and video recognition, generation, and translation, as well as text-to-image translations, which can be used for training robots, medical imaging, satellite imagery, and to optimize supply chain operations that may reduce business cost and the wastage of production inputs.

Considering the improvement and progress made throughout 2018-2019, OpenAI continued to immerse itself in the research and development of AI. This led to even greater work being done on areas such as unsupervised third-person imitation learning which enables agents to learn through observation of human demonstrations without having any interactions, as well as learning through imitation by modelling minds, cooperation, and communication with humans, and experience rewards through hindsight experience replay (OpenAI 2023d; Stadie et al., 2017; Andrychowicz et al., 2018). Amidst these activities the most prominent were OpenAI Five, and Generative Pre-Trained Transformers (GPT), i.e., GPT-1 and GPT-2, which were released in 2018 and 2019.

According to OpenAI (2023e), OpenAI Five is a computer program that is used to play against simulated online games like Dota 2. The training and development of OpenAI Five, generated several benefits, such as learning to advance strategies through self-play, improving computational efficiency through the rapid generation of training data and reinforcement learning, and most importantly developing an ability to become teammates with humans which is indicative of AI's ability to collaborate and support human beings (OpenAI, 2023e).

Generative Pre-Training (GPT) was used to improve natural language understanding of various tasks. To do this, first language models are first trained (unsupervised generative pre-training) using a wide array of unlabeled text, after which each specific task is discriminative fine-tuned (Radford et al., 2018). Since the models are training on a broad range of real-world data and situations, they can enhance the performance and success of many specific tasks by using common-sense reasoning, answering questions and textual entailment (Radford, 2018). The difference between GPT-1 and GPT-2 is based on their training, so while GPT-1 was trained on a large dataset of books, GPT-2 had 1.5bn parameters that allowed it to generate more comprehensible text.

Following these developments, in the time between 2020-2021, while OpenAI became a for-profit company, they continued to focus on the development of AI through many different avenues including the creation of activation atlases, and scaling laws (OpenAI, 2023d). The most important AI advancements during this period, however, came with the setting up and release of a suite of AI tools, such as Image GPT, DALL-E, WebGPT, and GPT-3 (Carter et al., 2019).

Touching briefly on each of these tools, GPT-3 is the largest language model, comprising 175bn parameters, and 96bn layers trained on 499bn tokens of web content (Dale, 2021). Because of its expansiveness, the text that is generated is much more complex and coherent human-like text, as it can perform a wide range of tasks such as generating computer code, music, stories, and writing essays (Dale 2021; Floridi & Chiriatti, 2020). WebGPT is used to improve the accuracy of these tasks in an online environment through web browsing. The models are trained using imitation learning, and human feedback, to produce accurate responses (Nakano et al., 2021).

Image GPT is simply a variation of GPT but instead of text, it is trained using an array of transformers to auto-regressively envision pixels that allow the multimodal system to process both the images and text, to produce accurate images (Chen et al., 2020). Unlike Image GPT, DALL-E uses text description based on natural language text prompts to generate images on a wide range of topics. It is similar to GPT-3, in that it is also a transformer language model, that enables DALL-E to create images from scratch, and based on existing images (Ramesh et al., 2021).

Finally, throughout 2022-2023, OpenAI concentrated most of its efforts on improving the performance of GPT-3, by releasing an AI Chatbot, called ChatGPT, which was also later integrated into the services provided by Microsoft, such as Microsoft 365, and Microsoft Bing. Trained using reinforcement learning, ChatGPT enables its users to have a human-like conversation, that can be fine-tuned from feedback by the user to improve the quality of the response being generated (Morgan, 2023; OpenAI, 2023f). This was then followed by the unveiling of GPT-4, which according to OpenAI (2023g, 1), "can accept image and text inputs and produce text outputs." Displaying a human-level performance, GPT-4 can use the most complex instruction given by users for real-world scenarios, to produce creative and reliable responses (OpenAI, 2023h).

THE RELATIONSHIP BETWEEN ARTIFICIAL INTELLIGENCE (AI) AND MULTI-FACTOR PRODUCTIVITY (MFP)

Considering the rapid growth and development of generative and language models developed by OpenAI during 2015-2023, it is not surprising that such AI models are likely to have a significant impact on productivity. AI-related tasks can influence a vast array of areas in the production process such as the automation of tasks, and as a result, it has the potential to change the productivity growth of business enterprises in Trinidad and Tobago, as well as the labour dynamics of these businesses in both the short and long term (Furman & Seamans, 2019). However, before examining the connection that AI has with MFP, a short discussion on MFP also known as Total-Factor Productivity (TFP) and its measures will be undertaken.

Multi-Factor Productivity (MFP) and its Measures

According to the Organization for Economic Co-operation and Development (OECD) (2023a), "Multifactor productivity (MFP) reflects the overall efficiency with which labour and capital inputs are used together in the production process." MFP is a productivity measure, so any shifts in this portion are likely to be indicative of adjustments made to the production process through factor inputs that may improve the overall productivity of either a business or an economy (Roser, 2013). For this reason, the entire concept of economic growth is based on MFP, however, its theoretical perspectives tend to differ based on the school of thought, where for example, Romer (1986) explains that MFP depends on external factors such as human capital, whereas Solow (1956) who also agrees that MFP is based on external factors but instead is driven by time.

Usually presented as either an index or annual growth rate, MFP reflects not only a growth in the quality and quantity of these conventional factor inputs of labour and capital but also how efficiently these inputs can be used (Franklin, 2018). Further to this, the inputs used in the measurement of MFP are weighted, so that they incorporate the relative importance of the inputs to industry output. While MFP can be derived at the sector, industry, and country level, it is often adopted by the business sector, broad economic sectors, and industries as a tool to evaluate their productive capacity, making it a comprehensive measure of technological change and efficiency, (Verges-Jamie, 2021). Notwithstanding this, although within the literature, there are many ways of measuring MFP, such as the growth regressions, frontier methods, the Tornqvist methods, and the Hicks-Moorsteen Approach, for purposes of this chapter emphasis will be placed on the most traditional measure of MFP, i.e., (1) the growth accounting method (Apostolides, 2008; Ahmed & Bhatti, 2020).

The growth accounting method is also known as the Solow Residual. With this method, MFP is determined by first breaking down the observed economic growth into its factor inputs and technical progress and then analyzing how these factors contribute to the overall level of economic growth (Solow, 1956). In the case of the latter, i.e., technological change is often deemed to be unexplained, is considered to be the Solow Residual as it is that aspect of economic growth that cannot be explained by the growth of either labour or capital (Solow, 1957). To derive the Solow Residual, Solow (1956, 1957) used the standard Cobb-Douglas production function as a starting point when adapted for this study as follows.

$$Y = F(K, L) \tag{1}$$

where Y refers to the output, K refers to capital, and L refers to labour. Given that Solow (1957) assumed that productivity was driven by time (t), and accumulated shifts in time A(t), equation (1) when rewritten to incorporate this component becomes,

$$Y=F(K, L, t) \tag{2}$$

$$Y= A(t)\, F(K, L) \tag{3}$$

By including A(t), it allows for technical change to take place, which shifts the entire production function. To show this shift when equation (3) is differentiated with t it becomes,

$$\frac{\frac{dY}{dt}}{Y} = \frac{\frac{dA}{dt}}{A} + A\left[\frac{\partial F}{\partial K}.\frac{\frac{dK}{dt}}{Y}\right] + A\left[\frac{\partial F}{\partial L}.\frac{\frac{dL}{dt}}{Y}\right] \tag{4}$$

equation (4) can be simplified further with the dots as time derivations so that it becomes,

$$\frac{\dot{Y}}{Y} = \frac{\dot{A}}{A} + A\left[\frac{\partial F}{\partial K}.\frac{\dot{K}}{Y}\right] + A\left[\frac{\partial F}{\partial L}.\frac{\dot{L}}{Y}\right] \tag{5}$$

where $\left[\frac{\partial Q}{\partial K}.\frac{\dot{K}}{Y}\right]$ and $\left[\frac{\partial Q}{\partial L}.\frac{\dot{L}}{Y}\right]$ are the relative factor shares of capital and labour, while $\frac{\dot{A}}{A}$ refers to any shift of the production function resulting from technical change or MFP. Assuming an aggregate production function,

$$Y=AK^{\alpha}L^{1-\alpha} \tag{6}$$

where α in equation (6) which can be between $0<\alpha<1$, refers to the elasticity of the production function, where A is shown below in equation (7) as the Solow Residual.

$$A= \frac{Y}{K^{\alpha} L^{1-\alpha}} \tag{7}$$

Notwithstanding the derivation of the Solow residual, this method to determine the MFP is primarily used within the literature because the parameters of the factor shares can be varied, while the aggregate production function does not need to take a specific form (Ahmed & Bhatti, 2020). However, the main drawbacks of using this method are that it assumes that the rate of return used to determine the factor shares is even across countries, it is sensitive to both the rank of the countries and the data on capital and labour, as well as it ignores natural capital as a factor input and environmental changes that may influence such growth (Ahmed & Bhatti, 2020; Ai et al., 2023).

For this reason, the measure can be improved by not only considering environmental changes such as greenhouse gas (GHG) emissions which led to the creation of Green MFP (MFPG), but also including indicators that reflect the quality of labour and capital (Brandolini & Cipollone, 2001; Ai et al., 2023; Rodriguez et al., 2018; Lauraitiene & Vitunskiene, 2022). The latter may cause A to become biased, as the economic growth rates of countries may be different as their long and short-term growth policy vary (Ai et al., 2023). To get around this problem, the alternative measures of MFP which are also extensions of the growth accounting method, such as Growth regressions and the Hicks-Moorsteen Approach can be used. In the case of the latter, the Hicks-Moorsteen Approach does not use the aggregate production function to determine the MFP can be used, as it defines productivity as the ratio of output and input index numbers as shown in equation (8),

$$A= \frac{Y}{K^{\beta} L^{\alpha}} \tag{8}$$

where α and β are the weights. Whereas in the case of the former growth regressions approach, structural equations are used to estimate the growth in MFP as shown in equation (9) where δ_1 refers to trends in time, δ_2 and δ_3 refers to the elasticity associated with capital and labour, while $\dot{K}_t$ and $\dot{L}_t$ are the growth rates associated with capital and labour,

$$MFP_t = \delta_1 + \left(\delta_2 + \delta_3 - 1\right)\left(\delta_2 \dot{K}_t + \delta_3 \dot{L}_t\right) \tag{9}$$

While this method is quite flexible as it is not sensitive like the Hicks-Moorsteen Approach and does not need data on capital and production to estimate MFP, it avoids the role that efficiency plays in productivity. MFP has a special relationship with labour productivity growth. In instances where capital and labour are used more efficiently in the production process, it can cause both labour productivity and MFP growth to improve (OECD, 2023b). However, during periods of economic crisis as the Covid-19 pandemic in 2020, and the 2007/2008 Global Financial Crisis, where there was a slowdown in labour productivity, it would make a smaller contribution to MFP, therefore causing a stagnation in MFP growth rates during these periods. In addition to this, the estimates produced by MFP can be used as indicators of the productive and capital efficiency and capacity of firms, and industries, as they can be indicative of its return on capital employed (ROCE) (Chadha & Adams, 1992).

Many factor inputs can influence MFP, such as adjustments in the economies of scale, i.e., increasing production at a larger scale, changes in businesses and industrial management practices, adjustment costs linked to any changes made to the production process, product modifications made to the marketing of items such as its branding and packaging, spillover and networking effects from production factors, structural changes in the organization and industry, the level of imperfect competition occurring within the market, and measurement errors in inputs and outputs, as well as improvements made to human capital, i.e., in terms of knowledge and expertise of the labour force, and technological advancements (OECD, 2023c). Other factors affecting MFP also include domestic fiscal policies, foreign direct investment, and their openness to trade ventures (Ahmed & Bhatti, 2020).

Connecting Artificial Intelligence (AI) to Changes in Multi-Factor Productivity (MFP)

Generally speaking, MFP, or TFP can also be viewed as a measure of technical change because such changes can be embedded within the previously mentioned factor inputs. However, in reality, this only reflects disembodied technological change, which are the changes that are incorporated within these factor inputs that lead to spillovers from production factors, and better management practices and organizational changes (OECD, 2023b). At the turn of the 21st century, Information and Communications Technology (ICT), the Internet of Things (IoT), and AI have been the primary cause of the growth in labour productivity, because it fosters a more significant reallocation of resources across industries. The increased use of AI in the manufacturing sector, as well as its integration into the business, finance, and trade sectors, amongst others, have led to productivity gains and higher MFP gains (Zhong et al., 2023).

The creation of AI-based systems such as generative and language models developed by Open AI within the last decade, has led to the growth of industrial intelligence, i.e., where AI is integrated into the industry to improve the efficiency of the industrial process, and the products produced. The integration of AI into the industry, as exhibited by industries in China, has led to not only growth in its MFP but also changed the labour market structure of industries through increased demand for highly skilled workers (An et al., 2022). This is because growing industrial intelligence plays a significant role in reducing labour costs, which are realized when the use of such intelligence researches a high level (Quian & Wang, 2022).

In addition, within the literature patents which are issued for AI-based innovations and intellectual property protection, by industries are also noted to have an impact on MFP and earnings. Firms particularly those operating in the areas of Financial technology (fintech) and Small and Medium Enterprises (SMEs) not only had a greater amount of AI patents but also displayed higher levels of MFP, which enabled them to offer their workers higher wages, as the use of AI increased their productivity and contributed to labour retention (Bassetti et al., 2020; Damioli et al., 2021). This is likely to be the case, as fintech firms use a wide array of technologies including blockchain networks, and mobile applications, as well as cryptocurrency that changes both the way services are offered meaning that most tasks become automated, and how the consumer interacts with the products and services offered which are likely to be more personalized and conducted at a faster pace. The development of regional blockchains in China was also likely to positively impact the MFP of firms, however, such an impact was more pronounced amongst firms that operated at their optimal capacity, and who initially had a higher use of blockchain technologies to increase productivity (Cao et al., 2022). Creating an environment which promotes digital inclusive finance improves the MFP of both non-state-owned commercial banks.

Like the finance industry, the increased use of AI by Chinese manufacturing firms has also had a positive impact on their MFP (Zhou & Chen, 2022). The growth in MFP was higher amongst manufacturing firms located along the eastern coast, as opposed to non-coastal areas, because this area had fewer bottlenecks in their labour force, meaning that they had a sufficient number of qualified workers, which sustained production levels, and had higher technology use, which permitted manufacturing firms to assimilate digital forms of technology to improve their productive capacity (Chang et al., 2023). If, however, cities were to implement a Smart City Policy (SCP) and Information Infrastructure Construction Policy (IICP) like, in the case of China, the MFP of firms would grow as it would strengthen the market position of the firm, reduce the development imbalance of firms located in coastal and non-coastal areas in China, and improve employment structures as these policies itself would encourage firms to invest in technological innovations to improve technical efficiency, that may attract investors and skilled workers (Chen, 2022; He et al., 2023). The renewal of real economy enterprises through AI-based technologies, that produce goods and services for sale on the market, can experience growth of their MFP. Although the initial growth in MFP is slow in these enterprises with the introduction of Al-based technologies, after they have surpassed their profitability threshold, their MFP increases considerably allowing them to produce at a higher level of efficiency (Cheng et al., 2023).

The integration of digital technologies into low-carbon strategies to reduce GHG emissions is also a driver of improvements in MFP in the agriculture industry. The move towards creating an economy that is much greener in terms of its resource use, the prioritization of sustainable natural resources and its low carbon development have seen AI technologies playing a great role in accomplishing this (Chen & Zhang 2023). AI's integration in the agricultural industry, for example, helps to optimize the use of resources and crop yields through the automation of its production and marketing process. It not only creates a sustainable means of producing food, environmental regulation, and identifying reliable sources of renewable energy but also advances the growth of agricultural MFP in underdeveloped areas (Vinuesa et al., 2020; Fu & Zhang, 2022). Such improvements have had a positive impact on the MFP of firms in the agricultural industry and have acted as a feedback mechanism, as they encourage firms to accelerate the digital transformation of their firms by using more sophisticated machinery and robotics. This had the dual effect of boosting the MFP created by both the agricultural and finance industries, as greater financial inclusion led to business enterprises gaining more access to the financial resources needed to use green agricultural technologies.

In the context of the green economy, digital improvements across industries and the creation of smart cities, have also led to improvements in Green MFP (Green TFP), i.e., the MFP that considers environmental and resource indicators in its calculation, as it can measure the environmental performance of firms in the context of sustainable development (Rusiawan et al., 2015). Such a positive relationship between the digital economy and green innovations in urban areas has improved MFP in forestry and spillover effects from Green MFP in countries like Indonesia and China (Chen et al., 2023; Fan et al., 2023). Furthermore, the use of green technology while increasing the MFP of business enterprises, simultaneously enforces environmental regulation, as it encourages heavily polluting companies to increase their willingness to engage in corporate social responsibility (CSR) methods that promote a cleaner means of production in the short and long term.

Apart from integrating AI into industries to transform them into smart industries, it is also important to do the same to governing bodies, from the perspective of governance. Creating an institutional framework that is heavily digitalized, i.e., e-governance, is also another positive driver of MFP, as it enables the public services offered by governments, local governments, and micro-state enterprises to be optimized (Li et al., 2023). There are numerous benefits of creating and sustaining a digital government such as providing services 24 hours on any digital platform, increased participation by the public, greater collaboration between state departments, improved efficiency, and reduced labour costs, which enhances MFP by improving technical efficiency and lessening the technological gap.

INTEGRATING AI IN TRINIDAD AND TOBAGO: THE CASE OF THE ENERGY AND MANUFACTURING SECTORS

Artificial Intelligence (AI) has become increasingly important to how many industries operate, because of the positive impact that it has on the MFP. As highlighted in the previous section, the integration of AI-based tools throughout business enterprises in various types of industries, and countries around the world, has led to a significant increase in productivity, innovation, and capital accumulation (An et al., 2022). However, to realize such benefits, industries can assimilate AI to increase their MFP through several means such as investing in AI-based tools and technologies and using AI-powered robotics to further automate their production process. For purposes of this chapter, emphasis will be placed on examining how AI can be integrated with the business entities in the two major revenue earners for Trinidad and Tobago, i.e., the energy sector, and the manufacturing sector, which have contributed 29%, and 17.2% respectively to the Gross Domestic Product (GDP) in 2022 (MPD-CSO, 2023).

Opportunities for Businesses Implementing AI in the Energy Sector

In many countries across the world, inclusive of Trinidad and Tobago, the energy sector is often deemed to be the life force of their economies and industries, as without a functioning energy system, other non-energy industries would not be sustainable. Trinidad and Tobago's energy sector's primary source of non-renewable energy is that of natural gas, and petroleum, and is comprised of extractive, processing, and downstream business entities. The efficient operation of the energy industry has a significant impact on Trinidad and Tobago's economy because it is not only viewed as an important stimulus for job creation, but also for boosting economic activity, promoting energy efficiency, encouraging foreign direct investment in local business entities, and most importantly for generating revenue (Ounmaa, 2021).

Notwithstanding the importance of the energy sector to the survival of Trinidad and Tobago's economy, extractive industries tend to do a great deal of harm to the environment, and society, by contributing to the pollution of the environment through the dumping of toxic waste, polluting underground reservoirs, and GHG emissions, that exacerbate changes in the climate (UN, 2021). Although, much larger countries like China, the United States (US), India, and EU27 are the largest net emitters of GHGs, smaller countries like Trinidad and Tobago also contribute (0.09% in

2022) to the world's total emissions, and therefore have a responsibility to reduce its emissions (Crippa et al., 2023). When used properly, AI can be an effective tool to aid in the reduction of emissions as network analyses, neural networks, machine learning algorithms, deep learning models and opensource programs like eco2AI, can be used by Trinidad and Tobago's energy sector to calculate and forecast its carbon emissions (Gaur et al., 2023; Budennyy et al., 2022). This information can then be used to design and implement policies to reduce its overall carbon footprint. A case study investigating the socio-economic impact of climate change on the energy sector in Trinidad and Tobago and the Caribbean region as a whole, by Martin et al., (2013), used an Artificial Neural Network to examine this impact, and in doing do found that if the energy sector is restructured then this would lead to a significant reduction in per capita CO2 emissions, as more than 50% of electricity generated will be from renewable sources.

AI can also be used in Trinidad and Tobago's energy sector to optimize both its decision-making process, and its energy grids, by managing the flow of energy used by households, as well as both the public and private sector businesses, while detecting faults in the power system network, to reduce energy waste and disruptions in power supply (Szczepaniuk & Szczepaniuk, 2023). To do this, power-generating companies in Trinidad and Tobago can use AI to collect data from these energy grids by using smart grids, renewable grids, and super grid infrastructure, and use the information collected by these grids to perform data analytics, to design better power use frameworks that can save energy, and to detect weaknesses in the power system network that can be vulnerable to cyberattacks (Ahmad et al., 2021). The use of AI, together with machine learning tools, and metaheuristic algorithms has the potential to optimize the entire value chain of the energy sector by improving energy generation, distribution, consumption, and trading of energy (Franki et al., 2023). One case study which looked at the use of Neural Networks by Shell Trinidad and the Gulf of Mexico offshore fields to predict logs using drilling and mudlogging data has provided a more accurate representation of the data used by conventional logging systems, leading to the production of higher resolution logs and drilling optimization (Gan et al., 2019). Aming (2021), goes on to explain that AI, and ML technologies can also be used to minimize geological and geotechnical risks in the Exploration and Production (E&P) Operations conducted by Petroleum companies in Trinidad and Tobago.

Focusing on the latter area of Energy Trading, AI can be used to make energy trading more efficient, by forecasting data on energy demands and prices, that can be supplied to Trinidad and Tobago's energy trading partners and companies alike, to assist them in their decisions as to when to buy and sell energy. As the demand for energy in Trinidad and Tobago grows, AI can be used to help with the coordination and supply management, so in instances where there are unfavourable weather and production conditions, AI can detect these issues and suggest alternative forms of energy such as renewable energies and biofuels, that can be used to supplement energy demands and consumption (Mahmoud & Slama, 2023). To aid in energy trading and supply management, energy companies can use generative AI to generate data to be used to train machine learning models, and block-chain peer-to-peer (P2P) energy trading with smart grids and microgrids, to operationalize efficiency and use of energy in Trinidad and Tobago (Singh et al., 2022). Such improvements to energy trading can enable consumers and producers to exchange energy in real-time on the energy market, which improves the resilience of the energy system while encouraging the use of renewable forms of energy. Developing countries with similar economies like Trinidad and Tobago have employed smart grids and have enhanced their energy generation, by monitoring energy use, and mitigating against unauthorized power connections (Raihan, 2023).

AI can be used to help energy providers in Trinidad and Tobago to become more knowledgeable about the use of energy by its customers, and to reduce their consumption and usage habits. Further to this, in an economy which has been traditionally powered by petroleum and natural gas, active customer engagement, will also aid domestic providers in Trinidad and Tobago to easily integrate renewable forms of energy on a large scale by using virtual power plants (VPPs) to shift the perception and acceptance of customers of renewable energy (Behi et al., 2021). Such plants are likely to help providers engage customers, while monitoring, and managing the use of renewable energy particularly solar energy (photovoltaic solar energy, solar thermal energy, and concentrated solar power), hydropower (hydroelectric dams, wave power and tidal power) systems, and even the use of alternate forms of transportation such as electric vehicles (Ullah et al., 2018). A case study developed by Hosein et al., (2020) showed that Neural network models can be used to predict the Renewable Energy (RN) targets for Trinidad and Tobago (10%), which can be met by increasing the price of electricity domestically, whose surplus revenue can be diverted into investments in renewable energy sources.

Opportunities for Businesses Implementing AI in the Manufacturing Sector

Like the energy sector, the manufacturing sector plays an important role in revenue generation in Trinidad and Tobago, and as a result, the use of AI across the manufacturing value chain has the potential to revolutionize the industry. There are several ways in which AI can be used in the manufacturing industry, such as predictive maintenance (PdM) through the use of sensing technologies, machine/deep learning, cyber-physical systems, industrial Internet of Things (IoT), and visual analytics (Cheng et al., 2022).

In the case of the latter, AI-based technology can collect data to help domestic manufacturers in Trinidad and Tobago forecast the occurrence of potential equipment failure so that maintenance can be done before it occurs. Thus, reducing long-term damage to machines, efficiency, and financial losses, while minimizing machine downtime (Achouch et al., 2022). In this regard, AI can be a useful tool in planning and production floor operations where smart manufacturing machines can be self-optimizing, as they use predictive maintenance to detect defects and schedule their maintenance (Nacchia et al., 2021). Although many Small and Medium Enterprises (SMEs) within developing countries and countries with similar economies like Trinidad and Tobago have encountered delays in implementing intelligent manufacturing, when implemented have increased the value of manufacturing firms through improved flexibility, efficiency, reliability, and Speed to Market (Atieh, et al., 2023).

Apart from detecting problems with manufacturing equipment, AI can also help manufacturers in Trinidad and Tobago to detect deformities in the products produced along the production line, by using imaging processing techniques. The automation of such an inspection throughout the production process can assist in improving quality control so that the end product is of high quality. This has led to the term quality 4.0 being associated with the digitization of the manufacturing industry, where these industries adopt cloud-based innovations such as AI-powered root cause analysis, to clear up any hidden quality issues cost-effectively and comprehensively (Javaid et al., 2021). Further automation of complex tasks, together with the use of robotics in the manufacturing of products also reduces the need for human intervention, as robots can operate continuously with the potential of making fewer mistakes, and errors, than human workers (Sahoo & Lo, 2022). The investment into automation technologies for smart production such as Computer Vision like Google Cloud Visual Inspection AI, Biometrics, Robotics, and Robotic Process Automation (RPA), will undoubtedly transition the traditional manufacturing processes, into one which is much smarter, efficient, and can handle high-volume processes (Chakraborty et al., 2023). According to King & Rameshwar (2017), local manufacturing firms in Trinidad and Tobago have already begun implementing elements of industry 4.0 technologies into their operation, through the use of cloud computing, smart sensors, systems integration, multilevel customer interaction and profiling, autonomous robots, location detection, and IoT platforms.

Different types of AI like AI Sensors with IoT, Machine Learning, Augmented reality, and Deep Neural Networks, can also assist in Supply Chain Management in the domestic manufacturing sector, by collecting data on their observations of consumer demand patterns in Trinidad and Tobago (Fasso et al., 2021). When data analytics is conducted using this data it can provide manufacturers with information on the tastes and preferences of consumers that they can then use to forecast the demand for their best-selling products and simulate outcomes to optimize their inventory (Rizvi et al., 2021). While using the information on poorly performing products to engage in new product development and the reformulation of old products to meet the needs of specific consumer groups that demand these products (Liu et al., 2020). Further to this, Sangster et al., (2016) explain that the Advanced Manufacturing Technologies used by domestic manufacturers in Trinidad and Tobago such as Programmable Logic Control Machines, and High-Speed Machining have not only increased the competitive advantage of their company, but also given them a higher level of competitive advantage, increased efficiency, flexibility, and quality.

Challenges and Solutions for Businesses Implementing AI in both the Energy and Manufacturing Sectors

Notwithstanding the many benefits of implementing AI-based technologies by businesses operating in the energy sector, the challenge remains, however, that Trinidad and Tobago's energy sector may not have the capacity to implement such AI models as these models consume large amounts of energy to operate effectively, which may increase the level of emissions (Budennyy et al., 2022). Further to this, for AI systems to make effective and informed decisions, large amounts of high-quality data are needed to train models. Unfortunately, the non-availability of such data may become a barrier as countries like Trinidad and Tobago have limited capacity and resources to collect and manage data.

The exorbitant cost of implementing a smart power grid system, as well as establishing industrywide data-sharing practices and outdated infrastructure may prevent businesses from accessing and using AI tools. The main complication of energy trading is that the use of different P2P trading schemes like microgrid P2P, intra-microgrid P2P, Peer microgrid and centralized or hybrid markets, may encourage bias and inequitable use and sharing of assets (Yap et al., 2021). Businesses operating in the manufacturing sector in Trinidad and Tobago, like that of India, may also experience similar challenges in implementing AI, some of which include high implementation costs associated with investing in new hardware and software to support AI systems, the merging of multiple manufacturing databases may not be possible as they use different systems to collect data, the lack of human resources (skills and training) to support the integration of AI systems (Sony et al., 2021; Sharma et al., 2022).

To address these challenges, businesses within both the energy and manufacturing sectors are using AI-based technologies by investing and modernizing the Information and Communications (ICT) infrastructure used, so that it can easily accommodate the integration of AI. By investing in more technologically advanced tools and applications businesses in Trinidad and Tobago will be better able to collect high-quality and representative data. At the same time, businesses also need to invest in the training of their workers using AI training programmes, to not only use AI tools but also troubleshoot any issues that may arise. Moreover, given that the legislative framework for the used of AI in developing countries like Palestine is ineffective at dealing with and keeping pace with the advancement of the technologies, emphasis should be placed on developing a legal framework and strategy for the use and implementation of AI in Trinidad and Tobago at the national level (Demaidi, 2023). In this regard, governments need to understand the challenges experienced by individual sectors and design appropriate mitigation strategies to deal with problems by partnering with AI implementation agencies, development partners and research organizations to identify and develop AI-based business models that are sustainable (Donahue, 2019).

ARTIFICIAL INTELLIGENCE (AI) AND LABOR MARKET PRODUCTIVITY IN TRINIDAD AND TOBAGO

The Impact of AI on Trinidad and Tobago's Labor Market

The impact that AI has on the labour market of countries around the world is a topic which has been discussed quite extensively because the integration of AI-based technologies within industries has demonstrated its ability to optimize both plant and human resources to the point that it has a positive effect on the MFP, it can be both a blessing and a curse. In that while the integration of AI technologies is no doubt advantageous in terms of boosting human productivity, critical thinking, and job satisfaction, it can also displace workers, and accelerate income inequality. Thus, for this chapter, emphasis will be placed on discussing both the positive and negative effects of the key aspects of AI in Trinidad and Tobago's labour market.

Job Creation and Displacement

The increased use of AI is expected to have a profound effect on the job market in Trinidad and Tobago because as it replaces some jobs due to the automation of tasks, there are new jobs to be created. However, the impact that this has on job creation, depends on a multitude of factors such as the pace at which industries in Trinidad and Tobago can adapt to these AI-based technologies, the type of the industry itself, as well as the skill level of the workers and their ability to use AI. For this reason, it is expected that even though many industries in Trinidad and Tobago in the areas of finance, healthcare, manufacturing, energy and retail, can embrace AI in their production process by hiring engineers, production managers, and business developers, who specialize in AI, and AI-based tools, like robotics, natural language processing, and machine learning, the amount of job creation taking place may be concentrated on AI-based occupations (Albanesi et al., 2023). Thus, industries may target their job openings to younger highly skilled workers, who may be more likely to adapt faster to the changes in the technological environment than semi-skilled and unskilled workers, who along with their AI-relevant skills, have a high level of cognition and creative problem-solving skills (soft skills) (Manca, 2023).

In addition, while global digital platforms continue to grow at a rapid pace, the use of digital technologies is also likely to encourage the growth of gig work and the expansion of the domestic gig economy. This allows countries like Trinidad and Tobago in the Global South to become part of the global outsourcing industry as key digital suppliers of labour through online platforms to business entities around the world regardless of their location (Fietz & Jann, 2023; Le Ludec et al., 2023). Furthermore, AI may also help to make more visible, the invisible workforce, i.e., persons who work remotely from their homes through their digital devices, or in factory-like workplaces in the technology industry, who are underpaid, and whose work goes unacknowledged (Gilbert, 2023). Through the use of AI, the growth in the exposure of the invisible workforce may legitimize their occupations, while reducing their inherent precarity and inequalities.

As technological progress continues to accelerate at a fast rate, the increased demand for highly skilled and knowledgeable workers is also likely to contribute to the changes in the labour market in Trinidad and Tobago. As a result of this, workers have to invest in their upskilling so that they do not become displaced by the integration of AI in domestic industries. There are however, several challenges that may occur, in that current workers may become resistant to such training as it signals that there will be changes in the way businesses operate domestically in Trinidad and Tobago, and it may deepen inequalities between workers as the cost of such training may be costly and not be accessible to low-income workers and workers whose employers are unwilling to cover the financial costs of upskilling particularly if their jobs are less exposed to automation and AI (Anger et al., 2023).

Further to this, despite the benefits of Language Learning Models (LLMs) to the working environment in Trinidad and Tobago, the use of GPT Chat to increase productivity and quality of the service provided, can cause significant disruptions in the current labour market across all wage levels, with higher paying jobs having the potential to be more affected (Ayoub et al., 2023; Eloundou et al., 2023). Such disruptions can include the augmentation of white-collar jobs such as tellers, bookkeeping, accounting, auditing clerks, legal and administrative assistants, as well as insurance underwriters, biomedical engineers, and database administrators, through generative AI-based tools like ChatGPT (Chelliah, 2017; WEF, 2023). Transformative digitalization in these particular occupations and the industries in which they are concentrated can enhance the productivity of current and future workers, as the tasks of these workers can be transformed rather than becoming fully automated (Carbonero et al., 2023).

In comparison, the displacement of workers by AI often depends on the occupation itself, as some occupations like credit authorizers, telemarketers, information and file clerks, and management analysts are more prone to destructive digitalization than others as they can be easily automated (Carbonero et al., 2023; WEF, 2023). The increased use of digital labour through the integration of AI bots for example during current and subsequent waves of advanced automation can displace workers in the types of occupations as they are routine and repetitive tasks that do not require a great deal of interpersonal communication (Zhang, 2022). The continued automation of these occupations and AI innovations in Trinidad and Tobago, may reduce the share of national income produced by the labour market, encourage the growth of income inequality among workers, and give rise to technological unemployment (Mutascu & Hegerty, 2023). The aforementioned inequality however depends on the workers' education and skill level, and their field of training, as highly educated and skilled workers for example in the fields of finance, engineering, law and medicine may be more vulnerable to AI (OECD, 2023d).

Legislation and Trade Union Representation

Another contentious issue in which AI is likely to affect the labour market is the regulation of AI through legislation. The use of AI can become a threat to the safety and security of workers, as the fragmented nature of data protection legislation in Trinidad and Tobago may not be adept at dealing with the risks associated with AI algorithms, as the Data Protection Act (DPA) Chapter 22:04 of 2011 while treating with the protection of personal data/information collected and processed by public and private sector entities, have neither enacted several aspects of the act concerning its enforcement nor made any provisions concerning the use of AI in business operations (MAGLA, 2016). This is a critical issue because the use of AI in the decision-making process of businesses if not transparent, can create a host of problems concerning the discrimination of workers, the unfair treatment of workers, the privacy of workers' personal information, ethical and security issues which can serve to amplify existing inequalities amongst workers, and undermine their fundamental rights to work (Aloisi & De Stefano, 2023).

Apart from the many benefits that AI is likely to have on Trinidad and Tobago's labour market, it is also important to discuss how such an engagement with AI and digital technologies influences the trade union movement in terms of its representation of workers. If trade unions in Trinidad and Tobago were to persistently engage with technology, particularly through social media, to organize and strengthen their membership, increase trade union membership and activism, and engage in a more organized form of industrial action, while supporting international trade union bodies (Geelan, 2021). However, the use of digital technologies to aid trade unions' representation and engagement with members is not without challenges as anti-union employers may retaliate against unionized employees who engage in online protest activities, and trade unions' websites and social media accounts may become prone to cyber-attacks.

For trade unions, with the growing integration of AI tools in the workplace, emphasis ought to be placed on ensuring that employers have effective data protection mechanisms in place to maintain the privacy of unionized workers' personal information as AI-based Human Resource (HR) systems may discriminate against workers if trained using discriminatory datasets (Krzywdzinski et al., 2023). Furthermore, the use of some HR processes through algorithmic management, to automate some aspects of the managerial decision-making process about the working conditions of the business environment, can become a major risk to employees as these systems collect information on their attributes from not only their keyboard movements but also wearable devices like ID-badges with built-in microphones, which violates workers right to privacy at work (Hassel & Ozkiziltan, 2023). Thus, these issues serve as an important point of reference as trade union representation is needed to deal with the direct risks associated with the use of AI by employers.

Ethical Considerations and Societal Impacts of AI Integration

As AI technologies continue to advance, the issue of ethics with AI is becoming increasingly connected because of the ethical issues that it raises. Although within the literature such issues are not new, but rather the same ethical dilemmas that are now being examined from a different perspective, i.e., AI-based technologies, these systems do indeed raise a multitude of issues concerning algorithmic bias, accountability and liability, and privacy, as well as several negative societal impacts such as job displacement, privacy concerns, bias and discrimination and social inequality (Niederman & Baker, 2022).

In particular, AI-based systems can exhibit biases that reflect the prejudices that exist within society. For example, in the human resource sector, although the use of AI could improve how potential employees are screened for jobs, if the underlying data used by AI models are skewed, meaning that they are influenced by human bias during the collection and input of the data, then this may create errors in the algorithm output (Saslow & Lorenz, 2019). As a result, this may lead to the discrimination and wrongful displacement of both current and potential workers from particular ethnic groups (Mujtaba & Mahapatra, 2019). The use of computational models and frameworks such as the ClosedLoops method, reweighting methods, independent auditing, and targeted data collection can be used to detect and mitigate against such bias by including sensitive features like that of ethnicity (Carol et al., 2022). By using these strategies, it reduces the risk of bias, while ensuring fair and equitable outcomes for all workers.

The use of AI can impact the privacy of workers in a variety of ways. Depending on how AI-based tools like employee monitoring systems, automated decision-making systems, and predictive analysis are used, although it may initially improve the skills and productivity of the worker, it can also compromise their privacy (Farhan, 2023). The constant monitoring of employees' physical movement, and email use within the workplace without their consent can not only reduce the perceived autonomy of workers and their sense of identity but also the transparency of job assessments during the hiring and promotion process (Mirbabaie et al., 2022). Further to this, the use of Open AI platforms and tools like TensorFlow, OpenCV, and PyTorch by employers can expose sensitive employee data, increase their risk of malicious activities such as cyber-attacks, and collect employee data without their consent. In light of these issues, changes in the legislation of countries like the US regarding electronic discovery or e-discovery using a two-tiered model of electronic discovery, to prevent employers from abusing technologies used in the workplace, while maintaining employee privacy (Kim, 2006). Apart from legislative changes, employee awareness and training programs on cybersecurity, together with the creation of a robust data privacy framework within the workplace to handle data, and respond to cybersecurity breaches (Jamal et al., 2024).

Finally, the implementation of ethical guidelines to ensure the use of AI-based technologies within the workplace can also maintain the privacy and security of employee data. The Guidelines such as the Montreal Declaration for Responsible Development of Artificial Intelligence in Canada and the Ethical Guidelines for Trustworthy AI in Europe often include set protocols to help protect employees from the potential harms of using AI-based technologies such as privacy and human rights violations, algorithmic biases and the misuse of data, by making employees aware of the risks and limitations of using such technologies (Vesnic-Alujevic et al., 2020). In this way, the use of ethical guidelines is more likely to ensure that the use of AI-based technologies and the output produced is better aligned with the socio-economic norms of the society (Gupta, 2023). Thus reducing discriminatory outcomes, and any social inequality that persons who do not either have access or limited access to technology may experience.

AI AND THE FUTURE OF WORK IN TRINIDAD AND TOBAGO

Bearing in mind the current impacts that the use of AI is likely to have on the labour market in Trinidad and Tobago and the issue of ethics, it is expected that as advancements in AI-based tools continue to evolve, it will have a significant impact on the future of work. AI is anticipated to influence the future of work is similar to what has been discussed earlier, in terms of job losses from automation, job creation in areas related to AI and data science, as well as innovation and productivity gains from the augmentation of human work, improvement in working conditions and the upskilling of workers. Despite these benefits, Trinidad and Tobago's labour market, and industries alike may encounter several challenges when integrating AI-based tools into their production process, which may limit the impact that AI has on the MFP of these industries.

In the case of Trinidad and Tobago, socio-economic issues in the areas of national security, healthcare, education, and the provision of public services may detract funding allocations away from national digital transformation to these areas. Any decline in financial investment in national digital transformation may worsen technological inequality domestically, as there may be an unequal distribution and access to technology and AI-based tools and digital technologies, by not only low-income households on the individual level but also private and public sector business enterprises at the organizational level, who may not have easy access to funding resources to invest in AI. The result of such unequal access to resources can lead to a decline in productivity and competitiveness of the business sector, reduced opportunities for economic mobility, as well as limited social participation (Dimaggio et al., 2004). In terms of the latter, limited use of the Internet and ownership of computers by low-income households further widens inequality and reduces the social participation of poorer households (Martin, 2003).

The exorbitant costs of implementing AI-based technologies within domestic industries in Trinidad and Tobago may also discourage them from using such technologies as external global funding from corporate entities like IBM, Google, and Amazon are shifting their investment in AI and technology to more economically advanced countries like the US and China, as their industries are already more automated (Alonso et al., 2020). Such a shift in investment to advanced economies can further widen the digital divide between developed and developing countries at the global level because the digital infrastructure in most countries like Trinidad and Tobago is not developed enough to encourage such investments as there is limited use of robotics, AI-based technologies, and the relevant policies to support these investments (Dewan et al., 2005). Thus, countries like Trinidad and Tobago with insufficient digital infrastructure, and capacity for robotics and AI may not experience the same benefits from its use as advanced economies (Carter et al., 2020). This may inadvertently lead to a reduction in the MFP and wages, which may encourage fewer incentives to be made available for robotics and AI in Trinidad and Tobago.

Further to this, given that AI-based systems are typically powered by the data that it is trained on, the lack of access to data may simply not be attainable, because domestic industries in Trinidad and Tobago may not have the capacity and technical know-how to collect, copy and edit such data. Apart from domestic industries, to fully transition to smart AI-based industries, the government of Trinidad and Tobago also needs to not only allocate resources for digital transformation, but also put regulations such as privacy laws which deal specifically with AI, in place that ease the access to data, and maintain privacy (Bak et al., 2022).

Depending on how and the type of data that is collected, it can also bring up intellectual property and regulatory issues, through the duplication of copyright material without consent, and the outsourcing of AI research to commercial entities that may not have the necessary infrastructure in place to secure the privacy of the data collected. This can lead AI models to develop inaccurate output, as the data used to train models may lack diversity, and may be biased towards certain groups of persons, which can lead to discrimination (Mannuru et al., 2023). Further to this, in cases where there are massive datasets available to train AI for Big Data Analytics, new issues such as the ownership and manipulation of such data come to light as it presents an important concern for safety, security, and ethics (Wakunuma et al., 2020).

ARTIFICIAL INTELLIGENCE AND ECONOMIC GROWTH

As discussed earlier, AI has the potential to significantly improve the total and multi-factor productivity across Trinidad and Tobago's economy, which can influence the growth and productivity of not only the major revenue generators like the energy and manufacturing sectors but a wide range of industries. Within the literature, several studies have shown that the integration of AI within the economy has great potential to generate higher rates of economic growth in the long run, but also that of sustainable development through its labour (labour employment and income effects), capital (capital accumulation and structure effect) and production technology (technological progress and efficiency effect) factors (Xu, 2022).

Several countries' studies done around the world have shown how they have harnessed AI to stimulate economic growth through its labour, capital, and production technology of different industries, such as Bilal et al., (2022), demonstrate that the use of AI-based electric vehicle charging stations in India has not only reduced optimization costs, but also its environmental impact. Satishkumar et al., (2023) have explained that in countries like India where 25% of its domestic revenue is generated by its Agricultural sector, the use of image processing and deep learning have played a pivotal role in the detection, classification, and treatment of diseases amongst crops, which reduces the crop losses, increases crop yields, while conserving resources.

These studies together with those highlighted on the opportunities that AI presents for businesses in the manufacturing and energy sector in Trinidad and Tobago, demonstrate that AI has the potential to drive economic growth across many industries by enhancing its productive capacity and generating solutions to industry problems. As highlighted earlier the use of generative AI within industries has major economic effects from driving labour costs down and raising productivity, but also resolving communication barriers between humans and machinery, higher probability for the occurrence of a productivity boom through job creation, upskilling, and greater job productivity of non-displaced workers (Hatzius et al., 2023). Furthermore, AI has the potential to improve green economic growth, like in countries like China, and Indonesia, in the long run by encouraging businesses to implement green supply chain practices, and use environmental technologies to reduce CO2 emissions (Abbas et al., 2019; Chen et al., 2022).

Although AI has great potential to improve the economic growth rates of Trinidad and Tobago, some of its limitations discussed earlier such as the lack of high-quality data, algorithmic bias, lack of transparency, regulatory and legislative problems, high implementation costs, as well as issues surrounding the displacement of workers, as well as privacy and security, all have the potential to hinder the trust in AI systems (Solodkyi & Polishchuk, 2023). This is primarily the case because AI can cause economic disruptions, encouraging the growth of inequality, by favouring high-income earners and boosting the capital returns of firms that can invest in AI (Cornelli et al., 2023). In light of these issues, it is important that governments also address the negative implications that AI is likely to have on economic growth by implementing mitigation strategies. Some of these strategies/recommendations include the creation of not only safety nets for vulnerable workers but also retraining programmes for those who have become displaced. Ensuring that the data used to train AI-based systems promotes Equity, Diversity and Inclusion (EDI) of all persons (diverse representation, as well as the use of Smart Information Sytems (SIS) and Fairness metrics to detect when there is a high likelihood of algorithmic biased and job destruction taking place can be used (Ryan et al., 2020; Wachter et al., 2021). Finally, using AI-based technologies as a job-creating mechanism, and implementing regulations and policies that ensure that AI systems are not only accountable but also transparent, can improve the societal benefit of AI (Ernst 2022).

CONCLUSION

The integration of AI-based technologies in manufacturing, energy, and other domestic industries in Trinidad and Tobago because the proper use of these technologies has the potential to significantly improve the MFP of these industries by boosting their overall productivity and efficiency. Investment in AI is important to countries like Trinidad and Tobago because it is expected to have a positive impact on both the economy and the labour market, as AI can help public and private sector business enterprises in specific industries design and offer innovative products and services that can increase productivity. Furthermore, with the assistance of AI domestic industries can come up with innovative solutions to the challenges that they experience to transform the industry.

The adoption of AI-based technologies, however, can also create many issues and concerns as Trinidad and Tobago may not have the financial capacity, and technical know-how to invest in AI as the AI-based systems, and techniques used in industries in the areas of energy and manufacturing are quite costly. In addition to this, from a legislative perspective, the data protection, intellectual property, and freedom of information acts of Trinidad and Tobago have neither been enacted, nor harmonized with the data protection laws around the world. The lack of such harmonization and regulation may deter businesses from investing in AI, which may reduce the productivity, competitiveness and market power of local industries which can all contribute to the erosion of its MFP.

Competing Interests: The author of this publication declares there are no competing interests.

Funding: This research received no specific grant from any funding agency in the public, commercial, or not-for-profit sectors. Funding for this research was covered by the author of the article.

REFERENCES

Abbas, B., Razak, A. A., & Wekke, I. S. (2019). Investigating green supply chain practices for economic growth. *Uncertain Supply Chain Management*, 783–792. doi:10.5267/j.uscm.2019.1.002

Achouch, M., Dimitrova, M., Ziane, K., Sattarpanah Karganroudi, S., Dhouib, R., Ibrahim, H., & Adda, M. (2022). On Predictive Maintenance in Industry 4.0: Overview, Models, and Challenges. *Applied Sciences (Basel, Switzerland)*, *12*(8081), 1–22. doi:10.3390/app12168081

Ahmad, T., Zhang, D., Huang, C., Zhang, H., Dai, N., Song, Y., & Chen, H. (2021). Artificial intelligence in sustainable energy industry: Status Quo, challenges, and opportunities. *Journal of Cleaner Production*, *289*(125834), 1–65. doi:10.1016/j.jclepro.2021.125834

Ahmed, T., & Bhatti, A. (2020). Measurement and Determinants of Multi-factor productivity: A Survey of the Literature. *Journal of Economic Surveys*, *34*(2), 293–319. doi:10.1111/joes.12360

Ai, X.-N., Gao, S.-J., Li, W.-M., & Liao, H. (2023). Greening China: Environmentally adjusted multifactor productivity in the last four decades. *Resources, Conservation and Recycling*, *192*(106918), 106918. Advance online publication. doi:10.1016/j.resconrec.2023.106918

Albanesi, S., da Silva, A. D., Jimeno, J. F., Lamo, A., & Wabitsch, A. (2023). *New Technologies and Jobs in Europe*. National Bureau of Economic Research (NBER), Cambridge, Massachusetts, United States. https://www.nber.org/papers/w31357

Aloisi, A., & De Stefano, V. (2023). Between risk mitigation and labour rights enforcement: Assessing the transatlantic race to govern AI-driven decision making through a comparative lens. *European Labour Law Journal*, *14*(2), 283–307. doi:10.1177/20319525231167982

Alonso, C., Kothari, S., & Rehman, S. (2020). How Artificial Intelligence Could Widen the Gap Between Rich and Poor Nations. International Monetary Fund (IMF). https://www.imf.org/en/Blogs/Articles/2020/12/02/blog-how-artificial-intelligence-could-widen-the-gap-between-rich-and-poor-nations

Altman, S. (2023). *Planning for AGI and beyond.* Open AI. https://openai.com/blog/planning-for-agi-and-beyond

Aming, A. (2021). Artificial Intelligence AI / Machine Learning ML Drives Increased Capital Efficiency and Minimizes Geological Risk in E&P Operations. Paper presented at the SPE Trinidad and Tobago Section Energy Resources Conference. 10.2118/200978-MS

An, K., Shan, Y., & Shi, S. (2022). Impact of Industrial Intelligence on Total Factor Productivity. *Sustainability (Basel)*, *14*(14535), 1–21. doi:10.3390/su142114535

Andrychowicz, M., Wolski, F., Ray, A., Schneider, J., Fong, R., Welinder, P., McGrew, B., Tobin, J., Abbeel, P., & Zaremba, W. (2018). *Highlight Experience Replay.* Cornell University, arXiv:1707.01495v3, 1-15. doi: /arXiv.1707.01495 doi:10.48550

Anger, S., Hess, P., Janssen, S., & Leber, U. (2023). Chapter 14 Employment-Related Further Traning in a Dynamic Labour Market. In S.Weinertetal.(Eds.), Education, Competence Development and Career Trajectories, Methodology of Educational Measurement and Assessment (pp. 319-336). Springer Nature, Switzerland, AG. doi:10.1007/978-3-031-27007-9_14

Apostolides, A. (2008). A Primer on Multifactor Productivity: Description, Benefits, and Uses. Bureau of Transportation Statistics. https://www7.bts.dot.gov/sites/bts.dot.gov/files/docs/browse-statistical-products-and-data/bts-publications/201991/multifactor-productivity.pdf

Atieh, A. M., Cooke, K. O., & Osiyevskyy, O. (2023). The role of intelligent manufacturing systems in the implementation of Industry 4.0 by small and medium enterprises in developing countries. *Engineering Reports*, *5*(3), e12578. doi:10.1002/eng2.12578

AyoubT. Y.AmamiA.HachaichiY. (2023). Expectations of AI Economic Impact & Giant AI Experiments: Case of Chat GPT 3.5. *Research Gate,* 1-9. doi:10.13140/RG.2.2.31305.62565

Bak, M., Madai, V. I., Fritzsche, M.-C., Mayrhofer, M. T., & McLennan, S. (2022). You Can't Have AI Both Ways: Balancing Health Data Privacy and Access Fairly. *Frontiers in Genetics*, *13*(929453), 1–7. doi:10.3389/fgene.2022.929453 PMID:35769991

Bassetti, T., Borbon Galvez, Y., Del Sorbo, M., & Pavesi, F. (2020). Artificial Intelligence – impact on total factor productivity, e-commerce & and fintech. [EU]. *European Union.* Advance online publication. doi:10.2760/333292

Behi, B., Arefi, A., Jennings, P., Gorjy, A., & Pivrikas, A. (2021). Advanced Monitoring and Control System for Virtual Power Plants for Enabling Customer Engagement and Market Participation. *Energies*, *14*(4), 1–14. doi:10.3390/en14041113

Bilal, M., Alsaidan, I., Alaraj, M., Almasoudi, F. M., & Rizwan, M. M. (2022). Techno-Economic and Environmental Analysis of Grid-Connected Electric Vehicle Charging Station Using AI-Based Algorithm. *Mathematics*, *10*(6), 924. doi:10.3390/math10060924

Brandolini, A., & Cipollone, P. (2001). *Multifactor Productivity and Labour Quality in Italy, 1981-2000*. Bank of Italy.

Brockman, G., Cheung, V., Pettersson, L., Schneider, J., Schulman, J., Tang, J., & Zaremba, W. (2016). *OpenAI Gym*. Cornell University, arXiv preprint: 1606.01540v1, 1-4. doi: /arXiv.1606.01540 doi:10.48550

Budennyy, S. A., Lazarev, V. D., Zakharenko, N. N., Korovin, A. N., Plosskaya, O. A., Dimitrov, D. V., Akhripkin, V. S., Pavlov, I. V., Oseledets, I. V., Barsola, I. S., Egorov, I. V., Kosterina, A. A., & Zhukov, L. E. (2022). eco2AI: Carbon Emissions Tracking of Machine Learning Models as the First Step Towards Sustainable AI. *Doklady Mathematics, 106*(1), S118–S128. doi:10.1134/S1064562422060230

Cao, Q., Li, J., Zhang, H., Liu, Y., & Luo, X. (2022). Blockchain and Firm Total Factor Productivity: Evidence from China. *Sustainability (Basel), 14*(10165), 1–15. doi:10.3390/su141610165

Carbonero, F., Davies, J., Ernst, E., Fossen, F. M., Samaan, D., & Sorgner, A. (2023). The impact of artificial intelligence on labour markets in developing countries: A new method with an illustration for Lao PDR and urban Viet Nam. *Journal of Evolutionary Economics, 33*(3), 1–30. doi:10.1007/s00191-023-00809-7 PMID:36811092

Carol, J. (2022). *McCall, F.M., DeCaprio, D., & Joseph Gartner, P.* The Measurement and Mitigation of Algorithmic Bias and Unfairness in Healthcare AI Models Developed for the CMS AI Health Outcomes Challenge.

Carter, L., Liu, D., & Cantrell, C. (2020). Exploring the Intersection of the Digital Divide and Artificial Intelligence: A Hermeneutic Literature Review. *AIS Transactions on Human-Computer Interaction, 12*(4), 253–275. doi:10.17705/1thci.00138

Carter, S., Armstrong, Z., Schubert, L., Johnson, I., & Olah, C. (2019). *Exploring Neural Networks with Activation Atlases*. Distill., doi:10.23915/distill.00015

Chadha, B., & Adams, C. (1992). *Growth, Productivity, and the Rate of Return on Capital. International Monetary Fund*. IMF., doi:10.5089/9781451978407.001.A001

Chakraborty, A., Bhattacharyya, S., De, D., Mahmud, M., & Banerjee, J. S. (2023). Intelligent Automation Framework Using AI and RPA: An Introduction. In S. Bhattacharyya, J. S. Banerjee, & D. De (Eds.), *Confluence of Artificial Intelligence and Robotic Process Automation. Smart Innovation, Systems and Technologies, 335*. Springer., doi:10.1007/978-981-19-8296-5_1

Chang, J., Lan, Q., Tang, W., Chen, H., Liu, J., & Duan, Y. (2023). Research on the Impact of Digital Economy on Manufacturing Total Factor Productivity. *Sustainability (Basel), 15*(5683), 1–21. doi:10.3390/su15075683

Chelliah, J. (2017). Will artificial intelligence usurp white-collar jobs? *Human Resource Management International Digest*, *25*(3), 1–3. doi:10.1108/HRMID-11-2016-0152

Chen, H., Ma, Z., Xiao, H., Li, J., & Chen, W. (2023). The Impact of Digital Economy Empowerment on Green Total Factor Productivity in Forestry. *Forests*, 14(1729):1-23. doi:10.3390/f14091729

Chen, M., Radford, A., Child, R., Wu, J., Jun, H., Luan, D., & Sutskever, I. (2020). Generative pretraining from pixels. *In International conference on machine learning*, 1691-1703). PMLR. https://cdn.openai.com/papers/Generative_Pretraining_from_Pixels_V2.pdf

Chen, M., & Zhang L. (2023). The econometric analysis of voluntary environmental regulations and total factor productivity in agribusiness under digitization. *PLoS ONE*, 18(9-e0291637): 1-22. doi:10.1371/journal.pone.0291637

Chen, P. (2022). The impact of smart city pilots on corporate total factor productivity. *Environmental Science and Pollution Research International*, *29*(55), 83155–83168. doi:10.1007/s11356-022-21681-1 PMID:35763146

Chen, S., Sohail, M. T., & Yang, M. (2022). Examining the effects of information and communications technology on green growth and environmental performance, socio-economic and environmental cost of technology generation: A pathway toward environment sustainability. *Frontiers in Psychology*, *13*, 1–9. doi:10.3389/fpsyg.2022.999045 PMID:36172239

Cheng, X., Chaw, J. K., Goh, K. M., Ting, T. T., Sahrani, S., Ahmad, M. N., Abdul Kadir, R., & Ang, M. C. (2022). Systematic Literature Review on Visual Analytics of Predictive Maintenance in the Manufacturing Industry. *Sensors (Basel)*, *22*(6321), 1–16. doi:10.3390/s22176321 PMID:36080780

Cheng, Y., Zhou, X., & Li, Y. (2023). The effect of digital transformation on real economy enterprises' total factor productivity. *International Review of Economics & Finance*, *85*, 488–501. doi:10.1016/j.iref.2023.02.007

Chuchro, R., & Gupta, D. (2017). Game playing with deep q-learning using openai gym. *Semantic Scholar,* 1-6. http://vision.stanford.edu/teaching/cs231n/reports/2017/pdfs/616.pdf

Cornelli, G., Frost, J., & Mishra, S. (2023). Artificial intelligence, services globalisation and income inequality. BIS Working Paper, 1135: 1-35. https://www.bis.org/publ/work1135.pdf

Creswell, A., White, T., Dumoulin, V., Arulkumaran, K., Sengupta, B., & Bharath, A. (2018). Generative Adversarial Networks: An Overview. *IEEE Signal Processing Magazine*, *35*(1), 53–65. doi:10.1109/MSP.2017.2765202

Crippa, M., Guizzardi, D., Pagani, F., Banja, M., Muntean, M., Schaaf E., Becker, W., Monforti-Ferrario, F., Quadrelli, R., Risquez Martin, A., Taghavi-Moharamli, P., Köykkä, J., Grassi, G., Rossi, S., Brandao De Melo, J., Oom, D., Branco, A., San-Miguel, J., & Vignati, E. (2023). GHG emissions of all world countries. European Union (EU), Luxembourg. doi:10.2760/953322

Dale, R. (2021). GPT-3: What's it good for? *Natural Language Engineering*, *27*(1), 113–118. doi:10.1017/S1351324920000601

Damioli, G., Van Roy, V., & Vertesy, D. (2021). The impact of artificial intelligence on labour productivity. *Eurasian Business Review*, *11*(1), 1–25. doi:10.1007/s40821-020-00172-8

Demaidi, M. N. (2023). Artificial intelligence national strategy in a developing country. *AI & Society*, •••, 1–13. doi:10.1007/s00146-023-01779-x

Dewan, S., & Riggins, F. J. (2005). The digital divide: Current and future research directions. *Journal of the Association for Information Systems*, *6*(12), 298–337. doi:10.17705/1jais.00074

Dimaggio, P., Hargittai, E., Celeste, C., & Shafer, S. (2004). Digital inequality: From unequal access to differentiated use. In *Social Inequality* (pp. 355–400). Russell Sage Foundation.

Donahue, M. Z. (2019). Q&A: AI for developing countries must be adaptable and low-cost. SciDev. net-Health.

Eloundou, T., Manning, S., Mishkin, P., & Rock, D. (2023). GPTs are GPTs: An Early Look at the Labor Market Impact Potential of Large Language Models. Cornell University, arXiv:2303.10130v5, 1-36. doi: /arXiv.2303.10130 doi:10.48550

Ernst, E. (2022). The AI trilemma: Saving the planet without ruining our jobs. *Frontiers in Artificial Intelligence*, *5*(886561), 1–20. doi:10.3389/frai.2022.886561 PMID:36337142

Fan, H., Zhang, N., & Su, H. (2023). The effects of smart city construction on urban green total factor productivity: evidence from China. *Economic Research-Ekonomska Istraživanja,* 36(1-2181840): 1-18. doi:10.1080/1331677X.2023.2181840

Farhan, A. (2023). The Impact of Artificial Intelligence on Human Workers. *Journal Of Communication Education.*, *17*(2), 93–104. doi:10.58217/joce-ip.v17i2.350

Fasso Wamba, S., Queiroz, M. M., Guthrie, C., & Braganza, A. (2021). Industry experiences of artificial intelligence (AI): Benefits and challenges in operations and supply chain management. *Production Planning and Control, 1-5*. Advance online publication. doi:10.1080/09537287.2021.1882695

Fietz, K., & Lay, J. (2023). Digitalisation and labour markets in developing countries. German Institute of Global and Area Studies (GIGA), Hamburg. http://hdl.handle.net/10419/272227

Floridi, L., & Chiriatti, M. (2020). GPT-3: Its Nature, Scope, Limits, and Consequences. *Minds and Machines*, *30*(4), 681–694. doi:10.1007/s11023-020-09548-1

Franki, V., Majnarić, D., & Višković, A. (2023). A Comprehensive Review of Artificial Intelligence (AI) Companies in the Power Sector. *Energies*, *16*(1077), 1–35. doi:10.3390/en16031077

Franklin, M. (2018). A simple guide to multi-factor productivity. Office for National Statistics (ONS). https://www.ons.gov.uk/economy/economicoutputandproductivity/productivitymeasures/methodologies/asimpleguidetomultifactorproductivity#multi-factor-productivity

Fu, W., & Zhang, R. (2022). Can Digitalization Levels Affect Agricultural Total Factor Productivity? Evidence From China. *Frontiers in Sustainable Food Systems*, *6*(860780), 1–16. doi:10.3389/fsufs.2022.860780

Furman, J., & Seamans, R. (2019). AI and the Economy. *Innovation Policy and the Economy*, *19*(1), 161–191. doi:10.1086/699936

Gan, T., Kumar, A., Ehiwario, M., Zhang, B., Semroski, C., de Jesus, O., Hoffmann, O., & Yasser, M. (2019). Artificial Intelligent Logs for Formation Evaluation Using Case Studies in the Gulf of Mexico and Trinidad & Tobago. Paper presented at the SPE Annual Technical Conference and Exhibition, Calgary, Alberta, Canada, September 2019. 10.2118/196064-MS

Gaur, L., Afaq, A., Arora, G. K., & Khan, N. (2023). Artificial intelligence for carbon emissions using a system of systems theory. *Ecological Informatics*, *76*(102165), 102165. Advance online publication. doi:10.1016/j.ecoinf.2023.102165

Geelan, T. (2021). Introduction to the Special Issue internet, social media and trade union revitalization: Still behind the digital curve or catching up? *New Technology, Work and Employment*, *36*(2), 123–139. doi:10.1111/ntwe.12205

George, A. S., & George, A. H. (2023). A review of ChatGPT AI's impact on several business sectors. *Partners Universal International Innovation Journal*, *1*(1), 9–23. doi:10.5281/zenodo.7644359

Gilbert, E. (2023). Beyond the usual suspects: Invisible labour(ers) in futures of work. *Geography Compass*, *17*(2, e12675), 1–12. doi:10.1111/gec3.12675

Gray, A. (2017). *5 global problems that AI could help us solve.* World Economic Forum (WEF). https://www.weforum.org/agenda/2017/02/5-global-problems-that-ai-could-help-us-solve/

Gupta, U. G. (2023). How to Bridge the Gap between AI Ethical Guidelines and Responsible Ethical Conduct. *AIMS International Journal of Management*, *17*(1), 41–53. doi:10.26573/2021.17.1.4

Hassel, A., & Ozkiziltan, D. (2023). Governing the work-related risks of AI: Implications for the German government and trade unions. *Transfer: European Review of Labour and Research*, *29*(1), 71–86. doi:10.1177/10242589221147228

Hatzius, J., Briggs, J., Kodnani, D., & Pierdomenico, G. (2023). The Potentially Large Effects of Artificial Intelligence on Economic Growth. Goldman and Sachs.

He, X., Liang, Y., Liang, D., & Deng, H. (2023). The impact of China's information infrastructure construction policy on green total factor productivity: Moving towards a green world. *Environmental Science and Pollution Research International*, *30*(46), 103017–103032. Advance online publication. doi:10.1007/s11356-023-29638-8 PMID:37676455

Hosein, G., Hosein, P., Bahadoorsingh, S., Martinez, R., & Sharma, C. (2020). Predicting Renewable Energy Investment Using Machine Learning. *Energies*, *13*(4494), 1–9. doi:10.3390/en13174494

Jamal, H., Ahmed Algeelani, N., & Al-Sammarraie, N. A. (2024). Safeguarding data privacy: Strategies to counteract internal and external hacking threats. *Computer Science and Information Technology*, *5*(1), 40–48. doi:10.11591/csit.v5i1.p40-48

Javaid, M., Haleem, A., Singh, R. P., & Suman, R. (2021). Significance of Quality 4.0 towards comprehensive enhancement in the manufacturing sector. *Sensors International*, *2*(100109), 1–13. doi:10.1016/j.sintl.2021.100109

Karpathy, A., Abbeel, P., Brockman, G., Chen, P., Cheung, V., Duan, Y., Goodfellow, I., Kingma, D., Ho, J., Houthooft, R., Saliman, T., Schulman, J., Sutskever, I., & Zaremba, W. (2016). *Generative models.* Open AI. https://openai.com/research/generative-models

Kim, E. (2006). The New Electronic Discovery Rules: A Place for Employee Privacy? *The Yale Law Journal*, *115*(6), 1481. doi:10.2307/20455660

King, G. S., & Rameshwar, J. R. (2017). *Stimulating Innovation through Industry 4.0 in a Small Commodity-Based Economy*. SPIM Innovation Summit – Building the Innovation Century.

Krzywdzinski, M., Gerst, D., & Butollo, F. (2023). Promoting human-centred AI in the workplace. Trade Unions and their strategies for regulating the use of AI in Germany. *Transfer: European Review of Labour and Research*, *29*(1), 53–70. doi:10.1177/10242589221142273

Lauraitiene, L., & Vitunskiene, V. (2022). A Theoretical Approach to Measuring Environmentally Sustainable Growth of Agriculture. *Scientific Papers. Series Management, Economic, Engineering in Agriculture and Rural Development*, *22*(1), 371–377.

Le Ludec, C., Cornet, M., & Casilli, A. A. (2023). The problem with annotation. Human labour and outsourcing between France and Madagascar. *Big Data & Society*, *10*(2), 1–13. doi:10.1177/20539517231188723

Li, E., Chen, Q., Zhang, X., & Zhang, C. (2023). Digital Government Development, Local Governments' Attention Distribution and Enterprise Total Factor Productivity: Evidence from China. *Sustainability (Basel)*, *15*(2472), 1–19. doi:10.3390/su15032472

Liu, J., Chang, H., Forrest, J. Y.-L., & Yang, B. (2020). Influence of artificial intelligence on technological innovation: Evidence from the panel data of China's manufacturing sectors. *Technological Forecasting and Social Change*, *158*(120142), 1–11. doi:10.1016/j.techfore.2020.120142

Mahmoud, M., & Slama, S. B. (2023). Peer-to-Peer Energy Trading Case Study Using an AI-Powered Community Energy Management System. *Applied Sciences (Basel, Switzerland)*, *13*(13), 1–19. doi:10.3390/app13137838

Manca, F. (2023). *Six questions about the demand for artificial intelligence skills in labour markets*. OECD., doi:10.1787/ac1bebf0-

Mannuru, N. R., Shahriar, S., Teel, Z. A., Wang, T., Lund, B. D., Tijani, S., Pohboon, C. O., Agbaji, D., Alhassan, J., Galley, J., Kousari, R., Ogbadu-Oladapo, L., Saurav, S. K., Srivastava, A., Tummuru, S. P., Uppala, S., & Vaidya, P. (2023). Artificial intelligence in developing countries: The impact of generative artificial intelligence (AI) technologies for development. *Information Development*, *0*(0), 02666669231200628. Advance online publication. doi:10.1177/02666669231200628

Martín, R., Gomes, C., Alleyne, D., & Phillips, W. (2013). An assessment of the economic and social impacts of climate change on the energy sector in the Caribbean. ECLAC. https://repositorio.cepal.org/server/api/core/bitstreams/59eea92d-9401-4309-a808-b58e7bd2de2a/content

Martin, S. (2003). Is the digital Divide Really Closing? A Critique of Inequality Measurement in A Nation Online. *ITandSociety*, *1*(4), 1–13.

Ministry of Planning and Development (MPD)Central Statistical Office. (CSO). (2023). *National Accounts.* CSO. https://cso.gov.tt/subjects/national-accounts/

Ministry of the Attorney General and Legal Affairs (MAGLA). (2016). Data Protection Act Chapter 22:04 Act 13 of 2011. MAGLA, Port-of-Spain, Trinidad, and Tobago. https://agla.gov.tt/downloads/laws/22.04.pdf

Mirbabaie, M., Brünker, F., Möllmann, N. R., & Stieglitz, S. (2022). The rise of artificial intelligence–understanding the AI identity threat at the workplace. *Electronic Markets*, *32*(1), 73–99. doi:10.1007/s12525-021-00496-x

Mujtaba, D. F., & Mahapatra, N., N. R. (2019). Ethical Considerations in AI-Based Recruitment, *2019 IEEE International Symposium on Technology and Society (ISTAS)*, Medford, MA, USA, 1-7. 10.1109/ISTAS48451.2019.8937920

Mutascu, M., & Hegerty, S. C. (2023). Predicting the contribution of artificial intelligence to unemployment rates: An artificial neural network approach. *Journal of Economics and Finance*, *47*(2), 400–416. doi:10.1007/s12197-023-09616-z

Nacchia, M., Fruggiero, F., Lambiase, A., & Bruton, K. (2021). A Systematic Mapping of the Advancing Use of Machine Learning Techniques for Predictive Maintenance in the Manufacturing Sector. *Applied Sciences (Basel, Switzerland)*, *11*(2546), 1–34. doi:10.3390/app11062546

Nakano, R., Hilton, J., Balaji, S., Wu, J., Ouyang, L., Kim, C., Hesse, C., Jain, S., Kosaraju, V., Saunders, W., & Jiang, X. (2021). *WebGPT: Browser-assisted question-answering with human feedback.* Cornell University, arXiv preprint: 2112.09332, 1-32. https://arxiv.org/pdf/2112.09332.pdf

Niederman, F., & Baker, E. W. (2022). Ethics and AI Issues: Old Container with New Wine? *Information Systems Frontiers*, *25*(1), 9–28. doi:10.1007/s10796-022-10305-1

OpenA. I. (2023a). *About.* Open AI. https://openai.com/about

Open, A. I. (2023b). *OpenAI Charter.* OpenAI. Retrieved from https://openai.com/charter

Open, A. I. (2023c). *Our Structure.* OpenAI. https://openai.com/our-structure

Open, A. I. (2023d). *Research Index.* Open AI. https://openai.com/research

Open, A. I. (2023e). *OpenAL Five defeats Dota 2 world Champions.* OpenAI. https://openai.com/research/openai-five-defeats-dota-2-world-champions

Open, A. I. (2023f). *Introducing ChatGPT.* OpenAI. https://openai.com/blog/chatgpt

Open, A. I. (2023g). *GPT-4 Technical Report.* Cornell University, arXiv:2303.08774v3, 1-100. doi: /arXiv.2303.08774 doi:10.48550

Open, A. I. (2023h). GPT-4. OpenAI. https://openai.com/research/gpt-4

Organization for Economic Co-operation and Development (OECD). (2023a). Multifactor productivity. OECD. https://data.oecd.org/lprdty/multifactor-productivity.htm

Organization for Economic Co-operation and Development (OECD). (2023b). OECD Compendium of Productivity Indicators 2023. OECD. https://www.oecd-ilibrary.org/sites/74623e5b-en/index.html?itemId=/content/publication/74623e5b-en

Organization for Economic Co-operation and Development (OECD). (2023c). Multifactor Productivity. *OECDiLibrary.* doi:10.1787/a40c5025-en

Organization for Economic Co-operation and Development (OECD). (2023d). *OECD Employment Outlook 2023 Artificial Intelligence and the Labour Market.* OECD., doi:10.1787/08785bba-

Ounmaa, L. (2021). What are the socio-economic impacts of an energy transition? United Nations Development Programme (UNDP). https://www.undp.org/eurasia/blog/what-are-socio-economic-impacts-energy-transition

Qian, W., & Wang, Y. (2022). How Do Rising Labor Costs Affect Green Total Factor Productivity? Based on the Industrial Intelligence Perspective. *Sustainability (Basel), 14*(13653), 1–19. doi:10.3390/su142013653

Radford, A. (2018). *Improving language understanding with unsupervised learning.* OpenAI. https://openai.com/research/language-unsupervised

Radford, A., Narasimhan, K., Salimans, T., & Sutskever, I. (2018). *Improving language understanding by generative pre-training.* OpenAI. https://cdn.openai.com/research-covers/language-unsupervised/language_understanding_paper.pdf

Raihan, A. (2023). A comprehensive review of artificial intelligence and machine learning applications in the energy sector. *Journal of Technology Innovations and Energy*, *2*(4), 1–26. doi:10.56556/jtie.v2i4.608

Ramesh, A., Pavlov, M., Goh, G., & Gray, S. (2021). *DALL-E: Creating images from text.* OpenAI. https://openai.com/research/dall-e

Rizvi, A. T., Haleem, A., Bahl, S., & Javaid, M. (2021). Artificial Intelligence (AI) and Its Applications in Indian Manufacturing: A Review. In S. K. Acharya & D. P. Mishra (Eds.), *Current Advances in Mechanical Engineering. Lecture Notes in Mechanical Engineering*. Springer., doi:10.1007/978-981-33-4795-3_76

Rodriguez, M. C., Hascic, I., & Souchier, M. (2018). Environmentally Adjusted Multifactor Productivity: Methodology and Empirical Results of OECD and G20 Countries. *Ecological Economics*, *153*, 147–160. doi:10.1016/j.ecolecon.2018.06.015

Romer, P. M. (1986). Increasing returns and long-run growth. *Journal of Political Economy*, *94*(5), 1002–1037. https://www.jstor.org/stable/1833190. doi:10.1086/261420

Roser, M., Ritchie, H., & Mathieu, E. (2023). "Technological Change". Our World In Data. https://ourworldindata.org/technological-change

Rusiawan, W., Tjiptoherijanto, P., Suganda, E., & Darmajanti, L. (2015). Assessment of Green Total Factor Productivity Impact on Sustainable Indonesia Productivity Growth. *Procedia Environmental Sciences*, *28*, 493–501. doi:10.1016/j.proenv.2015.07.059

Ryan, M., Antoniou, J., Brooks, L. D., Jiya, T., Macnish, K., & Stahl, B. C. (2020). The Ethical Balance of Using Smart Information Systems for Promoting the United Nations' Sustainable Development Goals. *Sustainability (Basel)*, *12*(4826), 1–22. doi:10.3390/su12124826

Sahoo, S., & Lo, C.-Y. (2022). Smart manufacturing powered by recent technological advancements: A review. *Journal of Manufacturing Systems*, *64*, 236–250. doi:10.1016/j.jmsy.2022.06.008

Sangster, N., Duke, R., Lalla, T., Persad, P., & Ameerali, A. (2016). Investigating the use of advanced manufacturing technologies in the manufacturing assembly sector in a small developing country. *International Journal of Materials Mechanics and Manufacturing*, *4*(4), 266–272.

SaslowK.LorenzP. (2019). Artificial Intelligence Needs Human Rights: How the Focus on Ethical AI Fails to Address Privacy, Discrimination and Other Concerns. PsychRN: Attitudes & Social Cognition, 1-25. doi:10.2139/ssrn.3589473

Seamans, R., & Raj, M. (2018). *AI, labour, productivity, and the need for firm-level data (No. w24239)*. National Bureau of Economic Research. doi:10.3386/w24239

Sharma, M., Luthra, S., Joshi, S., & Kumar, A. (2022). Implementing challenges of artificial intelligence: Evidence from the public manufacturing sector of an emerging economy. *Government Information Quarterly*, *39*(4), 101624. doi:10.1016/j.giq.2021.101624

Singh, R., Akram, S. V., Gehlot, A., Buddhi, D., Priyadarshi, N., & Twala, B. (2022). Energy System 4.0: Digitalization of the Energy Sector with Inclination towards Sustainability. *Sensors (Basel)*, *22*(6619), 1–42. doi:10.3390/s22176619 PMID:36081087

Solodkyi, V. V., &, Polishchuk, Y. A. (2023). Artificial intelligence implementation in Ukrainian banks: perspectives and limitations. Economic Bulletin of Dnipro University of Technology, 119-127. doi:10.33271/ebdut/82.119

Solow, R. M. (1956). A Contribution to the Theory of Economic Growth. *The Quarterly Journal of Economics*, *70*(1), 65–94. https://www.jstor.org/stable/1884513?origin=JSTOR-pdf. doi:10.2307/1884513

Solow, R. M. (1957). Technical Change and the Aggregate Production Function. *The Review of Economics and Statistics*, *39*(3), 312–320. https://www.jstor.org/stable/1926047?origin=JSTOR-pdf. doi:10.2307/1926047

Sony, M., Antony, J., Mc Dermott, O., & Garza-Reyes, J. A. (2021). An empirical examination of benefits, challenges, and critical success factors of Industry 4.0 in manufacturing and service sector. *Technology in Society*, *67*, 101754. doi:10.1016/j.techsoc.2021.101754

Stadie, B., Abbeel, P., & Sutskever, I. (2017). *Third-Person Imitation Learning*. Cornell University, arXiv:1703.01703v2, 1-16. doi: /arXiv.1703.01703 doi:10.48550

Szczepaniuk, H., & Szczepaniuk, E. K. (2023). Applications of Artificial Intelligence Algorithms in the Energy Sector. *Energies*, *16*(347), 1–24. doi:10.3390/en16010347

Ullah, A., Aimin, W., & Ahmed, M. (2018). Smart Automation, Customer Experience and Customer Engagement in Electric Vehicles. *Sustainability (Basel)*, *10*(5), 1–11. doi:10.3390/su10051350

United Nations (UN). (2021). Policy Brief: Transforming Extractive Industries for Sustainable Development. UN. https://www.un.org/sites/un2.un.org/files/sg_policy_brief_extractives.pdf

Verges-Jamie, J. (2021). The Misinterpretation of Productivity Measures. *Challenge, 64*(2), 1–16. doi:10.1080/05775132.2020.1866907

Vesnic-Alujevic, L., Nascimento, S., & Polvora, A. (2020). Societal and ethical impacts of artificial intelligence: Critical notes on European policy frameworks. *Telecommunications Policy*, *44*(6), 101961. doi:10.1016/j.telpol.2020.101961

Vinuesa, R., Azizpour, H., Leite, I., Balaam, M., Dignum, V., Domisch, S., Fellander, A., Langhans, S. D., Tegmark, M., & Nerini, F. F. (2020). The role of artificial intelligence in achieving the Sustainable Development Goals. *Nature Communications*, *11*(233), 1–10. doi:10.1038/s41467-019-14108-y PMID:31932590

Wachter, S., Mittelstadt, B. D., & Russell, C. (2021). Bias Preservation in Machine Learning: The Legality of Fairness Metrics Under EU Non-Discrimination Law. SSRN *Electronic Journal,* 123(3):1-51. https://doi.org/ doi:10.2139/SSRN.3792772

Wakunuma, K., Jiya, T., & Aliyu, S. (2020). Socio-ethical implications of using AI in accelerating SDG3 in Least Developed Countries. *Journal of Responsible Technology*, *4*(100006), 1–10. doi:10.1016/j.jrt.2020.100006

World Economic Forum (WEF). (2023). Jobs of Tomorrow: Large Language Models and Jobs. Geneva, Switzerland. https://www3.weforum.org/docs/WEF_Jobs_of_Tomorrow_Generative_AI_2023.pdf

Xu, Z. (2022). The Influence of Robot-Assisted Industry Using Deep Learning on the Economic Growth Rate of Manufacturing Industry in the Era of Artificial Intelligence. *Wireless Communications and Mobile Computing*, *2022*, 1–12. doi:10.1155/2022/4594858

Yap, Y.-H., Tan, W.-S., Wong, J., Ahmad, N. A., Wooi, C.-L., Wu, Y.-K., & Ariffin, A. E. (2021). A two-stage multi microgrid p2p energy trading with motivational game-theory: A case study in Malaysia. *The Institute of Engineering and Technology (IET). Renewable Power Generation, 15*, 2615–2628. doi:10.1049/rpg2.12205

ZhangB. (2022). No Rage Against the Machines: Threat of Automation Does Not Change Policy Preferences. *Social Science Research Network,* 1-8. doi:10.2139/ssrn.3455501

Zhong, Y., Xu, F., & Zhang, L. (2023). *Influence of artificial intelligence applications on total factor productivity of enterprises-evidence from textual analysis of annual reports of Chinese-listed companies*. Applied Econometrics., doi:10.1080/00036846.2023.2244246

Zhou, M., & Chen, Y. (2022). Research on the Impact of Artificial Intelligence on Green Total Factor Productivity in Manufacturing. *Advances in Economics, Business, and Management*, *650*, 47–50. doi:10.2991/aebmr.k.220402.010

KEY TERMS AND DEFINITIONS

Open AI: Open AI is a private research company based in San Francisco, United States. Founded in 2015, the company develops artificial intelligence (AI) systems such as generative models that can benefit humanity.

Generative models: Generative models are a specific type of machine learning model that is run on neural networks, which are capable of learning to identify underlying patterns found in large data sets, that can be used to generate new data.

Big Data: Big Data is commonly referred to as large datasets which contain structured or unstructured information gathered from various sources such as social media. Big Data is frequently used in machine learning models.

AI-based technologies: AI-based technologies refer to the tools and technologies used by companies to gain a competitive advantage in their specific market. The most common AI-based technologies include Natural Language Generation/Processing, Virtual Agents, Machine Learning, Robotics and Deep Learning.

MultiFactor Productivity (MFP): MFP is commonly referred to as a measure of economic performance that compares the amount of inputs of capital and labour, with that of outputs utilized in the production process. In particular, it measures the overall productive efficiency with which labour and capital are used in this process.

Solow Residual: The Solow Residual also known as the Total Factor Productivity(TFP) is a measurement of productivity growth that is the result of advancements in technology and efficiency.

Chapter 9
Crafting the Future: OpenAI's Strategies and Sustainable Innovation

T. Premavathi
Marwadi University, India

Ayush Shekhar
Marwadi University, India

Aayush Raj
Marwadi University, India

Shreya Agrawal
Marwadi University, India

Damodharan Palaniappan
Marwadi University, India

ABSTRACT

Crafting the Future: OpenAI's Strategies and Sustainable Innovation examines OpenAI's innovative ideas in the ever-changing AI landscape. The chapter highlights OpenAI's safety, transparency, and social benefit. This lets us examine the organization's research environment, focused on sophisticated language models and their groundbreaking applications in numerous domains. Sustainability is prioritised over scientific advancement and an inclusive AI ecosystem at OpenAI. The chapter discusses OpenAI's collaborative frameworks, partnerships, and community involvement to democratise and ethically deploy AI. OpenAI's proactive approach to social consequences and ethics, including bias reduction and AI development's ethical problems, is also examined. Crafting the Future informs academics, politicians, and enthusiasts about OpenAI's impact on global AI laws and standards. OpenAI's trajectory poses ethical, collaborative, and revolutionary questions throughout the chapter. Beyond cutting-edge technology, OpenAI seeks to change the world.

DOI: 10.4018/979-8-3693-1198-1.ch009

1. INTRODUCTION

In the ever-evolving landscape of artificial intelligence (AI), OpenAI stands as a formidable force, its impact transcending mere technological innovation. OpenAI's inception was fuelled by a visionary pursuit — a commitment to ensuring that artificial general intelligence (AGI) benefits all of humanity. This foundational vision, encapsulated within the OpenAI Charter, becomes the guiding star for the organization's methodologies and strategic decisions (Ahn et al., 2015). Beyond being a purveyor of cutting-edge language models, OpenAI is fundamentally distinguished by its commitment to ethical AI. Ethical considerations aren't auxiliary; they are woven into the very fabric of OpenAI's identity. The organization navigates the intricate balance between technological innovation and ethical responsibility, a theme that reverberates through its language models, particularly the transformative Generative Pre-trained Transformer (GPT) series (Parida, Westerberg, & Frishammar, 2012). However, OpenAI's impact is not confined to the realms of algorithms and neural networks; it extends to collaborative frameworks exemplified by the OpenAI Gym (Parida, Westerberg, & Frishammar, 2012). More than a mere framework for reinforcement learning, OpenAI Gym symbolizes a philosophy of collaboration as a catalyst for progress, embodying the ethos of shared knowledge and collective advancement.

Navigating the intricate balance between technological innovation and ethical responsibility, OpenAI's impact extends far beyond the algorithms and neural networks it pioneers. This delicate equilibrium is most evident in the transformative Generative Pre-trained Transformer (GPT) series (Pundziene et al., 2021), where ethical considerations are seamlessly integrated into the core of the technology. However, OpenAI's influence doesn't stop at the borders of algorithms; it encompasses collaborative frameworks exemplified by the OpenAI Gym (Bostrom, 2018). Going beyond being a mere framework for reinforcement learning, OpenAI Gym embodies a philosophy of collaboration as a driving force for progress—a manifestation of the ethos of shared knowledge and collective advancement.

Within the pages of this chapter, we embark on a comprehensive exploration of OpenAI's methodologies, peeling back the layers to reveal the intricacies of its strategies. These strategies extend beyond the realm of technological prowess to encompass ethical considerations, collaborative frameworks, and a proactive stance on societal impact. OpenAI emerges not only as a technological trailblazer but as a conscientious steward of responsible AI innovation, actively shaping a future where the benefits of AI are expansive, inclusive, and firmly grounded in ethics. Through a meticulous examination, this chapter seeks to unravel the multifaceted dimensions of OpenAI's strategies and sustainable innovation, shedding light on how the organization is actively sculpting the trajectory of AI's evolution.

2. FOUNDATIONAL PRINCIPLES AND VALUES

In navigating the forefront of the technological frontier, OpenAI's bedrock is formed by a set of core principles and values that shape its mission. OpenAI recognizes the profound impact of artificial intelligence on society and proactively engages in the responsible development of AI technologies. These guiding principles ensure that OpenAI's innovations respect ethical issues, push the boundaries of research and advancement, and positively impact a sustainable and inclusive AI landscape.

- **Emphasis on Transparency:**

OpenAI, this involves a profound reflection on the lifecycle of data – from generation and recording to curation, processing, dissemination, sharing, and utilization. It understands how important it is to help the general public, governments, and researchers alike understand the complexity of artificial intelligence (Gama & Magistretti, 2023). This transparency serves a dual purpose: firstly, to empower the general public, enabling individuals to comprehend the intricacies of AI, make informed decisions, and engage in meaningful discourse about its societal implications. Secondly, it extends to governments and researchers, fostering a collaborative environment where shared understanding and collective efforts can contribute to the responsible development and ethical deployment of AI technologies.

- **Fostering Trust:**

The goal of OpenAI's principle priority is to increase stakeholder confidence. In order to build confidence in the research and application of AI, the organization feels that transparency is essential, whether working with other institutions, industry, or the general public. OpenAI is building trust in AI by making AI systems explainable, ensuring safety and risk mitigation, promoting fairness and non-discrimination, encouraging collaboration and openness, and engaging with stakeholders (Rane et al., 2023a). The community at large gains confidence in OpenAI's endeavours as a result of its ongoing efforts to improve accountability and governance frameworks, which demonstrate the organization's dedication to responsible and reliable AI development.

- **Reduce Pressure to Compromise Safety:**

In the relentless pursuit of artificial intelligence innovation, OpenAI places paramount importance on safeguarding the ethical and safety considerations inherent in the development and deployment of advanced AI systems. This commitment is enshrined in the organization's ethical charter, where the principles of responsible AI usage are articulated as a guiding light. OpenAI employs a transparent decision-making process, allowing external scrutiny and input to foster a collective approach to safety considerations. Recognizing the collaborative nature of addressing safety challenges, OpenAI actively engages with external stakeholders, from policymakers to advocacy groups, fostering a proactive understanding of the broader societal implications of AI technologies. The organization conducts iterative risk assessments throughout the development lifecycle, staying agile in responding to emerging challenges and refining safety protocols. Community engagement is a cornerstone, with OpenAI actively seeking feedback to ensure that the development of AI aligns with collective values. The establishment of clear red lines, delineating ethical boundaries, and the gradual release of advanced systems reflect a cautious approach, allowing for meticulous monitoring of their impact before widespread deployment (Motlagh et al., 2023). OpenAI also invests in ongoing research to stay ahead of potential risks, addressing not only technical safety measures but also societal and policy aspects. Through these multifaceted strategies, OpenAI exemplifies a proactive stance, ensuring that the pressure to compromise safety is consistently mitigated, and AI advancements align with ethical principles, transparency, and the collective well-being of society.

- **Collaborative Approach:**

OpenAI takes a cooperative stance that emphasizes the value of interacting with outside experts, groups, and the general public. Considering the intricacy and possible social repercussions of artificial intelligence, OpenAI actively looks for a range of viewpoints to contribute to the creation and application of its technology. Initiatives like requesting public feedback on artificial intelligence in education and establishing alliances with outside research institutes are prime examples of this collaborative mindset. Through the inclusion of diverse perspectives, OpenAI seeks to reduce prejudices, improve equity, and take ethical issues into account while developing and deploying its AI systems. Beyond its walls, the organization emphasizes open communication and knowledge-sharing with the larger scientific and research community as part of its commitment to collaboration.

This strategy not only strengthens the validity and reliability of OpenAI's inventions but also promotes an atmosphere of accountability and shared responsibility for the development of artificial intelligence. Through shared ideals and joint skills, the collaborative ethos represents a proactive approach to creating a more transparent, inclusive, and trustworthy AI ecosystem.

- **Policy and Standard Sharpening:**

OpenAI is dedicated to upholding rigorous standards in the development of artificial intelligence. The organization prioritizes continuous improvement through standard sharpening processes, refining models to enhance their precision and effectiveness. This commitment extends to addressing potential biases and ensuring that models consistently meet ethical guidelines (Rane et al., 2024a). By actively engaging in the standard sharpening of its models, OpenAI aims to not only maintain high-quality performance but also to adapt to evolving challenges in the AI landscape. This approach reflects the organization's proactive stance in refining and optimizing AI technologies to meet the highest standards of safety, reliability, and ethical conduct.

3. EVOLUTION OF ADVANCE LANGUAGE MODELS

The evolution of advanced language models under the stewardship of OpenAI is a captivating narrative marked by remarkable milestones, each contributing to a paradigm shift in natural language processing. Embarking from the inception of foundational models like GPT-1, OpenAI unveiled the potential of machines to comprehend and generate coherent text at an unprecedented level (Rane et al., 2023b). This initial leap served as a catalyst, igniting curiosity and laying the groundwork for subsequent advancements.

The journey of iterative refinement and enhancement unfolds prominently in the iterations of the Generative Pre-trained Transformer (GPT) series. GPT-2, with its vast scale comprising millions of parameters, represented a significant leap forward in language understanding and generation capabilities (Rane et al., 2024b). The model showcased a remarkable ability to generate nuanced and contextually relevant text across diverse domains, underscoring OpenAI's commitment to pushing the boundaries of AI language models.

However, it is with GPT-3 that the evolutionary trajectory reaches unparalleled heights. This model, boasting a staggering 175 billion parameters, stands as a milestone in natural language processing, establishing a new standard for AI capabilities (Dergaa et al., 2023). GPT-3's immense scale empowers it with a sophisticated understanding of context, enabling the generation of text with an unprecedented level of coherence and context-awareness. It marks a transformative moment, not just in AI but in reshaping our understanding of the potential of machines to comprehend and generate human-like language.

Beyond sheer scale and technical prowess, OpenAI's language models signify a profound shift from mere text generators to tools capable of profound comprehension and interaction. GPT-3, in particular, demonstrates an ability to answer questions, engage in meaningful conversations, and grasp the intricacies of human communication. This transition positions OpenAI's contributions as instrumental in the journey toward achieving genuine natural language understanding, departing from earlier models that primarily produced contextually relevant text.

Importantly, OpenAI's commitment extends beyond technological innovation to encompass ethical considerations and responsible development. As language models evolve, OpenAI proactively addresses societal implications, implementing mechanisms to mitigate biases, ensure transparency, and solicit input from the wider community (Singh et al., 2023). The evolution of OpenAI's language models is not merely a technical trajectory but a comprehensive exploration of how advanced AI can be harnessed responsibly, aligning with ethical principles and societal values. This section illuminates the intricate layers of OpenAI's pivotal role in advancing the field of natural language processing and shaping language models that transcend technical achievements to become ethically grounded and socially responsible innovations.

4. COLLABORATION AND PARTNERSHIPS

OpenAI stands at the forefront of artificial intelligence innovation, with collaboration and strategic partnerships serving as the linchpin of its mission. The organization's commitment to advancing the field extends well beyond individual brilliance, embracing a collaborative ethos that underscores the interconnected nature of progress in artificial intelligence. In navigating the complex landscape of AI research, OpenAI actively forges partnerships with esteemed research institutions across the globe. These collaborations transcend geographical boundaries, fostering an environment where cutting-edge ideas and groundbreaking research projects can be shared openly. Through co-authored publications and joint research endeavours, OpenAI not only contributes to the global academic discourse but also harnesses the collective intelligence of the broader research community.

The canvas of OpenAI's collaboration extends beyond the realms of academia to include robust partnerships with industry leaders and organizations spanning diverse sectors. This expansive approach signifies OpenAI's commitment not just to theoretical advancements but to the practical applications of AI technologies. By strategically aligning with entities at the forefront of various industries, OpenAI endeavours to bridge the gap between theoretical innovation and tangible real-world impact. These partnerships are not mere transactions; they embody a shared commitment to responsible and ethical AI deployment, ensuring that the benefits of AI are distributed equitably across society.

Within the intricate tapestry of collaborative models, OpenAI employs a multifaceted approach. From foundational research collaborations that delve into the theoretical underpinnings of AI to applied partnerships addressing immediate societal challenges, OpenAI's engagements cover a spectrum. The organization's adaptability in tailoring collaboration models to meet specific challenges showcases its agility and responsiveness to the dynamic landscape of AI research. The commitment to transparency is a guiding principle, with OpenAI viewing openness not merely as a strategic choice but as a manifestation of its core values. This commitment fosters an ecosystem where breakthroughs become collective achievements, propelling the entire AI community forward.

As this chapter unfolds, it seeks to delve into the intricacies of OpenAI's collaboration strategies. Through a nuanced exploration of key partnerships, collaborative frameworks, and the guiding philosophy that shapes its approach, the chapter aims to offer a panoramic view of how OpenAI's commitment to collaboration serves as a catalyst in shaping the trajectory of artificial intelligence. By peeling back the layers of complexity in these collaborative endeavours, the narrative aims to illuminate OpenAI's role as a collaborative powerhouse, propelling innovation and steering the ethical evolution of AI in harmony with the broader global community. In doing so, it contributes to the broader discourse on collaborative models in AI research and development, highlighting the significance of collective intelligence in navigating the frontiers of artificial intelligence.

5. COMMUNITY ENGAGEMENT AND EDUCATION INITIATIVES

OpenAI's unwavering commitment to community engagement and education initiatives serves as a cornerstone in its broader mission to democratize access to artificial intelligence and cultivate a nuanced understanding of its transformative potential. The organization recognizes that the profound impact of AI extends far beyond the confines of its research labs, necessitating active engagement with and empowerment of diverse communities.

Central to this commitment is OpenAI's dedication to inclusivity. The organization actively endeavours to bridge the gap between the rapidly evolving landscape of AI advancements and the varied perspectives of individuals who may not traditionally be immersed in the field. Through targeted outreach programs, OpenAI conducts workshops, webinars, and educational sessions that not only demystify complex AI concepts but also offer practical insights into its applications. This outreach extends globally, utilizing online platforms and collaborative partnerships to reach a wide audience. By doing so, OpenAI seeks to inspire and equip individuals from diverse backgrounds, fostering a broader and more representative participation in the discourse surrounding artificial intelligence.

In addition to traditional educational settings, OpenAI embraces a participatory model of community engagement. Actively seeking feedback and insights from a diverse set of stakeholders, the organization creates avenues for meaningful interactions. Forums, surveys, and open dialogues serve as conduits for a two-way exchange, ensuring that the concerns and perspectives of the community are not only heard but actively considered. This iterative process enriches OpenAI's understanding of the ethical, societal, and cultural dimensions that are integral to the responsible development of AI, reinforcing the collaborative nature of progress.

Parallel to its community engagement efforts, OpenAI places a significant emphasis on education initiatives. Recognizing the importance of cultivating a knowledgeable and diverse talent pool, the organization supports educational programs at various levels. This involves the provision of resources, development of curricula, and active support for AI education. The focus is not only on fostering technical expertise but also on creating pathways for individuals from underrepresented groups to enter and thrive in the AI community. OpenAI's commitment to diversity in AI education aligns with its broader mission of ensuring that the benefits of artificial intelligence are accessible to and shared by a wide spectrum of individuals.

This section of the book chapter provides a detailed exploration of OpenAI's multifaceted community engagement and education initiatives. By delving into specific programs, collaborative partnerships, and the underlying philosophy that guides these endeavors, the narrative aims to showcase how OpenAI actively shapes a more inclusive and informed future for artificial intelligence. Through concrete examples, case studies, and nuanced analysis, the chapter unfolds to reveal OpenAI's role not only as a pioneering force in AI research but also as a conscientious steward actively contributing to the cultivation of a diverse, knowledgeable, and ethically grounded AI community.

Figure 1. Community engagement

6. METHODOLOGY

The methodology employed in this study is characterized by a multifaceted approach that aims to provide a thorough and nuanced understanding of OpenAI's strategies and sustainable innovation. The investigation into OpenAI's initiatives involves the integration of diverse methodological tools, each tailored to scrutinize specific aspects of the organization's endeavours. The comprehensive analysis unfolds through the following key methodological components:

6.1. Research and Development Framework

The examination of OpenAI's research and development (R&D) framework within this study goes beyond a mere surface-level exploration by employing a comprehensive historical lens. This approach involves delving into the annals of OpenAI's evolution, meticulously tracing the trajectory of its R&D strategies from inception to the present. The historical analysis aims to elucidate the motivations behind pivotal decisions, the contextual factors that shaped OpenAI's R&D landscape, and the organization's adaptive responses to emerging challenges.

In dissecting OpenAI's R&D framework, the study scrutinizes a myriad of sources, including research publications, internal guidelines, and policy documents. This multidimensional analysis seeks to unveil the core principles that have consistently guided OpenAI's pursuit of advancements in artificial intelligence. By going beyond the superficial aspects of the OpenAI Charter, the research aims to uncover the intricate nuances embedded in the decision-making processes, ethical considerations, and strategic choices that define the organization's R&D trajectory.

Moreover, the historical exploration not only focuses on the "what" of OpenAI's R&D endeavours but delves into the essential "why" and "how." This holistic understanding provides a foundation for contextualizing OpenAI's current R&D initiatives within the broader landscape of technological progress and ethical imperatives. In essence, the study aims to offer a nuanced narrative that captures the dynamic interplay of factors shaping OpenAI's R&D framework, contributing to a richer comprehension of the organization's enduring impact on the field of artificial intelligence.

6.2. Ethical Review and Decision-Making

At the core of OpenAI's mission lies a commitment to ethical principles, positioning the scrutiny of ethical considerations and decision-making processes as pivotal aspects of this study. The examination extends to a granular level, dissecting the mechanisms employed by OpenAI to identify and address ethical challenges systematically. Instances where ethical considerations have directly influenced strategic decisions are scrutinized, shedding light on the tangible impact of ethical frameworks on the organization's trajectory. Furthermore, a detailed analysis unfolds to reveal the practical implementation of these ethical principles throughout the lifecycle of AI technologies, providing insights into how OpenAI navigates the complex terrain of responsible development and deployment. This thorough investigation aims to unveil the ethical underpinnings that not only guide but actively shape OpenAI's initiatives in the ever-evolving landscape of artificial intelligence.

6.3. Collaboration Models

The study employs a robust two-pronged approach, blending quantitative and qualitative analyses to comprehensively scrutinize OpenAI's collaboration models. Quantitatively, the research evaluates the impact of collaborative initiatives through meticulous measurement of co-authored publications, joint projects, and overall collaborative outputs. This quantitative assessment serves as a metric for the scale and reach of OpenAI's collaborative endeavours within the broader research community.

Qualitatively, the study delves into the nuanced nature of these collaborations, examining the effectiveness of engagements in fostering meaningful knowledge exchange and their contribution to advancements in artificial intelligence. This qualitative analysis aims to uncover the intricacies of collaborative dynamics, exploring how partnerships and cooperative efforts influence OpenAI's research landscape. By integrating both quantitative and qualitative dimensions, the study aspires to present a comprehensive and nuanced understanding of the role and impact of collaborative initiatives in shaping OpenAI's trajectory in the field of artificial intelligence.

6.4. Community Engagement Strategies

The investigation into OpenAI's community engagement strategies embraces a participatory research approach, placing a strong emphasis on soliciting input directly from the community itself. Through in-depth interviews, meticulously crafted surveys, and comprehensive content analysis, this study aims to unearth the intricacies of community perceptions, concerns, and feedback. By adopting this participatory stance, the research transcends mere observation, actively involving community members in the dialogue surrounding OpenAI's initiatives.

This approach seeks to delve beneath the surface, unravelling the nuanced dynamics of OpenAI's engagement practices with its community. The research strives not just to identify the approaches through which OpenAI engages with its stakeholders but also to assess how these interactions align with the varied expectations existing within the wider AI community. By incorporating the voices and perspectives of the community directly into the analysis, the research aspires to provide a holistic understanding of OpenAI's community engagement strategies and their impact on fostering collaboration, inclusivity, and responsible AI development.

6.5. Democratization of AI

The democratization of AI is a multidimensional aspect, and the study takes a meticulous approach to dissect the various strategies employed by OpenAI. Educational outreach programs, accessibility initiatives, and efforts to empower diverse users are scrutinized in detail. The study aims to evaluate not just the existence of democratization initiatives but their effectiveness in breaking down barriers and broadening access to AI capabilities. By delving into specific programs and initiatives, the analysis seeks to uncover the depth of OpenAI's commitment to democratizing AI.

6.6. Addressing Bias and Fairness

Addressing bias and promoting fairness in AI systems is a focal point, requiring an exhaustive examination of OpenAI's methodologies. This involves a detailed exploration of the organization's approaches to bias mitigation, fairness measures, and strategies for ensuring ethical AI development. By scrutinizing specific instances and methodologies employed, the study aims to provide a nuanced understanding of OpenAI's commitment to ethical AI development and the proactive measures taken to address biases.

6.7. Policy Advocacy and Global Engagement

OpenAI's involvement in policy advocacy and global engagement is probed through a multifaceted analysis. The study scrutinizes interactions with policymakers, contributions to global discussions on AI governance, and the influence exerted on policy frameworks. This involves not just a high-level overview but a granular examination of the mechanisms employed by OpenAI to advocate for policies aligned with ethical considerations. The study aims to reveal the depth of OpenAI's impact on global AI governance.

6.8. Societal Impact Assessment

The societal impact assessment undertakes a holistic evaluation of OpenAI's innovations. This involves a detailed examination of both positive and negative societal impacts, the methodology used to measure and mitigate potential harms, and the organization's commitment to maximizing positive contributions. By employing a comprehensive impact assessment framework, the study aims to provide insights into the real-world implications of OpenAI's initiatives on society at large.

6.9. Environmental Sustainability Practices

The study delves into OpenAI's environmental sustainability practices, scrutinizing them within the context of research and development. This involves a detailed analysis of efforts to minimize environmental impact, adopt energy-efficient practices, and any initiatives promoting sustainability in AI technology development. By exploring the intersection of AI innovation and environmental responsibility, the study aims to provide a nuanced understanding of OpenAI's commitment to sustainability.

6.10. Human-AI Collaboration Frameworks

Human-AI collaboration frameworks are examined in detail, investigating how OpenAI integrates human input into its AI development processes. The investigation navigates through the specific instances where human input intertwines with AI development processes, shedding light on the symbiotic relationship between human intelligence and artificial intelligence. Special attention is devoted to probing the ethical dimensions inherent in these collaborative interactions, encompassing considerations such as transparency, fairness, and accountability.

The study goes beyond the surface, elucidating the frameworks established by OpenAI to facilitate responsible and ethical human-AI collaboration. By dissecting these frameworks, the research aims to unravel the mechanisms ensuring meaningful collaboration, emphasizing OpenAI's commitment to ethical guidelines that underpin the development and deployment of AI systems. This nuanced analysis offers valuable insights into the evolving landscape of Human-AI partnerships, highlighting OpenAI's role in shaping responsible practices within this dynamic and transformative domain.

6.11. Open Source Contributions

In the comprehensive study, particular emphasis is placed on a dedicated assessment of OpenAI's open-source contributions, acknowledging their pivotal role in shaping the organization's ethos. This involves a granular examination of the diverse projects that OpenAI actively contributes to the open-source community. By probing the motivations driving the decision to open-source specific technologies, the research aims to uncover the underlying principles guiding OpenAI's commitment to knowledge sharing and collaboration.

Moreover, the study goes beyond mere acknowledgment by critically evaluating the tangible impact of OpenAI's open-source contributions on the broader AI ecosystem. This assessment seeks to quantify and qualify how these contributions influence technological advancements, foster innovation, and contribute to the collective growth of the artificial intelligence community. In essence, the study sheds light on OpenAI's role as a proactive participant in the collaborative evolution of AI, showcasing the organization's dedication to fostering a culture of transparency, inclusivity, and shared knowledge.

In conclusion, the methodological framework is meticulously structured to encompass an expansive array of dimensions within OpenAI's strategies and sustainable innovation. By employing diverse and thorough methodological approaches, the study aims to offer a nuanced, comprehensive, and detailed exploration of each dimension. This depth of analysis contributes to a holistic depiction of OpenAI's pivotal role in shaping the future of artificial intelligence.

Figure 2. R&D Framework, ethical review, collaboration model, community engagement

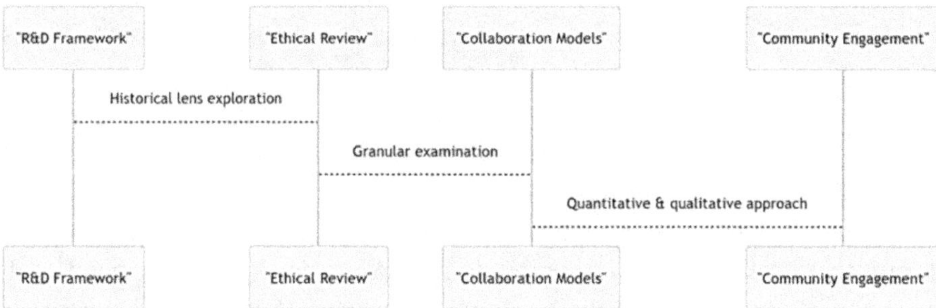

Figure 3. Democratics of AI, addressing bias and fairness, policy advocacy, societal impact assessment

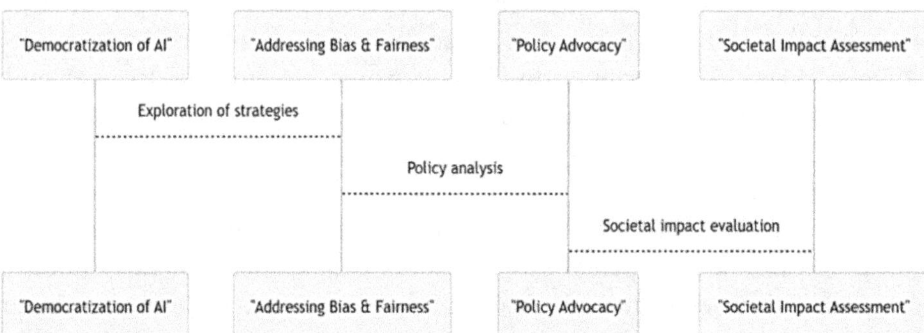

7. CHALLENGES FACED

OpenAI, at the forefront of AI innovation, encounters a myriad of challenges that underscore the intricate nature of navigating the evolving landscape of artificial intelligence. Central to these challenges is the ethical dimension inherent in AI research and development. As OpenAI pushes the boundaries of language models and cutting-edge technologies, it grapples with the nuanced ethical considerations that emerge. Striking a delicate balance between innovation and ethical responsibility becomes a continuous challenge, requiring ongoing refinement of methodologies to address biases, ensure fairness, and uphold ethical standards in the development process.

Societal impacts form another complex challenge for OpenAI. As its AI technologies integrate into various facets of daily life, understanding and mitigating potential negative consequences take centre stage. The organization faces the formidable task of minimizing societal harms related to privacy, security, and employment while maximizing the positive contributions of its innovations. A robust societal impact assessment framework is essential for OpenAI to make informed decisions that align with broader societal values.

While collaboration and openness are strengths, they also pose challenges. Collaborative models necessitate effective communication and coordination among diverse stakeholders, both within and beyond OpenAI. Negotiating global collaborations involves navigating cultural nuances, diverse perspectives, and varying regulatory environments. Sustaining constructive collaboration without compromising on foundational principles demands ongoing efforts to foster understanding and alignment of goals.

Democratizing AI, a core tenet of OpenAI's mission, introduces challenges related to accessibility and responsible use. Bridging the gap in access to AI capabilities must be done thoughtfully to avoid perpetuating inequalities or enabling harmful applications. Striking the right balance between empowerment and responsible use requires continuous refinement of strategies to ensure that the democratization of AI aligns with ethical considerations and societal well-being.

Additionally, the rapid evolution of the AI field itself presents an inherent challenge. Staying at the forefront of innovation demands continuous adaptation to emerging technologies, methodologies, and research trends. OpenAI must remain vigilant against potential risks and ethical pitfalls that may arise with the introduction of new advancements. The dynamic nature of the field necessitates a proactive approach to research and development to stay ahead of the curve.

In addition to these challenges, OpenAI also grapples with the imperative of addressing the environmental impact of AI technologies. As the computational demands of advanced models rise, mitigating the carbon footprint becomes a crucial challenge. Balancing the quest for technological advancement with a commitment to environmental sustainability adds an extra layer of complexity to OpenAI's endeavours.

This section of the book chapter delves into the intricacies of these challenges, providing a nuanced exploration of how OpenAI confronts and navigates these complex issues. Through detailed analysis, case studies, and a transparent examination of its ongoing efforts, the narrative seeks to offer a comprehensive understanding of the multifaceted challenges inherent in the responsible development and deployment of advanced AI technologies.

8. FUTURE SCOPE

The future trajectory of OpenAI's strategies and sustainable innovation presents a captivating panorama that holds the promise of reshaping the landscape of artificial intelligence. In the realm of technology advancement, OpenAI stands as a vanguard, and the unfolding years are expected to witness the organization pioneering novel approaches to language models and pushing the boundaries of AI applications. OpenAI's steadfast commitment to research and development positions it to be at the forefront of breakthroughs, potentially revolutionizing our understanding of AI capabilities and their real-world applications.

Collaboration emerges as a linchpin for the future endeavours of OpenAI. The organization's collaborative models are likely to evolve, extending partnerships to encompass a more extensive array of institutions, industries, and global communities. The richness of perspectives and expertise derived from diverse collaborations is anticipated to contribute to a more inclusive and globally impactful AI community. OpenAI's collaborative ethos is expected to foster an environment where knowledge exchange transcends geographical boundaries, laying the groundwork for collaborative breakthroughs that address complex challenges.

The democratization of AI is set to take centre stage in OpenAI's future initiatives. The organization may intensify its efforts to make AI knowledge and resources more accessible to a wider audience, including those from underrepresented groups. Educational outreach programs are poised to expand, equipping individuals with the tools and knowledge to actively participate in the AI discourse. OpenAI's commitment to addressing biases and ensuring fairness in AI systems could drive innovative solutions, setting benchmarks for ethical AI development and deployment.

Environmental sustainability is likely to emerge as a key focus in OpenAI's future roadmap. With increasing awareness of the environmental impact associated with advanced language models and computational processes, the organization may explore and implement strategies to minimize its carbon footprint. Proactive measures aligned with global environmental sustainability goals would not only showcase OpenAI's commitment to responsible innovation but also contribute to shaping a more eco-conscious AI landscape.

Beyond technological advancements, OpenAI's future scope extends to deeper societal impact assessments. The organization may refine its methodologies to comprehensively understand and address the broader implications of AI on communities, economies, and cultures. OpenAI's dedication to transparency and ethical considerations positions it as a frontrunner in developing frameworks that guide responsible AI deployment globally, ensuring that the societal impact of AI aligns with ethical and cultural values.

In conclusion, the future of OpenAI's strategies and sustainable innovation holds immense promise and possibility. This chapter serves as a foundational exploration of OpenAI's past and present, offering a lens through which to anticipate and analyse the organization's future contributions to the field of artificial intelligence. As OpenAI continues to navigate the dynamic landscape of AI, this chapter provides a starting point for ongoing exploration and scrutiny, contributing to the ongoing discourse on responsible and impactful AI development.

9. CONCLUSION: NAVIGATING THE FRONTIERS OF INNOVATION

In the intricate tapestry of OpenAI's strategies and sustainable innovation, this chapter has meticulously woven together the threads of the organization's historical landmarks, its present-day pursuits, and the compelling vision it holds for the future of artificial intelligence. OpenAI's journey, as illuminated in these pages, is not merely a chronological progression; it is a narrative that encapsulates the essence of responsible innovation, collaborative exploration, and ethical considerations.

From its inception, OpenAI has stood as a vanguard in the realm of artificial intelligence, spearheading groundbreaking advancements in language models and pushing the boundaries of what AI can achieve. What emerges from this exploration is not just a story of technological prowess but a narrative shaped by OpenAI's unwavering commitment to collaboration. The collaborative models forged by the organization extend beyond research papers; they represent a commitment to shared knowledge, collective progress, and a global community working towards the common goal of advancing AI responsibly.

This chapter has delved into the intricate web of OpenAI's collaborative ethos, shedding light on the nuanced dynamics of partnerships, community engagement, and educational initiatives. OpenAI's dedication to inclusivity is not a mere checkbox in its mission statement; it is a foundational principle that permeates its outreach efforts, education programs, and the very fabric of its collaborative endeavours.

The challenges encountered by OpenAI, whether ethical dilemmas, societal impacts, or the environmental footprint of AI, serve not as impediments but as crucibles for refinement. OpenAI's proactive approach to addressing these challenges paints a portrait of an organization keenly aware of its responsibilities and committed to navigating the complexities of AI development with a principled compass.

Looking to the future, OpenAI's trajectory appears poised for continued innovation and societal impact. The organization's collaborative models are likely to evolve, welcoming even more diverse voices into the global AI conversation. The democratization of AI, a core tenet, is expected to deepen, with educational initiatives expanding to empower a broader spectrum of individuals and communities.

As the chapter concludes, it beckons the reader to reflect not only on OpenAI's journey thus far but also on the unfolding narrative that lies ahead. The story of OpenAI is an invitation—a call to further exploration, analysis, and engagement. It prompts us to consider the profound implications of responsible AI development and the role organizations like OpenAI play in shaping a future where artificial intelligence is a force for positive transformation. The journey continues, and OpenAI remains at the forefront, navigating the frontiers of innovation with a commitment to excellence, collaboration, and the responsible stewardship of AI's vast potential.

REFERENCES

Ahn, J. M., Minshall, T., & Mortara, L. (2015). Open innovation: A new classification and its impact on firm performance in innovative SMEs. *Journal of Innovation Management, 3*(2), 33–54. doi:10.24840/2183-0606_003.002_0006

Bostrom, N. (2018). Strategic implications of openness in AI development. In *Artificial Intelligence Safety and Security* (pp. 145–164). Chapman and Hall/CRC. doi:10.1201/9781351251389-11

Dergaa, I., Saad, H. B., El Omri, A., Glenn, J., Clark, C., Washif, J., ... Chamari, K. (2023). Using artificial intelligence for exercise prescription in personalised health promotion: A critical evaluation of OpenAI's GPT-4 model. *Biology of Sport, 41*(2), 221–241. doi:10.5114/biolsport.2024.133661 PMID:38524814

Gama, F., & Magistretti, S. (2023). Artificial intelligence in innovation management: A review of innovation capabilities and a taxonomy of AI applications. *Journal of Product Innovation Management*, jpim.12698. doi:10.1111/jpim.12698

Motlagh, N. Y., Khajavi, M., Sharifi, A., & Ahmadi, M. (2023). The impact of artificial intelligence on the evolution of digital education: A comparative study of openAI text generation tools including ChatGPT, Bing Chat, Bard, and Ernie. *arXiv preprint arXiv:2309.02029.*

Parida, V., Westerberg, M., & Frishammar, J. (2012). Inbound open innovation activities in high-tech SMEs: The impact on innovation performance. *Journal of Small Business Management, 50*(2), 283–309. doi:10.1111/j.1540-627X.2012.00354.x

Pundziene, A., Nikou, S., & Bouwman, H. (2021). The nexus between dynamic capabilities and competitive firm performance: The mediating role of open innovation. *European Journal of Innovation Management*, *25*(6), 152–177. doi:10.1108/EJIM-09-2020-0356

Rane, N., Choudhary, S., & Rane, J. (2023a). *Integrating ChatGPT, Bard, and leading-edge generative artificial intelligence in building and construction industry: applications, framework, challenges, and future scope*. Academic Press.

Rane, N., Choudhary, S., & Rane, J. (2023b). *Integrating Building Information Modelling (BIM) with ChatGPT, Bard, and similar generative artificial intelligence in the architecture, engineering, and construction industry: applications, a novel framework, challenges, and future scope. Bard, and similar generative artificial intelligence in the architecture, engineering, and construction industry: applications, a novel framework, challenges, and future scope*. Academic Press.

RaneN.ChoudharyS.RaneJ. (2024a). *Contribution of ChatGPT and Similar Generative Artificial Intelligence for Enhanced Climate Change Mitigation Strategies.* doi:10.2139/ssrn.4681720

RaneN.ChoudharyS.RaneJ. (2024b). *A new era of automation in the construction industry: Implementing leading-edge generative artificial intelligence, such as ChatGPT or Bard*. doi:10.2139/ssrn.4681747

Singh, J., Samborowski, L., & Mentzer, K. (2023). A Human Collaboration with ChatGPT: Developing Case Studies with Generative AI. In *Proceedings of the ISCAP Conference* (*Vol. 2473*, p. 4901). Academic Press.

Compilation of References

Abbas, B., Razak, A. A., & Wekke, I. S. (2019). Investigating green supply chain practices for economic growth. *Uncertain Supply Chain Management*, 783–792. doi:10.5267/j.uscm.2019.1.002

Acemoglu, D., Hazell, J., & Restrepo, P. (2022). Artificial Intelligence and Jobs: Evidence from Online Vacancies. *Journal of Labor Economics*, *40*(S1), S293–S340. doi:10.1086/718327

Acemoglu, D., Lelarge, C., & Restrepo, P. (2020). Competing With Robots: Firm-Level Evidence from France. *AEA Papers and Proceedings. American Economic Association*, *110*, 383–388. doi:10.1257/pandp.20201003

Acemoglu, D., & Restrepo, P. (2022). Tasks, automation, and the rise in U.S. wage inequality. *Econometrica*, *90*(5), 1973–2016. doi:10.3982/ECTA19815

Achouch, M., Dimitrova, M., Ziane, K., Sattarpanah Karganroudi, S., Dhouib, R., Ibrahim, H., & Adda, M. (2022). On Predictive Maintenance in Industry 4.0: Overview, Models, and Challenges. *Applied Sciences (Basel, Switzerland)*, *12*(8081), 1–22. doi:10.3390/app12168081

Aghion, P., & Howitt, P. (1990). A Model of Growth through Creative Destruction. NBER Working Paper 3223 (National Bureau of Economic Research, Cambridge, MA).

Aghion, P., & Howitt, P. (1994). Growth and Unemployment. *The Review of Economic Studies*, *61*(3), 477–494. doi:10.2307/2297900

Ahmad, T., Zhang, D., Huang, C., Zhang, H., Dai, N., Song, Y., & Chen, H. (2021). Artificial intelligence in sustainable energy industry: Status Quo, challenges, and opportunities. *Journal of Cleaner Production*, *289*(125834), 1–65. doi:10.1016/j.jclepro.2021.125834

Ahmed, T., & Bhatti, A. (2020). Measurement and Determinants of Multi-factor productivity: A Survey of the Literature. *Journal of Economic Surveys*, *34*(2), 293–319. doi:10.1111/joes.12360

Ahn, J. M., Minshall, T., & Mortara, L. (2015). Open innovation: A new classification and its impact on firm performance in innovative SMEs. *Journal of Innovation Management*, *3*(2), 33–54. doi:10.24840/2183-0606_003.002_0006

Ai, X.-N., Gao, S.-J., Li, W.-M., & Liao, H. (2023). Greening China: Environmentally adjusted multifactor productivity in the last four decades. *Resources, Conservation and Recycling*, *192*(106918), 106918. Advance online publication. doi:10.1016/j.resconrec.2023.106918

Akhtar, W. H., Watanabe, C., Tou, Y., & Neittaanmäki, P. (2022). A New Perspective on the Textile and Apparel Industry in the Digital Transformation Era. *Textiles*, *2*(4), 633–656. doi:10.3390/textiles2040037

Al Shaher, S., Yanzhe, M., & Zreik, M. (2023). Navigating the Digital Frontier: Responsible Innovation in China's Digital Silk Road. *Migration Letters : An International Journal of Migration Studies*, *20*(S9), 1297–1315.

Alani, J. (2012). Effects of Productivity Growth on Employment Generation, Capital Accumulation and Economic Growth in Uganda. International Journal of Trade. *Economics and Finance*, *3*(3), 170–175. doi:10.7763/IJTEF.2012.V3.194

Albanesi, S., da Silva, A. D., Jimeno, J. F., Lamo, A., & Wabitsch, A. (2023). *New Technologies and Jobs in Europe*. National Bureau of Economic Research (NBER), Cambridge, Massachusetts, United States. https://www.nber.org/papers/w31357

Almurshidee, K. A. (2017). The Implementation of TQM in Higher Education Institutionsin Saudi Arabia: Marketing Prospective, *17*(1), 0–8.

Aloisi, A., & De Stefano, V. (2023). Between risk mitigation and labour rights enforcement: Assessing the transatlantic race to govern AI-driven decision making through a comparative lens. *European Labour Law Journal*, *14*(2), 283–307. doi:10.1177/20319525231167982

Alonso, C., Kothari, S., & Rehman, S. (2020). How Artificial Intelligence Could Widen the Gap Between Rich and Poor Nations. International Monetary Fund (IMF). https://www.imf.org/en/Blogs/Articles/2020/12/02/blog-how-artificial-intelligence-could-widen-the-gap-between-rich-and-poor-nations

Altman, S. (2023). *Planning for AGI and beyond.* Open AI. https://openai.com/blog/planning-for-agi-and-beyond

Alzubaidi, L. (2017). Program outcomes assessment using key performance indicators. *Proceedings of 62nd ISERD International Conference*, (January 2017), 20–24.

Aming, A. (2021). Artificial Intelligence AI / Machine Learning ML Drives Increased Capital Efficiency and Minimizes Geological Risk in E&P Operations. Paper presented at the SPE Trinidad and Tobago Section Energy Resources Conference. 10.2118/200978-MS

Anger, S., Hess, P., Janssen, S., & Leber, U. (2023). Chapter 14 Employment-Related Further Traning in a Dynamic Labour Market. In S.Weinertetal.(Eds.), Education, Competence Development and Career Trajectories, Methodology of Educational Measurement and Assessment (pp. 319-336). Springer Nature, Switzerland, AG. doi:10.1007/978-3-031-27007-9_14

An, K., Shan, Y., & Shi, S. (2022). Impact of Industrial Intelligence on Total Factor Productivity. *Sustainability (Basel)*, *14*(14535), 1–21. doi:10.3390/su142114535

Apostolides, A. (2008). A Primer on Multifactor Productivity: Description, Benefits, and Uses. Bureau of Transportation Statistics. https://www7.bts.dot.gov/sites/bts.dot.gov/files/docs/browse-statistical-products-and-data/bts-publications/201991/multifactor-productivity.pdf

Arntz, M., Gregory, T., & Zierahn, U. (2016). The Risk of Automation for Jobs. In *OECD Countries: A Comparative Analysis. OECD Social, Employment and Migration Working Paper, 189*. OECD Publishing., Available at www.ifuturo.org/sites/default/files/docs/automation.pdf

Ashima, R., Haleem, A., Bahl, S., Javaid, M., Mahla, S. K., & Singh, S. (2021). Automation and manufacturing of smart materials in Additive Manufacturing technologies using Internet of Things towards the adoption of Industry 4.0. *Materials Today: Proceedings*, *45*, 5081–5088. doi:10.1016/j.matpr.2021.01.583

Ashok, M., Madan, R., Joha, A., & Sivarajah, U. (2022). Ethical framework for Artificial Intelligence and Digital technologies. *International Journal of Information Management*, *62*, 102433. doi:10.1016/j.ijinfomgt.2021.102433

Åström, J., Reim, W., & Parida, V. (2022). Value creation and value capture for AI business model innovation: A three-phase process framework. *Review of Managerial Science*, *16*(7), 2111–2133. doi:10.1007/s11846-022-00521-z

Atieh, A. M., Cooke, K. O., & Osiyevskyy, O. (2023). The role of intelligent manufacturing systems in the implementation of Industry 4.0 by small and medium enterprises in developing countries. *Engineering Reports*, *5*(3), e12578. doi:10.1002/eng2.12578

Auzina-Emsina, A. (2014). Labour Productivity, Economic Growth and Global Competitiveness in Post-crisis Period. *Procedia: Social and Behavioral Sciences*, *156*, 317–321. doi:10.1016/j.sbspro.2014.11.195

Avent, R. (September 19, 2016). A world without work is coming – It could be utopia or it could be hell. The Guardian. Available at https://www.theguardian.com/commentisfree/2016/sep/19/world-without-work-utopia-hell-human-labour-obsolete

Ayadat, T., Ahmed, D., Chowdhury, S., & Asiz, A. (2020). Measurable performance indicators of student learning outcomes: A case study. *Global Journal of Engineering Education*, *22*(1), 40–50.

AyoubT. Y.AmamiA.HachaichiY. (2023). Expectations of AI Economic Impact & Giant AI Experiments: Case of Chat GPT 3.5. *Research Gate,* 1-9. doi:10.13140/RG.2.2.31305.62565

B˙ohm, S., Carrington, M., Cornelius, N., de Bruin, B., Greenwood, M., Hassan, L., & Shaw, D. (2022). Ethics at the centre of global and local challenges: Thoughts on the future of business ethics. *Journal of Business Ethics*, 180(3), 835–861.

Bak, M., Madai, V. I., Fritzsche, M.-C., Mayrhofer, M. T., & McLennan, S. (2022). You Can't Have AI Both Ways: Balancing Health Data Privacy and Access Fairly. *Frontiers in Genetics*, *13*(929453), 1–7. doi:10.3389/fgene.2022.929453 PMID:35769991

Banafa, A. The Future of Cybersecurity: Predictions and Trends. BBVA Openmind. 2023. Available from: https://www.bbvaopenmind.com/en/technology/digital-world/future-of-cybersecurity-predictions-trends. Accessed 19 Jun 2023.

Bansal, R. (2024). Unveiling the Potential of ChatGPT for Enhancing Customer Engagement. In *Leveraging ChatGPT and Artificial Intelligence for Effective Customer Engagement* (pp. 111–128). IGI Global. doi:10.4018/979-8-3693-0815-8

Bartelsman, E., Haltiwanger, J., & Scarpetta, S. (2004). *Microeconomic Evidence of Creative Destruction in Industrial and Developing Countries.* World Bank.

Bassetti, T., Borbon Galvez, Y., Del Sorbo, M., & Pavesi, F. (2020). Artificial Intelligence – impact on total factor productivity, e-commerce & and fintech. [EU]. *European Union.* Advance online publication. doi:10.2760/333292

Beaudreau, B. C. (2020). *The Economics of Speed: Machine Speed as the Key Factor in Productivity.* Springer. doi:10.1007/978-3-030-26713-1

Becker, B. (2015). Public R&D Policies and Private R&D Investment: A Survey of the Empirical Evidence. *Journal of Economic Surveys, 29*(5), 917–942. doi:10.1111/joes.12074

Bécue, A., Praça, I., & Gama, J. (2021). Artificial intelligence, cyber-threats and Industry 4.0: Challenges and opportunities. *Artificial Intelligence Review, 54*(5), 3849–3886. doi:10.1007/s10462-020-09942-2

Behi, B., Arefi, A., Jennings, P., Gorjy, A., & Pivrikas, A. (2021). Advanced Monitoring and Control System for Virtual Power Plants for Enabling Customer Engagement and Market Participation. *Energies, 14*(4), 1–14. doi:10.3390/en14041113

Bessen, J. (2018). AI and Jobs: The role of demand. NBER Working Paper No. 24235. Available at https://www.nber.org/papers/w24235. Accessed September 07, 2023.

Bhattacharya, P., Chatterjee, S., Datt, R., Verma, A., & Dutta, P. K. (2023). A Permissioned Blockchain Approach for Real-Time Embedded Control Systems. In S. Kadry & R. Prasath (Eds.), Lecture Notes in Computer Science: Vol. 13924. *Mining Intelligence and Knowledge Exploration. MIKE 2023.* Springer., doi:10.1007/978-3-031-44084-7_32

Bilal, M., Alsaidan, I., Alaraj, M., Almasoudi, F. M., & Rizwan, M. M. (2022). Techno-Economic and Environmental Analysis of Grid-Connected Electric Vehicle Charging Station Using AI-Based Algorithm. *Mathematics, 10*(6), 924. doi:10.3390/math10060924

Bishop, J. (2019). Assisting human interaction (United States Patent) [Review of Assisting human interaction]. https://patents.google.com/patent/US10467916B2

Bishop, J. (2015). Supporting communication between people with social orientation impairments using affective computing technologies: Rethinking the autism spectrum. In *Assistive technologies for physical and cognitive disabilities* (pp. 42–55). IGI Global. doi:10.4018/978-1-4666-7373-1.ch003

Bishop, J., & Reddy, M. (2003). The role of the Internet for educating individuals with social orientation impairments. *Journal of Computer Assisted Learning, 19*(4), 546–556. doi:10.1046/j.0266-4909.2003.00057.x

Blackman, R. (2020, October 15). *A Practical Guide to Building Ethical AI*. Retrieved fromhttps://hbr.org/2020/10/a-practical-guide-to-building-ethical-ai

Bloom, N., Van Reenen, J., & Williams, H. (2019). A toolkit of policies to promote innovation. *The Journal of Economic Perspectives*, *33*(3), 163–184. doi:10.1257/jep.33.3.163

Boman, S. (2023). Improving customer support efficiency through decision support powered by machine learning.

Bostrom, N. (2018). Strategic implications of openness in AI development. In*Artificial Intelligence Safety and Security* (pp. 145–164). Chapman and Hall/CRC. doi:10.1201/9781351251389-11

Bowles, J. (July 24, 2014). The computerisation of European Jobs. Bruegel blog. Available at bruegel.org/2014/07/the-computerisation-of-european-jobs/.

Brandolini, A., & Cipollone, P. (2001). *Multifactor Productivity and Labour Quality in Italy, 1981-2000*. Bank of Italy.

Braun, T., Fung, B. C., Iqbal, F., & Shah, B. (2018). Security and privacy challenges in smart cities. *Sustainable Cities and Society*, *39*, 499–507. doi:10.1016/j.scs.2018.02.039

Breslow, L. (2014). Methods of Measuring Learning Outcomes and Value Added, *44*(3), 72. Retrieved from www.et-foundation.co.uk%5Cn10.1080/02615470020028364%5Cnhttp://ludwig.lub.lu.se/login?url=http://search.ebscohost.com/login.aspx?direct=true&AuthType=ip,uid&db=a9h&AN=4139623&site=ehost-live%5Cnhttp://dx.doi.org/10.1016/j.tate.2014.08.004%5Cnhttp://dx.doi

Brito, D., & Curl, R. F. (2020). *Automation Does Not Kill Jobs. It Increases Inequality*. Baker Institute Report no. 11.06.20. Rice University's Baker Institute for Public Policy, Houston, Texas.

Brynjolfsson, E. and G. Petropoulos (2021) 'The coming productivity boom', MIT Technology Review, 10 June

Brynjolfsson, E., & Petropoulos, G. (2022). Advancing a More Productive Tech Economy. A White Paper for the Stanford Institute for Human – Centered Artificial Intelligence and the Stanford Digital Economy Lab.

Brynjolfsson, E., Li, D., & Raymond, L. R. (2023) Generative AI at Work. National Bureau of Economic Research working paper 31161. https://www.nber.org/papers/w31161

Brynjolfsson, E., Mitchell, T., & Rock, D. (2018). What can machines learn and what does it mean for occupations and the economy. *The American Economic Review*, *108*, 43–47.

Brynjolfsson, E., & Petropoulos, G. (2021). *The coming productivity boom*. MIT Technology Review.

Brynjolfsson, E., Rock, D., & Syverson, C. (2021). The Productivity J-Curve: How Intangibles Complement General Purpose Technologies. *American Economic Journal. Macroeconomics*, *13*(1), 333–372. doi:10.1257/mac.20180386

Brzeski, C., & Burk, C. (2015). Die Roboter kommen: Folgen der Automatisierung für den deutschen Arbeitsmarkt (The Robots are coming: Consequences of Automation for the German Labor Market) [German.]. *INGDiBa Econ Res*, *30*, 1–7.

Budennyy, S. A., Lazarev, V. D., Zakharenko, N. N., Korovin, A. N., Plosskaya, O. A., Dimitrov, D. V., Akhripkin, V. S., Pavlov, I. V., Oseledets, I. V., Barsola, I. S., Egorov, I. V., Kosterina, A. A., & Zhukov, L. E. (2022). eco2AI: Carbon Emissions Tracking of Machine Learning Models as the First Step Towards Sustainable AI. *Doklady Mathematics*, *106*(1), S118–S128. doi:10.1134/S1064562422060230

Burns, E. (2023). Machine Learning. *TechTarget network*. https://www.techtarget.com/searchenterpriseai/definition/machine-learning-ML

Calvo, R. A., & D'Mello, S. (2010). Affect detection: An interdisciplinary review of models, methods, and their applications. *IEEE Transactions on Affective Computing*, *1*(1), 18–37. doi:10.1109/T-AFFC.2010.1

Cambria, E., Olsher, D., & Rajagopal, D. (2014). SenticNet 3: A common and common-sense knowledge base for cognition-driven sentiment analysis. *Proceedings of the AAAI Conference on Artificial Intelligence*, *28*(1). Advance online publication. doi:10.1609/aaai.v28i1.8928

Cao, Q., Li, J., Zhang, H., Liu, Y., & Luo, X. (2022). Blockchain and Firm Total Factor Productivity: Evidence from China. *Sustainability (Basel)*, *14*(10165), 1–15. doi:10.3390/su141610165

Cao, Y., & Li, X. (2014). Quality and quality assurance in Chinese private higher education. *Quality Assurance in Education*, *22*(1), 65–87. doi:10.1108/QAE-09-2011-0061

Carbonero, F., Davies, J., Ernst, E., Fossen, F. M., Samaan, D., & Sorgner, A. (2023). The impact of artificial intelligence on labour markets in developing countries: A new method with an illustration for Lao PDR and urban Viet Nam. *Journal of Evolutionary Economics*, *33*(3), 1–30. doi:10.1007/s00191-023-00809-7 PMID:36811092

Carol, J. (2022). *McCall, F.M., DeCaprio, D., & Joseph Gartner, P.* The Measurement and Mitigation of Algorithmic Bias and Unfairness in Healthcare AI Models Developed for the CMS AI Health Outcomes Challenge.

Carter, L., Liu, D., & Cantrell, C. (2020). Exploring the Intersection of the Digital Divide and Artificial Intelligence: A Hermeneutic Literature Review. *AIS Transactions on Human-Computer Interaction*, *12*(4), 253–275. doi:10.17705/1thci.00138

Carter, S., Armstrong, Z., Schubert, L., Johnson, I., & Olah, C. (2019). *Exploring Neural Networks with Activation Atlases*. Distill., doi:10.23915/distill.00015

Carufel, R. (Dec. 18, 2019). Companies embrace AI, but execs cite challenges on alignment, ethics. Agility, PR Solutions. Retrieved from: https://www.agilitypr.com/pr-news/public-relations/companies-embrace-ai-but-execs-

Cavusgil, S. T., Deligonul, S., Kardes, I., & Cavusgil, E. (2018). Middle-class consumers in emerging markets: Conceptualization, propositions, and implications for international marketers. *Journal of International Marketing*, *26*(3), 94–108. doi:10.1509/jim.16.0021

Cedefop. (2009). *The shift to learning outcomes: Policies and practices in Europe. European Centre for the Development of Vocational Training*. doi:10.1108/et.2009.00451cab.002

Chadha, B., & Adams, C. (1992). *Growth, Productivity, and the Rate of Return on Capital. International Monetary Fund.* IMF., doi:10.5089/9781451978407.001.A001

Chakraborty, A., Bhattacharyya, S., De, D., Mahmud, M., & Banerjee, J. S. (2023). Intelligent Automation Framework Using AI and RPA: An Introduction. In S. Bhattacharyya, J. S. Banerjee, & D. De (Eds.), *Confluence of Artificial Intelligence and Robotic Process Automation. Smart Innovation, Systems and Technologies, 335*. Springer., doi:10.1007/978-981-19-8296-5_1

Chang, A. C. (2020). *Intelligence-based medicine: artificial intelligence and human cognition in clinical medicine and healthcare*. Academic Press.

Chang, J., Lan, Q., Tang, W., Chen, H., Liu, J., & Duan, Y. (2023). Research on the Impact of Digital Economy on Manufacturing Total Factor Productivity. *Sustainability (Basel)*, *15*(5683), 1–21. doi:10.3390/su15075683

Chang, L., Taghizadeh-Hesary, F., & Mohsin, M. (2023). Role of artificial intelligence on green economic development: Joint determinates of natural resources and green total factor productivity. *Resources Policy*, *82*, 103508. doi:10.1016/j.resourpol.2023.103508

Chelliah, J. (2017). Will artificial intelligence usurp white-collar jobs? *Human Resource Management International Digest*, *25*(3), 1–3. doi:10.1108/HRMID-11-2016-0152

Chen, H., Ma, Z., Xiao, H., Li, J., & Chen, W. (2023). The Impact of Digital Economy Empowerment on Green Total Factor Productivity in Forestry. *Forests*, 14(1729):1-23. doi:10.3390/f14091729

Chen, M., & Zhang L. (2023). The econometric analysis of voluntary environmental regulations and total factor productivity in agribusiness under digitization. *PLoS ONE*, 18(9-e0291637): 1-22. doi:10.1371/journal.pone.0291637

Chen, M., Radford, A., Child, R., Wu, J., Jun, H., Luan, D., & Sutskever, I. (2020). Generative pretraining from pixels. *In International conference on machine learning,* 1691-1703). PMLR. https://cdn.openai.com/papers/Generative_Pretraining_from_Pixels_V2.pdf

Cheng, X., Chaw, J. K., Goh, K. M., Ting, T. T., Sahrani, S., Ahmad, M. N., Abdul Kadir, R., & Ang, M. C. (2022). Systematic Literature Review on Visual Analytics of Predictive Maintenance in the Manufacturing Industry. *Sensors (Basel)*, *22*(6321), 1–16. doi:10.3390/s22176321 PMID:36080780

Cheng, Y., Zhou, X., & Li, Y. (2023). The effect of digital transformation on real economy enterprises' total factor productivity. *International Review of Economics & Finance*, *85*, 488–501. doi:10.1016/j.iref.2023.02.007

Chen, P. (2022). The impact of smart city pilots on corporate total factor productivity. *Environmental Science and Pollution Research International*, *29*(55), 83155–83168. doi:10.1007/s11356-022-21681-1 PMID:35763146

Chen, S., Sohail, M. T., & Yang, M. (2022). Examining the effects of information and communications technology on green growth and environmental performance, socio-economic and environmental cost of technology generation: A pathway toward environment sustainability. *Frontiers in Psychology*, *13*, 1–9. doi:10.3389/fpsyg.2022.999045 PMID:36172239

Chen, W., & Wellman, B. (2004). The global digital divide–within and between countries. *ITandSociety*, *1*(7), 39–45.

Christensen, L. R., Cummings, D., & Jorgenson, D. W. (1980). Economic Growth, 1947-1973: An International Comparison. In J. W. Kendrick & B. Vaccara (Eds.), *New Developments in Productivity Measurement* (pp. 17–131). University of Chicago Press.

Chuchro, R., & Gupta, D. (2017). Game playing with deep q-learning using openai gym. *Semantic Scholar,* 1-6. http://vision.stanford.edu/teaching/cs231n/reports/2017/pdfs/616.pdf

Converso, G., Gallo, M., Murino, T., & Vespoli, S. (2023). Predicting Failure Probability in Industry 4.0 Production Systems: A Workload-Based Prognostic Model for Maintenance Planning. *Applied Sciences (Basel, Switzerland), 13*(3), 1938. doi:10.3390/app13031938

Cornelli, G., Frost, J., & Mishra, S. (2023). Artificial intelligence, services globalisation and income inequality. BIS Working Paper, 1135: 1-35. https://www.bis.org/publ/work1135.pdf

Crawford, K. (2021). *The atlas of AI: Power, politics, and the planetary costs of artificial intelligence.* Yale University Press.

Creamer, D. B., Dobrovolsky, S. B., & Borenstein, I. (2015). *Capital in manufacturing and mining: Its formation and financing*. Princeton University Press.

Creswell, A., White, T., Dumoulin, V., Arulkumaran, K., Sengupta, B., & Bharath, A. (2018). Generative Adversarial Networks: An Overview. *IEEE Signal Processing Magazine*, *35*(1), 53–65. doi:10.1109/MSP.2017.2765202

Crippa, M., Guizzardi, D., Pagani, F., Banja, M., Muntean, M., Schaaf E., Becker, W., Monforti-Ferrario, F., Quadrelli, R., Risquez Martin, A., Taghavi-Moharamli, P., Köykkä, J., Grassi, G., Rossi, S., Brandao De Melo, J., Oom, D., Branco, A., San-Miguel, J., & Vignati, E. (2023). GHG emissions of all world countries. European Union (EU), Luxembourg. doi:10.2760/953322

CrowdStrike. Small Business Cyberattack Analysis: The Most Targeted SMB Sectors. CrowdStrike Blog. Available from: https://www.crowdstrike.com/blog/small-business-cyberattack-analysis-most-targeted-smb-sectors/. Accessed 17 Aug 2023.

Dai, Y., Liu, A., & Lim, C. P. (2023). Reconceptualizing ChatGPT and generative AI as a student-driven innovation in higher education.

Dale, R. (2021). GPT-3: What's it good for? *Natural Language Engineering*, *27*(1), 113–118. doi:10.1017/S1351324920000601

Damioli, G., Van Roy, V., & Vertesy, D. (2021). The impact of artificial intelligence on labour productivity. *Eurasian Business Review*, *11*(1), 1–25. doi:10.1007/s40821-020-00172-8

Daugherty, P. R., & Wilson, H. J. (2018). *Human+ machine: Reimagining work in the age of AI*. Harvard Business Press.

Dauth, W., Findeisen, S., Südekum, J., & Woessner, N. (2017). German robots – The impact of industrial robots on workers. IAB Discussion Paper 30/2017 (Institute for Employment Research, Nuremberg, Germany).

Dauth, W., Findeisen, S., & Suedekum, J. (2017). Trade and Manufacturing Jobs in Germany. *The American Economic Review*, *107*(5), 337–342. doi:10.1257/aer.p20171025

Davenport, T. H. (2018). *The AI advantage: How to put the artificial intelligence revolution to work*. MIT Press. doi:10.7551/mitpress/11781.001.0001

David, H., & Dorn, D. (2013). The Growth of Low-Skill Service Jobs and the Polarization of the US Labor Market. *The American Economic Review*, *103*(5), 1553–1597. doi:10.1257/aer.103.5.1553

De Grip, A., & Van Loo, J. (2002), "The economics of skills obsolescence: A review", de Grip, A., van Loo, J. and Mayhew, K. (Ed.) The Economics of Skills Obsolescence (Research in Labor Economics, Vol. 21), Emerald Group Publishing Limited, Bingley, pp. 1-26. doi:10.1016/S0147-9121(02)21003-1

Demaidi, M. N. (2023). Artificial intelligence national strategy in a developing country. *AI & Society*, •••, 1–13. doi:10.1007/s00146-023-01779-x

Dergaa, I., Saad, H. B., El Omri, A., Glenn, J., Clark, C., Washif, J., ... Chamari, K. (2023). Using artificial intelligence for exercise prescription in personalised health promotion: A critical evaluation of OpenAI's GPT-4 model. *Biology of Sport*, *41*(2), 221–241. doi:10.5114/biolsport.2024.133661 PMID:38524814

Derks, D., Fischer, A. H., & Bos, A. E. R. (2008). The role of emotion in computer-mediated communication: A Review. *Computers in Human Behavior*, *24*(3), 766–785. doi:10.1016/j.chb.2007.04.004

Devlin, J., Chang, M. W., Lee, K., & Toutanova, K. (2018). BERT: Pre-training of deep bidirectional transformers for language understanding.

Dewan, S., & Riggins, F. J. (2005). The digital divide: Current and future research directions. *Journal of the Association for Information Systems*, *6*(12), 298–337. doi:10.17705/1jais.00074

Dimaggio, P., Hargittai, E., Celeste, C., & Shafer, S. (2004). Digital inequality: From unequal access to differentiated use. In *Social Inequality* (pp. 355–400). Russell Sage Foundation.

Donahue, M. Z. (2019). Q&A: AI for developing countries must be adaptable and low-cost. SciDev. net-Health.

Drucker, P. F. (2018). The new productivity challenge. In *Quality in Higher Education* (pp. 37–46). Routledge. doi:10.4324/9781351293563-2

Dwivedi, V. J., & Joshi, Y. C. (2019). Productivity in 21st Century Indian Higher Education Institutions. *International Journal of Human Resource Management and Research*, *9*(4), 61–80. doi:10.24247/ijhrmraug20197

Ernst, E. (2022). The AI trilemma: Saving the planet without ruining our jobs. *Frontiers in Artificial Intelligence*, *5*(886561), 1–20. doi:10.3389/frai.2022.886561 PMID:36337142

Fan, H., Zhang, N., & Su, H. (2023). The effects of smart city construction on urban green total factor productivity: evidence from China. *Economic Research-Ekonomska Istraživanja,* 36(1-2181840): 1-18. doi:10.1080/1331677X.2023.2181840

Farhan, A. (2023). The Impact of Artificial Intelligence on Human Workers. *Journal Of Communication Education.*, *17*(2), 93–104. doi:10.58217/joce-ip.v17i2.350

Farrell, C. (February 11, 2013). Will Robots Create Economic Utopia? Bloomberg. Available at https://www.bloomberg.com/news/articles/2013-02-11/will-robotscreate-economic-utopia

Fasso Wamba, S., Queiroz, M. M., Guthrie, C., & Braganza, A. (2021). Industry experiences of artificial intelligence (AI): Benefits and challenges in operations and supply chain management. *Production Planning and Control*, *1-5*. Advance online publication. doi:10.1080/09537287.2021.1882695

Feldman, J., Zhang, D. J., Liu, X., & Zhang, N. (2022). Customer choice models vs. machine learning: Finding optimal product displays on Alibaba. *Operations Research*, *70*(1), 309–328. doi:10.1287/opre.2021.2158

Felzmann, H., Fosch-Villaronga, E., Lutz, C., & Tamò-Larrieux, A. (2020). Towards transparency by design for artificial intelligence. *Science and Engineering Ethics*, *26*(6), 3333–3361. doi:10.1007/s11948-020-00276-4 PMID:33196975

Fietz, K., & Lay, J. (2023). Digitalisation and labour markets in developing countries. German Institute of Global and Area Studies (GIGA), Hamburg. http://hdl.handle.net/10419/272227

Filipkowski, B. What is the future of cybersecurity? Fieldeffect. 2023. Available from: https://fieldeffect.com/blog/what-is-the-future-of-cyber-security. Accessed 19 Jun 2023.

Floridi, L., & Chiriatti, M. (2020). GPT-3: Its Nature, Scope, Limits, and Consequences. *Minds and Machines*, *30*(4), 681–694. doi:10.1007/s11023-020-09548-1

Franki, V., Majnarić, D., & Višković, A. (2023). A Comprehensive Review of Artificial Intelligence (AI) Companies in the Power Sector. *Energies*, *16*(1077), 1–35. doi:10.3390/en16031077

Franklin, M. (2018). A simple guide to multi-factor productivity. Office for National Statistics (ONS). https://www.ons.gov.uk/economy/economicoutputandproductivity/productivitymeasures/methodologies/asimpleguidetomultifactorproductivity#multi-factor-productivity

Frase, P. (2016). *Four Futures: Life after Capitalism.* Verso Books.

Frey, C.B. and Osborne, M.A. (2017). "The future of employment: How susceptible are jobs to computerisation?" Technol Forecast Soc Change, 114, Pp, 254–280.

Furman, J., & Seamans, R. (2019). AI and the Economy. *Innovation Policy and the Economy, 19*(1), 161–191. doi:10.1086/699936

Fu, W., & Zhang, R. (2022). Can Digitalization Levels Affect Agricultural Total Factor Productivity? Evidence From China. *Frontiers in Sustainable Food Systems, 6*(860780), 1–16. doi:10.3389/fsufs.2022.860780

Fu, X., Woo, W. T., & Hou, J. (2016). Technological innovation policy in China: The lessons, and the necessary changes ahead. *Economic Change and Restructuring, 49*(2-3), 139–157. doi:10.1007/s10644-016-9186-x

Gama, F., & Magistretti, S. (2023). Artificial intelligence in innovation management: A review of innovation capabilities and a taxonomy of AI applications. *Journal of Product Innovation Management*, jpim.12698. doi:10.1111/jpim.12698

Gan, T., Kumar, A., Ehiwario, M., Zhang, B., Semroski, C., de Jesus, O., Hoffmann, O., & Yasser, M. (2019). Artificial Intelligent Logs for Formation Evaluation Using Case Studies in the Gulf of Mexico and Trinidad & Tobago. Paper presented at the SPE Annual Technical Conference and Exhibition, Calgary, Alberta, Canada, September 2019. 10.2118/196064-MS

Gaur, L., Afaq, A., Arora, G. K., & Khan, N. (2023). Artificial intelligence for carbon emissions using a system of systems theory. *Ecological Informatics, 76*(102165), 102165. Advance online publication. doi:10.1016/j.ecoinf.2023.102165

Geelan, T. (2021). Introduction to the Special Issue internet, social media and trade union revitalization: Still behind the digital curve or catching up? *New Technology, Work and Employment, 36*(2), 123–139. doi:10.1111/ntwe.12205

George, A. H., Hameed, A. S., George, A. S., & Baskar, T. (2022). Study on Quantitative Understanding and Knowledge of Farmers in Trichy District. *Partners Universal International Research Journal, 1*(2), 5–8.

George, A. S., & George, A. H. (2023). A review of ChatGPT AI's impact on several business sectors. *Partners Universal International Innovation Journal, 1*(1), 9–23.

George, A. S., George, A. H., Baskar, T., & Pandey, D. (2022). The Transformation of the workspace using Multigigabit Ethernet. *Partners Universal International Research Journal, 1*(3), 34–43.

Ghosh, S. The biggest data breaches in India, CSO Online tracks recent major data breaches in India. CSO Online. 2021. Available from: https://www.csoonline.com/article/3541148/the-biggest-data-breaches-in-india.html

Gilbert, E. (2023). Beyond the usual suspects: Invisible labour(ers) in futures of work. *Geography Compass*, *17*(2, e12675), 1–12. doi:10.1111/gec3.12675

Gopinath, G. (Jun 5, 2023). *The Power and Perils of the "Artificial Hand": Considering AI Through the Ideas of Adam Smith Speech to commemorate 300th anniversary of Adam Smith's birth University of Glasgow.* International Monetary Fund. Retrieved from https://www.imf.org/en/News/Articles/2023/06/05/sp060523-fdmd-ai-adamsmith?cid=em-COM-123-46688

Gordon, R. J. (2018). Why Has Economic Growth Slowed When Innovation Appears to be Accelerating? NBER Working Paper 24554. National Bureau for Economic Research.

Gordon, R. J. (2016). *The rise and fall of American growth: The US standard of living since the Civil War.* Princeton University Press. doi:10.1515/9781400873302

Graetz, G., & Michaels, G. (2018). Robots at work. *The Review of Economics and Statistics*, *100*(5), 753–768. doi:10.1162/rest_a_00754

Gray, A. (2017). *5 global problems that AI could help us solve.* World Economic Forum (WEF). https://www.weforum.org/agenda/2017/02/5-global-problems-that-ai-could-help-us-solve/

Gries, T., & Naudié, W. (2018). Artificial intelligence, jobs, inequality and productivity: Does aggregate demand matter? IZA DP No. 12005, Bonn.

Griffiths, S., Sovacool, B. K., Kim, J., Bazilian, M., & Uratani, J. M. (2022). Decarbonizing the oil refining industry: A systematic review of sociotechnical systems, technological innovations, and policy options. *Energy Research & Social Science*, *89*, 102542. doi:10.1016/j.erss.2022.102542

Griliches, Z. (1990). Patent statistics as economic indicators: A survey. *Journal of Economic Literature*, *18*, 1661–1707.

Gupta, U. G. (2023). How to Bridge the Gap between AI Ethical Guidelines and Responsible Ethical Conduct. *AIMS International Journal of Management*, *17*(1), 41–53. doi:10.26573/2021.17.1.4

Hakiki, M., Fadli, R., Samala, A. D., Fricticarani, A., Dayurni, P., Rahmadani, K., & Astiti, A. D. (2023). Exploring the impact of using Chat-GPT on student learning outcomes in technology learning: The comprehensive experiment. *Advances in Mobile Learning Educational Research*, *3*(2), 859–872. doi:10.25082/AMLER.2023.02.013

Haluza, D., & Jungwirth, D. (2023). Artificial Intelligence and Ten Societal Megatrends: An Exploratory Study Using GPT-3. *Systems*, *11*(3), 120. doi:10.3390/systems11030120

Hassel, A., & Ozkiziltan, D. (2023). Governing the work-related risks of AI: Implications for the German government and trade unions. *Transfer: European Review of Labour and Research*, *29*(1), 71–86. doi:10.1177/10242589221147228

Hatzius, J., Briggs, J., Kodnani, D., & Pierdomenico, G. (2023). The Potentially Large Effects of Artificial Intelligence on Economic Growth. Goldman and Sachs.

Hentzen, J. K., Hoffmann, A., Dolan, R., & Pala, E. (2022). Artificial intelligence in customer-facing financial services: A systematic literature review and agenda for future research. *International Journal of Bank Marketing*, *40*(6), 1299–1336. doi:10.1108/IJBM-09-2021-0417

He, X., Liang, Y., Liang, D., & Deng, H. (2023). The impact of China's information infrastructure construction policy on green total factor productivity: Moving towards a green world. *Environmental Science and Pollution Research International*, *30*(46), 103017–103032. Advance online publication. doi:10.1007/s11356-023-29638-8 PMID:37676455

Hilal, W., Gadsden, S. A., & Yawney, J. (2022). Financial fraud: A review of anomaly detection techniques and recent advances. *Expert Systems with Applications*, *193*, 116429. doi:10.1016/j.eswa.2021.116429

Hosein, G., Hosein, P., Bahadoorsingh, S., Martinez, R., & Sharma, C. (2020). Predicting Renewable Energy Investment Using Machine Learning. *Energies*, *13*(4494), 1–9. doi:10.3390/en13174494

Humlum, A. (2020). *Robot Adoption and Labor Market Dynamics*, Working paper, University of Chicago.

Ip, G. (August 2, 2017). We survived spreadsheets, and we'll survive AI. Wall Street Journal. Available at https://www.wsj.com/articles/wesurvived-spreadsheetsand-well-survive-ai-1501688765

Jackson, K. (April 25, 1993). The World's First Motel Rests Upon Its Memories. Seattle Times. Available at www.community.seattletimes.nwsource.com/archive/?date=19930425&slug=1697701

Jaimovitch-López, G., Ferri, C., Hernández-Orallo, J., Martínez-Plumed, F., & Ramírez-Quintana, M. J. (2023). Can language models automate data wrangling? *Machine Learning*, *112*(6), 2053–2082. doi:10.1007/s10994-022-06259-9

Jamal, H., Ahmed Algeelani, N., & Al-Sammarraie, N. A. (2024). Safeguarding data privacy: Strategies to counteract internal and external hacking threats. *Computer Science and Information Technology*, *5*(1), 40–48. doi:10.11591/csit.v5i1.p40-48

Jarrahi, M. H. (2018). Artificial intelligence and the future of work: Human-AI symbiosis in organizational decision making. *Business Horizons*, *61*(4), 577–586. doi:10.1016/j.bushor.2018.03.007

Javaid, M., Haleem, A., Singh, R. P., & Suman, R. (2021). Significance of Quality 4.0 towards comprehensive enhancement in the manufacturing sector. *Sensors International*, *2*(100109), 1–13. doi:10.1016/j.sintl.2021.100109

Javaid, M., Haleem, A., Singh, R. P., Suman, R., & Gonzalez, E. S. (2022). Understanding the adoption of Industry 4.0 technologies in improving environmental sustainability. *Sustainable Operations and Computers*, *3*, 203–217. doi:10.1016/j.susoc.2022.01.008

Johannessen, J. A. (2021). *China's innovation economy: artificial intelligence and the new silk road.* Routledge. doi:10.4324/9781003211907

Jorgenson, D. W. (2009). *Productivity and Economic Growth.* doi:10.4337/9781784712891

Jungwirth, D., & Haluza, D. (2023). Artificial intelligence and public health: An exploratory study. *International Journal of Environmental Research and Public Health, 20*(5), 4541. doi:10.3390/ijerph20054541 PMID:36901550

Karpathy, A., Abbeel, P., Brockman, G., Chen, P., Cheung, V., Duan, Y., Goodfellow, I., Kingma, D., Ho, J., Houthooft, R., Saliman, T., Schulman, J., Sutskever, I., & Zaremba, W. (2016). *Generative models.* Open AI. https://openai.com/research/generative-models

Katar, O., ÖZKAN, D., YILDIRIM, Ö., & Acharya, U. R. (2023). Evaluation of GPT-3 AI language model in research paper writing. *Turkish Journal of Science and Technology, 18*(2), 311–318.

Keshavarz, M. (2011). Measuring course learning outcomes. *Journal of Learning Design, 4*(4), 1–9. doi:10.5204/jld.v4i4.84

Khan, J. Y., & Uddin, G. (2022, October). Automatic code documentation generation using gpt-3. In *Proceedings of the 37th IEEE/ACM International Conference on Automated Software Engineering* (pp. 1-6).

Kim, E. (2006). The New Electronic Discovery Rules: A Place for Employee Privacy? *The Yale Law Journal, 115*(6), 1481. doi:10.2307/20455660

King, G. S., & Rameshwar, J. R. (2017). *Stimulating Innovation through Industry 4.0 in a Small Commodity-Based Economy.* SPIM Innovation Summit – Building the Innovation Century.

Kirchschläger, P. G. (2021). *Digital transformation and ethics: ethical considerations on the robotization and automation of society and the economy and the use of artificial intelligence.* Nomos Verlag. doi:10.5771/9783845285504

Kočenda, E., & Alexandr, Č. (2014). *Elements of Time Series Econometrics: An Applied Approach.* Karolinum Press.

Korkmaz, S., & Korkmaz, O. (2017). The Relationship between Labor Productivity and Economic Growth in OECD Countries. *International Journal of Economics and Finance, 9*(5), 71–76. doi:10.5539/ijef.v9n5p71

Kralj Novak, P., Smailović, J., Sluban, B., & Mozetič, I. (2015). Sentiment of Emojis. *PLoS One, 10*(12), e0144296. Advance online publication. doi:10.1371/journal.pone.0144296 PMID:26641093

Krzywdzinski, M., Gerst, D., & Butollo, F. (2023). Promoting human-centred AI in the workplace. Trade Unions and their strategies for regulating the use of AI in Germany. *Transfer: European Review of Labour and Research, 29*(1), 53–70. doi:10.1177/10242589221142273

Kuah, A. T., & Wang, P. (2017). Fast-Expanding "Online" Markets in South Korea and China: Are They Worth Pursuing? *Thunderbird International Business Review*, *59*(1), 63–77. doi:10.1002/tie.21779

Kuhn, T. (1962). *The structure of scientific revolutions*. University of Chicago Press.

Kumar Sharma, A., & Sharma, R. (2023). The role of generative pre-trained transformers (GPTs) in revolutionising digital marketing: A conceptual model. *Journal of Cultural Marketing Strategy*, *8*(1), 80–92.

Kumar, A., Gupta, N., & Bapat, G. (2023). Who is making the decisions? How retail managers can use the power of ChatGPT. *The Journal of Business Strategy*.

Kushwaha, A. K., & Kar, A. K. (2021). *MarkBot – A Language Model-Driven Chatbot for Interactive Marketing in Post-Modern World*. Retrieved January 31, 2023, from Information Systems Frontiers. . doi:10.1007/s10796-021-10184-y

Lauraitiene, L., & Vitunskiene, V. (2022). A Theoretical Approach to Measuring Environmentally Sustainable Growth of Agriculture. *Scientific Papers. Series Management, Economic, Engineering in Agriculture and Rural Development*, *22*(1), 371–377.

Lauriola, I., Lavelli, A., & Aiolli, F. (2022). An introduction to deep learning in natural language processing: Models, techniques, and tools. *Neurocomputing*, *470*, 443–456. doi:10.1016/j.neucom.2021.05.103

Lauterbach, A. (2019). Artificial intelligence and policy: Quo vadis? *Digital Policy. Regulation & Governance*, *21*(3), 238–263. doi:10.1108/DPRG-09-2018-0054

Le Ludec, C., Cornet, M., & Casilli, A. A. (2023). The problem with annotation. Human labour and outsourcing between France and Madagascar. *Big Data & Society*, *10*(2), 1–13. doi:10.1177/20539517231188723

Lee, C. T., Pan, L. Y., & Hsieh, S. H. (2022). Artificial intelligent chatbots as brand promoters: A two-stage structural equation modeling-artificial neural network approach. *Internet Research*, *32*(4), 1329–1356. doi:10.1108/INTR-01-2021-0030

Leippold, M. (2023). Sentiment spin: Attacking financial sentiment with GPT-3. *Finance Research Letters*, *55*, 103957. doi:10.1016/j.frl.2023.103957

Levy, D. H. F., & Murnane, R. J. (2003). The Skill Content of Recent Technological Change: An Empirical Exploration. *The Quarterly Journal of Economics*, *118*(4), 1279–1333. https://www.jstor.org/stable/25053940. doi:10.1162/003355303322552801

Liang, S., Yang, J., & Ding, T. (2022). Performance evaluation of AI driven low carbon manufacturing industry in China: An interactive network DEA approach. *Computers & Industrial Engineering*, *170*, 108248. doi:10.1016/j.cie.2022.108248

Li, E., Chen, Q., Zhang, X., & Zhang, C. (2023). Digital Government Development, Local Governments' Attention Distribution and Enterprise Total Factor Productivity: Evidence from China. *Sustainability (Basel)*, *15*(2472), 1–19. doi:10.3390/su15032472

LiJ. (2023). Advancing Personalized Learning with Multi-modal Embedding Open Learner Model and GPT Prompt. doi:10.36227/techrxiv.24087288.v1

Liu, J., Chang, H., Forrest, J. Y.-L., & Yang, B. (2020). Influence of artificial intelligence on technological innovation: Evidence from the panel data of China's manufacturing sectors. *Technological Forecasting and Social Change*, *158*(120142), 1–11. doi:10.1016/j.techfore.2020.120142

Li, Y., Yi, J., Chen, H., & Peng, D. (2021). Theory and application of artificial intelligence in financial industry. *Data Science in Finance and Economics*, *1*(2), 96–116. doi:10.3934/DSFE.2021006

Lokman, A. S., & Ameedeen, M. A. (2018). *Modern chatbot systems: A technical review. Proceedings of the Future Technologies Conference* (pp. 1012–1023). Cham: Springer, (November).10.1007/978-3-030-02683-7_75

Mahmoud, M., & Slama, S. B. (2023). Peer-to-Peer Energy Trading Case Study Using an AI-Powered Community Energy Management System. *Applied Sciences (Basel, Switzerland)*, *13*(13), 1–19. doi:10.3390/app13137838

Majumder, E. (2022). ChatGPT-what is it and how does it work exactly?. *Geek Culture, 18*.

Mak, K. K., & Pichika, M. R. (2019). Artificial intelligence in drug development: Present status and future prospects. *Drug Discovery Today*, *24*(3), 773–780. doi:10.1016/j.drudis.2018.11.014 PMID:30472429

Makridakis, S. (2017). The forthcoming artificial intelligence (AI) revolution: Its impact on society and firms. *Futures*, *90*, 46–60. doi:10.1016/j.futures.2017.03.006

Manca, F. (2023). *Six questions about the demand for artificial intelligence skills in labour markets*. OECD., doi:10.1787/ac1bebf0-

Mannuru, N. R., Shahriar, S., Teel, Z. A., Wang, T., Lund, B. D., Tijani, S., Pohboon, C. O., Agbaji, D., Alhassan, J., Galley, J., Kousari, R., Ogbadu-Oladapo, L., Saurav, S. K., Srivastava, A., Tummuru, S. P., Uppala, S., & Vaidya, P. (2023). Artificial intelligence in developing countries: The impact of generative artificial intelligence (AI) technologies for development. *Information Development*, *0*(0), 02666669231200628. Advance online publication. doi:10.1177/02666669231200628

Marín, F. M. (2023). *De las humanidades digitales a la Inteligencia Artificial General*. University of Texas at San Antonio.

Martín, R., Gomes, C., Alleyne, D., & Phillips, W. (2013). An assessment of the economic and social impacts of climate change on the energy sector in the Caribbean. ECLAC. https://repositorio.cepal.org/server/api/core/bitstreams/59eea92d-9401-4309-a808-b58e7bd2de2a/content

Martinelli, A., Mina, A., & Moggi, M. (2021). The enabling technologies of industry 4.0: Examining the seeds of the fourth industrial revolution. *Industrial and Corporate Change*, *30*(1), 161–188. doi:10.1093/icc/dtaa060

Martin, S. (2003). Is the digital Divide Really Closing? A Critique of Inequality Measurement in A Nation Online. *ITandSociety*, *1*(4), 1–13.

Mehrabi, M. G., Ulsoy, A. G., & Koren, Y. (2000). Reconfigurable manufacturing systems: Key to future manufacturing. *Journal of Intelligent Manufacturing*, *11*(4), 403–419. doi:10.1023/A:1008930403506

Mert, M. (2017). "Technological Progress, Labour Productivity And Economic Growth: Disentangling The Negative And Positive Effects" *28th International Academic Conference*, Tel Aviv. 10.20472/IAC.2017.028.012

Ministry of Planning and Development (MPD)Central Statistical Office. (CSO). (2023). *National Accounts.* CSO. https://cso.gov.tt/subjects/national-accounts/

Ministry of the Attorney General and Legal Affairs (MAGLA). (2016). Data Protection Act Chapter 22:04 Act 13 of 2011. MAGLA, Port-of-Spain, Trinidad, and Tobago. https://agla.gov.tt/downloads/laws/22.04.pdf

Mirbabaie, M., Brünker, F., Möllmann, N. R., & Stieglitz, S. (2022). The rise of artificial intelligence–understanding the AI identity threat at the workplace. *Electronic Markets*, *32*(1), 73–99. doi:10.1007/s12525-021-00496-x

Mishel, L., & Bivens, J. (2021). The Productivity-Median Compensation Gap in the United States: The Contribution of Increased Wage Inequality and the Role of Policy Choices. *International Productivity Monitor*, (41), 61+. https://link.gale.com/apps/doc/A689169156/AONE?u=anon~10ba8f08&sid=googleScholar&xid=5119dfa8

Mishra, A. Cyber-attacks that shook Indian firms in 2022: Critical infra, healthcare most targeted. ET Insights. 2022. Available from: https://etinsights.et-edge.com/cyber-attacks-that-shook-indian-firms-in-2022-critical-infra-healthcare-most-targeted/

Mitchell, A. (January 25, 2023). ChatGPT could make these jobs obsolete: 'The wolf is at the door.' *New York Post*. Retrieved from https://nypost.com/2023/01/25/chat-gpt-could-make-these-jobs-obsolete/

Morrison, J., Roth McDuffie, A., & French, B. (2015). Identifying key components of teaching and learning in a STEM school. *School Science and Mathematics*, *115*(5), 244–255. doi:10.1111/ssm.12126

Motlagh, N. Y., Khajavi, M., Sharifi, A., & Ahmadi, M. (2023). The impact of artificial intelligence on the evolution of digital education: A comparative study of openAI text generation tools including ChatGPT, Bing Chat, Bard, and Ernie. *arXiv preprint arXiv:2309.02029.*

Mujtaba, D. F., & Mahapatra, N., N. R. (2019). Ethical Considerations in AI-Based Recruitment, *2019 IEEE International Symposium on Technology and Society (ISTAS)*, Medford, MA, USA, 1-7. 10.1109/ISTAS48451.2019.8937920

Mutascu, M., & Hegerty, S. C. (2023). Predicting the contribution of artificial intelligence to unemployment rates: An artificial neural network approach. *Journal of Economics and Finance*, *47*(2), 400–416. doi:10.1007/s12197-023-09616-z

Nacchia, M., Fruggiero, F., Lambiase, A., & Bruton, K. (2021). A Systematic Mapping of the Advancing Use of Machine Learning Techniques for Predictive Maintenance in the Manufacturing Sector. *Applied Sciences (Basel, Switzerland)*, *11*(2546), 1–34. doi:10.3390/app11062546

Nakano, R., Hilton, J., Balaji, S., Wu, J., Ouyang, L., Kim, C., Hesse, C., Jain, S., Kosaraju, V., Saunders, W., & Jiang, X. (2021). *WebGPT: Browser-assisted question-answering with human feedback*. Cornell University, arXiv preprint: 2112.09332, 1-32. https://arxiv.org/pdf/2112.09332.pdf

Naone, E. (November 11, 2009). "The Dark Side of The Technology Utopia". MIT Technology Review. Available at https://www.technologyreview.com/s/416244/the-dark-side-of-the-technology-utopia/

NCAAA. (2022). Key Performance Indicators for Higher Education Institutions. https://www.etec.gov.sa/ar/service/Institutional accreditation/servicedocuments

Neaher, G., Bray, D., Mueller-Kaler, J. & Schatz, B. (2021). *Standardizing the future: How can the United States navigate the geopolitics of international technology standards?* Atlantic Council Report.

Ngutsav, S. A. (2018, June). And Ijirshar, V.U. "Labour Productivity and Economic Growth in Nigeria: A Disaggregated Sector Analysis". *Lafia Journal of Economics and Management Sciences*, *3*(1), 256–276.

Niederman, F., & Baker, E. W. (2022). Ethics and AI Issues: Old Container with New Wine? *Information Systems Frontiers*, *25*(1), 9–28. doi:10.1007/s10796-022-10305-1

NoyS.ZhangW. (2023). Experimental Evidence on the Productivity Effects of Generative Artificial Intelligence. Available at SSRN: https://ssrn.com/abstract=4375283 or doi:10.2139/ssrn.4375283

OECD. (2019). AI Policy Observatory. Available at https://oecd.ai/en/ai-principles

OECD. (2021). *Artificial Intelligence, Machine Learning and Big Data in Finance: Opportunities, Challenges, and Implications for Policy Makers,* https://www.oecd.org/finance/artificial-intelligence-machine-learning-big-data-in-finance.htm

OECD. (2021). Productivity and economic growth. In OECD Compendium of Productivity Indicators 2021. OECD Publishing., Retrieved September 09, 2023, from, doi:10.1787/f8c31e3c-

Okerlund, J., Klasky, E., Middha, A., Kim, S., Rosenfeld, H., Kleinman, M., & Parthasarathy, S. (2022). What's in the chatterbox? Large language models, why they matter, and what we should do about them.

Oosthuizen, K., Botha, E., Robertson, J., & Montecchi, M. (2021). Artificial intelligence in retail: The AI-enabled value chain. *Australasian Marketing Journal*, *29*(3), 264–273. doi:10.1016/j.ausmj.2020.07.007

Open, A. I. (2023b). *OpenAI Charter.* OpenAI. Retrieved from https://openai.com/charter

Open, A. I. (2023c). *Our Structure.* OpenAI. https://openai.com/our-structure

Open, A. I. (2023d). *Research Index.* Open AI. https://openai.com/research

Open, A. I. (2023e). *OpenAL Five defeats Dota 2 world Champions.* OpenAI. https://openai.com/research/openai-five-defeats-dota-2-world-champions

Open, A. I. (2023f). *Introducing ChatGPT.* OpenAI. https://openai.com/blog/chatgpt

Open, A. I. (2023h). GPT-4. OpenAI. https://openai.com/research/gpt-4

OpenA. I. (2023a). *About.* Open AI. https://openai.com/about

Organization for Economic Co-operation and Development (OECD). (2023a). Multifactor productivity. OECD. https://data.oecd.org/lprdty/multifactor-productivity.htm

Organization for Economic Co-operation and Development (OECD). (2023b). OECD Compendium of Productivity Indicators 2023. OECD. https://www.oecd-ilibrary.org/sites/74623e5b-en/index.html?itemId=/content/publication/74623e5b-en

Organization for Economic Co-operation and Development (OECD). (2023c). Multifactor Productivity. *OECDiLibrary.* doi:10.1787/a40c5025-en

Organization for Economic Co-operation and Development (OECD). (2023d). *OECD Employment Outlook 2023 Artificial Intelligence and the Labour Market.* OECD., doi:10.1787/08785bba-

Ounmaa, L. (2021). What are the socio-economic impacts of an energy transition? United Nations Development Programme (UNDP). https://www.undp.org/eurasia/blog/what-are-socio-economic-impacts-energy-transition

Pajarinen, M., Rouvinen, P., & Ekeland, A. (2015). "Computerization threatens one-third of Finnish and Norwegian employment". ETLA Brief 34. Available at https://www.etla.fi/wp-content/uploads/ETLA-Muistio-Brief-34.pdf

Pan, H., & Koehler, J. (2007). Technological change in energy systems: Learning curves, logistic curves and input–output coefficients. *Ecological Economics*, *63*(4), 749–758. doi:10.1016/j.ecolecon.2007.01.013

Parida, V., Westerberg, M., & Frishammar, J. (2012). Inbound open innovation activities in high-tech SMEs: The impact on innovation performance. *Journal of Small Business Management, 50*(2), 283–309. doi:10.1111/j.1540-627X.2012.00354.x

Peng, S., Kalliamvakou, E., Cihon, P., & Demirer, M. (2023). The Impact of AI on Developer Productivity: Evidence from GitHub Copilot. Available at Arxiv: https://arxiv.org/abs/2302.06590 or https://doi.org//arXiv.2302.06590 doi:10.48550

Pesaran, M. H., Shin, Y., & Smith, R. J. (2001). Bounds testing approaches to the analysis of level relationships. *Journal of Applied Econometrics, 16*(3), 289–326. doi:10.1002/jae.616

Philips, A. Q. (2018). Have your cake and eat it too? Cointegration and dynamic inference from autoregressive distributed lag models. *American Journal of Political Science, 62*(1), 230–244. doi:10.1111/ajps.12318

Picard, R. W. (2000). *Affective computing*. MIT Press. doi:10.7551/mitpress/1140.001.0001

Potter, W. (27 January 2023) 'This is not crying wolf... the wolf is at the door': Fears AI could make white collar jobs obsolete as Microsoft pumps multibillion-dollar investment into ChatGPT after laying off 10,000 workers. *Dailymail.com.* retrieved from https://www.dailymail.co.uk/news/article-11683901/ChatGPT-make-white-collar-jobs-obsolete-Microsoft-pumps-billions-AI.html

Pundziene, A., Nikou, S., & Bouwman, H. (2021). The nexus between dynamic capabilities and competitive firm performance: The mediating role of open innovation. *European Journal of Innovation Management, 25*(6), 152–177. doi:10.1108/EJIM-09-2020-0356

QAA. (2018a). UK Quality Code for Higher Education: Advice and Guidance -. *Learning and Teaching*, (November), 1–11. https://www.qaa.ac.uk/en/Publications/Documents/quality-code-brief-guide.pdf

QAA. (2018b). UK Quality Code for Higher Education: Advise and Guidance - Assessment, (November), 1–14. Retrieved from https://www.qaa.ac.uk/en/Publications/Documents/quality-code-brief-guide.pdf

QAA. (2019). Annex D: Outcome classification descriptions for FHEQ Level 6 and FQHEIS Level 10 degrees, 1–9. Retrieved from https://www.qaa.ac.uk/docs/qaa/quality-code/annex-d-outcome-classification-descriptions-for-fheq-level-6-and-fqheis-level-10-degrees.pdf?sfvrsn=824c981_10

Qian, W., & Wang, Y. (2022). How Do Rising Labor Costs Affect Green Total Factor Productivity? Based on the Industrial Intelligence Perspective. *Sustainability (Basel), 14*(13653), 1–19. doi:10.3390/su142013653

Qiu, R. G., Ha, H., Ravi, R., Qiu, L., & Badr, Y. (2016). A Big Data based Smart Evaluation System using Public Opinion Aggregation. *Proceedings of the 18th International Conference on Enterprise Information Systems, 1*(Iceis), 520–527. 10.5220/0005867805200527

Qiu, R. G., Ravi, R. R., & Qiu, L. L. (2015). Aggregating and visualizing public opinions and sentiment trends on the US higher education. *Proceedings of the 17th International Conference on Information Integration and Web-Based Applications &Services - IiWAS '15*, 1–5. 10.1145/2837185.2837261

Quality Assurance Agency. (2014). The Frameworks for Higher Education Qualifications of UK Degree-Awarding Bodies. *The Frameworks for Higher Education Qualifications of UK Degree-Awarding Bodies*, (October). Retrieved from https://www.qaa.ac.uk/docs/qaa/quality-code/qualifications-frameworks.pdf

Radford, A. (2018). *Improving language understanding with unsupervised learning*. OpenAI. https://openai.com/research/language-unsupervised

Radford, A., Narasimhan, K., Salimans, T. and Sutskever, I. (2018) *Improving Language Understanding with Unsupervised Learning*. Technical Report, OpenAI.

Radford, A., Narasimhan, K., Salimans, T., & Sutskever, I. (2018). *Improving language understanding by generative pre-training*. OpenAI. https://cdn.openai.com/research-covers/language-unsupervised/language_understanding_paper.pdf

Raihan, A. (2023). A comprehensive review of artificial intelligence and machine learning applications in the energy sector. *Journal of Technology Innovations and Energy*, *2*(4), 1–26. doi:10.56556/jtie.v2i4.608

Ramadhan, R., & Suhendra. (2021). The effect of distance learning during Covid-19 pandemics on the mathematical learning results. *Journal of Physics: Conference Series*, *1806*(1), 012096. Advance online publication. doi:10.1088/1742-6596/1806/1/012096

Ramesh, A., Pavlov, M., Goh, G., & Gray, S. (2021). *DALL-E: Creating images from text*. OpenAI. https://openai.com/research/dall-e

Rane, N., Choudhary, S., & Rane, J. (2023a). *Integrating ChatGPT, Bard, and leading-edge generative artificial intelligence in building and construction industry: applications, framework, challenges, and future scope*. Academic Press.

Rane, N., Choudhary, S., & Rane, J. (2023b). *Integrating Building Information Modelling (BIM) with ChatGPT, Bard, and similar generative artificial intelligence in the architecture, engineering, and construction industry: applications, a novel framework, challenges, and future scope. Bard, and similar generative artificial intelligence in the architecture, engineering, and construction industry: applications, a novel framework, challenges, and future scope*. Academic Press.

RaneN.ChoudharyS.RaneJ. (2024a). *Contribution of ChatGPT and Similar Generative Artificial Intelligence for Enhanced Climate Change Mitigation Strategies*. doi:10.2139/ssrn.4681720

RaneN.ChoudharyS.RaneJ. (2024b). *A new era of automation in the construction industry: Implementing leading-edge generative artificial intelligence, such as ChatGPT or Bard*. doi:10.2139/ssrn.4681747

Rasul, T., Nair, S., Kalendrs, D., Robin, M., Santini, F. de O., Ladeira, W. J., ... Heathcote, L. (2023). The role of ChatGPT in higher education: Benefits, Challenges, and future research directions. *Journal of Applied Learning & Teaching*, *6*(1), 41–56. https://doi.org/https://doi.org/10.37074/jalt.2023.6.1.29

Rauflab, C. (2023). The Ethics of Artificial Intelligence. Available at https://www.swissinfo.ch/eng/45808880/45808880

Rizvi, A. T., Haleem, A., Bahl, S., & Javaid, M. (2021). Artificial Intelligence (AI) and Its Applications in Indian Manufacturing: A Review. In S. K. Acharya & D. P. Mishra (Eds.), *Current Advances in Mechanical Engineering. Lecture Notes in Mechanical Engineering*. Springer., doi:10.1007/978-981-33-4795-3_76

Rodriguez, M. C., Hascic, I., & Souchier, M. (2018). Environmentally Adjusted Multifactor Productivity: Methodology and Empirical Results of OECD and G20 Countries. *Ecological Economics*, *153*, 147–160. doi:10.1016/j.ecolecon.2018.06.015

Romer, P. M. (1986). Increasing returns and long-run growth. *Journal of Political Economy*, *94*(5), 1002–1037. https://www.jstor.org/stable/1833190. doi:10.1086/261420

Roser, M., Ritchie, H., & Mathieu, E. (2023). "Technological Change". Our World In Data. https://ourworldindata.org/technological-change

Rusiawan, W., Tjiptoherijanto, P., Suganda, E., & Darmajanti, L. (2015). Assessment of Green Total Factor Productivity Impact on Sustainable Indonesia Productivity Growth. *Procedia Environmental Sciences*, *28*, 493–501. doi:10.1016/j.proenv.2015.07.059

Ryan, M., Antoniou, J., Brooks, L. D., Jiya, T., Macnish, K., & Stahl, B. C. (2020). The Ethical Balance of Using Smart Information Systems for Promoting the United Nations' Sustainable Development Goals. *Sustainability (Basel)*, *12*(4826), 1–22. doi:10.3390/su12124826

Sachs, G. (2023). Generative AI could raise global GDP by 7%. Available at https://www.goldmansachs.com/intelligence/pages/generative-ai-could-raise-global-gdp-by-7-percent.html

Sacks, G. (05 April 2023). Generative AI could raise global GDP by 7% Artificial Intelligence Retrieved from https://www.goldmansachs.com/intelligence/pages/generative-ai-could-raise-global-gdp-by-7-percent.html

Sagarikabiswas (02 Apr 2023). ChatGPT: 7 IT Jobs That AI Can't Replace. Retrieved from https://www.geeksforgeeks.org/chatgpt-7-it-jobs-that-ai-cant-replace/

Sahay, B. S. (2005). Multi-factor productivity measurement model for service organisation. *International Journal of Productivity and Performance Management*, *54*(1), 7–22. doi:10.1108/17410400510571419

Sahoo, S., & Lo, C.-Y. (2022). Smart manufacturing powered by recent technological advancements: A review. *Journal of Manufacturing Systems*, *64*, 236–250. doi:10.1016/j.jmsy.2022.06.008

Sangster, N., Duke, R., Lalla, T., Persad, P., & Ameerali, A. (2016). Investigating the use of advanced manufacturing technologies in the manufacturing assembly sector in a small developing country. *International Journal of Materials Mechanics and Manufacturing*, *4*(4), 266–272.

Santarisi, N. S., & Tarazi, A. H. (2008). The Effect of TQM Practices on Higher Education Performance : The Faculty of Engineering and Technology at the University of Jordan as a Case Study. *Dirasat. Engineering and Science*, *35*(2), 84–96.

Sarkodie, S. A., Strezov, V., Weldekidan, H., Asamoah, E. F., Owusu, P. A., & Doyi, I. N. Y. (2019). Environmental sustainability assessment using dynamic autoregressive-distributed lag simulations—Nexus between greenhouse gas emissions, biomass energy, food and economic growth. *The Science of the Total Environment*, *668*, 318–332. doi:10.1016/j.scitotenv.2019.02.432 PMID:30852209

SaslowK.LorenzP. (2019). Artificial Intelligence Needs Human Rights: How the Focus on Ethical AI Fails to Address Privacy, Discrimination and Other Concerns. PsychRN: Attitudes & Social Cognition, 1-25. doi:10.2139/ssrn.3589473

Schumpeter, J. (1949). *The Theory of Economic Development, An Inquiry into Profits, Capital, Credit, Interest and the Business Cycle*. Harvard University Press.

Schumpeter, J. (1994). *Capitalism, Socialism and democracy*. Routledge.

Seamans, R., & Raj, M. (2018). *AI, labour, productivity, and the need for firm-level data (No. w24239)*. National Bureau of Economic Research. doi:10.3386/w24239

Sharifi, A., Khavarian-Garmsir, A. R., & Kummitha, R. K. R. (2021). Contributions of smart city solutions and technologies to resilience against the COVID-19 pandemic: A literature review. *Sustainability (Basel)*, *13*(14), 1–28. doi:10.3390/su13148018

Sharma, M., Luthra, S., Joshi, S., & Kumar, A. (2022). Implementing challenges of artificial intelligence: Evidence from the public manufacturing sector of an emerging economy. *Government Information Quarterly*, *39*(4), 101624. doi:10.1016/j.giq.2021.101624

Sheehan, J., & Tessmer, M. (1997). A Construct Validation of the Mental Models Learning Outcome Using Explaratory Factor Analysis. *Eric*, 363–381.

Shenkar, O., Luo, Y., & Chi, T. (2021). *International business*. Routledge. doi:10.4324/9781003034315

Singh, J., Samborowski, L., & Mentzer, K. (2023). A Human Collaboration with ChatGPT: Developing Case Studies with Generative AI. In *Proceedings of the ISCAP Conference* (*Vol. 2473*, p. 4901). Academic Press.

Singh, R., Akram, S. V., Gehlot, A., Buddhi, D., Priyadarshi, N., & Twala, B. (2022). Energy System 4.0: Digitalization of the Energy Sector with Inclination towards Sustainability. *Sensors (Basel)*, *22*(6619), 1–42. doi:10.3390/s22176619 PMID:36081087

Smolansky, A., Cram, A., Raduescu, C., Zeivots, S., Huber, E., & Kizilcec, R. F. (2023). Educator and Student Perspectives on the Impact of Generative AI on Assessments in Higher Education. *L@S 2023 - Proceedings of the 10th ACM Conference on Learning @ Scale*, 378–382. 10.1145/3573051.3596191

Solodkyi, V. V., &, Polishchuk, Y. A. (2023). Artificial intelligence implementation in Ukrainian banks: perspectives and limitations. Economic Bulletin of Dnipro University of Technology, 119-127. doi:10.33271/ebdut/82.119

Solow, R. M. (1956). A Contribution to the Theory of Economic Growth. *The Quarterly Journal of Economics*, *70*(1), 65–94. https://www.jstor.org/stable/1884513?origin=JSTOR-pdf. doi:10.2307/1884513

Solow, R. M. (1957). Technical Change and the Aggregate Production Function. *The Review of Economics and Statistics*, *39*(3), 312–320. https://www.jstor.org/stable/1926047?origin=JSTOR-pdf. doi:10.2307/1926047

Somers, J. (2018). "How the Artificial-Intelligence Program AlphaZero Mastered Its Games". The New Yorker. Available at: https://www.newyorker.com/science/elements/howthe-artificial-intelligence-program-alphazero-mastered-its-games

Sonntag, G. (2008). We Have Evidence, They Are Learning: Using Multiple Assessments to Measure Student Information Literacy Learning Outcomes. *World Library and Information Congress: 74th IFLA General Conference and Council*, 14.

Sony, M., Antony, J., Mc Dermott, O., & Garza-Reyes, J. A. (2021). An empirical examination of benefits, challenges, and critical success factors of Industry 4.0 in manufacturing and service sector. *Technology in Society*, *67*, 101754. doi:10.1016/j.techsoc.2021.101754

Sorour, A., Atkins, A. S., Stanier, C., Alharbi, F., & Campion, R. (2022). The Development of Business Intelligence Dashboard for Monitoring Quality in Higher Education Institutions in Saudi Arabia Including Sentiment Analysis From Social Media. *INTED2022 Proceedings, 1*(March), 1391–1399. 10.21125/inted.2022.0413

Sorour, A., & Atkins, A. (2024). Big data challenge for monitoring quality in higher education institutions using business intelligence dashboards. *Journal of Electronic Science and Technology*, *22*(1).

Sorour, A., Atkins, A. S., Stanier, C., & Alharbi, F. (2019). The Role of Business Intelligence and Analytics in Higher Education Quality: A Proposed Architecture. *International Conference on Advances in the Emerging Computing Technologies, Islamic Un*(February 10-12).

Sorour, A., Atkins, A., Alharbi, F., Stanier, C., & Campion, R. (2020). Integrated Dashboards With Social Media Analysis Capabilities For Monitoring Quality in Higher Education Institutions. *12th International Conference on Education and New Learning Technologies, 6-7 July*, 2862–2870. 10.21125/edulearn.2020.0861

Strauss, D. (June 4, 2023). Generative AI's 'productivity revolution' will take time to pay off. Financial Times. Retrieved from https://www.ft.com/content/21384711-3506-4901-830c-7ecc3ae6b32a

Su, B., & Heshmati, A. (2011). "Development and Sources of Labor Productivity in Chinese Provinces". IZA Discussion Paper, (No 6263), 1-30. Retrieved from http://ftp.iza.org/dp6263.pdf

Sulindawati, N. L. G. E. (2021). Improving Learning Outcomes through Learning Media in Making Financial Reports at the Hospitality Board. *Journal of Education Research and Evaluation*, *5*(4), 580–586. doi:10.23887/jere.v5i4.34888

Szczepaniuk, H., & Szczepaniuk, E. K. (2023). Applications of Artificial Intelligence Algorithms in the Energy Sector. *Energies*, *16*(347), 1–24. doi:10.3390/en16010347

The 3 Biggest Challenges to Securing Company Data. WHOA.com. Available from: https://whoa.com/the-3-biggest-challenges-to-securing-company-data. Accessed 15 Jun 2023.

Top 5 Ransomware Attacks in India to Watch Out for in 2023. LinkedIn. 2023. Available from: https://www.linkedin.com/pulse/top-5-ransomware-attacks-india-watch-out-2023

Townley, B. (2019). Foucault, power/knowledge, and its relevance for human resource management. In *Postmodern management theory* (pp. 215–242). Routledge. doi:10.4324/9780429431678-11

Tsai, D. C. L., Huang, A. Y. Q., Lu, O. H. T., & Yang, S. J. H. (2021). Automatic question generation for repeated testing to improve student learning outcome. *Proceedings - IEEE 21st International Conference on Advanced Learning Technologies, ICALT 2021*, (1), 339–341. 10.1109/ICALT52272.2021.00108

Tyagi, S., Tyagi, D. R. K., Dutta, D. P. K., & Dubey, D. P. Next Generation Phishing Detection and Prevention System using Machine Learning. *1st International Conference on Advanced Innovations in Smart Cities (ICAISC)*, Jeddah, Saudi Arabia; 2023. p. 1-6. 10.1109/ICAISC56366.2023.10085529

Ullah, A., Aimin, W., & Ahmed, M. (2018). Smart Automation, Customer Experience and Customer Engagement in Electric Vehicles. *Sustainability (Basel)*, *10*(5), 1–11. doi:10.3390/su10051350

United Nations (UN). (2021). Policy Brief: Transforming Extractive Industries for Sustainable Development. UN. https://www.un.org/sites/un2.un.org/files/sg_policy_brief_extractives.pdf

Vaswani, A., Shazeer, N., Parmar, N., Uszkoreit, J., Jones, L., Gomez, A. N., & Polosukhin, I. (2017). *Attention is all you need. Advances in neural information processing systems,* 30. 31st Conference on Neural Information Processing Systems. CA, USA: Long Beach, (Available at) https://proceedings.neurips.cc/paper/2017/file/ 3f5ee243547dee91fbd053c1c4a845aa-Paper.pdf

Vaswani, A., Shazeer, N., Parmar, N., Uszkoreit, J., Jones, L., Gomez, A. N., ... Polosukhin, I. (2017). Attention is all you need. *31st Conference on Neural Information Processing Systems (NIPS 2017).*

Verganti, R., Vendraminelli, L., & Iansiti, M. (2020). Innovation and design in the age of artificial intelligence. *Journal of Product Innovation Management*, *37*(3), 212–227. doi:10.1111/jpim.12523

Verges-Jamie, J. (2021). The Misinterpretation of Productivity Measures. *Challenge*, *64*(2), 1–16. doi:10.1080/05775132.2020.1866907

Vesnic-Alujevic, L., Nascimento, S., & Polvora, A. (2020). Societal and ethical impacts of artificial intelligence: Critical notes on European policy frameworks. *Telecommunications Policy*, *44*(6), 101961. doi:10.1016/j.telpol.2020.101961

Vinuesa, R., Azizpour, H., Leite, I., Balaam, M., Dignum, V., Domisch, S., Fellander, A., Langhans, S. D., Tegmark, M., & Nerini, F. F. (2020). The role of artificial intelligence in achieving the Sustainable Development Goals. *Nature Communications*, *11*(233), 1–10. doi:10.1038/s41467-019-14108-y PMID:31932590

Wachter, S., Mittelstadt, B. D., & Russell, C. (2021). Bias Preservation in Machine Learning: The Legality of Fairness Metrics Under EU Non-Discrimination Law. SSRN *Electronic Journal,* 123(3):1-51. https://doi.org/ doi:10.2139/SSRN.3792772

Wakunuma, K., Jiya, T., & Aliyu, S. (2020). Socio-ethical implications of using AI in accelerating SDG3 in Least Developed Countries. *Journal of Responsible Technology*, *4*(100006), 1–10. doi:10.1016/j.jrt.2020.100006

Wallace, R. S. (2008). The Anatomy of A.L.I.C.E. In Parsing the Turing test: Philosophical and methodological issues in the quest for the thinking computer (pp. 181–210). essay, Springer.

Wan, C. (2023). How Predictive Maintenance Is Transforming Manufacturing. Retrieved January 31, 2024, from https://www.thefastmode.com/expert-opinion/32863-how-predictive-maintenance-is-transforming-manufacturing

Wang, J., Lu, Y., Fan, S., Hu, P., & Wang, B. (2022). How to survive in the age of artificial intelligence? Exploring the intelligent transformations of SMEs in central China. *International Journal of Emerging Markets*, *17*(4), 1143–1162. doi:10.1108/IJOEM-06-2021-0985

Weblink: https://www.computerworld.com/article/3687614/how-enterprises-can-use-chatgpt-and-gpt-3.html

Weissglass, D. E. (2022). Contextual bias, the democratization of healthcare, and medical artificial intelligence in low- and middle-income countries. *Bioethics*, *36*(2), 201–209. doi:10.1111/bioe.12927 PMID:34460977

What are Cybersecurity Threats? RiskOptics (reciprocity.com). 2022. Available from: https://www.reciprocity.com/what-are-cybersecurity-threats. Accessed 15 Jun 2023.

What is Cybersecurity? Cisco. Available from: https://www.cisco.com/c/en_in/products/security/what-is-cybersecurity.html

What is cybersecurity? IBM. Available from: https://www.ibm.com/topics/cybersecurity

Williams, J. (2023). ChatGPT and Its Use in the Finance and Banking Industry [2023]. Its ChatGPT, 3.

Williams, J. (2023). How AI Will Enhance Human Capabilities. *Forbes*. Retrieved from https://www.forbes.com/sites/forbescommunicationscouncil/2018/03/19/how-ai-will-enhance-human-capabilities/?sh=1d37cd1e366f

Wong, L. (2013). Student Engagement with Online Resources and Its Impact on Learning Outcomes. *Journal of Information Technology Education: Innovations in Practice*, *12*, 129–146. doi:10.28945/1829

World Economic Forum (WEF). (2023). Jobs of Tomorrow: Large Language Models and Jobs. Geneva, Switzerland. https://www3.weforum.org/docs/WEF_Jobs_of_Tomorrow_Generative_AI_2023.pdf

Xu, Z. (2022). The Influence of Robot-Assisted Industry Using Deep Learning on the Economic Growth Rate of Manufacturing Industry in the Era of Artificial Intelligence. *Wireless Communications and Mobile Computing*, *2022*, 1–12. doi:10.1155/2022/4594858

Yang, J., Luo, B., Zhao, C., & Zhang, H. (2022). Artificial intelligence healthcare service resources adoption by medical institutions based on TOE framework. *Digital Health*, *8*, 20552076221126034. doi:10.1177/20552076221126034 PMID:36211801

Yap, Y.-H., Tan, W.-S., Wong, J., Ahmad, N. A., Wooi, C.-L., Wu, Y.-K., & Ariffin, A. E. (2021). A two-stage multi microgrid p2p energy trading with motivational game-theory: A case study in Malaysia. *The Institute of Engineering and Technology (IET). Renewable Power Generation*, *15*, 2615–2628. doi:10.1049/rpg2.12205

Yogesh, K., & ... . (2023). “So, what if ChatGPT wrote it?” Multidisciplinary perspectives on opportunities, challenges, and implications of generative conversational AI for research, practice, and policy. *International Journal of Information Management*, *71*, 102642. https://www.sciencedirect.com/science/article/pii/S0268401223000233. doi:10.1016/j.ijinfomgt.2023.102642

Zhang, Z., Zohren, S., & Roberts, S. (2020). Deep learning for portfolio optimization. *The Journal of Financial Data Science*.

ZhangB. (2022). No Rage Against the Machines: Threat of Automation Does Not Change Policy Preferences. *Social Science Research Network,* 1-8. doi:10.2139/ssrn.3455501

Zhong, Y., Xu, F., & Zhang, L. (2023). *Influence of artificial intelligence applications on total factor productivity of enterprises-evidence from textual analysis of annual reports of Chinese-listed companies*. Applied Econometrics., doi:10.1080/00036846.2023.2244246

Zhou, M., & Chen, Y. (2022). Research on the Impact of Artificial Intelligence on Green Total Factor Productivity in Manufacturing. *Advances in Economics, Business, and Management*, *650*, 47–50. doi:10.2991/aebmr.k.220402.010

Zreik, M. (2023a). Navigating HRM Challenges in Post-Pandemic China: Multigenerational Workforce, Skill Gaps, and Emerging Strategies. In A. Even & B. Christiansen (Eds.), *Enhancing Employee Engagement and Productivity in the Post-Pandemic Multigenerational Workforce* (pp. 171–188). IGI Global., doi:10.4018/978-1-6684-9172-0.ch008

Zreik, M. (2023b). Sustainable and Smart Supply Chains in China: A Multidimensional Approach. In B. Bentalha, A. Hmioui, & L. Alla (Eds.), *Integrating Intelligence and Sustainability in Supply Chains* (pp. 179–197). IGI Global., doi:10.4018/979-8-3693-0225-5.ch010

Zreik, M. (2023c). Harnessing the Power of Blockchain Technology in Modern China: A Comprehensive Exploration. In L. Ferreira, M. Cruz, E. Cruz, H. Quintela, & M. Cunha (Eds.), *Supporting Technologies and the Impact of Blockchain on Organizations and Society* (pp. 94–112). IGI Global., doi:10.4018/978-1-6684-5747-4.ch007

Related References

Contemporary Management Approaches to the Global Hospitality and Tourism Industry

To continue our tradition of advancing information science and technology research, we have compiled a list of recommended IGI Global readings. These references will provide additional information and guidance to further enrich your knowledge and assist you with your own research and future publications.

Abdul Razak, R., & Mansor, N. A. (2021). Instagram Influencers in Social Media-Induced Tourism: Rethinking Tourist Trust Towards Tourism Destination. In M. Dinis, L. Bonixe, S. Lamy, & Z. Breda (Eds.), *Impact of New Media in Tourism* (pp. 135-144). IGI Global. https://doi.org/10.4018/978-1-7998-7095-1.ch009

Abir, T., & Khan, M. Y. (2022). Importance of ICT Advancement and Culture of Adaptation in the Tourism and Hospitality Industry for Developing Countries. In C. Ramos, S. Quinteiro, & A. Gonçalves (Eds.), *ICT as Innovator Between Tourism and Culture* (pp. 30–41). IGI Global. https://doi.org/10.4018/978-1-7998-8165-0.ch003

Abir, T., & Khan, M. Y. (2022). Importance of ICT Advancement and Culture of Adaptation in the Tourism and Hospitality Industry for Developing Countries. In C. Ramos, S. Quinteiro, & A. Gonçalves (Eds.), *ICT as Innovator Between Tourism and Culture* (pp. 30–41). IGI Global. https://doi.org/10.4018/978-1-7998-8165-0.ch003

Abtahi, M. S., Behboudi, L., & Hasanabad, H. M. (2017). Factors Affecting Internet Advertising Adoption in Ad Agencies. *International Journal of Innovation in the Digital Economy*, *8*(4), 18–29. doi:10.4018/IJIDE.2017100102

Afenyo-Agbe, E., & Mensah, I. (2022). Principles, Benefits, and Barriers to Community-Based Tourism: Implications for Management. In I. Mensah & E. Afenyo-Agbe (Eds.), *Prospects and Challenges of Community-Based Tourism and Changing Demographics* (pp. 1–29). IGI Global. doi:10.4018/978-1-7998-7335-8.ch001

Agbo, V. M. (2022). Distributive Justice Issues in Community-Based Tourism. In I. Mensah & E. Afenyo-Agbe (Eds.), *Prospects and Challenges of Community-Based Tourism and Changing Demographics* (pp. 107–129). IGI Global. https://doi.org/10.4018/978-1-7998-7335-8.ch005

Agrawal, S. (2017). The Impact of Emerging Technologies and Social Media on Different Business(es): Marketing and Management. In O. Rishi & A. Sharma (Eds.), *Maximizing Business Performance and Efficiency Through Intelligent Systems* (pp. 37–49). Hershey, PA: IGI Global. doi:10.4018/978-1-5225-2234-8.ch002

Ahmad, A., & Johari, S. (2022). Georgetown as a Gastronomy Tourism Destination: Visitor Awareness Towards Revisit Intention of Nasi Kandar Restaurant. In M. Valeri (Ed.), *New Governance and Management in Touristic Destinations* (pp. 71–83). IGI Global. https://doi.org/10.4018/978-1-6684-3889-3.ch005

Alkhatib, G., & Bayouq, S. T. (2021). A TAM-Based Model of Technological Factors Affecting Use of E-Tourism. *International Journal of Tourism and Hospitality Management in the Digital Age*, *5*(2), 50–67. https://doi.org/10.4018/IJTHMDA.20210701.oa1

Altinay Ozdemir, M. (2021). Virtual Reality (VR) and Augmented Reality (AR) Technologies for Accessibility and Marketing in the Tourism Industry. In C. Eusébio, L. Teixeira, & M. Carneiro (Eds.), *ICT Tools and Applications for Accessible Tourism* (pp. 277-301). IGI Global. https://doi.org/10.4018/978-1-7998-6428-8.ch013

Anantharaman, R. N., Rajeswari, K. S., Angusamy, A., & Kuppusamy, J. (2017). Role of Self-Efficacy and Collective Efficacy as Moderators of Occupational Stress Among Software Development Professionals. *International Journal of Human Capital and Information Technology Professionals*, *8*(2), 45–58. doi:10.4018/IJHCITP.2017040103

Aninze, F., El-Gohary, H., & Hussain, J. (2018). The Role of Microfinance to Empower Women: The Case of Developing Countries. *International Journal of Customer Relationship Marketing and Management, 9*(1), 54–78. doi:10.4018/IJCRMM.2018010104

Antosova, G., Sabogal-Salamanca, M., & Krizova, E. (2021). Human Capital in Tourism: A Practical Model of Endogenous and Exogenous Territorial Tourism Planning in Bahía Solano, Colombia. In V. Costa, A. Moura, & M. Mira (Eds.), *Handbook of Research on Human Capital and People Management in the Tourism Industry* (pp. 282–302). IGI Global. https://doi.org/10.4018/978-1-7998-4318-4.ch014

Arsenijević, O. M., Orčić, D., & Kastratović, E. (2017). Development of an Optimization Tool for Intangibles in SMEs: A Case Study from Serbia with a Pilot Research in the Prestige by Milka Company. In M. Vemić (Ed.), *Optimal Management Strategies in Small and Medium Enterprises* (pp. 320–347). Hershey, PA: IGI Global. doi:10.4018/978-1-5225-1949-2.ch015

Aryanto, V. D., Wismantoro, Y., & Widyatmoko, K. (2018). Implementing Eco-Innovation by Utilizing the Internet to Enhance Firm's Marketing Performance: Study of Green Batik Small and Medium Enterprises in Indonesia. *International Journal of E-Business Research, 14*(1), 21–36. doi:10.4018/IJEBR.2018010102

Asero, V., & Billi, S. (2022). New Perspective of Networking in the DMO Model. In M. Valeri (Ed.), *New Governance and Management in Touristic Destinations* (pp. 105–118). IGI Global. https://doi.org/10.4018/978-1-6684-3889-3.ch007

Atiku, S. O., & Fields, Z. (2017). Multicultural Orientations for 21st Century Global Leadership. In N. Baporikar (Ed.), *Management Education for Global Leadership* (pp. 28–51). Hershey, PA: IGI Global. doi:10.4018/978-1-5225-1013-0.ch002

Atiku, S. O., & Fields, Z. (2018). Organisational Learning Dimensions and Talent Retention Strategies for the Service Industries. In N. Baporikar (Ed.), *Global Practices in Knowledge Management for Societal and Organizational Development* (pp. 358–381). Hershey, PA: IGI Global. doi:10.4018/978-1-5225-3009-1.ch017

Atsa'am, D. D., & Kuset Bodur, E. (2021). Pattern Mining on How Organizational Tenure Affects the Psychological Capital of Employees Within the Hospitality and Tourism Industry: Linking Employees' Organizational Tenure With PsyCap. *International Journal of Tourism and Hospitality Management in the Digital Age, 5*(2), 17–28. https://doi.org/10.4018/IJTHMDA.2021070102

Ávila, L., & Teixeira, L. (2018). The Main Concepts Behind the Dematerialization of Business Processes. In M. Khosrow-Pour, D.B.A. (Ed.), Encyclopedia of Information Science and Technology, Fourth Edition (pp. 888-898). Hershey, PA: IGI Global. https://doi.org/ doi:10.4018/978-1-5225-2255-3.ch076

Ayorekire, J., Mugizi, F., Obua, J., & Ampaire, G. (2022). Community-Based Tourism and Local People's Perceptions Towards Conservation: The Case of Queen Elizabeth Conservation Area, Uganda. In I. Mensah & E. Afenyo-Agbe (Eds.), *Prospects and Challenges of Community-Based Tourism and Changing Demographics* (pp. 56–82). IGI Global. https://doi.org/10.4018/978-1-7998-7335-8.ch003

Baleiro, R. (2022). Tourist Literature and the Architecture of Travel in Olga Tokarczuk and Patti Smith. In R. Baleiro & R. Pereira (Eds.), *Global Perspectives on Literary Tourism and Film-Induced Tourism* (pp. 202-216). IGI Global. https://doi.org/10.4018/978-1-7998-8262-6.ch011

Barat, S. (2021). Looking at the Future of Medical Tourism in Asia. *International Journal of Tourism and Hospitality Management in the Digital Age*, *5*(1), 19–33. https://doi.org/10.4018/IJTHMDA.2021010102

Barbosa, C. A., Magalhães, M., & Nunes, M. R. (2021). Travel Instagramability: A Way of Choosing a Destination? In M. Dinis, L. Bonixe, S. Lamy, & Z. Breda (Eds.), *Impact of New Media in Tourism* (pp. 173-190). IGI Global. https://doi.org/10.4018/978-1-7998-7095-1.ch011

Bari, M. W., & Khan, Q. (2021). Pakistan as a Destination of Religious Tourism. In E. Alaverdov & M. Bari (Eds.), *Global Development of Religious Tourism* (pp. 1-10). IGI Global. https://doi.org/10.4018/978-1-7998-5792-1.ch001

Bartens, Y., Chunpir, H. I., Schulte, F., & Voß, S. (2017). Business/IT Alignment in Two-Sided Markets: A COBIT 5 Analysis for Media Streaming Business Models. In S. De Haes & W. Van Grembergen (Eds.), *Strategic IT Governance and Alignment in Business Settings* (pp. 82–111). Hershey, PA: IGI Global. doi:10.4018/978-1-5225-0861-8.ch004

Bashayreh, A. M. (2018). Organizational Culture and Organizational Performance. In W. Lee & F. Sabetzadeh (Eds.), *Contemporary Knowledge and Systems Science* (pp. 50–69). Hershey, PA: IGI Global. doi:10.4018/978-1-5225-5655-8.ch003

Bechthold, L., Lude, M., & Prügl, R. (2021). Crisis Favors the Prepared Firm: How Organizational Ambidexterity Relates to Perceptions of Organizational Resilience. In A. Zehrer, G. Glowka, K. Schwaiger, & V. Ranacher-Lackner (Eds.), *Resiliency Models and Addressing Future Risks for Family Firms in the Tourism Industry* (pp. 178–205). IGI Global. https://doi.org/10.4018/978-1-7998-7352-5.ch008

Bedford, D. A. (2018). Sustainable Knowledge Management Strategies: Aligning Business Capabilities and Knowledge Management Goals. In N. Baporikar (Ed.), *Global Practices in Knowledge Management for Societal and Organizational Development* (pp. 46–73). Hershey, PA: IGI Global. doi:10.4018/978-1-5225-3009-1.ch003

Bekjanov, D., & Matyusupov, B. (2021). Influence of Innovative Processes in the Competitiveness of Tourist Destination. In J. Soares (Ed.), *Innovation and Entrepreneurial Opportunities in Community Tourism* (pp. 243–263). IGI Global. https://doi.org/10.4018/978-1-7998-4855-4.ch014

Bharwani, S., & Musunuri, D. (2018). Reflection as a Process From Theory to Practice. In M. Khosrow-Pour, D.B.A. (Ed.), Encyclopedia of Information Science and Technology, Fourth Edition (pp. 1529-1539). Hershey, PA: IGI Global. doi:10.4018/978-1-5225-2255-3.ch132

Bhatt, G. D., Wang, Z., & Rodger, J. A. (2017). Information Systems Capabilities and Their Effects on Competitive Advantages: A Study of Chinese Companies. *Information Resources Management Journal, 30*(3), 41–57. doi:10.4018/IRMJ.2017070103

Bhushan, M., & Yadav, A. (2017). Concept of Cloud Computing in ESB. In R. Bhadoria, N. Chaudhari, G. Tomar, & S. Singh (Eds.), *Exploring Enterprise Service Bus in the Service-Oriented Architecture Paradigm* (pp. 116–127). Hershey, PA: IGI Global. doi:10.4018/978-1-5225-2157-0.ch008

Bhushan, S. (2017). System Dynamics Base-Model of Humanitarian Supply Chain (HSCM) in Disaster Prone Eco-Communities of India: A Discussion on Simulation and Scenario Results. *International Journal of System Dynamics Applications, 6*(3), 20–37. doi:10.4018/IJSDA.2017070102

Binder, D., & Miller, J. W. (2021). A Generations' Perspective on Employer Branding in Tourism. In V. Costa, A. Moura, & M. Mira (Eds.), *Handbook of Research on Human Capital and People Management in the Tourism Industry* (pp. 152–174). IGI Global. https://doi.org/10.4018/978-1-7998-4318-4.ch008

Birch Freeman, A. A., Mensah, I., & Antwi, K. B. (2022). Smiling vs. Frowning Faces: Community Participation for Sustainable Tourism in Ghanaian Communities. In I. Mensah & E. Afenyo-Agbe (Eds.), *Prospects and Challenges of Community-Based Tourism and Changing Demographics* (pp. 83–106). IGI Global. https://doi.org/10.4018/978-1-7998-7335-8.ch004

Biswas, A., & De, A. K. (2017). On Development of a Fuzzy Stochastic Programming Model with Its Application to Business Management. In S. Trivedi, S. Dey, A. Kumar, & T. Panda (Eds.), *Handbook of Research on Advanced Data Mining Techniques and Applications for Business Intelligence* (pp. 353–378). Hershey, PA: IGI Global. doi:10.4018/978-1-5225-2031-3.ch021

Boragnio, A., & Faracce Macia, C. (2021). "Taking Care of Yourself at Home": Use of E-Commerce About Food and Care During the COVID-19 Pandemic in the City of Buenos Aires. In M. Korstanje (Ed.), *Socio-Economic Effects and Recovery Efforts for the Rental Industry: Post-COVID-19 Strategies* (pp. 45–71). IGI Global. https://doi.org/10.4018/978-1-7998-7287-0.ch003

Borges, V. D. (2021). Happiness: The Basis for Public Policy in Tourism. In A. Perinotto, V. Mayer, & J. Soares (Eds.), *Rebuilding and Restructuring the Tourism Industry: Infusion of Happiness and Quality of Life* (pp. 1–25). IGI Global. https://doi.org/10.4018/978-1-7998-7239-9.ch001

Bücker, J., & Ernste, K. (2018). Use of Brand Heroes in Strategic Reputation Management: The Case of Bacardi, Adidas, and Daimler. In A. Erdemir (Ed.), *Reputation Management Techniques in Public Relations* (pp. 126–150). Hershey, PA: IGI Global. doi:10.4018/978-1-5225-3619-2.ch007

Buluk Eşitti, B. (2021). COVID-19 and Alternative Tourism: New Destinations and New Tourism Products. In M. Demir, A. Dalgıç, & F. Ergen (Eds.), *Handbook of Research on the Impacts and Implications of COVID-19 on the Tourism Industry* (pp. 786–805). IGI Global. https://doi.org/10.4018/978-1-7998-8231-2.ch038

Bureš, V. (2018). Industry 4.0 From the Systems Engineering Perspective: Alternative Holistic Framework Development. In R. Brunet-Thornton & F. Martinez (Eds.), *Analyzing the Impacts of Industry 4.0 in Modern Business Environments* (pp. 199–223). Hershey, PA: IGI Global. doi:10.4018/978-1-5225-3468-6.ch011

Buzady, Z. (2017). Resolving the Magic Cube of Effective Case Teaching: Benchmarking Case Teaching Practices in Emerging Markets – Insights from the Central European University Business School, Hungary. In D. Latusek (Ed.), *Case Studies as a Teaching Tool in Management Education* (pp. 79–103). Hershey, PA: IGI Global. doi:10.4018/978-1-5225-0770-3.ch005

Camillo, A. (2021). *Legal Matters, Risk Management, and Risk Prevention: From Forming a Business to Legal Representation*. IGI Global. doi:10.4018/978-1-7998-4342-9.ch004

Căpusneanu, S., & Topor, D. I. (2018). Business Ethics and Cost Management in SMEs: Theories of Business Ethics and Cost Management Ethos. In I. Oncioiu (Ed.), *Ethics and Decision-Making for Sustainable Business Practices* (pp. 109–127). Hershey, PA: IGI Global. doi:10.4018/978-1-5225-3773-1.ch007

Chan, R. L., Mo, P. L., & Moon, K. K. (2018). Strategic and Tactical Measures in Managing Enterprise Risks: A Study of the Textile and Apparel Industry. In K. Strang, M. Korstanje, & N. Vajjhala (Eds.), *Research, Practices, and Innovations in Global Risk and Contingency Management* (pp. 1–19). Hershey, PA: IGI Global. doi:10.4018/978-1-5225-4754-9.ch001

Charlier, S. D., Burke-Smalley, L. A., & Fisher, S. L. (2018). Undergraduate Programs in the U.S: A Contextual and Content-Based Analysis. In J. Mendy (Ed.), *Teaching Human Resources and Organizational Behavior at the College Level* (pp. 26–57). Hershey, PA: IGI Global. doi:10.4018/978-1-5225-2820-3.ch002

Chumillas, J., Güell, M., & Quer, P. (2022). The Use of ICT in Tourist and Educational Literary Routes: The Role of the Guide. In C. Ramos, S. Quinteiro, & A. Gonçalves (Eds.), *ICT as Innovator Between Tourism and Culture* (pp. 15–29). IGI Global. https://doi.org/10.4018/978-1-7998-8165-0.ch002

Dahlberg, T., Kivijärvi, H., & Saarinen, T. (2017). IT Investment Consistency and Other Factors Influencing the Success of IT Performance. In S. De Haes & W. Van Grembergen (Eds.), *Strategic IT Governance and Alignment in Business Settings* (pp. 176–208). Hershey, PA: IGI Global. doi:10.4018/978-1-5225-0861-8.ch007

Damnjanović, A. M. (2017). Knowledge Management Optimization through IT and E-Business Utilization: A Qualitative Study on Serbian SMEs. In M. Vemić (Ed.), *Optimal Management Strategies in Small and Medium Enterprises* (pp. 249–267). Hershey, PA: IGI Global. doi:10.4018/978-1-5225-1949-2.ch012

Daneshpour, H. (2017). Integrating Sustainable Development into Project Portfolio Management through Application of Open Innovation. In M. Vemić (Ed.), *Optimal Management Strategies in Small and Medium Enterprises* (pp. 370–387). Hershey, PA: IGI Global. doi:10.4018/978-1-5225-1949-2.ch017

Daniel, A. D., & Reis de Castro, V. (2018). Entrepreneurship Education: How to Measure the Impact on Nascent Entrepreneurs. In A. Carrizo Moreira, J. Guilherme Leitão Dantas, & F. Manuel Valente (Eds.), *Nascent Entrepreneurship and Successful New Venture Creation* (pp. 85–110). Hershey, PA: IGI Global. doi:10.4018/978-1-5225-2936-1.ch004

David, R., Swami, B. N., & Tangirala, S. (2018). Ethics Impact on Knowledge Management in Organizational Development: A Case Study. In N. Baporikar (Ed.), *Global Practices in Knowledge Management for Societal and Organizational Development* (pp. 19–45). Hershey, PA: IGI Global. doi:10.4018/978-1-5225-3009-1.ch002

De Uña-Álvarez, E., & Villarino-Pérez, M. (2022). Fostering Ecocultural Resources, Identity, and Tourism in Inland Territories (Galicia, NW Spain). In G. Fernandes (Ed.), *Challenges and New Opportunities for Tourism in Inland Territories: Ecocultural Resources and Sustainable Initiatives* (pp. 1-16). IGI Global. https://doi.org/10.4018/978-1-7998-7339-6.ch001

Delias, P., & Lakiotaki, K. (2018). Discovering Process Horizontal Boundaries to Facilitate Process Comprehension. *International Journal of Operations Research and Information Systems*, *9*(2), 1–31. doi:10.4018/IJORIS.2018040101

Denholm, J., & Lee-Davies, L. (2018). Success Factors for Games in Business and Project Management. In *Enhancing Education and Training Initiatives Through Serious Games* (pp. 34–68). Hershey, PA: IGI Global. doi:10.4018/978-1-5225-3689-5.ch002

Deshpande, M. (2017). Best Practices in Management Institutions for Global Leadership: Policy Aspects. In N. Baporikar (Ed.), *Management Education for Global Leadership* (pp. 1–27). Hershey, PA: IGI Global. doi:10.4018/978-1-5225-1013-0.ch001

Deshpande, M. (2018). Policy Perspectives for SMEs Knowledge Management. In N. Baporikar (Ed.), *Knowledge Integration Strategies for Entrepreneurship and Sustainability* (pp. 23–46). Hershey, PA: IGI Global. doi:10.4018/978-1-5225-5115-7.ch002

Dezdar, S. (2017). ERP Implementation Projects in Asian Countries: A Comparative Study on Iran and China. *International Journal of Information Technology Project Management*, *8*(3), 52–68. doi:10.4018/IJITPM.2017070104

Domingos, D., Respício, A., & Martinho, R. (2017). Reliability of IoT-Aware BPMN Healthcare Processes. In C. Reis & M. Maximiano (Eds.), *Internet of Things and Advanced Application in Healthcare* (pp. 214–248). Hershey, PA: IGI Global. doi:10.4018/978-1-5225-1820-4.ch008

Dosumu, O., Hussain, J., & El-Gohary, H. (2017). An Exploratory Study of the Impact of Government Policies on the Development of Small and Medium Enterprises in Developing Countries: The Case of Nigeria. *International Journal of Customer Relationship Marketing and Management*, *8*(4), 51–62. doi:10.4018/IJCRMM.2017100104

Durst, S., Bruns, G., & Edvardsson, I. R. (2017). Retaining Knowledge in Smaller Building and Construction Firms. *International Journal of Knowledge and Systems Science*, *8*(3), 1–12. doi:10.4018/IJKSS.2017070101

Edvardsson, I. R., & Durst, S. (2017). Outsourcing, Knowledge, and Learning: A Critical Review. *International Journal of Knowledge-Based Organizations*, *7*(2), 13–26. doi:10.4018/IJKBO.2017040102

Edwards, J. S. (2018). Integrating Knowledge Management and Business Processes. In M. Khosrow-Pour, D.B.A. (Ed.), Encyclopedia of Information Science and Technology, Fourth Edition (pp. 5046-5055). Hershey, PA: IGI Global. doi:10.4018/978-1-5225-2255-3.ch437

Eichelberger, S., & Peters, M. (2021). Family Firm Management in Turbulent Times: Opportunities for Responsible Tourism. In A. Zehrer, G. Glowka, K. Schwaiger, & V. Ranacher-Lackner (Eds.), *Resiliency Models and Addressing Future Risks for Family Firms in the Tourism Industry* (pp. 103–124). IGI Global. https://doi.org/10.4018/978-1-7998-7352-5.ch005

Eide, D., Hjalager, A., & Hansen, M. (2022). Innovative Certifications in Adventure Tourism: Attributes and Diffusion. In R. Augusto Costa, F. Brandão, Z. Breda, & C. Costa (Eds.), *Planning and Managing the Experience Economy in Tourism* (pp. 161-175). IGI Global. https://doi.org/10.4018/978-1-7998-8775-1.ch009

Ejiogu, A. O. (2018). Economics of Farm Management. In *Agricultural Finance and Opportunities for Investment and Expansion* (pp. 56–72). Hershey, PA: IGI Global. doi:10.4018/978-1-5225-3059-6.ch003

Ekanem, I., & Abiade, G. E. (2018). Factors Influencing the Use of E-Commerce by Small Enterprises in Nigeria. *International Journal of ICT Research in Africa and the Middle East*, *7*(1), 37–53. doi:10.4018/IJICTRAME.2018010103

Ekanem, I., & Alrossais, L. A. (2017). Succession Challenges Facing Family Businesses in Saudi Arabia. In P. Zgheib (Ed.), *Entrepreneurship and Business Innovation in the Middle East* (pp. 122–146). Hershey, PA: IGI Global. doi:10.4018/978-1-5225-2066-5.ch007

El Faquih, L., & Fredj, M. (2017). Ontology-Based Framework for Quality in Configurable Process Models. *Journal of Electronic Commerce in Organizations, 15*(2), 48–60. doi:10.4018/JECO.2017040104

Faisal, M. N., & Talib, F. (2017). Building Ambidextrous Supply Chains in SMEs: How to Tackle the Barriers? *International Journal of Information Systems and Supply Chain Management, 10*(4), 80–100. doi:10.4018/IJISSCM.2017100105

Fernandes, T. M., Gomes, J., & Romão, M. (2017). Investments in E-Government: A Benefit Management Case Study. *International Journal of Electronic Government Research, 13*(3), 1–17. doi:10.4018/IJEGR.2017070101

Figueira, L. M., Honrado, G. R., & Dionísio, M. S. (2021). Human Capital Management in the Tourism Industry in Portugal. In V. Costa, A. Moura, & M. Mira (Eds.), *Handbook of Research on Human Capital and People Management in the Tourism Industry* (pp. 1–19). IGI Global. doi:10.4018/978-1-7998-4318-4.ch001

Gao, S. S., Oreal, S., & Zhang, J. (2018). Contemporary Financial Risk Management Perceptions and Practices of Small-Sized Chinese Businesses. In I. Management Association (Ed.), Global Business Expansion: Concepts, Methodologies, Tools, and Applications (pp. 917-931). Hershey, PA: IGI Global. doi:10.4018/978-1-5225-5481-3.ch041

Garg, R., & Berning, S. C. (2017). Indigenous Chinese Management Philosophies: Key Concepts and Relevance for Modern Chinese Firms. In B. Christiansen & G. Koc (Eds.), *Transcontinental Strategies for Industrial Development and Economic Growth* (pp. 43–57). Hershey, PA: IGI Global. doi:10.4018/978-1-5225-2160-0.ch003

Gencer, Y. G. (2017). Supply Chain Management in Retailing Business. In U. Akkucuk (Ed.), *Ethics and Sustainability in Global Supply Chain Management* (pp. 197–210). Hershey, PA: IGI Global. doi:10.4018/978-1-5225-2036-8.ch011

Gera, R., Arora, S., & Malik, S. (2021). Emotional Labor in the Tourism Industry: Strategies, Antecedents, and Outcomes. In V. Costa, A. Moura, & M. Mira (Eds.), *Handbook of Research on Human Capital and People Management in the Tourism Industry* (pp. 73–91). IGI Global. https://doi.org/10.4018/978-1-7998-4318-4.ch004

Giacosa, E. (2018). The Increasing of the Regional Development Thanks to the Luxury Business Innovation. In L. Carvalho (Ed.), *Handbook of Research on Entrepreneurial Ecosystems and Social Dynamics in a Globalized World* (pp. 260–273). Hershey, PA: IGI Global. doi:10.4018/978-1-5225-3525-6.ch011

Glowka, G., Tusch, M., & Zehrer, A. (2021). The Risk Perception of Family Business Owner-Manager in the Tourism Industry: A Qualitative Comparison of the Intra-Firm Senior and Junior Generation. In A. Zehrer, G. Glowka, K. Schwaiger, & V. Ranacher-Lackner (Eds.), *Resiliency Models and Addressing Future Risks for Family Firms in the Tourism Industry* (pp. 126–153). IGI Global. https://doi.org/10.4018/978-1-7998-7352-5.ch006

Glykas, M., & George, J. (2017). Quality and Process Management Systems in the UAE Maritime Industry. *International Journal of Productivity Management and Assessment Technologies*, *5*(1), 20–39. doi:10.4018/IJPMAT.2017010102

Glykas, M., Valiris, G., Kokkinaki, A., & Koutsoukou, Z. (2018). Banking Business Process Management Implementation. *International Journal of Productivity Management and Assessment Technologies*, *6*(1), 50–69. doi:10.4018/IJPMAT.2018010104

Gomes, J., & Romão, M. (2017). The Balanced Scorecard: Keeping Updated and Aligned with Today's Business Trends. *International Journal of Productivity Management and Assessment Technologies*, *5*(2), 1–15. doi:10.4018/IJPMAT.2017070101

Gomes, J., & Romão, M. (2017). Aligning Information Systems and Technology with Benefit Management and Balanced Scorecard. In S. De Haes & W. Van Grembergen (Eds.), *Strategic IT Governance and Alignment in Business Settings* (pp. 112–131). Hershey, PA: IGI Global. doi:10.4018/978-1-5225-0861-8.ch005

Goyal, A. (2021). Communicating and Building Destination Brands With New Media. In M. Dinis, L. Bonixe, S. Lamy, & Z. Breda (Eds.), *Impact of New Media in Tourism* (pp. 1-20). IGI Global. https://doi.org/10.4018/978-1-7998-7095-1.ch001

Grefen, P., & Turetken, O. (2017). Advanced Business Process Management in Networked E-Business Scenarios. *International Journal of E-Business Research*, *13*(4), 70–104. doi:10.4018/IJEBR.2017100105

Guasca, M., Van Broeck, A. M., & Vanneste, D. (2021). Tourism and the Social Reintegration of Colombian Ex-Combatants. In J. da Silva, Z. Breda, & F. Carbone (Eds.), *Role and Impact of Tourism in Peacebuilding and Conflict Transformation* (pp. 66-86). IGI Global. https://doi.org/10.4018/978-1-7998-5053-3.ch005

Haider, A., & Saetang, S. (2017). Strategic IT Alignment in Service Sector. In S. Rozenes & Y. Cohen (Eds.), *Handbook of Research on Strategic Alliances and Value Co-Creation in the Service Industry* (pp. 231–258). Hershey, PA: IGI Global. doi:10.4018/978-1-5225-2084-9.ch012

Hajilari, A. B., Ghadaksaz, M., & Fasghandis, G. S. (2017). Assessing Organizational Readiness for Implementing ERP System Using Fuzzy Expert System Approach. *International Journal of Enterprise Information Systems, 13*(1), 67–85. doi:10.4018/IJEIS.2017010105

Haldorai, A., Ramu, A., & Murugan, S. (2018). Social Aware Cognitive Radio Networks: Effectiveness of Social Networks as a Strategic Tool for Organizational Business Management. In H. Bansal, G. Shrivastava, G. Nguyen, & L. Stanciu (Eds.), *Social Network Analytics for Contemporary Business Organizations* (pp. 188–202). Hershey, PA: IGI Global. doi:10.4018/978-1-5225-5097-6.ch010

Hall, O. P. Jr. (2017). Social Media Driven Management Education. *International Journal of Knowledge-Based Organizations, 7*(2), 43–59. doi:10.4018/IJKBO.2017040104

Hanifah, H., Halim, H. A., Ahmad, N. H., & Vafaei-Zadeh, A. (2017). Innovation Culture as a Mediator Between Specific Human Capital and Innovation Performance Among Bumiputera SMEs in Malaysia. In N. Ahmad, T. Ramayah, H. Halim, & S. Rahman (Eds.), *Handbook of Research on Small and Medium Enterprises in Developing Countries* (pp. 261–279). Hershey, PA: IGI Global. doi:10.4018/978-1-5225-2165-5.ch012

Hartlieb, S., & Silvius, G. (2017). Handling Uncertainty in Project Management and Business Development: Similarities and Differences. In Y. Raydugin (Ed.), *Handbook of Research on Leveraging Risk and Uncertainties for Effective Project Management* (pp. 337–362). Hershey, PA: IGI Global. doi:10.4018/978-1-5225-1790-0.ch016

Hass, K. B. (2017). Living on the Edge: Managing Project Complexity. In Y. Raydugin (Ed.), *Handbook of Research on Leveraging Risk and Uncertainties for Effective Project Management* (pp. 177–201). Hershey, PA: IGI Global. doi:10.4018/978-1-5225-1790-0.ch009

Hawking, P., & Carmine Sellitto, C. (2017). Developing an Effective Strategy for Organizational Business Intelligence. In M. Tavana (Ed.), *Enterprise Information Systems and the Digitalization of Business Functions* (pp. 222–237). Hershey, PA: IGI Global. doi:10.4018/978-1-5225-2382-6.ch010

Hawking, P., & Sellitto, C. (2017). A Fast-Moving Consumer Goods Company and Business Intelligence Strategy Development. *International Journal of Enterprise Information Systems, 13*(2), 22–33. doi:10.4018/IJEIS.2017040102

Hawking, P., & Sellitto, C. (2017). Business Intelligence Strategy: Two Case Studies. *International Journal of Business Intelligence Research, 8*(2), 17–30. doi:10.4018/IJBIR.2017070102

Hee, W. J., Jalleh, G., Lai, H., & Lin, C. (2017). E-Commerce and IT Projects: Evaluation and Management Issues in Australian and Taiwanese Hospitals. *International Journal of Public Health Management and Ethics*, *2*(1), 69–90. doi:10.4018/IJPHME.2017010104

Hernandez, A. A. (2018). Exploring the Factors to Green IT Adoption of SMEs in the Philippines. *Journal of Cases on Information Technology*, *20*(2), 49–66. doi:10.4018/JCIT.2018040104

Hollman, A., Bickford, S., & Hollman, T. (2017). Cyber InSecurity: A Post-Mortem Attempt to Assess Cyber Problems from IT and Business Management Perspectives. *Journal of Cases on Information Technology*, *19*(3), 42–70. doi:10.4018/JCIT.2017070104

Ibrahim, F., & Zainin, N. M. (2021). Exploring the Technological Impacts: The Case of Museums in Brunei Darussalam. *International Journal of Tourism and Hospitality Management in the Digital Age*, *5*(1), 1–18. https://doi.org/10.4018/IJTHMDA.2021010101

Igbinakhase, I. (2017). Responsible and Sustainable Management Practices in Developing and Developed Business Environments. In Z. Fields (Ed.), *Collective Creativity for Responsible and Sustainable Business Practice* (pp. 180–207). Hershey, PA: IGI Global. doi:10.4018/978-1-5225-1823-5.ch010

Iwata, J. J., & Hoskins, R. G. (2017). Managing Indigenous Knowledge in Tanzania: A Business Perspective. In P. Jain & N. Mnjama (Eds.), *Managing Knowledge Resources and Records in Modern Organizations* (pp. 198–214). Hershey, PA: IGI Global. doi:10.4018/978-1-5225-1965-2.ch012

Jain, P. (2017). Ethical and Legal Issues in Knowledge Management Life-Cycle in Business. In P. Jain & N. Mnjama (Eds.), *Managing Knowledge Resources and Records in Modern Organizations* (pp. 82–101). Hershey, PA: IGI Global. doi:10.4018/978-1-5225-1965-2.ch006

James, S., & Hauli, E. (2017). Holistic Management Education at Tanzanian Rural Development Planning Institute. In N. Baporikar (Ed.), *Management Education for Global Leadership* (pp. 112–136). Hershey, PA: IGI Global. doi:10.4018/978-1-5225-1013-0.ch006

Janošková, M., Csikósová, A., & Čulková, K. (2018). Measurement of Company Performance as Part of Its Strategic Management. In R. Leon (Ed.), *Managerial Strategies for Business Sustainability During Turbulent Times* (pp. 309–335). Hershey, PA: IGI Global. doi:10.4018/978-1-5225-2716-9.ch017

Jean-Vasile, A., & Alecu, A. (2017). Theoretical and Practical Approaches in Understanding the Influences of Cost-Productivity-Profit Trinomial in Contemporary Enterprises. In A. Jean Vasile & D. Nicolò (Eds.), *Sustainable Entrepreneurship and Investments in the Green Economy* (pp. 28–62). Hershey, PA: IGI Global. doi:10.4018/978-1-5225-2075-7.ch002

Joia, L. A., & Correia, J. C. (2018). CIO Competencies From the IT Professional Perspective: Insights From Brazil. *Journal of Global Information Management, 26*(2), 74–103. doi:10.4018/JGIM.2018040104

Juma, A., & Mzera, N. (2017). Knowledge Management and Records Management and Competitive Advantage in Business. In P. Jain & N. Mnjama (Eds.), *Managing Knowledge Resources and Records in Modern Organizations* (pp. 15–28). Hershey, PA: IGI Global. doi:10.4018/978-1-5225-1965-2.ch002

K., I., & A, V. (2018). Monitoring and Auditing in the Cloud. In K. Munir (Ed.), *Cloud Computing Technologies for Green Enterprises* (pp. 318-350). Hershey, PA: IGI Global. https://doi.org/ doi:10.4018/978-1-5225-3038-1.ch013

Kabra, G., Ghosh, V., & Ramesh, A. (2018). Enterprise Integrated Business Process Management and Business Intelligence Framework for Business Process Sustainability. In A. Paul, D. Bhattacharyya, & S. Anand (Eds.), *Green Initiatives for Business Sustainability and Value Creation* (pp. 228–238). Hershey, PA: IGI Global. doi:10.4018/978-1-5225-2662-9.ch010

Kaoud, M. (2017). Investigation of Customer Knowledge Management: A Case Study Research. *International Journal of Service Science, Management, Engineering, and Technology, 8*(2), 12–22. doi:10.4018/IJSSMET.2017040102

Katuu, S. (2018). A Comparative Assessment of Enterprise Content Management Maturity Models. In N. Gwangwava & M. Mutingi (Eds.), *E-Manufacturing and E-Service Strategies in Contemporary Organizations* (pp. 93–118). Hershey, PA: IGI Global. doi:10.4018/978-1-5225-3628-4.ch005

Khan, M. Y., & Abir, T. (2022). The Role of Social Media Marketing in the Tourism and Hospitality Industry: A Conceptual Study on Bangladesh. In C. Ramos, S. Quinteiro, & A. Gonçalves (Eds.), *ICT as Innovator Between Tourism and Culture* (pp. 213–229). IGI Global. https://doi.org/10.4018/978-1-7998-8165-0.ch013

Kinnunen, S., Ylä-Kujala, A., Marttonen-Arola, S., Kärri, T., & Baglee, D. (2018). Internet of Things in Asset Management: Insights from Industrial Professionals and Academia. *International Journal of Service Science, Management, Engineering, and Technology, 9*(2), 104–119. doi:10.4018/IJSSMET.2018040105

Klein, A. Z., Sabino de Freitas, A., Machado, L., Freitas, J. C. Jr, Graziola, P. G. Jr, & Schlemmer, E. (2017). Virtual Worlds Applications for Management Education. In L. Tomei (Ed.), *Exploring the New Era of Technology-Infused Education* (pp. 279–299). Hershey, PA: IGI Global. doi:10.4018/978-1-5225-1709-2.ch017

Kővári, E., Saleh, M., & Steinbachné Hajmásy, G. (2022). The Impact of Corporate Digital Responsibility (CDR) on Internal Stakeholders' Satisfaction in Hungarian Upscale Hotels. In M. Valeri (Ed.), *New Governance and Management in Touristic Destinations* (pp. 35–51). IGI Global. https://doi.org/10.4018/978-1-6684-3889-3.ch003

Kożuch, B., & Jabłoński, A. (2017). Adopting the Concept of Business Models in Public Management. In M. Lewandowski & B. Kożuch (Eds.), *Public Sector Entrepreneurship and the Integration of Innovative Business Models* (pp. 10–46). Hershey, PA: IGI Global. doi:10.4018/978-1-5225-2215-7.ch002

Kumar, J., Adhikary, A., & Jha, A. (2017). Small Active Investors' Perceptions and Preferences Towards Tax Saving Mutual Fund Schemes in Eastern India: An Empirical Note. *International Journal of Asian Business and Information Management, 8*(2), 35–45. doi:10.4018/IJABIM.2017040103

Latusi, S., & Fissore, M. (2021). Pilgrimage Routes to Happiness: Comparing the Camino de Santiago and Via Francigena. In A. Perinotto, V. Mayer, & J. Soares (Eds.), *Rebuilding and Restructuring the Tourism Industry: Infusion of Happiness and Quality of Life* (pp. 157–182). IGI Global. https://doi.org/10.4018/978-1-7998-7239-9.ch008

Lavassani, K. M., & Movahedi, B. (2017). Applications Driven Information Systems: Beyond Networks toward Business Ecosystems. *International Journal of Innovation in the Digital Economy, 8*(1), 61–75. doi:10.4018/IJIDE.2017010104

Lazzareschi, V. H., & Brito, M. S. (2017). Strategic Information Management: Proposal of Business Project Model. In G. Jamil, A. Soares, & C. Pessoa (Eds.), *Handbook of Research on Information Management for Effective Logistics and Supply Chains* (pp. 59–88). Hershey, PA: IGI Global. doi:10.4018/978-1-5225-0973-8.ch004

Lechuga Sancho, M. P., & Martín Navarro, A. (2022). Evolution of the Literature on Social Responsibility in the Tourism Sector: A Systematic Literature Review. In G. Fernandes (Ed.), *Challenges and New Opportunities for Tourism in Inland Territories: Ecocultural Resources and Sustainable Initiatives* (pp. 169–186). IGI Global. https://doi.org/10.4018/978-1-7998-7339-6.ch010

Lederer, M., Kurz, M., & Lazarov, P. (2017). Usage and Suitability of Methods for Strategic Business Process Initiatives: A Multi Case Study Research. *International Journal of Productivity Management and Assessment Technologies*, *5*(1), 40–51. doi:10.4018/IJPMAT.2017010103

Lee, I. (2017). A Social Enterprise Business Model and a Case Study of Pacific Community Ventures (PCV). In V. Potocan, M. Ünğan, & Z. Nedelko (Eds.), *Handbook of Research on Managerial Solutions in Non-Profit Organizations* (pp. 182–204). Hershey, PA: IGI Global. doi:10.4018/978-1-5225-0731-4.ch009

Leon, L. A., Seal, K. C., Przasnyski, Z. H., & Wiedenman, I. (2017). Skills and Competencies Required for Jobs in Business Analytics: A Content Analysis of Job Advertisements Using Text Mining. *International Journal of Business Intelligence Research*, *8*(1), 1–25. doi:10.4018/IJBIR.2017010101

Levy, C. L., & Elias, N. I. (2017). SOHO Users' Perceptions of Reliability and Continuity of Cloud-Based Services. In M. Moore (Ed.), *Cybersecurity Breaches and Issues Surrounding Online Threat Protection* (pp. 248–287). Hershey, PA: IGI Global. doi:10.4018/978-1-5225-1941-6.ch011

Levy, M. (2018). Change Management Serving Knowledge Management and Organizational Development: Reflections and Review. In N. Baporikar (Ed.), *Global Practices in Knowledge Management for Societal and Organizational Development* (pp. 256–270). Hershey, PA: IGI Global. doi:10.4018/978-1-5225-3009-1.ch012

Lewandowski, M. (2017). Public Organizations and Business Model Innovation: The Role of Public Service Design. In M. Lewandowski & B. Kożuch (Eds.), *Public Sector Entrepreneurship and the Integration of Innovative Business Models* (pp. 47–72). Hershey, PA: IGI Global. doi:10.4018/978-1-5225-2215-7.ch003

Lhannaoui, H., Kabbaj, M. I., & Bakkoury, Z. (2017). A Survey of Risk-Aware Business Process Modelling. *International Journal of Risk and Contingency Management*, *6*(3), 14–26. doi:10.4018/IJRCM.2017070102

Li, J., Sun, W., Jiang, W., Yang, H., & Zhang, L. (2017). How the Nature of Exogenous Shocks and Crises Impact Company Performance?: The Effects of Industry Characteristics. *International Journal of Risk and Contingency Management*, *6*(4), 40–55. doi:10.4018/IJRCM.2017100103

Lopez-Fernandez, M., Perez-Perez, M., Serrano-Bedia, A., & Cobo-Gonzalez, A. (2021). Small and Medium Tourism Enterprise Survival in Times of Crisis: "El Capricho de Gaudí. In D. Toubes & N. Araújo-Vila (Eds.), *Risk, Crisis, and Disaster Management in Small and Medium-Sized Tourism Enterprises* (pp. 103–129). IGI Global. doi:10.4018/978-1-7998-6996-2.ch005

Mahajan, A., Maidullah, S., & Hossain, M. R. (2022). Experience Toward Smart Tour Guide Apps in Travelling: An Analysis of Users' Reviews on Audio Odigos and Trip My Way. In R. Augusto Costa, F. Brandão, Z. Breda, & C. Costa (Eds.), *Planning and Managing the Experience Economy in Tourism* (pp. 255-273). IGI Global. https://doi.org/10.4018/978-1-7998-8775-1.ch014

Malega, P. (2017). Small and Medium Enterprises in the Slovak Republic: Status and Competitiveness of SMEs in the Global Markets and Possibilities of Optimization. In M. Vemić (Ed.), *Optimal Management Strategies in Small and Medium Enterprises* (pp. 102–124). Hershey, PA: IGI Global. doi:10.4018/978-1-5225-1949-2.ch006

Malewska, K. M. (2017). Intuition in Decision-Making on the Example of a Non-Profit Organization. In V. Potocan, M. Ünğan, & Z. Nedelko (Eds.), *Handbook of Research on Managerial Solutions in Non-Profit Organizations* (pp. 378–399). Hershey, PA: IGI Global. doi:10.4018/978-1-5225-0731-4.ch018

Maroofi, F. (2017). Entrepreneurial Orientation and Organizational Learning Ability Analysis for Innovation and Firm Performance. In N. Baporikar (Ed.), *Innovation and Shifting Perspectives in Management Education* (pp. 144–165). Hershey, PA: IGI Global. doi:10.4018/978-1-5225-1019-2.ch007

Marques, M., Moleiro, D., Brito, T. M., & Marques, T. (2021). Customer Relationship Management as an Important Relationship Marketing Tool: The Case of the Hospitality Industry in Estoril Coast. In M. Dinis, L. Bonixe, S. Lamy, & Z. Breda (Eds.), Impact of New Media in Tourism (pp. 39-56). IGI Global. https://doi.org/doi:10.4018/978-1-7998-7095-1.ch003

Martins, P. V., & Zacarias, M. (2017). A Web-based Tool for Business Process Improvement. *International Journal of Web Portals*, *9*(2), 68–84. doi:10.4018/IJWP.2017070104

Matthies, B., & Coners, A. (2017). Exploring the Conceptual Nature of e-Business Projects. *Journal of Electronic Commerce in Organizations*, *15*(3), 33–63. doi:10.4018/JECO.2017070103

Mayer, V. F., Fraga, C. C., & Silva, L. C. (2021). Contributions of Neurosciences to Studies of Well-Being in Tourism. In A. Perinotto, V. Mayer, & J. Soares (Eds.), *Rebuilding and Restructuring the Tourism Industry: Infusion of Happiness and Quality of Life* (pp. 108–128). IGI Global. https://doi.org/10.4018/978-1-7998-7239-9.ch006

McKee, J. (2018). Architecture as a Tool to Solve Business Planning Problems. In M. Khosrow-Pour, D.B.A. (Ed.), Encyclopedia of Information Science and Technology, Fourth Edition (pp. 573-586). Hershey, PA: IGI Global. doi:10.4018/978-1-5225-2255-3.ch050

McMurray, A. J., Cross, J., & Caponecchia, C. (2018). The Risk Management Profession in Australia: Business Continuity Plan Practices. In N. Bajgoric (Ed.), *Always-On Enterprise Information Systems for Modern Organizations* (pp. 112–129). Hershey, PA: IGI Global. doi:10.4018/978-1-5225-3704-5.ch006

Meddah, I. H., & Belkadi, K. (2018). Mining Patterns Using Business Process Management. In R. Hamou (Ed.), *Handbook of Research on Biomimicry in Information Retrieval and Knowledge Management* (pp. 78–89). Hershey, PA: IGI Global. doi:10.4018/978-1-5225-3004-6.ch005

Melian, A. G., & Camprubí, R. (2021). The Accessibility of Museum Websites: The Case of Barcelona. In C. Eusébio, L. Teixeira, & M. Carneiro (Eds.), *ICT Tools and Applications for Accessible Tourism* (pp. 234–255). IGI Global. https://doi.org/10.4018/978-1-7998-6428-8.ch011

Mendes, L. (2017). TQM and Knowledge Management: An Integrated Approach Towards Tacit Knowledge Management. In D. Jaziri-Bouagina & G. Jamil (Eds.), *Handbook of Research on Tacit Knowledge Management for Organizational Success* (pp. 236–263). Hershey, PA: IGI Global. doi:10.4018/978-1-5225-2394-9.ch009

Menezes, V. D., & Cavagnaro, E. (2021). Communicating Sustainable Initiatives in the Hotel Industry: The Case of the Hotel Jakarta Amsterdam. In F. Brandão, Z. Breda, R. Costa, & C. Costa (Eds.), *Handbook of Research on the Role of Tourism in Achieving Sustainable Development Goals* (pp. 224-234). IGI Global. https://doi.org/10.4018/978-1-7998-5691-7.ch013

Menezes, V. D., & Cavagnaro, E. (2021). Communicating Sustainable Initiatives in the Hotel Industry: The Case of the Hotel Jakarta Amsterdam. In F. Brandão, Z. Breda, R. Costa, & C. Costa (Eds.), *Handbook of Research on the Role of Tourism in Achieving Sustainable Development Goals* (pp. 224-234). IGI Global. https://doi.org/10.4018/978-1-7998-5691-7.ch013

Mitas, O., Bastiaansen, M., & Boode, W. (2022). If You're Happy, I'm Happy: Emotion Contagion at a Tourist Information Center. In R. Augusto Costa, F. Brandão, Z. Breda, & C. Costa (Eds.), *Planning and Managing the Experience Economy in Tourism* (pp. 122-140). IGI Global. https://doi.org/10.4018/978-1-7998-8775-1.ch007

Mnjama, N. M. (2017). Preservation of Recorded Information in Public and Private Sector Organizations. In P. Jain & N. Mnjama (Eds.), *Managing Knowledge Resources and Records in Modern Organizations* (pp. 149–167). Hershey, PA: IGI Global. doi:10.4018/978-1-5225-1965-2.ch009

Mokoqama, M., & Fields, Z. (2017). Principles of Responsible Management Education (PRME): Call for Responsible Management Education. In Z. Fields (Ed.), *Collective Creativity for Responsible and Sustainable Business Practice* (pp. 229–241). Hershey, PA: IGI Global. doi:10.4018/978-1-5225-1823-5.ch012

Monteiro, A., Lopes, S., & Carbone, F. (2021). Academic Mobility: Bridging Tourism and Peace Education. In J. da Silva, Z. Breda, & F. Carbone (Eds.), *Role and Impact of Tourism in Peacebuilding and Conflict Transformation* (pp. 275-301). IGI Global. https://doi.org/10.4018/978-1-7998-5053-3.ch016

Muniapan, B. (2017). Philosophy and Management: The Relevance of Vedanta in Management. In P. Ordóñez de Pablos (Ed.), *Managerial Strategies and Solutions for Business Success in Asia* (pp. 124–139). Hershey, PA: IGI Global. doi:10.4018/978-1-5225-1886-0.ch007

Murad, S. E., & Dowaji, S. (2017). Using Value-Based Approach for Managing Cloud-Based Services. In A. Turuk, B. Sahoo, & S. Addya (Eds.), *Resource Management and Efficiency in Cloud Computing Environments* (pp. 33–60). Hershey, PA: IGI Global. doi:10.4018/978-1-5225-1721-4.ch002

Mutahar, A. M., Daud, N. M., Thurasamy, R., Isaac, O., & Abdulsalam, R. (2018). The Mediating of Perceived Usefulness and Perceived Ease of Use: The Case of Mobile Banking in Yemen. *International Journal of Technology Diffusion*, *9*(2), 21–40. doi:10.4018/IJTD.2018040102

Naidoo, V. (2017). E-Learning and Management Education at African Universities. In N. Baporikar (Ed.), *Management Education for Global Leadership* (pp. 181–201). Hershey, PA: IGI Global. doi:10.4018/978-1-5225-1013-0.ch009

Naidoo, V., & Igbinakhase, I. (2018). Opportunities and Challenges of Knowledge Retention in SMEs. In N. Baporikar (Ed.), *Knowledge Integration Strategies for Entrepreneurship and Sustainability* (pp. 70–94). Hershey, PA: IGI Global. doi:10.4018/978-1-5225-5115-7.ch004

Naumov, N., & Costandachi, G. (2021). Creativity and Entrepreneurship: Gastronomic Tourism in Mexico. In J. Soares (Ed.), *Innovation and Entrepreneurial Opportunities in Community Tourism* (pp. 90–108). IGI Global. https://doi.org/10.4018/978-1-7998-4855-4.ch006

Nayak, S., & Prabhu, N. (2017). Paradigm Shift in Management Education: Need for a Cross Functional Perspective. In N. Baporikar (Ed.), *Management Education for Global Leadership* (pp. 241–255). Hershey, PA: IGI Global. doi:10.4018/978-1-5225-1013-0.ch012

Nedelko, Z., & Potocan, V. (2017). Management Solutions in Non-Profit Organizations: Case of Slovenia. In V. Potocan, M. Üngan, & Z. Nedelko (Eds.), *Handbook of Research on Managerial Solutions in Non-Profit Organizations* (pp. 1–22). Hershey, PA: IGI Global. doi:10.4018/978-1-5225-0731-4.ch001

Nedelko, Z., & Potocan, V. (2017). Priority of Management Tools Utilization among Managers: International Comparison. In V. Wang (Ed.), *Encyclopedia of Strategic Leadership and Management* (pp. 1083–1094). Hershey, PA: IGI Global. doi:10.4018/978-1-5225-1049-9.ch075

Nedelko, Z., Raudeliūnienė, J., & Črešnar, R. (2018). Knowledge Dynamics in Supply Chain Management. In N. Baporikar (Ed.), *Knowledge Integration Strategies for Entrepreneurship and Sustainability* (pp. 150–166). Hershey, PA: IGI Global. doi:10.4018/978-1-5225-5115-7.ch008

Nguyen, H. T., & Hipsher, S. A. (2018). Innovation and Creativity Used by Private Sector Firms in a Resources-Constrained Environment. In S. Hipsher (Ed.), *Examining the Private Sector's Role in Wealth Creation and Poverty Reduction* (pp. 219–238). Hershey, PA: IGI Global. doi:10.4018/978-1-5225-3117-3.ch010

Obicci, P. A. (2017). Risk Sharing in a Partnership. In *Risk Management Strategies in Public-Private Partnerships* (pp. 115–152). Hershey, PA: IGI Global. doi:10.4018/978-1-5225-2503-5.ch004

Obidallah, W. J., & Raahemi, B. (2017). Managing Changes in Service Oriented Virtual Organizations: A Structural and Procedural Framework to Facilitate the Process of Change. *Journal of Electronic Commerce in Organizations*, *15*(1), 59–83. doi:10.4018/JECO.2017010104

Ojo, O. (2017). Impact of Innovation on the Entrepreneurial Success in Selected Business Enterprises in South-West Nigeria. *International Journal of Innovation in the Digital Economy*, *8*(2), 29–38. doi:10.4018/IJIDE.2017040103

Okdinawati, L., Simatupang, T. M., & Sunitiyoso, Y. (2017). Multi-Agent Reinforcement Learning for Value Co-Creation of Collaborative Transportation Management (CTM). *International Journal of Information Systems and Supply Chain Management*, *10*(3), 84–95. doi:10.4018/IJISSCM.2017070105

Olivera, V. A., & Carrillo, I. M. (2021). Organizational Culture: A Key Element for the Development of Mexican Micro and Small Tourist Companies. In J. Soares (Ed.), *Innovation and Entrepreneurial Opportunities in Community Tourism* (pp. 227–242). IGI Global. doi:10.4018/978-1-7998-4855-4.ch013

Ossorio, M. (2022). Corporate Museum Experiences in Enogastronomic Tourism. In R. Augusto Costa, F. Brandão, Z. Breda, & C. Costa (Eds.), Planning and Managing the Experience Economy in Tourism (pp. 107-121). IGI Global. https://doi.org/ doi:10.4018/978-1-7998-8775-1.ch006

Ossorio, M. (2022). Enogastronomic Tourism in Times of Pandemic. In G. Fernandes (Ed.), *Challenges and New Opportunities for Tourism in Inland Territories: Ecocultural Resources and Sustainable Initiatives* (pp. 241–255). IGI Global. https://doi.org/10.4018/978-1-7998-7339-6.ch014

Özekici, Y. K. (2022). ICT as an Acculturative Agent and Its Role in the Tourism Context: Introduction, Acculturation Theory, Progress of the Acculturation Theory in Extant Literature. In C. Ramos, S. Quinteiro, & A. Gonçalves (Eds.), *ICT as Innovator Between Tourism and Culture* (pp. 42–66). IGI Global. https://doi.org/10.4018/978-1-7998-8165-0.ch004

Pal, K. (2018). Building High Quality Big Data-Based Applications in Supply Chains. In A. Kumar & S. Saurav (Eds.), *Supply Chain Management Strategies and Risk Assessment in Retail Environments* (pp. 1–24). Hershey, PA: IGI Global. doi:10.4018/978-1-5225-3056-5.ch001

Palos-Sanchez, P. R., & Correia, M. B. (2018). Perspectives of the Adoption of Cloud Computing in the Tourism Sector. In J. Rodrigues, C. Ramos, P. Cardoso, & C. Henriques (Eds.), *Handbook of Research on Technological Developments for Cultural Heritage and eTourism Applications* (pp. 377–400). Hershey, PA: IGI Global. doi:10.4018/978-1-5225-2927-9.ch018

Papadopoulou, G. (2021). Promoting Gender Equality and Women Empowerment in the Tourism Sector. In F. Brandão, Z. Breda, R. Costa, & C. Costa (Eds.), Handbook of Research on the Role of Tourism in Achieving Sustainable Development Goals (pp. 152-174). IGI Global. https://doi.org/ doi:10.4018/978-1-7998-5691-7.ch009

Papp-Váry, Á. F., & Tóth, T. Z. (2022). Analysis of Budapest as a Film Tourism Destination. In R. Baleiro & R. Pereira (Eds.), *Global Perspectives on Literary Tourism and Film-Induced Tourism* (pp. 257-279). IGI Global. https://doi.org/10.4018/978-1-7998-8262-6.ch014

Patiño, B. E. (2017). New Generation Management by Convergence and Individual Identity: A Systemic and Human-Oriented Approach. In N. Baporikar (Ed.), *Innovation and Shifting Perspectives in Management Education* (pp. 119–143). Hershey, PA: IGI Global. doi:10.4018/978-1-5225-1019-2.ch006

Patro, C. S. (2021). Digital Tourism: Influence of E-Marketing Technology. In M. Dinis, L. Bonixe, S. Lamy, & Z. Breda (Eds.), *Impact of New Media in Tourism* (pp. 234-254). IGI Global. https://doi.org/10.4018/978-1-7998-7095-1.ch014

Pawliczek, A., & Rössler, M. (2017). Knowledge of Management Tools and Systems in SMEs: Knowledge Transfer in Management. In A. Bencsik (Ed.), *Knowledge Management Initiatives and Strategies in Small and Medium Enterprises* (pp. 180–203). Hershey, PA: IGI Global. doi:10.4018/978-1-5225-1642-2.ch009

Pejic-Bach, M., Omazic, M. A., Aleksic, A., & Zoroja, J. (2018). Knowledge-Based Decision Making: A Multi-Case Analysis. In R. Leon (Ed.), *Managerial Strategies for Business Sustainability During Turbulent Times* (pp. 160–184). Hershey, PA: IGI Global. doi:10.4018/978-1-5225-2716-9.ch009

Perano, M., Hysa, X., & Calabrese, M. (2018). Strategic Planning, Cultural Context, and Business Continuity Management: Business Cases in the City of Shkoder. In A. Presenza & L. Sheehan (Eds.), *Geopolitics and Strategic Management in the Global Economy* (pp. 57–77). Hershey, PA: IGI Global. doi:10.4018/978-1-5225-2673-5.ch004

Pereira, R., Mira da Silva, M., & Lapão, L. V. (2017). IT Governance Maturity Patterns in Portuguese Healthcare. In S. De Haes & W. Van Grembergen (Eds.), *Strategic IT Governance and Alignment in Business Settings* (pp. 24–52). Hershey, PA: IGI Global. doi:10.4018/978-1-5225-0861-8.ch002

Pérez-Uribe, R. I., Torres, D. A., Jurado, S. P., & Prada, D. M. (2018). Cloud Tools for the Development of Project Management in SMEs. In R. Perez-Uribe, C. Salcedo-Perez, & D. Ocampo-Guzman (Eds.), *Handbook of Research on Intrapreneurship and Organizational Sustainability in SMEs* (pp. 95–120). Hershey, PA: IGI Global. doi:10.4018/978-1-5225-3543-0.ch005

Petrisor, I., & Cozmiuc, D. (2017). Global Supply Chain Management Organization at Siemens in the Advent of Industry 4.0. In L. Saglietto & C. Cezanne (Eds.), *Global Intermediation and Logistics Service Providers* (pp. 123–142). Hershey, PA: IGI Global. doi:10.4018/978-1-5225-2133-4.ch007

Pierce, J. M., Velliaris, D. M., & Edwards, J. (2017). A Living Case Study: A Journey Not a Destination. In N. Silton (Ed.), *Exploring the Benefits of Creativity in Education, Media, and the Arts* (pp. 158–178). Hershey, PA: IGI Global. doi:10.4018/978-1-5225-0504-4.ch008

Pipia, S., & Pipia, S. (2021). Challenges of Religious Tourism in the Conflict Region: An Example of Jerusalem. In E. Alaverdov & M. Bari (Eds.), *Global Development of Religious Tourism* (pp. 135-148). IGI Global. https://doi.org/10.4018/978-1-7998-5792-1.ch009

Poulaki, P., Kritikos, A., Vasilakis, N., & Valeri, M. (2022). The Contribution of Female Creativity to the Development of Gastronomic Tourism in Greece: The Case of the Island of Naxos in the South Aegean Region. In M. Valeri (Ed.), *New Governance and Management in Touristic Destinations* (pp. 246–258). IGI Global. https://doi.org/10.4018/978-1-6684-3889-3.ch015

Radosavljevic, M., & Andjelkovic, A. (2017). Multi-Criteria Decision Making Approach for Choosing Business Process for the Improvement: Upgrading of the Six Sigma Methodology. In J. Stanković, P. Delias, S. Marinković, & S. Rochhia (Eds.), *Tools and Techniques for Economic Decision Analysis* (pp. 225–247). Hershey, PA: IGI Global. doi:10.4018/978-1-5225-0959-2.ch011

Radovic, V. M. (2017). Corporate Sustainability and Responsibility and Disaster Risk Reduction: A Serbian Overview. In M. Camilleri (Ed.), *CSR 2.0 and the New Era of Corporate Citizenship* (pp. 147–164). Hershey, PA: IGI Global. doi:10.4018/978-1-5225-1842-6.ch008

Raghunath, K. M., Devi, S. L., & Patro, C. S. (2018). Impact of Risk Assessment Models on Risk Factors: A Holistic Outlook. In K. Strang, M. Korstanje, & N. Vajjhala (Eds.), *Research, Practices, and Innovations in Global Risk and Contingency Management* (pp. 134–153). Hershey, PA: IGI Global. doi:10.4018/978-1-5225-4754-9.ch008

Raman, A., & Goyal, D. P. (2017). Extending IMPLEMENT Framework for Enterprise Information Systems Implementation to Information System Innovation. In M. Tavana (Ed.), *Enterprise Information Systems and the Digitalization of Business Functions* (pp. 137–177). Hershey, PA: IGI Global. doi:10.4018/978-1-5225-2382-6.ch007

Rao, Y., & Zhang, Y. (2017). The Construction and Development of Academic Library Digital Special Subject Databases. In L. Ruan, Q. Zhu, & Y. Ye (Eds.), *Academic Library Development and Administration in China* (pp. 163–183). Hershey, PA: IGI Global. doi:10.4018/978-1-5225-0550-1.ch010

Ravasan, A. Z., Mohammadi, M. M., & Hamidi, H. (2018). An Investigation Into the Critical Success Factors of Implementing Information Technology Service Management Frameworks. In K. Jakobs (Ed.), *Corporate and Global Standardization Initiatives in Contemporary Society* (pp. 200–218). Hershey, PA: IGI Global. doi:10.4018/978-1-5225-5320-5.ch009

Rezaie, S., Mirabedini, S. J., & Abtahi, A. (2018). Designing a Model for Implementation of Business Intelligence in the Banking Industry. *International Journal of Enterprise Information Systems, 14*(1), 77–103. doi:10.4018/IJEIS.2018010105

Richards, V., Matthews, N., Williams, O. J., & Khan, Z. (2021). The Challenges of Accessible Tourism Information Systems for Tourists With Vision Impairment: Sensory Communications Beyond the Screen. In C. Eusébio, L. Teixeira, & M. Carneiro (Eds.), *ICT Tools and Applications for Accessible Tourism* (pp. 26–54). IGI Global. https://doi.org/10.4018/978-1-7998-6428-8.ch002

Rodrigues de Souza Neto, V., & Marques, O. (2021). Rural Tourism Fostering Welfare Through Sustainable Development: A Conceptual Approach. In A. Perinotto, V. Mayer, & J. Soares (Eds.), *Rebuilding and Restructuring the Tourism Industry: Infusion of Happiness and Quality of Life* (pp. 38–57). IGI Global. https://doi.org/10.4018/978-1-7998-7239-9.ch003

Romano, L., Grimaldi, R., & Colasuonno, F. S. (2017). Demand Management as a Success Factor in Project Portfolio Management. In L. Romano (Ed.), *Project Portfolio Management Strategies for Effective Organizational Operations* (pp. 202–219). Hershey, PA: IGI Global. doi:10.4018/978-1-5225-2151-8.ch008

Rubio-Escuderos, L., & García-Andreu, H. (2021). Competitiveness Factors of Accessible Tourism E-Travel Agencies. In C. Eusébio, L. Teixeira, & M. Carneiro (Eds.), *ICT Tools and Applications for Accessible Tourism* (pp. 196–217). IGI Global. https://doi.org/10.4018/978-1-7998-6428-8.ch009

Rucci, A. C., Porto, N., Darcy, S., & Becka, L. (2021). Smart and Accessible Cities?: Not Always – The Case for Accessible Tourism Initiatives in Buenos Aries and Sydney. In C. Eusébio, L. Teixeira, & M. Carneiro (Eds.), *ICT Tools and Applications for Accessible Tourism* (pp. 115–145). IGI Global. https://doi.org/10.4018/978-1-7998-6428-8.ch006

Ruhi, U. (2018). Towards an Interdisciplinary Socio-Technical Definition of Virtual Communities. In M. Khosrow-Pour, D.B.A. (Ed.), Encyclopedia of Information Science and Technology, Fourth Edition (pp. 4278-4295). Hershey, PA: IGI Global. doi:10.4018/978-1-5225-2255-3.ch371

Ryan, L., Catena, M., Ros, P., & Stephens, S. (2021). Designing Entrepreneurial Ecosystems to Support Resource Management in the Tourism Industry. In V. Costa, A. Moura, & M. Mira (Eds.), *Handbook of Research on Human Capital and People Management in the Tourism Industry* (pp. 265–281). IGI Global. https://doi.org/10.4018/978-1-7998-4318-4.ch013

Sabuncu, I. (2021). Understanding Tourist Perceptions and Expectations During Pandemic Through Social Media Big Data. In M. Demir, A. Dalgıç, & F. Ergen (Eds.), *Handbook of Research on the Impacts and Implications of COVID-19 on the Tourism Industry* (pp. 330–350). IGI Global. https://doi.org/10.4018/978-1-7998-8231-2.ch016

Safari, M. R., & Jiang, Q. (2018). The Theory and Practice of IT Governance Maturity and Strategies Alignment: Evidence From Banking Industry. *Journal of Global Information Management*, *26*(2), 127–146. doi:10.4018/JGIM.2018040106

Sahoo, J., Pati, B., & Mohanty, B. (2017). Knowledge Management as an Academic Discipline: An Assessment. In B. Gunjal (Ed.), *Managing Knowledge and Scholarly Assets in Academic Libraries* (pp. 99–126). Hershey, PA: IGI Global. doi:10.4018/978-1-5225-1741-2.ch005

Saini, D. (2017). Relevance of Teaching Values and Ethics in Management Education. In N. Baporikar (Ed.), *Management Education for Global Leadership* (pp. 90–111). Hershey, PA: IGI Global. doi:10.4018/978-1-5225-1013-0.ch005

Sambhanthan, A. (2017). Assessing and Benchmarking Sustainability in Organisations: An Integrated Conceptual Model. *International Journal of Systems and Service-Oriented Engineering*, *7*(4), 22–43. doi:10.4018/IJSSOE.2017100102

Sambhanthan, A., & Potdar, V. (2017). A Study of the Parameters Impacting Sustainability in Information Technology Organizations. *International Journal of Knowledge-Based Organizations*, *7*(3), 27–39. doi:10.4018/IJKBO.2017070103

Sánchez-Fernández, M. D., & Manríquez, M. R. (2018). The Entrepreneurial Spirit Based on Social Values: The Digital Generation. In P. Isaias & L. Carvalho (Eds.), *User Innovation and the Entrepreneurship Phenomenon in the Digital Economy* (pp. 173–193). Hershey, PA: IGI Global. doi:10.4018/978-1-5225-2826-5.ch009

Sanchez-Ruiz, L., & Blanco, B. (2017). Process Management for SMEs: Barriers, Enablers, and Benefits. In M. Vemić (Ed.), *Optimal Management Strategies in Small and Medium Enterprises* (pp. 293–319). Hershey, PA: IGI Global. doi:10.4018/978-1-5225-1949-2.ch014

Sanz, L. F., Gómez-Pérez, J., & Castillo-Martinez, A. (2018). Analysis of the European ICT Competence Frameworks. In V. Ahuja & S. Rathore (Eds.), *Multidisciplinary Perspectives on Human Capital and Information Technology Professionals* (pp. 225–245). Hershey, PA: IGI Global. doi:10.4018/978-1-5225-5297-0.ch012

Sarvepalli, A., & Godin, J. (2017). Business Process Management in the Classroom. *Journal of Cases on Information Technology, 19*(2), 17–28. doi:10.4018/JCIT.2017040102

Saxena, G. G., & Saxena, A. (2021). Host Community Role in Medical Tourism Development. In M. Singh & S. Kumaran (Eds.), *Growth of the Medical Tourism Industry and Its Impact on Society: Emerging Research and Opportunities* (pp. 105–127). IGI Global. https://doi.org/10.4018/978-1-7998-3427-4.ch006

Saygili, E. E., Ozturkoglu, Y., & Kocakulah, M. C. (2017). End Users' Perceptions of Critical Success Factors in ERP Applications. *International Journal of Enterprise Information Systems, 13*(4), 58–75. doi:10.4018/IJEIS.2017100104

Saygili, E. E., & Saygili, A. T. (2017). Contemporary Issues in Enterprise Information Systems: A Critical Review of CSFs in ERP Implementations. In M. Tavana (Ed.), *Enterprise Information Systems and the Digitalization of Business Functions* (pp. 120–136). Hershey, PA: IGI Global. doi:10.4018/978-1-5225-2382-6.ch006

Schwaiger, K. M., & Zehrer, A. (2021). The COVID-19 Pandemic and Organizational Resilience in Hospitality Family Firms: A Qualitative Approach. In A. Zehrer, G. Glowka, K. Schwaiger, & V. Ranacher-Lackner (Eds.), *Resiliency Models and Addressing Future Risks for Family Firms in the Tourism Industry* (pp. 32–49). IGI Global. https://doi.org/10.4018/978-1-7998-7352-5.ch002

Scott, N., & Campos, A. C. (2022). Cognitive Science of Tourism Experiences. In R. Augusto Costa, F. Brandão, Z. Breda, & C. Costa (Eds.), Planning and Managing the Experience Economy in Tourism (pp. 1-21). IGI Global. https://doi.org/ doi:10.4018/978-1-7998-8775-1.ch001

Seidenstricker, S., & Antonino, A. (2018). Business Model Innovation-Oriented Technology Management for Emergent Technologies. In M. Khosrow-Pour, D.B.A. (Ed.), Encyclopedia of Information Science and Technology, Fourth Edition (pp. 4560-4569). Hershey, PA: IGI Global. doi:10.4018/978-1-5225-2255-3.ch396

Selvi, M. S. (2021). Changes in Tourism Sales and Marketing Post COVID-19. In M. Demir, A. Dalgıç, & F. Ergen (Eds.), *Handbook of Research on the Impacts and Implications of COVID-19 on the Tourism Industry* (pp. 437–460). IGI Global. doi:10.4018/978-1-7998-8231-2.ch021

Senaratne, S., & Gunarathne, A. D. (2017). Excellence Perspective for Management Education from a Global Accountants' Hub in Asia. In N. Baporikar (Ed.), *Management Education for Global Leadership* (pp. 158–180). Hershey, PA: IGI Global. doi:10.4018/978-1-5225-1013-0.ch008

Sensuse, D. I., & Cahyaningsih, E. (2018). Knowledge Management Models: A Summative Review. *International Journal of Information Systems in the Service Sector, 10*(1), 71–100. doi:10.4018/IJISSS.2018010105

Seth, M., Goyal, D., & Kiran, R. (2017). Diminution of Impediments in Implementation of Supply Chain Management Information System for Enhancing its Effectiveness in Indian Automobile Industry. *Journal of Global Information Management, 25*(3), 1–20. doi:10.4018/JGIM.2017070101

Seyal, A. H., & Rahman, M. N. (2017). Investigating Impact of Inter-Organizational Factors in Measuring ERP Systems Success: Bruneian Perspectives. In M. Tavana (Ed.), *Enterprise Information Systems and the Digitalization of Business Functions* (pp. 178–204). Hershey, PA: IGI Global. doi:10.4018/978-1-5225-2382-6.ch008

Shaqrah, A. A. (2018). Analyzing Business Intelligence Systems Based on 7s Model of McKinsey. *International Journal of Business Intelligence Research, 9*(1), 53–63. doi:10.4018/IJBIR.2018010104

Sharma, A. J. (2017). Enhancing Sustainability through Experiential Learning in Management Education. In N. Baporikar (Ed.), *Management Education for Global Leadership* (pp. 256–274). Hershey, PA: IGI Global. doi:10.4018/978-1-5225-1013-0.ch013

Shetty, K. P. (2017). Responsible Global Leadership: Ethical Challenges in Management Education. In N. Baporikar (Ed.), *Innovation and Shifting Perspectives in Management Education* (pp. 194–223). Hershey, PA: IGI Global. doi:10.4018/978-1-5225-1019-2.ch009

Sinthupundaja, J., & Kohda, Y. (2017). Effects of Corporate Social Responsibility and Creating Shared Value on Sustainability. *International Journal of Sustainable Entrepreneurship and Corporate Social Responsibility, 2*(1), 27–38. doi:10.4018/IJSECSR.2017010103

Škarica, I., & Hrgović, A. V. (2018). Implementation of Total Quality Management Principles in Public Health Institutes in the Republic of Croatia. *International Journal of Productivity Management and Assessment Technologies, 6*(1), 1–16. doi:10.4018/IJPMAT.2018010101

Skokic, V. (2021). How Small Hotel Owners Practice Resilience: Longitudinal Study Among Small Family Hotels in Croatia. In A. Zehrer, G. Glowka, K. Schwaiger, & V. Ranacher-Lackner (Eds.), *Resiliency Models and Addressing Future Risks for Family Firms in the Tourism Industry* (pp. 50–73). IGI Global. doi:10.4018/978-1-7998-7352-5.ch003

Smuts, H., Kotzé, P., Van der Merwe, A., & Loock, M. (2017). Framework for Managing Shared Knowledge in an Information Systems Outsourcing Context. *International Journal of Knowledge Management*, *13*(4), 1–30. doi:10.4018/IJKM.2017100101

Sousa, M. J., Cruz, R., Dias, I., & Caracol, C. (2017). Information Management Systems in the Supply Chain. In G. Jamil, A. Soares, & C. Pessoa (Eds.), *Handbook of Research on Information Management for Effective Logistics and Supply Chains* (pp. 469–485). Hershey, PA: IGI Global. doi:10.4018/978-1-5225-0973-8.ch025

Spremic, M., Turulja, L., & Bajgoric, N. (2018). Two Approaches in Assessing Business Continuity Management Attitudes in the Organizational Context. In N. Bajgoric (Ed.), *Always-On Enterprise Information Systems for Modern Organizations* (pp. 159–183). Hershey, PA: IGI Global. doi:10.4018/978-1-5225-3704-5.ch008

Steenkamp, A. L. (2018). Some Insights in Computer Science and Information Technology. In *Examining the Changing Role of Supervision in Doctoral Research Projects: Emerging Research and Opportunities* (pp. 113–133). Hershey, PA: IGI Global. doi:10.4018/978-1-5225-2610-0.ch005

Stipanović, C., Rudan, E., & Zubović, V. (2022). Reaching the New Tourist Through Creativity: Sustainable Development Challenges in Croatian Coastal Towns. In M. Valeri (Ed.), *New Governance and Management in Touristic Destinations* (pp. 231–245). IGI Global. https://doi.org/10.4018/978-1-6684-3889-3.ch014

Tabach, A., & Croteau, A. (2017). Configurations of Information Technology Governance Practices and Business Unit Performance. *International Journal of IT/Business Alignment and Governance*, *8*(2), 1–27. doi:10.4018/IJITBAG.2017070101

Talaue, G. M., & Iqbal, T. (2017). Assessment of e-Business Mode of Selected Private Universities in the Philippines and Pakistan. *International Journal of Online Marketing*, *7*(4), 63–77. doi:10.4018/IJOM.2017100105

Tam, G. C. (2017). Project Manager Sustainability Competence. In *Managerial Strategies and Green Solutions for Project Sustainability* (pp. 178–207). Hershey, PA: IGI Global. doi:10.4018/978-1-5225-2371-0.ch008

Tambo, T. (2018). Fashion Retail Innovation: About Context, Antecedents, and Outcome in Technological Change Projects. In I. Management Association (Ed.), Fashion and Textiles: Breakthroughs in Research and Practice (pp. 233-260). Hershey, PA: IGI Global. https://doi.org/ doi:10.4018/978-1-5225-3432-7.ch010

Tantau, A. D., & Frăţilă, L. C. (2018). Information and Management System for Renewable Energy Business. In *Entrepreneurship and Business Development in the Renewable Energy Sector* (pp. 200–244). Hershey, PA: IGI Global. doi:10.4018/978-1-5225-3625-3.ch006

Teixeira, N., Pardal, P. N., & Rafael, B. G. (2018). Internationalization, Financial Performance, and Organizational Challenges: A Success Case in Portugal. In L. Carvalho (Ed.), *Handbook of Research on Entrepreneurial Ecosystems and Social Dynamics in a Globalized World* (pp. 379–423). Hershey, PA: IGI Global. doi:10.4018/978-1-5225-3525-6.ch017

Teixeira, P., Teixeira, L., Eusébio, C., Silva, S., & Teixeira, A. (2021). The Impact of ICTs on Accessible Tourism: Evidence Based on a Systematic Literature Review. In C. Eusébio, L. Teixeira, & M. Carneiro (Eds.), *ICT Tools and Applications for Accessible Tourism* (pp. 1–25). IGI Global. doi:10.4018/978-1-7998-6428-8.ch001

Trad, A., & Kalpić, D. (2018). The Business Transformation Framework, Agile Project and Change Management. In M. Khosrow-Pour, D.B.A. (Ed.), Encyclopedia of Information Science and Technology, Fourth Edition (pp. 620-635). Hershey, PA: IGI Global. https://doi.org/ doi:10.4018/978-1-5225-2255-3.ch054

Trad, A., & Kalpić, D. (2018). The Business Transformation and Enterprise Architecture Framework: The Financial Engineering E-Risk Management and E-Law Integration. In B. Sergi, F. Fidanoski, M. Ziolo, & V. Naumovski (Eds.), *Regaining Global Stability After the Financial Crisis* (pp. 46–65). Hershey, PA: IGI Global. doi:10.4018/978-1-5225-4026-7.ch003

Trengereid, V. (2022). Conditions of Network Engagement: The Quest for a Common Good. In R. Augusto Costa, F. Brandão, Z. Breda, & C. Costa (Eds.), *Planning and Managing the Experience Economy in Tourism* (pp. 69-84). IGI Global. https://doi.org/10.4018/978-1-7998-8775-1.ch004

Turulja, L., & Bajgoric, N. (2018). Business Continuity and Information Systems: A Systematic Literature Review. In N. Bajgoric (Ed.), *Always-On Enterprise Information Systems for Modern Organizations* (pp. 60–87). Hershey, PA: IGI Global. doi:10.4018/978-1-5225-3704-5.ch004

Vargas-Hernández, J. G. (2017). Professional Integrity in Business Management Education. In N. Baporikar (Ed.), *Management Education for Global Leadership* (pp. 70–89). Hershey, PA: IGI Global. doi:10.4018/978-1-5225-1013-0.ch004

Varnacı Uzun, F. (2021). The Destination Preferences of Foreign Tourists During the COVID-19 Pandemic and Attitudes Towards: Marmaris, Turkey. In M. Demir, A. Dalgıç, & F. Ergen (Eds.), *Handbook of Research on the Impacts and Implications of COVID-19 on the Tourism Industry* (pp. 285–306). IGI Global. https://doi.org/10.4018/978-1-7998-8231-2.ch014

Vasista, T. G., & AlAbdullatif, A. M. (2017). Role of Electronic Customer Relationship Management in Demand Chain Management: A Predictive Analytic Approach. *International Journal of Information Systems and Supply Chain Management, 10*(1), 53–67. doi:10.4018/IJISSCM.2017010104

Vieru, D., & Bourdeau, S. (2017). Survival in the Digital Era: A Digital Competence-Based Multi-Case Study in the Canadian SME Clothing Industry. *International Journal of Social and Organizational Dynamics in IT, 6*(1), 17–34. doi:10.4018/IJSODIT.2017010102

Vijayan, G., & Kamarulzaman, N. H. (2017). An Introduction to Sustainable Supply Chain Management and Business Implications. In M. Khan, M. Hussain, & M. Ajmal (Eds.), *Green Supply Chain Management for Sustainable Business Practice* (pp. 27–50). Hershey, PA: IGI Global. doi:10.4018/978-1-5225-0635-5.ch002

Vlachvei, A., & Notta, O. (2017). Firm Competitiveness: Theories, Evidence, and Measurement. In A. Vlachvei, O. Notta, K. Karantininis, & N. Tsounis (Eds.), *Factors Affecting Firm Competitiveness and Performance in the Modern Business World* (pp. 1–42). Hershey, PA: IGI Global. doi:10.4018/978-1-5225-0843-4.ch001

Wang, C., Schofield, M., Li, X., & Ou, X. (2017). Do Chinese Students in Public and Private Higher Education Institutes Perform at Different Level in One of the Leadership Skills: Critical Thinking?: An Exploratory Comparison. In V. Wang (Ed.), *Encyclopedia of Strategic Leadership and Management* (pp. 160–181). Hershey, PA: IGI Global. doi:10.4018/978-1-5225-1049-9.ch013

Wang, J. (2017). Multi-Agent based Production Management Decision System Modelling for the Textile Enterprise. *Journal of Global Information Management, 25*(4), 1–15. doi:10.4018/JGIM.2017100101

Wiedemann, A., & Gewald, H. (2017). Examining Cross-Domain Alignment: The Correlation of Business Strategy, IT Management, and IT Business Value. *International Journal of IT/Business Alignment and Governance, 8*(1), 17–31. doi:10.4018/IJITBAG.2017010102

Wolf, R., & Thiel, M. (2018). Advancing Global Business Ethics in China: Reducing Poverty Through Human and Social Welfare. In S. Hipsher (Ed.), *Examining the Private Sector's Role in Wealth Creation and Poverty Reduction* (pp. 67–84). Hershey, PA: IGI Global. doi:10.4018/978-1-5225-3117-3.ch004

Yablonsky, S. (2018). Innovation Platforms: Data and Analytics Platforms. In *Multi-Sided Platforms (MSPs) and Sharing Strategies in the Digital Economy: Emerging Research and Opportunities* (pp. 72–95). Hershey, PA: IGI Global. doi:10.4018/978-1-5225-5457-8.ch003

Yaşar, B. (2021). The Impact of COVID-19 on Volatility of Tourism Stocks: Evidence From BIST Tourism Index. In M. Demir, A. Dalgıç, & F. Ergen (Eds.), *Handbook of Research on the Impacts and Implications of COVID-19 on the Tourism Industry* (pp. 23–44). IGI Global. https://doi.org/10.4018/978-1-7998-8231-2.ch002

Yusoff, A., Ahmad, N. H., & Halim, H. A. (2017). Agropreneurship among Gen Y in Malaysia: The Role of Academic Institutions. In N. Ahmad, T. Ramayah, H. Halim, & S. Rahman (Eds.), *Handbook of Research on Small and Medium Enterprises in Developing Countries* (pp. 23–47). Hershey, PA: IGI Global. doi:10.4018/978-1-5225-2165-5.ch002

Zacher, D., & Pechlaner, H. (2021). Resilience as an Opportunity Approach: Challenges and Perspectives for Private Sector Participation on a Community Level. In A. Zehrer, G. Glowka, K. Schwaiger, & V. Ranacher-Lackner (Eds.), *Resiliency Models and Addressing Future Risks for Family Firms in the Tourism Industry* (pp. 75–102). IGI Global. https://doi.org/10.4018/978-1-7998-7352-5.ch004

Zanin, F., Comuzzi, E., & Costantini, A. (2018). The Effect of Business Strategy and Stock Market Listing on the Use of Risk Assessment Tools. In *Management Control Systems in Complex Settings: Emerging Research and Opportunities* (pp. 145–168). Hershey, PA: IGI Global. doi:10.4018/978-1-5225-3987-2.ch007

Zgheib, P. W. (2017). Corporate Innovation and Intrapreneurship in the Middle East. In P. Zgheib (Ed.), *Entrepreneurship and Business Innovation in the Middle East* (pp. 37–56). Hershey, PA: IGI Global. doi:10.4018/978-1-5225-2066-5.ch003

About the Contributors

Festus Adedoyin is a Fellow of the Higher Education Academy and a Senior Lecturer at the Department of Computing and Informatics, Bournemouth University, U.K. Festus has led the Economics of Information Security unit since 2020, with current research interest is in the application of Machine and Deep Learning, and Econometrics tools to research stories in Energy and Tourism Economics as well as Finance and Digital Health.

Bryan Christiansen is an Adjunct Professor at Southern New Hampshire University where he teaches undergraduate business courses entirely online. Christiansen is also the Chief Executive Officer of the Idaho-based management consultancy, CYGERA, LLC. He is fluent in Chinese, Japanese, and Spanish with extensive exposure to Russian and Turkish. Christiansen has given presentations on his field of expertise at numerous universities in Europe, the Middle East, and North America.

Shreya Agrawal, born and raised in culturally rich city of Ayodhya, Uttar Pradesh. Currently, I am immersed in the dynamic field of Computer Engineering and specialization in Artificial Intelligence, pursuing my undergraduate degree at Marwadi University. As I navigate through the challenging yet fascinating realms of technology, my focus lies on the cutting-edge domain of Artificial Intelligence. Currently in my pre-final year, I am driven by a passion for exploring the limitless possibilities that AI presents. Join me on this exciting journey as I delve into the world of technology and innovation.

Elias Alexander I provide target list research, email research, lead generation, contact research, C-level contact research, primary research, secondary research, data cleansing, data validation, market research, competitive analysis through web research and database formatting in any volume through SQL, MS-Access and Excel with a highly experienced professionals.

Anthony Atkins BSc (Hons), MSc (Eng), PgC, PgD, MSc (CS), PhD, C Eng, PE, MBCS, SFHEA, Professor Emeritus in Digital Transformation and AI in the Faculty of Digital, Technology, Innovation and Business (DTIB), at Staffordshire University, United Kingdom. He is a Chartered Engineer and Professional Engineer and has been a Professor in both disciplines of Computing Science and Mining Engineering in the UK and USA with 40 years of industrial and academic experience. Published over 280 refereed publications consisting of 55 journals, 23 chapters in books, and conferences with colleagues and research students. Prof Atkins has supervised over 24 PhD students in the fields of Health Informatics, AI, Big Data Analytics, Gamification, Business Intelligence, Knowledge Management and Applied Computing. He has supervised 11 Post Doctorate Fellows, graduated 24 PhD students and over 100 master's students (UK, USA, and Australia). He has also examined over 40 PhD and MPhil degrees as External Examiner in the UK, USA, Australia, India, and Nepal. Prof Atkins has also held £3.4m research grants as principal investigator from the EU, EPSRC and from industry and NHS Trust. He is also the inventor of several large-scale industrial patents in UK, USA, Canada, and Australia using real time sensors in bioengineering and environmental engineering and was awarded a Churchill Fellowship. Quality Assurance Consultant in ICT and Education in Qatar, USA, UK, and India and a Visiting Professor in Germany, China, Thailand, India, and Hong Kong.

Robert Bilsland is a senior C# software engineer with a specialism in handling, processing, storing and displaying spatial information. I have over 20 years experience in developing web applications using Microsoft technologies currently targeting C#, .Net Core, Spatial C# Libraries, Blazor, SQL Server, Spatial SQL and Azure. Over 30 years experience in software development within the IT industry from mainframes through desktop PCs to web applications.

Jonathan Bishop is an information technology executive, researcher and writer. He founded Crocels Research in 2005, which works with Crocels Community Media Group members. Jonathan's research & development work generally falls within human-computer interaction. He has over 100 publications in this area, including on Internet trolling, digital addiction, affective computing, gamification; cyberlaw, multimedia forensics, cyber-stalking; Classroom 2.0, School 3.0, Digital Teens. In addition to his BSc(Hons) in Multimedia Studies and postgraduate degrees in law, business, economics and e-learning, Jonathan serves in local government as a councillor, and has been a school governor and contested numerous elections, including to the UK and Welsh parliaments. He is a an FBCS FCLIP FInstAM FInstLM FAPM FRAI FRSS FRSA, SMIEEE, MIET MACM MIITP MIMarEST, MarTech CITP CP. He has prizes for literary skills and was a finalist in national and local competitions for his environmental, community and equality work, often forming part of action research studies. Jonathan enjoys music, swimming and chess.

Amir Ahmad Dar is the Faculty in the Department of Mathematics at Lovely Professional University Punjab. The area of interest: Financial mathematics, financial economics, statistics and business mathematics.

Roshnie A. Doon, holds a Ph.D. in Economic Development Policy, MSc. Economics, and BSc. Economics from the University of the West Indies St. Augustine, Trinidad. She has completed a Ph.D. Master Class in International Business from the Henley School of Business at the University of Reading, U.K., and is currently a research affiliate of the Global Labor Organization (GLO), Essen Germany, and an executive committee member of the Caribbean Academy of Sciences Trinidad and Tobago Chapter (CAS-TT). Her academic interests are focused on Applied and Empirical Economics, in the areas of Labour, Gender, and Education Economics. Here she has published on a wide range of areas, which includes Higher Education Instruction, Economic and Social Implications of COVID-19, Migration, Returns to Schooling, Educational Mismatch, STEM Education, Wage Inequality, Gender Wage Gaps, and Economic Development Policy. Apart from being an academic editor, she has published her research in a wide array of journal and book publications, while sharing her research work through guest lectures, and conference presentations domestically, regionally, and internationally in Trinidad, Jamaica, Barbados, Guyana, the United States, the United Kingdom, Italy, Iceland, Australia, and New Zealand.

Pushan Kumar Dutta is a distinguished Assistant Professor Grade III in the Electronics and Communication Engineering Department at ASETK, Amity University Kolkata. He completed his PhD from Jadavpur University, Kolkata, in 2015, and later pursued a post-doctorate from the Erasmus Mundus Association. He is an accomplished editor, having edited multiple books in the field of healthcare, signal processing, industry 4.0, digital transformation and for IET, IGI Global, Degruyter, CRC, Elsevier and Springer with over 10 book chapters and as reviewer for Springer, Wiley, CRC, Apple Academic Press, and Taylor and Francis. In addition, he has published more than 70 articles in scopus indexed journals and 90 articles in total. In 2022, Dr. Dutta has already completed 10 book editorials, demonstrating his prolific contribution to the academic literature. He is a member of the technical programming committee for various prominent conferences in 2022 and 2023 and has delivered keynote speeches at international events.

Omar Guirette-Barbosa Bussines Management Ph D.Experience in quality systems based on ISO standards such as 9001, 17025, etc. Consultant on accreditation and certification issues, as well as on the application of continuous improvement tools and industrial engineering.

Wahid Hassan Data-driven professional with a strong work ethic and ability to adapt quickly. Have good knowledge of Python Programming Language, Data engineering, Database design and Web Development. A quick learner with ability to absorb new ideas as well as communicate clearly and effectively both orally and in writing within a team environment or on an individual basis.

Victor Ogunbiyi is a lecturer in strategic marketing in the School of Leadership, Management, and Marketing at De Montfort University, United Kingdom. His research interests are in the areas of international buyer behaviour, ethical marketing practices, sustainable food management practices, policy initiatives for food waste mitigation and Technology in Business Innovation. Victor, approach this area from a multi-stakeholder, collaborative perspective. He visited Vietnam on a funded project for the EC-Asia Research Network on the Integration of Global and Local Agri-Food Supply Chains towards Sustainable Food Security in 2022.

Damodharan Palaniappan received PhD degree from Anna University, Tamil Nadu, India. Presently he is working as an Associate Professor at Marwadi University, Rajkot, Gujarat. He has more than 17 years teaching experience. His research interests are Web Mining, Machine Learning, Image Processing and Big Data.

Aayush Raj In the realm of artificial intelligence and machine learning, I am an enthusiastic learner and contributor. My academic journey at Marwadi University has been marked by a deep exploration of the intersections between AI/ML and various disciplines. I have actively engages in discussions, workshops, and research activities, showcasing my commitment to staying at the forefront of technological advancements.

Ayush Shekhar, currently a dedicated student pursuing a Bachelor of Technology (B.Tech) degree in Computer Science with a specialization in Artificial Intelligence. My passion for Artificial Intelligence goes beyond the classroom. I actively engage in extracurricular projects and hands-on experiences, applying theoretical knowledge to real-world scenarios. As I progress in my academic journey, my goal is to contribute to the field of AI through research, innovation, and practical applications. I envision myself playing a role in developing AI solutions that address real-world challenges and contribute to the responsible and ethical advancement of technology.

Ali Sorour BSc, MBA, MSc (Computing), PhD, SOCPA, CIA, CISA, CPA, MBCS. He received the M.Sc. degree in Computing in 2017 and the Ph.D in Computer Science in 2022, both from Staffordshire University, United Kingdom. He have more than 10 years of academic and professional experience. Sorour is acting as an independent consultant for several public and private institutions in the field of performance management using AI-Driven technologies. He developed several BI dashboards for purposes such as monitoring risks and detection of money laundering transactions in audit firms. His research interests include artificial intelligence, business intelligence & analytics, and FinTech.

Premavathi T, I completed my M.E in Anna university and 13 +yrs experience in teaching. Currently pursuing a PhD in Deep learning.

Omar Vargas-González Professor and Head of Systems and Computing Department at Tecnologico Nacional de Mexico Campus Ciudad Guzman, professor at Telematic Engineering at Centro Universitario del Sur Universidad de Guadalajara with a master degree in Computer Systems. Has been trained in Innovation and Multidisciplinary Entrepreneurship at Arizona State University (2018) and a Generation of Ecosystems of Innovation, Entrepreneurship and Sustainability for Jalisco course by Harvard University T.H. Chan School of Health. At present conduct research on diverse fields such as Entrepreneurship, Economy, Statistics, Mathematics and Information and Computer Sciences. Has colaborated in the publication of over 20 scientific articles and conducted diverse Innovation and Technological Development projects.

Mohamad Zreik, a Postdoctoral Fellow at Sun Yat-sen University, is a recognized scholar in International Relations, specializing in China's Arab-region foreign policy. His recent work in soft power diplomacy compares China's methods in the Middle East and East Asia. His extensive knowledge spans Middle Eastern Studies, China-Arab relations, East Asian and Asian Affairs, Eurasian geopolitics, and Political Economy, providing him a unique viewpoint in his field. Dr. Zreik is a proud recipient of a PhD from Central China Normal University (Wuhan). He's written numerous acclaimed papers, many focusing on China's Belt and Road Initiative and its Arab-region impact. His groundbreaking research has established him as a leading expert in his field. Presently, he furthers his research on China's soft power diplomacy tactics at Sun Yat-sen University. His significant contributions make him a crucial figure in understanding contemporary international relations.

Index

G

H

I

L

M

N

O

P

R

S

X

www.ingramcontent.com/pod-product-compliance
Lightning Source LLC
LaVergne TN
LVHW080646011026
849160LV00014B/1332